From Status to Contract

Frontispiece Sir Henry Maine addressing the Indian Council, St James's, London, *c.* 1878. Autographed in Maine's hand. From a drawing by T. Blake Wigram.

From Status to Contract

A Biography of
Sir Henry Maine 1822–1888

George Feaver

Longmans

LONGMANS, GREEN AND CO LTD
London and Harlow

Associated companies, branches and representatives throughout the world

© *Longmans, Green & Co Ltd, 1969*
First published 1969

KD
F42x

Printed in Great Britain
by W & J Mackay & Co Ltd, Chatham

For D. S. F.

Contents

Illustrations

Acknowledgements

I wish to record my sincere thanks to the harrassed library staff of the British Library of Political and Economic Science, and especially to C. G. Allen, Keeper of Manuscripts, all of whom have been extremely helpful to me during the preparation of this study. Thanks are also due to Mrs Molly Poulter and Dr R. J. Bingle of the incomparably Dickensian India Office Library for their assistance at different stages of my researches, as well as to Dr J. F. A. Mason of Christ Church, Oxford; Dr A. P. Clark of the Princeton University Library; Miss E. G. Henderson of the Harvard Law School Library; D. W. Bridgewater and D. R. Watkins of the Yale University Library; Peter Walne, Berkshire County Archivist; Joyce Godber, Bedford County Archivist; D. C. Cargill of Edinburgh, and Miss Nancy Devine and other members of the library staff of Mount Holyoke College, Massachusetts, who lessened the inevitable difficulties of writing those sections completed in America.

While a separate list acknowledging primary sources is given elsewhere in this study, I must expressly thank the Fifth Marquess of Salisbury for generously allowing reproduction of materials from the manuscript papers of his grandfather. The Trustees of the Chartwell Literary Trust arranged for me to examine letters, written by Sir Henry Maine to Lord Randolph Churchill, in the historic surroundings of 27 Hyde Park Gate. The late Sir John Murray of the John Murray Publishing Company patiently met my many requests for information, and allowed me the pleasure of working at leisure on various papers amidst the splendid collection of Byronia that adorns his Albemarle Street offices. Mrs Sheila Sokolov-Grant kindly allowed me access to her valuable private collection of the papers of her grandfather, and Maine's previous biographer, Sir M. E. Grant Duff. I am indebted to Mr Henry C. S. Maine, C.M.G., M.V.O., Sir

Henry Maine's only grandson, for his reminiscences, and for the loan of family letters, clippings and photographs.

The researches and travels undertaken in conjunction with this biography, an earlier version of which was accepted as a PH.D. dissertation by the University of London, were made possible by the generous financial assistance of the Canada Council, the Leverhulme Trust, the Koerner Foundation, and the Central Research Fund of the University of London.

I wish also to thank Jeremy Gibson, Mark Gummer, Marie Dejey and Liz Spencer of the editorial and art departments at Longmans, for their help in preparing the final draft for publication.

My greatest acknowledgement is to all those who have been my teachers at the University of British Columbia and the University of London, and especially to Mr Maurice Cranston, who first led me to an interest in Sir Henry Maine and the political thought of the Victorians, and who has ever since been an unfailing source of insight and advice. Finally, the encouragement, editorial assistance and endless patience of my wife have contributed greatly, and in the usual unsung manner, to the completion of this book.

I wish to acknowledge the kind permission of the following to reproduce illustrative materials: Mr Henry C. S. Maine, C.M.G., M.V.O., for Plates 6, 7, 11, 12, 13 and 18; the National Portrait Gallery for Plates 1, 2, 3, 4, 8, 9, 14, 15 and 16; the Secretary of State for Commonwealth Affairs for the Frontispiece and Plate 5; and the Master and Fellows of Trinity College, Cambridge, for Plate 10. Plate 17 by courtesy of the Dean and Chapter of Westminster.

Abbreviations

BOOKS

AL   MAINE, SIR H. J. S., *Ancient Law*, London, Murray, 1861
EHI   —*Early History of Institutions*, London, Murray, 1875
ELC   —*Early Law and Custom*, London, Murray, 1883
PG   —*Popular Government*, London, Murray, 1885
VC   —*Village Communities in East and West*, London, Murray,
             1871 (3rd edn, 1876)
Memoir   GRANT DUFF, SIR M. E., *Memoir of Sir Henry Maine, with
             Indian Speeches and Minutes*, London, Murray, 1892

JOURNALS AND MANUSCRIPTS

C. W. Coll.   Sir Charles Wood Collection, India Office Library, London.
                Mss Eur. F78.
J. L. Coll.   Sir John Lawrence Collection (Lord Lawrence) India Office
                Library, London. Mss Eur. F90.
J. M. Arch.   John Murray Archives, John Murray Publishing Company.
L. E. Coll.   Lord Elgin Collection, India Office Library, London.
                Mss Eur. F83/16.
Sat. R.   *Saturday Review of Literature*, London, 1855–
St J. G.   *St James's Gazette*, London, 1880–

Introduction

Sir Henry Maine was one of Victorian England's great jurists, and his brilliant book on *Ancient Law*, first published in 1861, has guaranteed his importance as a writer in the field of legal antiquities. Living in an age that valued the man of general accomplishment, he was also a leading London journalist, and an Anglo-Indian administrator during a crucial phase of British imperial rule. He was an incisive Victorian spokesman for the cause of political conservatism, a noteworthy critic of modern democracy whose philosophical roots, like those of Edmund Burke, lay deeply embedded in the Whiggish tradition of British political thought. Maine was a university professor at a time when the performance of teaching duties was first beginning to be taken seriously in the older British universities. As such, he was prominent among a pioneering group of professional students of society who first attracted undergraduates to their lecture-halls during the middle years of the nineteenth century through their advocacy of new 'historical and comparative' methods which, as they thought, would eradicate conjectural approaches to social studies and replace these with a rigorously factual science of man.

Maine possessed unusual skills as a literary stylist. Woodrow Wilson, who as a young professor of politics was a great admirer of his work, saw this in entitling an *Atlantic Monthly* article on Maine 'A Lawyer With a Style'. Some years later, that controversial socialist, the late Professor Harold Laski, who was assuredly himself no sympathizer with Sir Henry's political views, reflected in a letter written to the ageing American jurist Oliver Wendell Holmes, Jr: 'If I had to name a book to tempt the outsider into a sense that jurisprudence was a great subject, I think I should ask him to read Maine, and then deny greatness at his peril.' Most Anglo-American lawyers of Holmes's generation would have agreed. Maine's imaginative pen would not rest within the restrictive bounds of a cautious empiricism, yet more than that of any legal theorist of his day, his ambitious scholarship encouraged the foundation of a new empirical approach to the study of the evolution of legal institutions, a radical departure virtually unknown in England prior to his appointment to the Cambridge Professorship of Civil Law in 1847. Urging the need to go beyond the linguistic preoccupations of the Austinian or 'analytical' school of jurisprudence in order to attain the fullest grasp of the nature of law, Sir Henry was a British legal scholar more in the tradition of continental Europeans of the stature of Montesquieu or Tocqueville, von Savigny and Vico, in his pursuit of meaning in large-scale historical patterns. The result, as Sir William Holdsworth once commented, was that 'Maine's books taught and still teach students to think historically'.

Maine acted as the intellectual heir of the eighteenth-century Scottish anthropologists in his persistent attempts to replace rationalist doctrines of social contract and natural law with descriptions of the rudiments of political society drawn directly from the surviving legal records of the past. He made his special domain the study of jurisprudence and political philosophy from the standpoint of the comparative philologist, and wrote, as one admiring contemporary suggested, as if he were a 'political embryologist'. While many of his novel theories have since been abandoned, a surprisingly great number of Maine's views are nowadays commonplace to even the relative newcomer to the study of law. As Sir Frederick Pollock pointed out in 1906:

> Any student who harbours doubt as to the extent of Maine's contributions to the historical philosophy of law may do well to ask himself, in what books legal and historical, of earlier date than *Ancient Law*, he could have found adequate perception, or any distinct perception, of such matters as these: the sentiment of reverence evoked by the mere . . . existence of law in early communities; the essential formalism of archaic law; the predominance of rules of procedure over rules of substance in early legal systems; the fundamental difference between ancient and modern ideas as to the legal proof; the relatively modern character of the individual citizen's disposing power, especially by will and

freedom of contract; and the still more modern appearance of true criminal law.

From among all Maine's many important ideas, however, there are two that particularly stand out through the influence they have exerted among students of society. By far the best known is the famous generalization, first outlined in *Ancient Law*, that the legal development of progressive societies involves a movement of the position of the individual in private law 'from status to contract', a thesis that was understandably well received in the great age of *laissez-faire* liberalism, but which has become more controversial in this century of growing government regulation of the traditionally private sector. In putting forward the theory, Maine, perhaps more than any scholar of his generation, provided an authoritative legal rationale and the guiding academic spirit of the middle-class entrepreneurial attitude. In the context of his own system of ideas, Maine's status to contract theory was the underlying link between his scholarly legal works and his pessimistic political philosophy. The second of Sir Henry's major theoretical contributions was his careful analytical distinction between two basic types of society, an histori- cally older variety in which membership was traced exclusively through kinship, and political authority was organized at the level of the extended family group, and a later one in which the notion of community comes to be associated with local contiguity and the common sharing of territory. No such rigorous distinction between the organizational patterns of traditional and modern society had been drawn before the appearance of *Ancient Law*.

Maine grew to philosophical maturity under the giant shadow of Jeremy Bentham, and in his professorial pursuits Sir Henry readily acknowledged his great debt to Bentham's juridical teachings. Yet his concern for individual freedom led Maine to register a major mid-Victorian dissent from the political thought of the architect of majoritarian hedonism. If Benthamite political theory rested ostensibly upon the twin cornerstones of discrete individualism and the natural harmony of particularized economic interests, Maine concluded that it posed a serious practical paradox in simultaneously holding to a belief in universal political equality. In his comparative studies in legal anthropology he had discovered evidence that the collectivism characteristic of static societies derived primarily from a stagnant legal equalitarianism that enslaved all alike to a fixed and immutable status. It followed for Maine that progress depended upon intellectual and economic inequalities, and that it was these which underlay the gradual infusion into strictly regimented social transactions of a wider degree of free contractual relations. Moreover, while Bentham had believed society could be radically transformed through the positive enactments of legislatures, Maine's historical and comparative studies taught him that the vast majority of mankind remain averse to change, that progressive societies have been rare and fragile in recorded history, and that the continuous activity of legislatures is an altogether modern phenomenon confined to the practices of a few enlightened peoples. Acting on these beliefs, Sir Henry worked during his years as an Indian lawgiver to modify the effects of the abstract administrative Benthamism of a previous generation of Anglo-Indian officials, while in domestic British affairs he was a tireless critic of the leading tenets of the Benthamite political firmament.

While acknowledged in his lifetime to be an English historian and political theorist of the calibre of Acton and Bagehot, Maine is by no means a well known figure today. This state of affairs can be partly attributed to there being no full-length study of his life and work. Since 1892 the standard reference on Maine has been Sir M. E. Grant Duff's *Memoir of Sir Henry Maine*. The volume consists of a collection of Maine's Indian Speeches and Minutes which were posthumously edited by his friend Whitley Stokes, and to these is added Grant Duff's short biographical preface, prepared at the behest of Sir Henry's literary executors. One reason that little has been written to supplement Grant Duff's *Memoir*, when it seems that so few stones have been left unturned among the historical quarries of the Victorian era, is that the primary source materials one would normally expect to consult are simply not available. What became of the great bulk of Sir Henry's library and personal papers, indeed, remains as much a mystery as ever. When Maine died unexpectedly in France during the early weeks of 1888, he left most of his large library and collection of papers to his eldest son, Charles Sumner, with the one proviso that to Lady Maine he first reserved the right 'to such of my books (not exceeding 200 in number) as she may be pleased to select'. Charles Sumner, a promising young barrister who met a tragically early death only a few months after that of his

xviii

famous father, in turn left the library to his infant son, Henry Cecil Sumner. In 1920, at the very advanced age of 93, Lady Maine died and left the 200 volumes she kept at a cottage at Walton on Thames, Surrey, to her grandson Henry Cecil as well, so that as late as the second decade of this century Maine's library must have been largely intact.

Today nothing remains of it, and one of the few books from the original collection, a volume of Carlyle's *Essays* bearing Sir Henry's unusual book-plate on the fly-leaf, is on my shelves as I write these lines. As to Sir Henry's personal papers, it is likely that these too remained in a single collection for some years after his death, and certainly there is evidence that Grant Duff had access to such a collection. By 1903 they had been dispersed. In that year Whitley Stokes sent several small packets of Maine's miscellaneous Indian correspondence to Alfred Lyall at the India Office, noting that Lady Maine had given them to him 'with a request that I should tell her what to do with them'. She was an elderly woman living in reduced circumstances, and seems to have had little sense of her husband's historical importance. According to her grandson, she threw away the contents of letters written to Sir Henry by prominent literary men like Thackeray and Dickens, after cutting off and selling their signatures! Although we cannot altogether exclude the possibility that there are Maine papers gathering dust in the corner of some musty attic, it is in the circumstances almost certain that little survives beyond what has been uncovered in the course of the present researches. There is perhaps some consolation in reflecting that the details of Sir Henry's professional existence would in all likelihood have held little general interest, for to borrow a memorable phrase from Robert Blake's recent study of Disraeli, his was a 'porty, snuffy, rather donnish world'. Yet it remains a wistful thought, to the present writer at least, that the full letter files of this Victorian worthy are lost to us.

While the special problems Maine presents to the prospective biographer are considerable, there is a brighter side to the picture. The remnants of what appears to have been the much larger collection of Sir Henry's manuscript books were purchased by Harold Laski in 1940, and eventually given as a gift to the London School of Economics. The discovery by M. M. Bevington of marked newspaper files, and of a further list by this writer, makes possible the identification of a great number of Maine's anonymous journal articles, and these throw new light on the contemporary significance of his political thought. My researches into the private papers of Maine's correspondents, in the United Kingdom and abroad, have brought fresh perspectives to other aspects of his career. While governed by the relative paucity of source materials, I am hopeful that the results represent a fuller appreciation of Maine's life than has hitherto been available.

It remains to add a word concerning the stylistic features of the book. The specialist will, I trust, have patience with the sometimes extensive summaries of the contents of Maine's works. On the assumption that Sir Henry's theories are no longer widely known these are intended to provide a convenient introduction for the general reader. Secondly, I have followed the policy in certain sections of the narrative of including lengthy direct quotations from manuscripts that are not easily accessible, and that, in the absence of a single collection of Maine's papers, seemed to me of some historical interest. In the chapters on India, I have attempted wherever possible to render spellings as they usually appear in current usage, but in certain instances involving direct quotation from manuscript sources, I have retained the style fashionable in Maine's time. Finally, may I say at the outset that every effort has been made to expunge unnecessary jargon, but that in some instances I have found it impossible to do without terms in common use among social scientists. Where reliance on these has been necessary, I have attempted to make their meaning clear from the contexts in which they occur.

London, 1967   G.F.

Origins of a Lawyer

Kelso, Roxburghshire, which lies on the north bank of the curving Tweed River at its junction with the Teviot, is notable as the site of the early twelfth-century Kelso Abbey, though nowadays little remains to remind one of the energetic devotion of its Benedictine monks except the west end of their great church. Sir Walter Scott lived in the picturesque Border town during his childhood, and his generous tribute to it as one of the most beautiful places in Scotland is still recalled with understandable pride by the soft-accented townspeople. By the turn of the nineteenth-century, Kelso was the major marketing centre for the region, and its population of close to 5,000 inhabitants made it somewhat larger than it is today. At about that time the noted Scots civil engineer, John Rennie, added to the topographical features of the town a further distinguishing landmark: a new type of elliptically arched bridge, which was later used by him as the model for London's Waterloo Bridge.[1]

In southern Scotland the word 'Mains' has long signified the principal or home farm of an estate, and while its origins as a surname are unclear, it seems probable that, like 'Mayne', it derived from some earlier association with the French province of Maine. At Kelso there was a 'John Mane' recorded as a tenant in lands of the Abbey as early as 1567.[2] In the later etymological corruption of the surname in the area, families with the related names of 'Main' and 'Mein' became common. The particular family line that interests us is that of Adam Main, innkeeper of the Cross Keys Hotel, Kelso, who died there in 1804. It seems clear that this obscure figure was the grandfather not only of Sir Henry Maine, but of his wife Lady Maine (*née* Jane Morton Main) as well. By his wife Ann Main (*née* Lowes), Adam Main fathered several children. Of these, the Kelso Baptismal Records include the following:

1803. Agnes–Born 15 June & Baptised 1 July, 1796.
Witnesses James Main & Dr Rutherford.
1803. *George–Born 1 December, 1797* & Baptised 24 December.
Witnesses Mrs Rutherford & James Main.
1810. *George–Born 1 December, 1798* & Baptised 15 January,
1799.
Witnesses Mrs Rutherford & Margt Rutherford.[3]

We know from independent sources that Sir Henry married his
first cousin, and from further records on deposit at Registry House,
Edinburgh, that the second of these two Georges was Lady Maine's
father. Sir Henry's father must therefore also have been a son of
Adam Main. Yet the name of his father was a 'Dr James Main(e)'.
While it is possible that a further Adam Main child bearing the
name 'James' was never baptized, what is striking about the excerpts
given above is that two consecutive sons should be given the name
'George', and that they should both be born on the same day, one
year apart. Moreover, these baptismal entries were made as long as
six and eleven years respectively after the event. Since no James
Main appears in the further birth and baptismal records of Kelso in
the entire period 1785–1810, either the registrar made an error in
transcription, or what seems more likely, he improvised the details
of these baptisms which had taken place so many years earlier. There
is every reason to assume that the first son of Adam and Ann Main
given above was in fact 'James [George] Main', Sir Henry Maine's
father, and that his recorded date of birth in 1797 is only an approxi-
mation.

Sir Henry's uncle, George Main, became a solicitor and edited
the *Kelso Mail* in his later years. For the last fifteen years of his life
he was also Bailie of the town. During the summer of 1825 George
married Eliza Routledge, the eldest daughter of the Reverend
William Routledge of the Barony Parish, Glasgow, and she bore him
five children—Ann (1826), Jane Morton (6 July 1827), William
(1828), Adam Woodman (1831) and George (1832)—before her
death in 1834. In September 1836, he married Ann Brown, relict
of one Andrew Henderson, a manufacturer in Leeds, and she
brought her six-year-old daughter, Alice Henderson, to the already
sizeable George Main household. The following January she gave
birth to another daughter, Eliza Sophia, and bore two more children

2

—Harriet (1839) and [?] Main (1841)—before her early death in 1843 at the age of thirty-six. The Eliza Maine born of this second marriage lived with Sir Henry and Lady Maine in Cornwall Gardens, London, in later life, and became a prolific writer of rather bad novels in the tradition of Trollope, which were published at regular intervals after 1870 by Smith, Elder and Company. She died at Llandudno, Wales, in 1891. The dauntless George Main married yet again after Ann Brown passed away, this third time to Margaret Slater of Glasgow, who lived on at Kelso until 1877. George died in 1857 and was interred in the Cloister Burying Ground of Kelso Abbey, as befitted a local dignitary.[4]

By the time George Main began his career as a solicitor in Kelso, his brother James had already left Scotland to seek his fortune in London. On 27 November 1818, he was awarded the M.D. degree of Aberdeen University *in absentia*, on the attestation of Dr Bateman of Shadwell and Dr Ley of Battersea, London,[5] yet no entry for a Dr James Main(e) is to be found in any of the Post Office lists or in Pigott's *London and Provincial Directories* for the entire period 1810–30. Around this time James must have adopted the anglicized version of 'Maine' as his surname, a not uncommon practice among provincials anxious to make their way in English society. He became a suitor to Eliza Joan (or Jane) Fell, fourth daughter of David (d. 1806) and Catherine Fell (d. 1824) of Mansion House, Caversham Grove, Oxfordshire, who apparently had family connections in Kelso. Since there were several brothers as well as five sisters in Eliza's large family, the dowry she brought to her eventual marriage to James, a portion of the modest fortune accumulated by her father through East India Company investments, cannot have been great.

We know few of the facts of the whereabouts of Sir Henry Maine's parents during this period, and indeed of Maine's origins. Perhaps the most reliable of several versions is Venn's *Alumni Cantabrigienses*, which gives Maine's birth as occuring at Hockcliffe, Bedfordshire on 15 August 1822 (the same as that of Matthew Arnold).[6] But I have been unsuccessful in my efforts to trace a baptismal certificate in either Bedfordshire or Oxfordshire records, nor is there any relevant information in the separate nonconformist lists housed at the Public Records Office, London. We do know that Maine had two brothers—Lewin George Maine, an Anglican priest, and another who emigrated to New Zealand[7]—and Grant Duff tells us further in

3

his *Memoir* of Maine that he spent his earliest years in Jersey, but that 'family difficulties soon supervening, he was removed to England, and was brought up thenceforward exclusively by his mother'.[8] The 'family difficulties' could feasibly have been the death of Eliza's mother, yet Grant Duff's concluding remark seems to be a circumspect Victorian way of avoiding an awkward personal subject bearing on the marriage of Maine's parents. At any rate, the *Lincoln's Inn Admission Records, 1800–1893*, list Dr James Maine as a resident of 'Hindustan'.[9] It is an interesting biographical note that Sir Henry Maine always seemed consciously secretive about his family background. Even Sir James Fitzjames Stephen, a lifelong friend and confidant, could recall only the barest details of Sir Henry's family in his unpublished autobiography, and these not always accurately. 'Maine', he wrote, 'was I believe the son of a clergyman, and he was the nephew of the Archbishop of Canterbury (Sumner). But I have never known such a mystery. Intimate as we have been, I know absolutely nothing of his family connections, except that he married his first cousin, and has brothers, to me unknown.'[10] Quite aside from the possibility that some potentially scandalous matter underlay the separation of Dr James Maine from his wife in 1824, Henry Maines' rather humble origins seem in themselves to have been a source of embarrassment to him in later life. Like Edmund Burke, while he loved the past, he longed to forget his own past. He fancied that his blood was derived from a noble French line,[11] and hinted at this in choosing as the inscription on his coat of arms the motto 'Je maintiendray', yet Eliza Maine perhaps came closer to the truth in the narrative of one of her novels, *Marchmont of Redlands*. Her heroines, the Scots cousins Christie and Amabel Home, are reflecting on their family history:

[The Homes] were neither rich nor poor. They were not endowed with the virtues of any remarkable ancestors, and had no 'family' to speak of; in fact, [Christie] was of opinion that theirs was a family *not* to speak of, for not so long ago [the Homes] had been hanged for Border robberies time and again. Sheep stealing had been common among them, and fighting and quarreling were their natural elements. And as for the mothers of the Homes, few records have been kept either of their sayings or doings. They had been worthy sort of women in their generations, with possibly here and there a lady among them to account for the signs of good blood which the 19th century Homes, whether they had the right to them or not, certainly possessed. They were respectable enough now, [the Homes], whatever their ancestors might have been.[12]

While Henry Maine was made to suffer the minor indignity of humble parentage, he must have felt most fortunate in his mother's choice of his godfather. When Maine was born in 1822, the Reverend John Bird Sumner, a cousin of his mother, was the colourful young vicar of St Margaret's, Mapledurham, not far from Eliza's family home at Caversham Grove. In 1816 his bold *Treatise on the Records of the Creation, and on the Moral Attributes of the Creator* had caused a stir in High Church circles, for Sumner had attempted to vindicate the Mosaic account of the creation of the world, while adhering to the evolutionary conclusions of the new science of geology. Mrs Maine apparently felt so much admiration for his courageous attempt to reconcile the teachings of the Anglican Church with the discoveries of modern science that she resolved to make him Henry's godfather. While Sumner presumably also baptized his godson 'Henry James Sumner Maine', there is no record of such in the baptismal register of St Margaret's, or in the further local records housed in the Bodleian Library, Oxford. Henry Maine seldom used the 'James' in his name, but he always gave prominence to the 'Sumner', for his godfather was destined for greater things than the pleasant sinecure of the Mapledurham vicarage. In 1828, he was named by Peel to the Bishopric of Chester, and in 1848, became Archbishop of Canterbury.

After the death of her mother, Eliza settled with her boys at Henley on Thames, and it was there that Henry Maine passed his childhood. He was a nervous and physically frail child from earliest years. Grant Duff tells us that 'he was all but poisoned at that early period of his life by an overdose of opium, administered by his doting mother and an equally devoted aunt'.[13] He was eventually enrolled at a day school in the 'Fair Mile' at Henley, run by Mrs Maine's former governess, a Mrs Lamb. He remained there until 1829, when his godfather, who was fortuitously a Governor of Christ's Hospital—the well-known charitable school which was at that time situated on the site of the King Edward Street Post Office, London—secured his entrance as a 'Blue Coat Boy'. Maine quickly developed a reputation among his peers for his unusual intellectual brilliance. His passion for classical history was first aroused by his introduction, while a 'Grecian' at Christ's Hospital, to 'the Psalter in Hebrew, and Ollivant's History of Joseph: Thucydides, Herodotus, Aeschylus, Sophocles, Euripides, Aristophanes, Demosthenes, and Valpry's Greek Testament'. He learned to prepare original essays in Greek and Latin as well as in English.

It was the practice in Maine's time at Christ's Hospital for the students to gather in Hall on Sunday evenings, to listen to the recitation of scripture and poetry. Maine was often called on, it seems, to present readings of his own compositions. Contemporaries later commented on the dramatic effect produced by the contrast of Henry's physically frail features with the power of his delivery. Years afterwards, for example, a schoolboy companion, D'Arcy Thompson, wistfully recalled an apparently typical Maine performance:

> Upon his pale and intellectually beautiful face, clearly visible between the two far-away lamps, the eyes of nearly a thousand listeners were fixed, and a sublime shudder passed over the whole assembly as, in tones rich, clear, and resonant, the solemn words were read.[14]

Maine's school friends thought it likely that he would devote his career to poetry and creative literature.

In 1838, when he was sixteen, Henry won the school prize for the best Latin Alcaic Ode. With the other senior scholars, he read his composition on St Matthew's Day before a crowded auditorium. He had written in praise of the recent abolition of slavery in the West Indies, and his recitation provided the basis for what was probably his earliest press notice. 'It was a very good piece of Latin verse', *The Times* judiciously reported, 'and very well spoken by Mr Henry James Sumner Maine, sixth Grecian.'[15] In his final year at Christ's Hospital, Maine was awarded the Thompson Classical Gold Medal as the scholar most proficient in classics. He prized the medal, the first of many such academic successes, throughout his life, eventually willing it to his younger son. His brilliant school career had assured Henry of at least some financial assistance with his further studies, and in 1840 he was awarded an exhibition or scholarship to Pembroke College, Cambridge. Young Maine's academic accomplishments had been closely followed in the large Kelso household of his uncle, George Main. In 1840 his second daughter, Jane Morton Main, a pretty girl talented at singing and languages, was thirteen years of age, and well acquainted with the school achievements of her cousin Henry, now a severely intellectual young university freshman. By the time the next Census of Kelso was taken in 1851, she was no longer among the children of George Main living in his household.[16] She had left the Border to live in England as Henry Maine's wife.

2

Pembroke College, Cambridge

When Henry Maine arrived at Cambridge in September 1840, as the new exhibitioner of Pembroke, he was a rather tall, slim young man with long, wavy brown hair, and inquisitive eyes. His complexion bore the delicate texture of one frequently troubled with illness. He wore silk bow-ties, and his jackets had the slightly ruffled look of one too occupied with intellectual matters to be meticulous about physical appearances. His poor health led friends to doubt whether Henry had the stamina to continue at the nervous pace he had set himself at Christ's Hospital. But Maine was ambitious; he was determined to succeed and did so. In 1841 he was elected a Foundation Scholar of Pembroke. In 1842 he was awarded three medals, including the Chancellor's Medal for English Verse, the Camden Medal for Latin Hexameters, and the Brown Medal for a Latin Ode. In the following year he accumulated a new distinction by becoming Craven University Scholar, in addition to winning two further medals for Greek and Latin epigrams. These academic achievements, among the most impressive undergraduate records in the long history of Cambridge University, were not made without certain sacrifices. Long hours of study apparently impaired Maine's already delicate constitution. 'It was hard to drag him away from his rooms and his books', a contemporary recollected of Maine's compulsive scholarship, 'even for the ordinary minimum of constitutional exercise.'

Maine's virtual monopoly of prizes was not unnoticed in Cambridge. Previously, it had been most unlikely that anyone other than a Trinity or St John's man would stand a chance in University prize competitions. One of Maine's close undergraduate friends, William Cory, wrote home to his parents in 1844 that 'Maine is winning his proud post in the teeth of popular ill will, being considered an upstart because he is to beat Trinity men, etc.' Maine was at a clear disadvantage in being in a small college in unreformed Cambridge. At that time, a substantial portion of teaching income was derived from the fees tutors charged students for admission to lectures and tutorials, and thus the better dons tended to gather in the larger and more lucrative colleges. Furthermore, the smaller colleges tended to have poorer library resources, and the best scholars therefore avoided them if they could. That Maine became such an outstanding classicist in these circumstances is itself a testament to his intellectual ability.

The few surviving student notebooks of Henry Maine offer interesting evidence of the vigour with which the young scholar pursued his studies. Hard-covered workbooks, now yellowed with age, are filled with exhaustive vocabulary lists written in Maine's distinctive, flowing hand. Some of the lists, which are systematically numbered, reach into the thousands. One occasionally encounters the lighter side of undergraduate life as well: a penned cartoon of a well-dressed young man with an exaggerated nose, playing snooker, stares up mutely at the reader.

Among the notebooks there are a group of essays Maine wrote during his first year at Cambridge, and they constitute the earliest of his extant writings. In the draft of an essay on Thucydides and Herodotus, the young scholar weighs historical evidence for its plausibility:

Thucydides

We know he had a daughter from the tradition that the eighth book was written by her . . . The principle events of his life are his hearing Herodotus read his history, which affected him to tears, his having the Plague (430 B.C.), and his banishment owing to occurrences at Amphipolis to the coast of Thrace (about 423 B.C.). *First event not probable.* Herodotus must have visited 456 or thereabouts when Thucydides was an infant.[1]

He drew elaborate maps of the ancient world of the Mediterranean and the Middle East, and already showed an appreciation of the importance of custom for the historian:

poor accounts and mere anecdotes of battles . . . much geographical detail. Speeches not characteristic of speakers or their nation, but much insight into custom is given.

9

Elsewhere Maine's scholarly appraisals betray the typical class bias of a Victorian university student. Discussing the structure of Roman government in an essay on Titus Livy's *History of Rome* he wrote that, by the 3rd century B.C.:

the government was in the hands of 35 tribes . . . as the rural tribes predominated, and those who had a stake in the country and were wealthy enough for the journey came, the Government was not yet in the hands of the Rabble.[2]

Nor was it, to his mind, in England as he wrote. As the product of a privileged educational background, Maine early found reason to believe in philosopher kings. In Plato and Aristotle there was ample justification for the view that democracy, where, as young Maine had put it, 'the Rabble' ruled, was an undesirable form of regime. 'A Democracy', he wrote in an essay in 1842, 'was where the magistrates were elected by the lot.' Maine never really progressed beyond this definition. Democracy remained for him, as one trained in classical literature, simply a leaderless *form* of government by the numerical majority. In later life he would bring this view to bear on his analysis of the prospects of modern democratic rule.

In 1843 Maine apparently made a thorough study of Plato. He composed a poem eulogizing the Greek philosopher and submitted it for the English prize contest he had won the year before. His name had become such a familiar one on the list of prize winners that everyone expected him to win. In fact, when the results were announced early in June, he learned that his friend William Cory had defeated him by a single vote. Cory, faithful to his competitor beyond the requirements of politeness, made it known that in his estimation Maine's poem was better than his, and that because it was 'more philosophical than the other entries, the judges would not take the trouble to look at it close enough'.[3] Whatever the relative merits of the two poems, Maine's entry concluded with the sentimental observation that:

> we who every hour
> Build grain by grain the mass of human power,
> Must bow before our Master, who but stood
> And nursed the juices working in the bud
> And might not tend the flowering, who but fed
> The stream of Science at its fountain head.[4]

In later life Maine's scholarship was characterized by his insistence that modern European man lives constantly in the intellectual shadow of Greek civilization. 'Except the blind forces of Nature', he was to write in a famous phrase of his Rede Lecture of 1875, 'nothing moves in this world which is not Greek in origin.'[5]

Maine's undergraduate life at Cambridge was of course not entirely confined to books. He had a small circle of intimates with whom he spent his leisure time. He chose his companions carefully, for he thought extracurricular activities should complement hours in a library. Thus, he loved to walk with his hand-picked friends in the gardens of Trinity, where they could engage in serious discussion of the leading events of the day, or of their latest reading in general literature.

When he won the two Latin prizes and the English poem prize in 1842, Maine became known in the larger colleges. One evening as he sat reading, a knock at the door announced two mysterious visitors. He was invited to membership in the exclusive Cambridge secret society, the Apostles' Club. From the date of his acceptance, membership in the Club became Henry's most absorbing social activity. The Apostles' was easily the most famous of the Cambridge clubs in the nineteenth century. Interest in 'higher philosophy' and 'contemporary problems of England' were its concerns. The criteria of membership was intellectual merit. The twelve 'Apostles' met at 8.30 every Saturday evening during term in the rooms of the member whose turn it was to read a paper. When all had arrived, tea, coffee, and toast were served, after which the group gathered in a semicircle around the fireplace while the host, seating himself at a table in the middle of the room, read his paper. Then the members in turn aired their views of the essay, and following lengthy debate, entered their votes in a record book. Before the meeting was adjourned, the member whose turn it was to speak at the next meeting suggested four possible topics, and the others chose one from among these.[6]

At one of these meetings Maine first met Henry Fitzmaurice Hallam, the brother of Arthur Hallam, whose tragic early death had moved the poet Alfred Tennyson to compose *In Memoriam*. Maine and Henry Fitzmaurice shared many hours together in discussion and in 'reading aloud the older English dramatists'. Hallam's greatest interests were history and theology. He became a Sunday-school teacher while at Cambridge in order to 'apply his theories of religious

11

education'. Maine shared his interest in history, but apparently felt little of his concern over religious matters. Even the Oxford Movement, which was at its height during Maine's undergraduate years, failed to arouse his curiosity. As his biographer, Grant Duff later recalled, 'although he was too civil to say so, except to those with whom he was very intimate, Maine regarded most of his Oxford contemporaries as just a little off their heads'.[7] After Henry Hallam graduated in 1846, Maine frequently visited at his home in Wilton Crescent, London. There he met Hallam's father, Henry Hallam Sr, who was at the time among England's foremost historians. His *Constitutional History of England* (1827) was one of the earliest attempts at a systematic interpretation of the modern history of English law.

Throughout these years, Henry Hallam was probably Maine's closest friend. Unfortunately, their friendship was to be short-lived. Hallam died during a trip to Italy when only twenty-six years old, depriving Maine of his companionship and providing an unpleasant parallel to the more famous Arthur Hallam – Alfred Tennyson friendship. Maine prepared a *Memoir* for his friend that was privately published, in which he declared that: 'For those united with him in a companionship more than ordinarily close, his friendship had taken on such a character as to have almost become a necessity of existence.'[8] When Maine's second son was born in 1857 he remembered their friendship sufficiently well to name the child 'Henry Hallam Maine'.

Through Henry Hallam, Maine met the young biologist, Francis Galton, a cousin of Charles Darwin who later gained wide recognition as the founder of the science of eugenics. In his autobiography, Galton recalled Maine's impressive intellect during their years together in Cambridge, his 'great charm of manner with much beauty of feature . . . one of the few non-Trinity men who became thoroughly at home in Trinity itself'. In later life the two spent many hours at the Athenaeum Club in Pall Mall, London, discussing topics connected with primitive culture. Galton appealed to Maine's interests in science, whereas several other of his early companions constituted his 'literary circle'. William Cory, Julian Fane, Franklin Lushington and Tom Taylor seem to have been frequent visitors at his rooms. Cory, who later became assistant master at Eton, admired Maine's 'mastery in conversation and argument' and like Maine's Christ's Hospital contemporaries, was convinced he should devote his

12

life to poetry. If he saw any shortcoming in Maine, it was that he felt his manner too stiff and dispassionate, at times even arrogant. Julian Fane, whom Maine thought 'the most intelligent' person he met at Cambridge, went on to a career in the Foreign Office. Franklin Lushington, who came from a distinguished London literary family through which he was related to Leslie Stephen and Virginia Woolf, remained devoted to Maine until his death. Tom Taylor was probably the most versatile of the group: he became a successful London playwright, then later a professor in the University of London, and for the last years of his life, was the editor of *Punch*.[9]

Perhaps the most important friendship Maine made at Cambridge began during the summer of 1845, when he was vacationing at Filey with one of his fellow Apostles, Frederick Gibbs. While on a walk early one morning he narrowly avoided being shot by a hunter who accidentally fired in his direction. The young marksman introduced himself and made hurried apologies. His name was James Fitzjames Stephen,[10] author in years to come of one of the leading works of British conservative thought in the nineteenth century, *Liberty Equality, Fraternity* (1873). His career, as lawyer, Indian administrator, and critic of democratic trends in England, shows striking similarities to that of Maine's. Robust and self-consciously masculine, opinionated and attracted to emotional argument, Stephen's personality stood in sharp contrast to that of the more reserved Maine. Yet Maine's speedy action in nominating Stephen for membership of the Apostles' during the term immediately following their meeting suggests that personality differences did not hinder their friendship. In an entry in his unpublished autobiography, now in the Cambridge University Library, Stephen recalled his first meeting with Maine, and their friendship in the Apostles':

The summer holidays of 1845 I stayed with Frederick Gibbs at Filey, 7 miles from Scarborough, whence he was reading for the fellowship which he got in October of that year. It was there I made the acquaintance of my dear and faithful friend H. S. Maine, with whom I have been intimately connected in every successive phase of my life . . . He was a year or two younger than FWG and had just taken his degree as Head of the Classical Tripos, with almost unequalled distinction . . . FWG and I were there together for perhaps 10 weeks, and HSM for a fortnight or

13

three weeks . . . He was a specially shining Apostle and in all discussions not only took by far the first and best part, but did it so well and unpretentiously and in a strain so much above what the rest of us could reach, that it was a good piece of education to hear him.

The subjects discussed at Apostles' meetings were very cosmopolitan. Before Maine went up to Cambridge, religious themes had tended to predominate: 'The Origin of Evil', 'The Derivation of Moral Sentiment', 'Prayer and the Personality of God' were apparently typical subjects that occupied the earnest young men, but by the 1840s, these religious topics seem to have given way to abstract discussions of political and historical theory. The society unanimously agreed at one meeting that 'so far from being a derogation from the moral dignity of man, the system of expediency is the only method consistent with the condition of his action'. In another paper Stephen argued that there was 'no foundation for a philosophy of history in the analogy between the progressive improvements of mankind and that of which individuals are capable', a subject which bears the imprint of ideas that were later incorporated in Maine's *Ancient Law*. Julian Fane delivered a paper in which he advocated the use of 'some elements of socialism . . . in the reconstruction of society, which the spirit of the age demands'. Maine, for reasons that we unfortunately do not know, supported him. Elsewhere, he boldly contended that 'Carlyle is not a truly philosophical historian'. Inquiry was, of course, not limited to political and historical subjects. William Cory wrote to his parents in 1845 that he was preparing 'an essay on naval tactics' for the society, and in the same period Maine wrote a paper on Shakespeare's *Midsummer Night's Dream*. It was thought to be of such outstanding quality that the *Edinburgh Review* published it, his first work to see print besides the prize poems. Some passages from the essay, with minor revisions in wording, would almost serve as an apologia for his later advocacy of the 'historical and comparative method' of legal studies. As he wrote:

> We are convinced that there is always a great advantage in attempting to trace the thread of purpose . . . As in waters which swarm with life and riches, something well worth letting down the net for will be drawn up at every cast, even if it be not exactly that which we are seeking: some admirable unison of thought will be manifested.[11]

14

Membership in the Apostles' Club was undoubtedly the most rewarding distraction of Maine's undergraduate career. The practical advantages of associating with a select group of the most promising young men of his Cambridge generation, and of having his ideas tested, criticized and encouraged by them, as well as the friendships he maintained with influential former Apostles' who met at annual dinners at the Star and Garter Inn at Richmond, proved of great value to him. He continued to be actively interested in the affairs of the society long after he left Cambridge.

The year 1844, the final year of Maine's undergraduate course, proved a very busy one for him. He was a candidate for the Classical Tripos Examinations, a voluntary set of papers set for outstanding students who had passed the B.A. requirements and had also placed on the Mathematical Tripos. The race for the highly coveted honour of Senior Classic and First Chancellor's Medallist, decided on the basis of performance on the Tripos, was early conceded to be a contest between Maine and W. G. Clark, a mathematics student who later became Orator of the University. Undergraduates took sides, and wagered money in favour of their choice. Maine, 'the Pembroke man', took the confidence placed in him very seriously, and embarked on an exhaustive programme of study in preparation. A contemporary later recalled[12] that he rushed around the college libraries, 'ransacked all manner of notebooks and collections of marked passages', and 'seized upon all the available English verse he could find to translate into Greek and Latin'. He did not have energy to work more than nine hours daily, so to protect his health, his supporters would 'haul him out by main force and compel him to take an hour's walk every day'. His rival, W. G. Clark, in contrast, was apparently not one to be easily ruffled. He sturdily declined to forego his regular evening game of whist! Maine's method, however, proved more effective, for he was placed first in the examinations and was subsequently named Senior Classic. Shortly after, he was also chosen over Clark as First Chancellor's Medallist. His supporters were jubilant, and somewhat more affluent than when the betting had begun.

By any measure, Maine had compiled a remarkable university record. He was thus ideal material for a tutorship. His own college did not have an available position, since it was then required that a fixed proportion of Fellows be in Holy Orders. Shortly, however, he was offered instead a Junior Tutorship at Trinity Hall, the Cambridge law college. After deliberation, he accepted. He took up rooms there in late summer of 1844, near the mathematical lecture room in the principal court.

3

Law Don

Maine was just twenty-two years old when he began the classics tutorship at Trinity Hall. One of his first pupils was Charles Bristed, an American who was the founder of 'The Epigram Club', another Cambridge society in which Maine held membership. Each of the members composed verses, sent them unsigned to Bristed, and then over port and cheese listened to them read aloud. Maine specialized in light-hearted imitations of Macaulay and Coleridge,[1] while W. G. Clark, his undergraduate rival who had also accepted a tutorship upon graduation, 'elaborated perfect burlesques of the Popeian versifications and the University Prize Poems', perhaps with an eye to revenging his defeat by Maine in the Senior Classic competition. Some of the epigrams were apparently published anonymously in *Punch*.

Charles Bristed later wrote a book on his years as a Cambridge undergraduate, which enjoyed a wide circulation in America. Fortunately, he preserved in it some first-hand impressions of Maine as a young tutor:

> I had some curiosity [he wrote] to see how this tutor of mine, so young as he was, about two years my junior and fresh from a team himself, would get on at first, and whether his known cleverness would help him or be in his way. The result removed all doubts and surpassed my most sanguine expectations. I could feel that I was being admirably jockeyed. He had the greatest dexterity in impressing his knowledge upon others, made explanations that came to the point at once, and could not be misunderstood, corrected mistakes in a way that one was not apt to forget, supplied you with endless variety of happy expressions for composition and dodges in translation—in short, I was conscious of making progress

17

with him every day, and only regretted that I could not continue with him through the Long.[2]

Bristed also recalled Maine's performances at high table, where, while 'backward to speak before his elders (he had the rare merit of being either a talker or listener, as circumstances demanded)', when he did contribute to conversation, he did so 'in keen and rapid remarks that told like knock-out blows'.[3]

When Maine first taught at Cambridge during the 1840s, there was a striking contrast between the general mediocrity of academic life in the colleges of the unreformed University, and the individual scientific achievements of some of its leading professors. Thus, William Whewell, Master of Trinity, had worked with Lyell and Faraday to create appropriate nomenclatures for their revolutionary discoveries in geology and electricity, and was a noted authority on mechanics and the theory of tides, as well as being the author of the influential *History of the Inductive Sciences* (1837). The Director of the Cambridge Observatory, James Challis, had held the attention of all of Europe during the summer of 1846, when he engaged in a race with the French astronomer Urbain Leverrier to locate the new planet Neptune, whose position in the skies had been independently predicted by the Cambridge mathematician John Adams, Fellow of Pembroke and, after 1860, Lowndean Professor of Astronomy. It was Cambridge's Professor of Botany, John Stephens Henslow, who had recommended one of his former students, Charles Darwin, as naturalist for the *Beagle* expedition of 1831, a fateful choice which led indirectly to the eventual publication of Darwin's *On the Origin of Species* (1859). And in the law faculty, Andrew Amos, who was appointed Downing Professor of the Laws of England in 1848, was widely recognized as a leading Benthamite champion of the 'scientific' study and teaching of the law. He had previously been the first Professor of English Law at University College London (an appointment subsequently held with distinction by both his son and grandson), and had succeeded Macaulay as Law Member of the Governor-General's Council in India during 1837–43, a post Maine himself later held.

Against a background of growing confidence in the successes of scientific method, Maine began the study of Roman law shortly after his appointment to the classics tutorship. He had not long embarked

18

on this new venture when on 21 June 1847, he was appointed to the Regius Professorship of Civil Law at Cambridge. James Fitzjames Stephen, who was then still an undergraduate, attempted in his autobiography to recall the unusual circumstances of Maine's early appointment:

> Frederick Campbell (the present half-idiotic Lord Campbell) mentioned Maine to Lord Campbell the first, I do not quite know at what stage of Lord C's career, but before he was either Chancellor or Chief Justice, and through this introduction Maine came to be appointed Professor of Civil Law at Cambridge. It was at that time what I have heard called an ill-paid sinecure, worth perhaps £100 a year, or a little more.[4]

Stephen was close to the truth in his description of the Professorship as an 'ill-paid sinecure'. There was at the time little interest in Roman Law or indeed in law teaching in general among English lawyers. Professor William Holdsworth, in his massive *History of English Law*, has concluded that until well into the nineteenth century the state of English legal education was 'a very melancholy topic . . . The law student was obliged to get his knowledge of law by means of undirected reading and discussion, and by attendance in chambers, in a law office, or in the courts.'[5] Admission to the Bar was regulated by each of the four ancient Inns of Court in London, where there were no lectures or examinations, and the keeping of terms was calculated according to the number of meals eaten at the prospective barrister's Inn. In 1833 the Incorporated Law Society, a quite separate body which controlled the admission of solicitors, instituted lectures for articled clerks on the 'practical' subjects of common law, equity and conveyancing, and after 1843 examinations came to be required of all candidates. While professorships of law existed at both Oxford and Cambridge, there had been little actual teaching since Blackstone, as the first incumbent of the Vinerian Chair at Oxford, had urged (with greater effect in America than England) the systematic study of the academic rather than the practical branches of law in the universities. Only at the new University College London, where Bentham's disciple John Austin held a professorship of jurisprudence long enough to prove himself a brilliant theorist and a miserable lecturer, and later at King's College, London, was there any university level legal teaching to speak of.

19

Jurisprudence was regarded with downright suspicion by many an English lawyer. There were occasional books by Englishmen which recommended to beginning law students a thorough preliminary grounding in the principles of English and Roman Law, but even the more successful of these, such as Nathaniel Lindley's *Introduction to the Study of Jurisprudence* (1855), were viewed as somewhat eccentric productions. And while the great name of Jeremy Bentham carried the weight of authority among influential legislators, there is no denying that his grandiose jurisprudence conjured up images of quackery to most 'practical' lawyers. So far as foreign writing was concerned, portions of the work of the great German historical jurist, von Savigny, had become available in French translations by M. Guenoux, but these were scarce, as was the limited English edition of his *Roman Law During the Middle Ages*.[6]

On the other hand, through the interest of John Stuart Mill the more general comparative methods of studying society, associated with the names of such continental scholars as Montesquieu and Tocqueville, were gradually becoming known in England by the 1840s. Moreover, a widely publicized Select Committee, appointed in 1846 to investigate the state of legal education in England and Ireland, concluded that British lawyers needed formal training in the principles of both English and Roman law, and that the best way to achieve this goal was to require them to pass examinations that covered previously neglected comparative and philosophical materials.[7] Maine's sympathy with these views was reflected in the close attention he bestowed on his evidence to the Oxford and Cambridge Commission of 1850. Maine informed the commissioners that the lectures he delivered at Cambridge dealt with general jurisprudence, illustrated by Roman and English law, and that related subjects of study were moral philosophy, legal history, and international law.[8] His students were required to translate Justinian's *Institutes*, and to have a command of conversational Latin. The order of topics dealt with followed that of Samuel Hallifax's *Analysis of the Civil Law* (1774).

Like his predecessor, Dr James Geldart, who had edited a new edition of Hallifax's book in 1836, Maine did not think the performance of an 'Act'—a formal Latin disputation in the syllogistic form on two questions of law—was an adequate measure of competence for the B.C.L. degree. He had therefore continued and strengthened

Dr Geldart's system of terminal examinations.[9] In hopes of rescuing the law school from its reputation as 'the refuge of the very idle',[10] Maine made several recommendations to the Commissioners. Most importantly, he called for the establishment of a Board of Legal Studies in Cambridge similar to the already existent Board of Mathematical Studies, which would administer a schedule of law lectures, and, along with one or two examiners attached to it, supervise the requirements for a new Law Tripos.

He further suggested that the required attendance at lectures of the Regius Professor be reduced to one term, the other two being devoted to the study of English law and moral philosophy. Finally, he urged careful attention to the fashioning of a law curriculum that would emphasize the historical, comparative and philosophical materials usually neglected in England.[11] When the Commission Report was published in 1852, the emphasis it placed on the future role of the universities as teachers of philosophical jurisprudence on the one hand, and as the link joining legal scholarship to other branches of social study on the other, must have greatly pleased Maine. As the Report concluded:

> We are of opinion that the instruction provided . . . shall not be confined to the laws of this country or to any particular code, but that, in addition to the study of English, Civil and International Law, it should embrace an examination of the principles on which existing systems of law are founded . . . and . . . should be extended to an investigation of the principles on which all laws ought to be founded: in other words, that the study of General Jurisprudence, and of the science of Legislation and of Morals in connection therewith, ought to be encouraged.[12]

In 1854 a Board of Legal Studies was established in Cambridge, and in 1858 the first Law Tripos results were published.[13]

The Report contained other news that must have been received with equal pleasure in the Maine household. In his evidence to the Commission Maine had complained that the endowments of the Cambridge Legal Professorships were 'not sufficient to buy lawyers of learning and talent out of their profession. . . . I myself am a practising barrister, my two immediate predecessors were beneficed clergymen, and in none of these cases can it be said that the University was the theatre of the Professor's most engrossing labours'.[14] He added that if the guaranteed income could not be increased, it was at least imperative that the method of accepting payment for attendance at lectures and admission to degrees be altered. 'Under the existing state of things,' he suggested, 'nothing but the personal character of the Professor can save him from the imputation of competing with the University for the fees on degrees by relaxing the stringency of the examination by which degrees are conferred.' Under the new system of Triposes recommended by the Commission, Maine was to receive a total of £319 2s 8d. from degree fees, lecture tickets, and a special parliamentary grant.[15] The increase conveniently coincided with a period of growing financial responsibility for the young law professor. On 20 December 1847 Maine had married his first cousin, Jane Main, at the Episcopal Church in Brisbane Place, Kelso.[16] The wedding service was conducted by the same Reverend Mr Kell who had married Jane's parents in the same church twenty-five years earlier. On 18 March 1850 Jane gave birth to the Maine's first child at their London home in Finchley Road.[17] The baby, a boy, was christened 'Charles Sumner', the second name given as was his father's, in honour of John Bird Sumner.

Apparently the regulated domestic routine imposed by marriage served for a time to better Maine's health. He visited William Cory at Eton shortly after his marriage, and had fully recovered from the extended illness that had brought him to the verge of a complete breakdown during the two previous years.[18] The two walked in the school park at Windsor reminiscing, and Maine talked at length of London literary and political gossip. Cory wrote in his diary afterwards: 'He is inexhaustibly lively and powerful: somewhat impetuous still, but thanks to marriage and hydropathy, more kind and gentle, and philanthropic.'[19]

The Maines took temporary lodgings in Cambridge during term, and seem to have done a good deal of entertaining. Through an introduction by the Reverend William Brookfield, one of the original Apostles', the Maines met the novelist William Makepeace Thackeray and he spent a weekend with them in Cambridge during March 1849. Thackeray wrote to Brookfield's wife that 'we brexf'sted with Mr and Mrs Mayne, and I thought him a most kind, gentle and loveable sort of man, and I liked her artlessness and simplicity'. The 'sumptuous breakfast' of broiled fowl was prelude to a morning of discussion between Maine and Thackeray, later joined by Julian Fane and Vernon Harcourt.[20] Maine and Thackeray continued to meet after their first introduction, and it was probably the young law professor's knowledge of general literature that made him an interesting companion for the novelist. Thackeray apparently found Maine's wife less appealing. Quite aside from her 'artlessness and simplicity', the author of *Vanity Fair* felt that 'Mrs Mayne . . . does not look so pretty mornings, as when candlelight illumines her simple beauties'.[21] Yet a letter written by Mrs Brookfield to the historian Henry Hallam, describing another of the Maine's parties, suggests that Thackeray may not have done full justice to her talents:

> According to agreement, I pen a few words descriptive of the festivities at Professor Maine's, but I rather fear they will be more briefly expressed than may meet your views.
>
> There were, I daresay, thirty or fourty people, Mrs Maine singing Italian as we came in, and subsequently the celebrated Scotch songs. Not knowing a human being rendered the first half-hour slightly depressing, but I was introduced to one or two ladies and to dear Harcourt and Holland, who were both of them affable and conversed agreeably with me for the rest of the evening.
>
> I thought it was a brisk little party, 'take it all for all', with a most sumptuous collation by way of supper. Trifles and pyramidal tipsey cakes and jellies of the most ornamental descriptions were flanked by the solid fowl and the energing sandwich, and people 'pitched in' tremendously. Mrs Maine has a very pretty voice and looked very nice doing the honours, and with her husband I am smitten, as I always was, you know.[22]

Maine's marriage to his first cousin in 1847 brought him little in the way of a dowry, and the circumstances of his early education as a Christ's Hospital 'Blue Coat Boy' suggest that his own family had been unable to contribute much to supplement his professional earnings in the period. Maine, while a passionate defender of the rights of wealth and landed privilege in his later political writings, was not himself a man of great financial resources, a factor that as much as his ill health placed serious obstacles in the path of his later career in public life. While he eventually realized a sizeable income from prudent investments in Indian stocks, he was never, by the standards of his contemporaries, a wealthy man, and was least of all so in his youth. Thus, while he welcomed the increase in his Cambridge salary recommended by the University Commission, he apparently continued to have financial worries during the 1850s. Ideally, since his physical presence was not always required at Cambridge, he hoped for a position in London that he could hold at the same time as the university professorship. For a lawyer, the obvious answer was private practice. Shortly after the birth of his first son, Maine did in fact become an attorney, and he practised for a time at the Common Law Bar. He travelled briefly on the Norfolk Circuit, and also tried his hand at the Equity branch, but in each instance, the pressures of private practice proved too great for his delicate constitution. Fortunately for academic jurisprudence, another opportunity presented itself. After the findings of the Select Committee of 1846 were published, several of the Inns of Court established lectureships, and the foundations were laid for closer co-operation between each of them. In 1852 the Council of Legal Education, a general co-ordinating body of the four institutions, came into being.[23] Five Readerships were created, and to one of these, that of Jurisprudence and Civil Law, Maine was appointed.

Maine brought to his London appointment the very freshness of approach that he had recommended for the law curriculum of Cambridge University. 'The fault of our legal system', he wrote in an article on the state of legal studies in England at the time, 'is that it is exclusively practical . . . with us, law is not a science.'[24] Maine's lectures on jurisprudence, given in the Middle Temple, apparently drew large numbers of young lawyers. In them he stressed the lessons to be learned by the English student of law from the study of Roman law, in which the various stages of Roman legal development, from its earliest written expression to the culmination of its juridical sophistication in the *Institutes* of Justinian, could be analysed alongside comparable stages, where they existed, in English legal growth. Yet while he laid the foundations of his historical jurisprudence in this period, it is an interesting fact that he seems to have known little of the detail of Roman civil law. According to J. F. Stephen, Maine's true greatness as an English jurist was as an inspired teacher and impassioned advocate, who used Roman law to breath new life into old truths:

Neither Maine himself, nor I suppose, anyone else in England, knew anything whatever about Roman Law at that time, & it is remarkable and characteristic that Maine himself, though he reintroduced the study of the subject into England, never, I believe, was much of a civilian. I suppose he knew the Institutes, but I doubt if he ever knew much of the Pandects. He knew the lack of the subject however. He was able to set Roman law in its proper position in relation to other subjects, He derived, in the most beautiful manner, applications of history and philosophy to Roman law. He found it, as he told me once (half in fun) in the Book of Revelation, in which, by the way, Renan had countenanced him a good deal. He was enabled to sniff at Bentham for knowing nothing about it, & writing in consequence about English law, in a merely revolutionary manner: in short, being a man of talent and originality, coming close to Genesis, he transfigured one of the driest of subjects into all sorts of beautiful things, without knowing or caring much of its details. [25]

While a lecturer at the Middle Temple, Maine first met M. E. Grant Duff, who eventually became his biographer. They were introduced in 1853, when Maine served as examiner for a studentship of fifty guineas won by Grant Duff. He found Maine a dedicated teacher and friend, later recalling: 'What struck me most about him as a companion at that time was the strange contrast between the excessive fragility of his appearance—for he was just recovering from an illness which had been all but fatal, and the vigour of his mind.'[26] Grant Duff kept detailed diaries from his undergraduate days, and these have been collected along with many of his other papers by a grand-daughter, Mrs Sheila Sokolov-Grant of Orford, Suffolk. But the volume for the 1850s, when as Grant Duff later wrote, he was 'extremely intimate' with Maine, is unfortunately missing. We are thus denied whatever information it might have contributed to the reconstruction of this formative period of Maine's career.

A mutual friend of Maine and Grant Duff at the Middle Temple, the studious Irishman Whitley Stokes, may well have influenced Maine's intellectual development. Stokes early in his career became an enthusiastic student of the new Germanic science of comparative philology, and one recent writer has claimed him as Ireland's greatest philologist. When Maine went to India in 1862, he made Stokes head of the new Legislative Department at Calcutta, and when his *Early History of Institutions* was published in 1875, which drew heavily on early Irish legal materials, Maine dedicated it to him, 'In Recollection of a Long Official Connection, and Still Longer Friendship'. Through the efforts of Max Müller and certain members of the Ethnological Society of London, the techniques of philology were becoming known to a larger audience in England, and Maine makes frequent reference to the subject in his published writings. It is quite feasible, as one historian of ideas has suggested, that this new science influenced him as much as did evolutionary biology.[27]

Frederic Harrison had been a reluctant law student on entering the Inns in 1856, yet listening to Maine's lectures he developed a keen interest in jurisprudence. He later recalled that 'I insisted on becoming Maine's pupil for six months, as a condition of keeping my reason during my study of law.'[28] Maine gave him private tutorials, and Harrison wrote to a friend at Oxford: 'To tell the impulse my studies have received in law from Maine, I cannot begin. I am quite employed all day & already 3 nights in the week are regularly taken up.'[29] In his *Memoirs*, Harrison remembered many mornings during the 1850s spent in Maine's chambers at 1 Stone Building, Chancery Lane, where he met 'W. Vernon Harcourt, George Venables, Fitzjames Stephen, Vaughan Johnson, etc., and we discussed a good deal of general literature and politics.' When they met in 1856, Harrison remembered Maine as 'in deplorable health . . . without court business, and in poor prospects even of life'.[30] Though his tutor was sickly, however, he impressed Harrison with his 'brilliant scholarship and analytical genius'. Maine set him a series of papers to write on Roman civil law during the winter of 1857, and according to Harrison, he was already at that time at work on *Ancient Law*.[31] He saw Maine as more historian than lawyer, and thought his Middle Temple lectures revealed his true academic character as more that of a social philosopher than of a jurist in the strict sense. Already when the two young men had met, Harrison had come under the influence of Auguste Comte, and had met the French social scientist in Paris the summer before taking up the study of law under Maine. Usually regarded as the moving spirit behind the foundation of modern sociology, Comte saw human history as an evolutionary pro-

26

cess that could be described by means of scientific laws of social continuity and change. Harrison must have brought his enthusiasm for the ambitious theories of Comte to his friendship with Maine.

To the period of his Readership at the Inns of Court belong Maine's first published legal writings. Although they do not bear the imprint of any one intellectual influence, they do clearly suggest an approach to legal studies that differed considerably from those familiar to English lawyers of his day. The earliest legal paper Maine published was the printed version of a lecture he delivered before the Juridical Society of London on 16 April 1855, entitled *The Conception of Sovereignty and its Importance in International Law*.[32] The discussion of John Austin is of special interest, for it was to be the achievement of Maine's mature legal writings to point out the weaknesses of Austin's influential 'analytical' jurisprudence, primarily set out in the *Province of Jurisprudence Determined*, one of the great systematic treatises of English legal literature in the nineteenth century. At the heart of Austin's analysis of the nature of law, which combined Hobbesian and Benthamite elements, was the assumption that the obligation of the citizenry to obey in any legal system depended primarily upon the theoretically complete power of a ruler to command obedience. Locating this 'sovereign', according to Austin, was reasonably straightforward. 'If a determinate human superior, not in the habit of obedience to a like superior, receive habitual obedience from the bulk of a given society', he wrote, 'that determinate superior is sovereign in that society.' While acknowledging Austin's undeniable brilliance at legal definition, Maine believed he had erred in according to the notion of 'sovereignty', as the positive commands of a ruler, such a central position in his system. His was a non-historical and culturally biased view, for the idea of 'territorial sovereignty', which lay at the basis of the Austinian notion of law, had no application to vast areas of human society.[33] In Maine's estimation, the elaborate linguistic analyses of Austin's *Province of Jurisprudence Determined* too frequently sacrificed the deeper understanding of the actual legal arrangements of diverse societies for mere logical symmetry.

In an important further paper on 'Roman Law and Legal Education', published during the following year and later reprinted in his *Village Communities*, Maine expanded his views in urging that the systematic study of Roman civil law would help to correct the limited

27

cultural scope of the Austinian approach. Using Roman legal records, the most complete remnants of a past system of legal practice, Maine believed it possible to infer similar general stages of development through which other progressive legal systems must pass before they ever attained the sophisticated and relatively modern stages described by Austin's jurisprudence. 'It is not because our own jurisprudence and that of Rome were once alike that they ought to be studied together', he argued, 'it is because they will be alike.'[34] That his ideas would need further elucidation was apparently clear to him at the time. He suggested in one of his papers that a fuller inquiry into the relationship between Roman legal institutions and the general science of jurisprudence 'would be obviously absurd to prosecute within the limits of an essay like the present'. He was already engaged in 1856 in the task of beginning to incorporate his 'historical and comparative' theories in a larger work. Maine was not, however, able to devote his full energies to these further legal studies. There were apparently recurring problems of financial insecurity. 'The salaries of the Readers are fixed at a rate so low', he complained of the Inns at the time, 'as to render private practice a necessary adjunct to their official position.'[35] For Maine, 'private practice' came largely to mean employment as an occasional journalist.

The *Saturday Review*

Maine had apparently already begun to write for the newspapers shortly after his marriage in 1847, when he contributed leaders to the *Morning Chronicle*. J. F. Stephen recalled in his unpublished autobiography that:

> Just as I was leaving college, the *Morning Chronicle* was in its palmy state. Sydney Herbert and some of the other Peelites, and W. Gladstone and some other of Sir R. Peel's followers, as they were then called, sank a mint of money in it. I have heard as much as £200,000, and as far as writing went, it was one of the best papers of the day. Maine was rather mysteriously a writer on it, and so were some of my other friends . . . The pay was very high, £3 10*s*. 0*d*. each article.[1]

Unfortunately, since it was then common practice for articles to be published unsigned, no record of Maine's writings for the *Morning Chronicle* seems to have survived. When Grant Duff composed his *Memoir* of Maine in 1892, he claimed to have had access to a marked file of articles on foreign and domestic politics that Maine published in the *Morning Chronicle* during 1849, but I have been unable to trace it. We know little beyond his observation that Maine's articles illustrated that his political sympathies at the time lay with the free-trade Peelite group within the unreformed Tory party, rather than with the protectionists.

Changes in the political world eventually brought the once proud *Chronicle* to the verge of bankruptcy. When Lord Aberdeen formed his coalition Government in December of 1852 he included a sizeable Peelite representation, yet he apparently initiated the practice of allowing *The Times* earlier copies of public documents than its competitors, and the Peelite *Chronicle* suffered steady setbacks in circulation and prestige.[2] In the autumn of 1854 circulation had fallen to only 2,500 copies daily, and the paper was shortly thereafter bought by Serjeant Glover, a Liberal party sympathizer. The fiery editor of the *Chronicle*, and one of the most colourful in Fleet Street history, James Douglas Cook, resigned, as did most of his Peelite Conservative contributors. Maine was not, however, for long without employment as a political journalist. Cook persuaded A. J. B. Beresford-Hope, a wealthy High Church Tory, to undertake the proprietorship of a new literary journal and Maine, who was enthusiastic, assisted him in recruiting contributors from the universities. Plans for the new weekly developed speedily. In the early weeks of September 1855 Maine spent a holiday at 'Eden', the family home of Grant Duff at Torlair, Banffshire. He was preoccupied from the time of his arrival there. Grant Duff recorded in his diary for September 11: 'Maine . . . is full of a new paper which is to appear this autumn, and for which he asked me to write . . . Maine . . . propose(s) to call it the *Saturday Review*'.[3] The first number of the famous literary journal was published shortly afterwards, on 3 November 1855.

Maine came to the *Saturday Review* as a veteran newspaper writer and an already accomplished stylist. As Frederic Harrison had found of his abilities at Middle Temple, he had 'a rare literary instinct'. After he and his wife moved to Albion Street near Marble Arch in 1853, Maine began buying small hard-covered work books at Hammond's Stationery Shop in Edgeware Road. The books could easily be carried on trips to the City. When a free moment presented itself at the Inns, he would jot down phrases that could later be worked into his articles. Several such work books are amongst Maine's manuscripts in the British Library of Political and Economic Science:

> The finest thoughts are like diamonds, formed by the pressure of enormous masses of thought . . . Cliqueism is the chrysalis-stage of opinion, which but for its kindly shelter would be early dashed to pieces against the rude projections of an inhospitable world . . .
> All the brilliance of his elaborate impromptu, and all the fervour of his factitious indignation . . .
> Frozen up like the tune in Munchausen's post-boy's horn . . .

Recession beyond the soundings of reason . . .
Point on which one piques oneself . . .[4]

he wrote in a tiny hand. He filled page after page with his literary phrases, often interspersing them among the London addresses of friends.

Until recently, it would have been impossible to identify Maine's articles in the *Saturday Review*, as like the *Morning Chronicle*, it followed a policy of leaving articles unsigned. Grant Duff, for example, was aware of Maine's close association with the journal, but made virtually no reference in his biography of Sir Henry to specific articles he wrote. Fortunately, however, J. F. Stephen, whom Maine recruited to the staff, left a marked file in his library which has come to light. M. M. Bevington made careful use of this file, and a similar one in the Columbia University Library, as a basic source for a definitive study of the early years of the *Saturday Review*.[5] Although Stephen's file extended over only the first three volumes of the review, it provides a clear idea of the extent of Maine's involvement. There are seventy articles attributed to him, in all probability only a fraction of the total number he submitted over the four or five years of his close attachment to the paper as a leader writer during the 1850s. With this sampling, however, we are able to enjoy a previously unavailable perspective on his lifelong political writings, and to see the direction of his political thought during the same period that he was composing *Ancient Law*.

As a young law professor writing for the *Saturday Review*, Maine constantly expressed his preference for a government that was conducted by an experienced, time-tested aristocracy. 'We will any day back the men of birth', he wrote without reservation in 1857. Granted that the great families of England had had something of a monopoly of political power in the past, he submitted that it was a monopoly which 'even political economists call a natural monopoly, and respect under that name'.[6] In his study of history, he found a sort of 'iron law of oligarchy', which showed that:

> for centuries to come, Parliament will be over-shadowed by aristocratic influence; and it is only once in a score of years that a Bright, a Gladstone, or a Disraeli will mount painfully to those niches in the legislature into which a Derby or a Palmerston half-contemptuously lounges. It is indeed certain that as years go

by, the aristocracy must lose, and the classes below it gain, in political power and influence. *But political power and influence only determine the interests which are to be attended to, and prove nothing of the statesmen who will be selected to attend to them.*[7]

Writing in the 1850s, well after the passage of the Great Reform Bill, Maine clearly realized that the old class aristocracy was in itself a declining force in practical politics, yet he held firmly to the view that in every generation, there is a relatively small group which, regardless of birth, forms the ruling segment of the community. In other words, Maine's conception of politics was from his earliest years based on the assumption that social and political power is inevitably exercised by privileged élites. The chief virtue of the old English élite, centred in the landed aristocracy, had in his estimation been its experience, and Maine believed such a quality of leadership equally important in the newer middle class rulers:

> A man may have been flogged into the condition of St Lawrence at Eton, and plucked as clean as an Irish goose at Oxford, but if he has lived ever since in the atmosphere of Parliament, he will know more than any man who ever endorsed bills of lading until he is forty can ever hope to know.[8]

Given these views, he understandably had little enthusiasm for the prospect of universal suffrage, a prospect made more immediate through the propagandistic efforts of the disciples of Jeremy Bentham. To give political power to the masses, he felt, must lead to tyranny, for while sovereignty might theoretically reside with the people, it would in fact be managed by the democratic politician. Maine's *Saturday Review* notion of politicians was different from his admiration of natural élites. He thought that the wider political power was distributed, the more abstract party slogans would become, and feared that these would be unscrupulously manipulated by opportunistic demagogues. Since most people, in Maine's estimation, are naïve, poorly informed and dissatisfied, they would be likely to build unwarranted expectations on the promises made by politicians in return for their votes, and when these were not fulfilled, to lose faith altogether in their rulers.

Maine was concerned about the attention newly given by statesmen to the 'public opinion' created by the popular press, and felt that responsible political leadership could be seriously endangered if the superficially informed readers of newspapers came to control influential opinion—the mass of indiscriminate Englishmen who, while claiming fair play as one of their leading characteristics, were 'in all matters except fisticuffs . . . terribly apt to apply the rule of give and take, by taking everything, and leaving nothing'.[9] Maine turned to the analysis of public opinion in many of his *Saturday Review* articles. Interestingly, it was often not the penny press he attacked, but the newspaper most associated with authoritative reporting, *The Times*. Far from denying its brilliance, he feared that its very calibre tended to produce among his contemporaries unquestioned acceptance of its reports. Maine thought newspapers provided a dangerous potential for political manipulation. 'Consider', he warned, 'that each of your literary rulers has been selected to govern you, not for his Absolute Wisdom, but for his peppery style and fertility of illusion.'[10] Already in 1855, he felt, the country was 'governed' to an alarming extent by Printing House Square:

> It is high time we began to realize the magnificent spectacle afforded by British freedom—30 millions of *Cives Romani* governed despotically by a newspaper . . . All conversation, all action, all literature is full of the proof that we live under a tyranny, and except a small protesting minority, nobody seems to mind it.[11]

Maine complained that even the once more responsible weeklies relied on the opinions of *The Times* as if they were 'Truth'.

Maine deplored the tendency for individual newspapers to become exclusively the spokesmen for political parties. 'From watching the papers daily', he wrote in one of his early articles, 'it is possible to see how the principles of Party Vituperation proceed.'[12] Maine questioned the advantages for England of a system of political organization which, as trends in the newspaper world suggested, would permit everyone with whom one did not agree 'to be painted as a prodigy of incapacity, a miracle of folly, or a monster of crime'. What was the purpose of the modern tendency to honour partisanship to the point that it effectively removed the possibility of an objective assessment of political reality? 'It first imputes evil', he asserted, 'and then denies the good which that evil may be supposed to carry with it. . . . It is, in short, the fruit of a hate so blind as to be afraid of the admissions with which it suspects its own evil-speaking to be pregnant.'[13] Maine had similarly bitter comments for journalists 'who employ the language of party'. He believed such writers to be 'exactly those who have become a proverb in the English press for the most childish imbecility and the most disgraceful ignorance'. Organized political parties, he suggested, had 'the charms which marriage has for a rake',[14] and added that modern party activists were guilty of following blindly the often inconsistent platforms constructed by their leaders for their party advantage:

> Already you are manifesting considerable aptitude for the policy which has conducted your leader to eminence—already the Jacobinal colouring of your language and argument shows that you are not indisposed to alternate Conservative commonplace with Revolutionary prose and Radical verse. All you have to learn is the art of diverting attention while you shift your views . . . when you have mastered that, the rest is quite simple.[15]

For Maine, Benjamin Disraeli was an apt example of the new brand of popular British politician. Maine wrote of Disraeli, whom he despised for his opposition to Peel's Corn Bill in 1846, that he displayed 'the same intensity of faith which animated General Bonaparte to profess Islam'. The only time, in his judgement, when one might serve a party and keep a clear conscience, was when genuine national crises created identifiable issues. Otherwise, it was 'difficult to get by without damaging your conscience or emasculating your intelligence'. He thought the inconsistencies of current party platforms made this clear, for a 'low-born Conservative makes a meal of Maynooth, the Sabbath, the extinction of Roman Catholic Chaplains, and the virtues of Mr Disraeli', while 'a plebian Liberal swallows the Ballot, the extension of the Suffrage, Financial Reform, and the Abolition of Church Rates'.[16]

A leading theme of Maine's *Saturday Review* articles was his concern over the erosion of traditional political authority in England, for as he observed, 'The Reign of her present Majesty is contemporaneous with the transition from a period of considerable court influence to a period in which that influence will have to succumb altogether to the power of public opinion.'[17] Authority for Maine, as his early political writings constantly illustrate, meant far more than simple legal capacity. It meant competence to lead, a special moral quality reserved for the natural élite whose functions would be

34

usurped in modern democracy. Without their leadership, there could be no stability *and* progress, for the mass of men were irresponsible and incapable of self-government.[18] They were also incapable of understanding their own best interests:

> A free people [Maine reflected] so far from habitually showing undue severity, is open to the exactly opposite reproach . . . it is indulgent to a fault . . . instead of turning fiercely on unlooked for ill-success, it retains its partialities in spite of failures almost ludicrous for their completeness . . . it is so offended by the very semblance of injustice as to be infinitely readier to condemn the official censor, who seems to have done little more than his duty, than to quarrel with the censured public servant, who appears to have done a little less.[19]

Maine wrote many *Saturday Review* articles on politics and society in France and America, where he believed 'mere numbers' counted most, and the modern theory of democracy has had its most thorough application to practice. In doing so, he clearly hoped to provide a lesson for his fellow Englishmen, before they wholeheartedly adopted the Benthamite doctrine of the greatest happiness of the greatest number as their leading standard of morals and legislation. The French revolutionary slogans of 1789, he repeatedly pointed out, had invariably resulted in the negation of meaningful freedom whenever they were taken seriously. Every French republican attempt at mass democracy had come to the same ending, 'a tyranny of which the parallel can only be found in ancient fable.'[20] He was less critical of American political institutions, for Maine thought the pernicious teachings of Rousseau, the chief prophet of modern European democracy, had not attained so fundamental an influence in the pragmatic democracy of the new world. His primary criticisms of American democracy, rather, were of a general cultural nature. He felt that democratic worship of the common man had led in America to lower cultural standards. The better class of Englishman would be less likely to be guilty of this than his American counterpart, according to Maine, because of 'the influence exerted over the former by the institution of kingship', that is, because the Englishman's sense of social status was based upon a clearly recognized hierarchy within which traditional aristocratic values were readily transmitted.[21] In Maine's rather uncharitable view, whether one examined the mass circulation news-papers invented by James Gordon Bennett of New York, or the narrative poetry of Walt Whitman, the current state of American letters offered sobering evidence to support his analysis of the probable cultural effects of introducing democracy to England.[22]

Maine's other writings, which dealt with such topical questions as civil service reform, the Crimean War, and the future of the British East India Company, reaffirm that whatever his ostensible subject, his chief *Saturday Review* purpose was a wide-ranging confrontation of the major tenets of later Benthamite radicalism. Indeed, his anonymous early journal writings represent a highly significant conservative response to the urgent, and in some instances alarmist, reform message of the philosophical radicals, which was propagated through the same medium in this period.[23] Maine's intention in these further articles was to deal explicitly with those who wished to harness the new power of popular opinion to force upon the ruling classes untested ideas that were bound to result in the total reorganization not only of the voting lists, but of the entire professional administration of British affairs.[24] He feared that the adoption of such schemes would be accompanied by a shift away from political individualism in the direction of state collectivism.

The Administrative Reform Association, founded by a group of London businessmen and politicians in May 1855, hoped to secure not only the speedy implementation of the famous Northcote-Trevelyan Report of 1854 on Civil Service reform, but through their further efforts, to effect a general reform of all government practices. Wedded to the twin goals of efficiency and publicity in politics,[25] the Association bore the brunt of many of Maine's anonymous critiques during these years. He wrote sarcastically of Arthur Roebuck, the radical parliamentary leader of the reformers and longstanding Benthamite, that he 'claims to represent the reform of a system—he holds himself out to the world as equal to a series of definite acts, as able to suggest and carry out the reorganization of complicated administrative machinery'.[26] While the Association urged that the introduction into government departments of the Benthamite idea of competitive examinations would lead to greater efficiency and the eradication of unearned privilege, Maine questioned where all the reformist fervour would end, and wondered aloud whether the result would actually prove to be a better system or merely a different one:

It seems to be commonly believed that the conception of a Competitive Examination suggests itself as naturally to the human mind as the ideas of Right and Duty. But the fact is, the very notion of competition, as a reliable criterion of knowledge and skill, would have been utterly strange in England before the dates of the Oxford Prize-lists and the Cambridge Triposes.[27]

Maine thought too extreme a reliance on examinations could lead to the eradication of 'practical knowledge' in British public life, and would tend to reward dullness.[28] Infinitely more important to the business of ruling, in his judgement, was 'a little forethought and knowledge of the world'.[29] Echoing Burke, he submitted that so far from it being desirable to honour efficiency to the point of 'turning Her Majesty's Government into what tradesmen call "a concern",'[30] efficiency must actually take second place to experience and compromise in the political education of Britain's rulers:

> Five centuries of free government, and nearly two of parliamentary omnipotence, have given us as their accumulated result, a special system of legislation; and it is by a perpetual play of compromise, by winning upon prejudices and cooling down enthusiasms, by taking a little here and giving a little there, that English Ministers produce laws—not, indeed, perfect in technical form—but worthy of all respect as the closest expression of a national will known to the civilized world.[31]

In statesmanship, what was appropriate could never be dispassionately assessed in advance with any precision, as if politics was 'a game of chess'. In the political market place, 'calculations can only be effected in the rough—apparent causes do not always, and cannot always, produce their expected effects—the greatest successes are frequently only the result of a favourable balance of blunders'.[32] Yet Maine thought his contemporaries were increasingly accustomed to accept the reformer's confident assertions that the complex world of politics could be explained and rearranged at will, if only enough publicity was brought to bear on its management:

> To the reader in his armchair, nothing can be clearer, more satisfactory, or more intelligible. Every movement is explained. Every event is assigned to its proper cause. The character of every leading

actor is analyzed, and the effect produced by every one of his moral and intellectual qualities on the undertaking which he conducted is traced out and described. But does any man in his senses believe it all? Did anybody who ever took part in the scenes depicted find his own recollections tally in the very least?[33]

Maine's *Saturday Review* articles were polemical in tone, and, appearing as they did at regular intervals, were largely composed of first thoughts on the leading issues of the day. Their good and bad points must in fairness be judged in that light. On the one hand, his prediction that modern public opinion would become increasingly monopolized by a few nationally powerful newspapers has been partially fulfilled by the demise, since he wrote, of a great number of privately owned and editorially independent journals. Similarly, we may admire his prescience in warning of the dangers to freedom when newspapers become exclusively the spokesmen for political parties. On the other hand, he underestimated the role of newspapers as guardians of the public interest. Those that have survived the economic tests of marketability in the liberal democracies have tended to offset each other's attempts to monopolize news coverage, and in doing so have encouraged the wider dissemination of knowledge about public affairs. Responsible reporting has been encouraged by the disappearance of anonymous journalism, and, among British papers, recent years have witnessed a steady development away from the direct affiliation of newspapers with specific political parties. And of course, Maine could not have seen that in modern political systems newspapers would by no means be the sole arbiters of public opinion: they compete with radio and television, as well as with interest groups, political parties, and independent scribblers, for the attention of the private citizen.

Maine's related views on the dangers inherent in popularly organized political parties finally come down to his personal preference for aristocratic politics. While he argued in the *Saturday Review* for a return to the system of parliamentary factions exercising the function of what Burke called the 'virtual representation' of general interests, democrats have regarded such views as misleadingly romantic reconstructions of the past, and believe that political parties that are directly dependent on the general support of a democratic electorate are the best means so far devised for attaining truly responsible government. While Maine further connected the notion that popular parties must be well disciplined to be effective, with the conclusion that this meant an oppressive degree of internal party control, the overall experience of western democracies suggests that competing groups, both within and among popular parties have often served as checks upon the theoretically complete power of their leadership. Finally, while few would dispute Maine's argument that experience is preferable to mere academic knowledge in those who govern us, it is today a more relevant point that modern government demands that both qualities be taken together.

Maine's *Saturday Review* articles reveal him as a passionate libertarian and a robust Whiggish defender of the value of practical knowledge over abstract ideas in politics.[34] Like John Stuart Mill, Maine was sensitive to the growing demands of social conformity in mid-Victorian England. In his professional duties at the Inns of Court, he was pointing forcefully to one of the chief legal characteristics of progressive societies as being the removal of ascriptive conditions of legal and social status, while simultaneously in the *Morning Chronicle* and *Saturday Review* he heralded the adoption of Free Trade under the Peelites as an important example of the continuation of progress towards free contract.[35] Yet the leading impression of Maine's *Saturday Review* articles may be expressed as a profound and rather melancholy concern that the advent of a democratic system of government in England might end by depriving of their right to maintain freedom of contract the minority of rational men who were otherwise capable of doing so, by imposing on all alike a regimented social equalitarianism. Already, years before he ever set foot in India, Maine was demonstrating the temperament of the Whitehall civil servant distrustful of the intrusions of democratic amateurs into the traditional preserves of England's privileged ruling classes.[36] The emphatic individualism of his earliest political writings suggests elements of that great tradition of English political philosophy originating in the writings of John Locke, while his persistent rejection of the politically doctrinaire, and his exaggerated respect for experience and good birth, recall the occasional pieces of David Hume[37] and the philosophical fervour of Burke. There is as well (perhaps more so in his later writings) much in Maine's political outlook that is reminiscent of Montesquieu.[38] Maine's first statement of political principles, published during the years of his association with the *Saturday Review*,[39] congratulated the vital English middle classes that in modern times had successfully adapted their energies to the service of the ancient institutions of the British Monarchy, and warned of the dangers to the continuation of that balanced partnership in the claims of popular government.

Ancient Law

In 1854 Maine resigned his Cambridge professorship, in order to focus full attention upon his interests in London. At about the time of his appointment as Reader at the Inns of Court, he had begun the preparation of a manuscript tracing the historical development of law in the ancient world. Separate portions of the work were apparently first set out in the form of juridical lectures, and the earliest drafts of these were delivered in the Middle Temple, London, during the autumn of 1855. In the years immediately following, as his surviving work-books indicate, Maine revised the essays with a thoroughness that suggests he had planned from the outset on their eventual publication. Some five years later, during the spring of 1860, he took a more positive step in that direction. Mr John Murray of Albemarle Street, Piccadilly, who had brought out Darwin's *Origin of Species* the previous year, agreed to undertake the publication of the book. Maine thought it flattering that the enterprising Mr Murray 'should propose to take the risk'.

Well over half of the final manuscript draft of *Ancient Law* was completed by the summer of 1860. The problem of deciding on an appropriate title for the as yet unnamed volume provided the subject for the earliest extant Maine correspondence I have been able to trace, a business letter written to his publisher from his chambers at 1 Stone Building, Lincoln's Inn, on 6 July 1860:

My dear Murray,
I hope to send you in a day or two the MS of rather more than half of the book.

I have not been very successful in my reflection on titles. The following are all that have struck me:

1. 'Ancient Law, and Its Relation to Modern Ideas'

2. 'Ancient Law, Its Connection with the Early History of
Society, and Its Relation to Modern Ideas'
3. 'Archaic Jurisprudence, etc., etc., etc.'
No. 3. strikes me as affected, No. 2. as too long.

The author wishes to describe himself as:

'Henry Sumner Maine, Reader in Jurisprudence and the Civil
Law at the Middle Temple, and formerly Regius Professor of
Civil Law in the University of Cambridge.'[1]

As a point of historical interest, Maine did not himself actually
choose the full title for *Ancient Law*. He wrote to Murray again on
11 July, noting somewhat reluctantly that 'I have on the whole
come to the conclusion that the title you have selected is the best,
though at first I rather preferred No. 1'.[2] Shortly afterwards, he
forwarded to him the completed chapters of manuscript, explaining
that these included 'one in my clerk's writing, one partially in mine
and partly in his, and three wholly in mine'.

Most of the remainder of *Ancient Law* was not written in England.
Maine apparently found his precarious health a decided handicap to
any concentrated effort of writing, and yearned to quit London
altogether for a prolonged period of recuperation. As he confided to
Murray, during a particularly despondent period:

We are pining for the fresh air and quiet of Wimbledon. So
disgusted with London are we that I have accepted an offer which
will rid me of my house altogether. I shall store all my furniture,
and after the legal Long Vacation, if we cannot make up our
minds to take a house in Lansdowne Road, I think we shall go
into lodgings at Wimbledon and keep a constant look out.

Maine did leave London shortly after writing this letter, and
passed most of the remainder of the summer of 1860 resting and
carrying on his writing in the more congenial atmosphere of a
fashionable continental spa. He had completed three more of his
chapters by the time of his return to Brighton in early October, and
wrote further from there to assure Murray of his steady progress:

I do not suppose you will care much to hear from me till I can
present myself with my MS complete in my hand, but still I
think I had better let you know that I am again in England. Of
the six chapters still unfinished, I have written three and a half,

and I hope to finish the other half chapter before I return to London at the end of the month. Two chapters will remain, but for these, I trust that the MSS of my lectures will serve without material alteration.

I should have made more progress than I have, if this horrible summer and autumn had not prevented me shaking off my augish symptoms. Mrs Maine, who is pretty well, desires her kind regards to Mrs Murray.[3]

The final two chapters of *Ancient Law*, dealing with the early history of contract and criminal law, were duly drawn from Maine's Middle Temple lecture notes, and in January 1861 the book was finally published. The author was among the first to receive copies, and he wrote to Murray the morning that publication was announced, observing with satisfaction that his was 'a very handsome volume indeed',[4] and adding that he would be happy to 'come to Albemarle Street for the purpose of writing my name in some presentation copies'.

The book was not long in attracting interest. Charles Merivale, the historian and contributor to the *Saturday Review*, wrote to his sister during April 1861:

Dear me!, what clever men there are in the world! I am enthusiastic just now . . . about Stanley's *Eastern Church* and Maine's *Ancient Law*, the latter perhaps the most original book we have had for a vast time. It comes just at a time to answer all sorts of questions I have been asking myself about the transition period of Roman Law, the shaking off of the old slough of the Twelve Tables, and the assumption of the principles which continue to leaven all European law at this present day. A revolution of one thousand years of constant progress, without a violent shock throughout![5]

Maine's generation of lawyers and historians, from the first appearance of *Ancient Law*, viewed it with much the same sort of enthusiasm as natural scientists had received Darwin's *Origin of Species*. There is certainly a sense of the profound impact made upon students of society by the publication of *Ancient Law*, following so quickly on the heels of Darwin, in an ebullient letter written from Harvard by the positivist historian John Fiske to his fiancée, shortly after a pirated edition of the book appeared in America:

Dear Abby,

I have passed through an era and entered upon a new Epoch of my life! Thursday evening I began reading Henry Sumner Maine's *Ancient Law* and read it all New Year's, finishing it at exactly midnight. No novel that I ever read enchained me more. I consider it almost next to Spencer. It has thrown all my ideas of law into definite shape. It has suggested to me many new and startling views of social progress. It has confirmed many new generalizations which were beginning to arise in my mind as faint suspicions. I scarcely ever read a work so exceedingly *suggestive*. In fact, it *suggests* far more than it says. Almost every proposition in it may be made the foundation of a long train of thought. But besides what it hints at, what it explains is wonderful . . . it is perfectly glorious! I am going to read it over and over until I know it by heart.

Years of study are richly rewarded when they enable one to experience such an intellectual ecstacy as I felt New Year's Day! When I came out to dinner and heard the fellows talking the small-talk about 'going on busts', and this actress being pretty and the play being good, and all—the *stuff* people talk when they have got nothing to let out—you can't imagine how dreadfully low and worthless their pursuits and ideas seemed to me. O my dear! . . . there is nothing in this world like SCIENCE, nothing as divine as the life of a scholar!6

Although with less exuberance, the periodical press similarly paid high tribute to *Ancient Law*. Both J. F. Stephen and Frederic Harrison favourably reviewed the book soon after its appearance, and Maine thought especially highly of Harrison's article, and another which appeared in the *Scotsman*.7 The *Saturday Review* compared Maine to Montesquieu, and heralded him as an English von Savigny, while boldly prophesying that the work would 'mark an era in the history of jurisprudence'.8 Even the *Westminster Review*, which had begun life in the 1820s as the spokesman for orthodox utilitarian views, warmly praised the volume. Maine's researches, and especially his searching analysis of the flimsy foundations of the political theories of natural law and social contract, the reviewer felt, provided the legalist with an important historical complement to the work of Bentham. While German and French writers had provided the basic materials for the history of law, it was, in the *Westminster's* opinion, only fitting that an English law professor had stepped forward to sketch the philosophy of that history.[9] Montague Bernard, writing in the *Quarterly Review*, observed in a similar vein that the brilliance of Maine's work was above all attributable to 'what we might be allowed to call a French facility of generalization, combined with the just observation of an English man of science'.[10]

In the years before the appearance of *Ancient Law* in 1861, current fashions in English legal studies had been dominated by the authority of Jeremy Bentham, and to a lesser extent, by his disciple John Austin, who thought the primary task of the jurist should be the close examination of present-day legal phenomena. Bentham was for most of his career essentially a law reformer, and Austin had been fundamentally interested in the precise analysis of legal terminology. Maine shared their assumption that the proper goal of the jurist was to place legal knowledge on a more 'scientific' basis, but thought, as he emphasized in his earliest juridical publications, that ignorance of history had led in each case to a needlessly narrow approach, one indeed which effectively barred the fullest understanding of the domain of law. When Maine set out to write *Ancient Law*, as he had further indicated in his report to the Education Commission during the 1850s, the little academic study of jurisprudence then in progress in England was conducted in almost total ignorance of contemporary European systems of law and of classical Roman legal history, even though dramatic manuscript discoveries in the early years of the century had led to a greatly increased interest in Roman legal development and its connection with modern usages in the major universities of continental Europe. In England, indeed, truly professional studies of the history of the common law itself were virtually non-existent at the time.

Maine hoped, through his *Ancient Law*, to demonstrate that a greater appreciation of the social basis of all legal institutions would be achieved when lawyers used the techniques of the historian to trace the implications, for all present systems of law, of the full course of legal development in the ancient world. 'These rudimentary ideas', Maine was convinced, 'are to the jurist what the primary crusts of the earth are to the geologist. They contain, potentially, all the forms in which law has subsequently exhibited itself.' Maine's method, and especially his heavy reliance on Roman legal materials, was reminiscent of that of the early nineteenth-century German historical school of Hugo, von Savigny and Ihering, without its abstract romanticism. Rejecting the rationalist assumptions of the English analytical jurists, moreover, Maine set out to construct a new sort of empirical history that could nonetheless be fitted into a theoretical framework explaining the general evolution of legal systems. While there is little evidence that his innovating methods owed anything much directly to the evolutionary discoveries of Darwin, the results of his own researches into lines of legal development in the ancient and modern world, as Sir Frederick Pollock later commented, did 'nothing less than create the natural history of law'.[11]

Maine believed the further back one penetrated into western history, the more one came to realize that the largely unquestioned importance assigned by the school of Bentham to the role of positive legislative actions, as the primary source of legal and social innovation, found no support in the actual practises of early society. He surmised that in the far reaches of history, 'no sort of legislature, not even a distinct author of law, is contemplated or conceived of'. In early times, heroic kings, like those in the Homeric poems, pronounced isolated judgements or *themistes* only as the need arose, in their role as priestly intermediaries and lawgivers. Without developed notions of precedent or uniformity, ancient legal rules were thus merely 'adjudications on insulated states of fact'. Maine held, paradoxically, that judgement must have preceded custom in earliest law.[12] In the western branches of Indo-European society, he thought, belief in the sacred powers of these kings eventually declined, giving rise to a general movement towards domination by military and political aristocracies. In eastern societies having such Aryan roots there developed, instead of this decisive transition in leadership and authority, systems for the sharing of power between kings and priestly élites.

In both branches the new aristocracies succeeded to the administration of law, basing their claims to legitimacy not on the kingly premise of sacred inspiration, but on possession of expert knowledge of the rules. Thus, tradition and precedent, according to Maine, first entered the law in something approaching a systematic fashion, for it was incumbent on these new aristocratic lawgivers to remember past rulings, and to pass this information on within their group. This

period of what Maine terms 'true customary law' was inevitably sur-
passed by the eventual modification of law in these societies, at which
time the customary rules hitherto preserved within the collective
memory of the aristocracy were set down on tablets, and thus made
available for greater publicity. Here, Maine felt, the furthest point
of the 'natural' evolution of legal systems was reached, and what
determined the future course of its law was the point in a society's
history when such codification took place.[13] In Roman history, the
customary law seemed to have been codified, so Maine argued, at a
remarkably early period in the general development of Roman
society. The Twelve Tables of Rome (c. 451–449 B.C.), believed to
be the earliest codification of Roman law and the chief source of the
fundamental legal rules of later Roman civilization on the Tiber,
were thus generally reflective of actual legal practises at the time of
their formulation. In the East, he thought, a plebeian element like
that which had forced the publication of laws at Rome, never gained
sufficient influence over kings and priests, and codification there was
achieved, by comparison with Rome, much later. By that time
customary law had already lived beyond its usefulness in practise.
As could be seen by examining fragments of the early Indian Code of
Manu, which probably originated at the beginning of the Christian
era, the codified Indian rules consisted largely of arid formulas.

Even after the era of codification, Maine continued, legal transactions remained bound to an extraordinary amount of ceremony,
and exhibited a slavish devotion to the minutest details of procedure.
Most societies, indeed, never pass beyond this stage, but in a few
a further evolution of the law, assisted by artificial means, does take
place. Maine relied primarily on Roman legal history during the long
course of its development, from the eighth century B.C. to the codi-
fications of Justinian in A.D. 565, as a model legal system to illustrate
his influential thesis that in such 'progressive societies', legal fictions,
equity and finally, legislation, represent an overlapping historical
sequence of reform agencies that serve to close the gap between the
needs of progressive social opinion, and the natural conservatism of
legal rules that persists even after codification.[14]

First, Maine demonstrated how the *responsa prudentium* of the
iuris prudentes, a class of persons 'learned in the law' who first came
to prominence at Rome during the fourth century B.C., broke down
the rigid monopoly of doctrinaire legal interpretation exercised in

the period following the codification of Roman law by the traditionalist *pontifices*, or lawyer-priests. These *responsa*, which were explanatory glosses of the Twelve Tables purporting merely to interpret the contents of the codified rules with no intention of changing them, were, according to Maine, in reality legal fictions which 'constantly modified, extended, limited or practically overruled the provisions of the Decimviral law',[15] just as in the early development of the modern English legal system, the case law changed received rules at the same time that it was assumed to be applying law that had always existed. Maine did not share Bentham's impatience with legal fictions, but stressed their historical importance in freeing legal systems from the danger of excessive rigidity, an important insight in his day. As he expressed it: 'They satisfy the desire for improvement, which is not quite wanting, at the same time that they do not offend the superstitious disrelish for change which is always present.'[16]

Maine next suggested that towards the end of the republican period in Roman history, a body of equity law began to replace the *responsa* as the chief instrument of Roman legal reform. He thought these new developments could be traced to the legal pronouncements of the *praetor peregrinis*, the Roman law official whose office was created (*c.* 247 B.C.) when military and commercial expansion brought increasingly complex conflicts between Roman civil law and that of other societies. It was the Greek philosophical notion of a law of nature, borrowed and applied in the Edicts of the *praetors* to assist the development of common points of law in the actual *ius gentium* or law of nations, that according to Maine now saved Roman law from stagnation, by providing principles of 'aequitas' existing alongside the civil law which were believed to transcend it in moral authority. Maine estimated that from the era of the first Punic War to the reign of Alexander Severus (A.D. 222–35), the expansion of Roman law was made possible through reliance upon these rules of equity, a development which he pointed out had its counterpart in the history of the growing role of the English Court of Chancery in the modern common law system down to the Chancellorship of Lord Eldon.[17]

As he had with legal fictions, Maine takes a rather cautious and conservative view of the quality and character of change that was initiated by these principles of equity. The Roman legal doctrine of

48

natural law was thus 'remedial, not revolutionary or anarchical', and its genius was that it kept alive the vision of a better type of law while it never encouraged a rejection of the obligation of existing laws, a habit of mind that would be fatal, in Maine's judgment, to the continued orderly evolution of all legal systems during periods of great stress. Only after Severus, beginning with the early consolidations of Augustus and culminating in the great Code of Justinian (A.D. 565), he concluded, was Roman legal reform effected by means of the Imperial constitutions. Contrary to the main emphases of Bentham's influential legislative theories for reforming law, the study of Roman legal history offered important evidence that only relatively late in the career of legal systems do legislatures come to play a prominent role in the reform of private law.[18]

Maine turned for the remainder of *Ancient Law* to examine 'the rudiments of the social state' as seen from the standpoint of ancient systems of law, and it is this aspect of the work that first attracted the interest of scholars outside the field of jurisprudence. He believed the insulated patriarchal family depicted in the earliest portions of Roman law, where an omniscient *paterfamilias* held absolute power over its members, was the form of primitive family organization that was once typical throughout Indo-European society.[19] Even before it had reached the level of the *themistes* of the heroic king, law was simply the word of the eldest male parent in the inner autonomy of the family. The earliest societies, Maine thus surmised, were not composed of individuals in any sense recognizable to the Victorian age, but of aggregations of families, not of single human beings but of groups.[20] By examining the historical growth of Roman contract law, moreover, Maine seemed to provide scholarly foundations for one of Hume's critiques of the individualistic social contract theory of the origins of political obligation. Showing contract to be in its earlier forms purely verbal, and encumbered with a preponderance of tedious procedure, he held that only slowly did the sense of mental obligation basic to advanced notions of contract become disentangled from the originally more important ceremonial technicalities, and finally surmount them as the sole ingredient of the contract.[21] If the ancient rules seemed to allow no scope for individuated contract, which Maine regarded as one of the corner-stones of high civilization, then it seemed likely that 'joint-ownership, and not separate ownership' had been 'the really archaic institution' of property, a

49

theme he later resumed in his *Village Communities in East and West.*

Setting Indian and Roman examples alongside the findings of recent studies of property holding in Russia, Serbia and Scotland, Maine concluded that general features of co-proprietorship must have been universal at an early stage of social development, and suggested that differences in the later organizational patterns of these societies indicated, if not a strict line of advance, at least separate modes of holding illustrative of 'the gradual disentanglement of the separate rights of individuals from the blended rights of a community'.[22] In Roman law, moreover, he found patterns in the development of more mobile forms of property out of an originally undifferentiated type that could be generalized to other historical instances. Tracing the gradual absorption of the rigid Roman law of *res mancipi* (land, slaves and beasts of burden strictly subject to Roman ownership, and requiring for their transfer the cumbersome ancient act of mancipation) into the more adaptable *res nec mancipi* (originally less important forms of property which could be transferred by simple delivery), Maine pointed to similar modern developments in English property law that had set in motion the gradual assimilation of the law of realty to the law of personalty. Other Roman techniques for assisting the reform of property law and encouraging the emergence of private property, seemed also to Maine to have their modern analogies, such as the rule of *usucapion*, or prescription, which allowed things possessed uninterruptedly for a certain period to become the property of the possessor, and the device of *cessio in jure*, or collusive recovery, that was similar to the fines and recoveries of medieval English property law.[23]

Maine thought the family in early society was strikingly—from the lawyers standpoint—like a small independent corporation, an insight that has since been amply confirmed by anthropologists in the field. Like the modern legal conception of the corporation sole, he noted, early family law 'takes a view of *life* wholly unlike any which appears in developed jurisprudence. Corporations *never* die, and accordingly primitive law considers the entities with which it deals, i.e., the patriarchal or family groups, as perpetual and indistinguishable.'[24] This explained to Maine why intestate inheritance is an older legal institution than testamentary succession. Observing[25] that in the early stages of Roman law wills did not settle property, and were neither revocable, secret or written, Maine suggested that they were originally devices for regulating succession to the *potestas* in the family group. The use of the testamentary form arose only to meet the situation of a complete failure in the line naturally entitled to the inheritance. Out of this earliest corporate family, which lived on after the death of the *paterfamilias*, eventually grew— Maine thought by the extensive use of the legal fiction of adoption, which allowed strangers into the brotherhood of the corporation—as if by 'a system of concentric circles which have gradually expanded from the same point', the more advanced notions of community and state. Maine stressed, in one of his most brilliant generalizations, that the differences separating the two basic forms of social and political organization—an older type based strictly on family tie, and a newer one on territoriality— were so great as to require the closest attention of future students of antiquities:

> All ancient societies regarded themselves as having proceeded from one original stock, and even laboured under an incapacity for comprehending any reason except this for their holding together in political union. The history of political ideas begins, in fact, with the assumption that kinship in blood is the sole possible ground of community in political functions, nor is there any of those subversions of feeling, which we term emphatically revolutions, so startling and so complete, as the change which is accomplished when some other principle—such as that, for instance, of *local contiguity*—establishes itself for the first time as the basis of common political action.[26]

Maine's legal studies led him to conclude that while in the earliest reaches of western history the sphere of civil law had been extremely small, it had tended steadily to enlarge itself in Roman practice through a process in which 'the individual is steadily substituted for the Family, as the unit of which civil laws take account',[27] just as a similar pattern seemed characteristic of the developing law of the modern 'progressive' European societies. Under the Roman *patria potestas*, the male parent had originally possessed an unqualified authority over the persons of his offspring, even in such matters as the right to dictate conditions of marriage and divorce, and to dispose of children by adoption or sale. It was not until well into the Imperial period that many of the former parental powers were transferred to the jurisdiction of civil magistrates. Maine thought there was ample evidence in Roman historical records of a corresponding decline of parental control over the property of his progeny. By the early years of the Empire, the operation of the *patria potestas* had been relaxed by means of the *castrense peculium*, so as to exclude property acquired by soldiers on service from paternal confiscation. Three centuries later, *quasi-castrense peculium* extended this form of 'permissive property' to cover the earnings of civil servants. Shortly afterwards Constantine further reduced the father's position by limiting his share of the property children might inherit from their mother to a *usufract*, or life interest. The furthest point was reached when Justinian enacted the rule that the rights of the father to the property of his children acquired from sources other than his own estate were to cease with the death of the *paterfamilias*, a reform which represented a remarkable historical development in Roman family law, although by modern English standards—where similar processes of family emancipation were taking place—it still left children under strict patriarchal control.[28] Maine found analogous trends in the Roman law governing the status of females. Under the various early Roman marriage forms of *confarreation, coemption* and *usus*, the husband acquired extensive rights over the *filius familius*, and was indeed regarded as her father. All her property became his, and after his death, she fell under the power of a guardian named by him. By the lifetime of Gaius, however, the assumption that the equality of the sexes was a principle of the law of nature had become a commonplace among leading Roman jurists, and the position of women transformed into one of 'great personal and proprietary independence'.[29] Maine pointed out that similarities could be traced in the development of the modern law of marriage, though here, under the influence of Christian and barbarian notions which were mixed with revived Roman jurisprudence during the medieval period, the evolution had been one in which the wife was being gradually emancipated from the legal personality of her husband, rather than of her blood-relations, a process by no means yet complete when Maine wrote *Ancient Law*. He used further examples from the development of the Roman law of master and slave to illustrate his theory of these liberating trends in the law of persons, pointing out that, however barbaric the institution itself might seem to a modern European, the slave in later Roman history was in a sense infinitely better off than his counterpart had been in the very infancy of

52

civilization, as a result of the recognition afforded him by principles of the law of nature.[30] And in modern European history, of course, the status of the slave was rapidly disappearing altogether and being replaced by the contractual relations of master and servant. Maine summarized his argument in a striking generalization that has become one of the most celebrated passages in English legal literature:

> Starting, as if from one terminus of history, from a condition of society in which all the relations of Persons are summed up in the relations of Family, we seem to have steadily moved towards a phase of social order in which all these relations arise from the free agreement of individuals . . .
>
> The word Status may be usefully employed to construct a formula expressing the law of progress thus indicated, which, whatever be its value, seems to me to be sufficiently ascertained. All the forms of Status taken notice of in the Law of Persons were derived from, and to some extent are still coloured by, the powers and privileges anciently residing in the Family. If then we employ Status, agreeably with the usage of the best writers, to signify these personal conditions only, and avoid applying the term to such conditions as are the immediate or remote result of agreement, we may say that the movement of the progressive societies has hitherto been a movement from Status to Contract.[31]

Maine's 'status to contract' theory, while the most renowned of his many well-known generalizations about early law, has also remained the most controversial, not least of all because it has been used to support particular political points of view. Based primarily on the history of the Roman law of persons, but intended to fit the circumstances of 'progressive' legal systems in general, the dictum was thus received by Maine's contemporaries as vindication of the leading ideological currents of European society during a period of optimistic industrial expansion. Here was a scholarly exposition of individualism manifesting itself in history, in which progressive western man was moving ever closer towards the apex of legal refinement, the freedom of individuals in principle to contract for themselves, and thus to determine their own status. Certainly in Maine's lifetime events lent support to the plausibility of that interpretation. Liberty of contract in the regulation of business and industry, liberty of association and liberty of testamentary succession, were accepted as established trends that parliament was accordingly expected to nurture and respect, and although family law was perhaps less outwardly affected than other branches of law in Victorian England, the series of Married Women's Property Acts passed during the century did free wives to enter into contracts and hold property in their own names. The Landlord and Tenant (Ireland) Act of 1860, passed just one year before the appearance of Maine's book, must have struck him as an example of the process he had described, basing the relationship of Irish landlord and tenant as it did on contract and not on tenure of service. In preparing the third edition of *Ancient Law* in 1865, moreover, Maine himself pointed beyond England to the recent abolition of slavery in Russia and America, as evidence in support of his thesis. In the great age of *laissez-faire*, liberals and conservatives alike accepted that the movement from 'status to contract', now given a scientific treatment in *Ancient Law*, was a beneficial catalyst to social advance likely to continue indefinitely in the west.[32]

Yet by the closing years of the nineteenth century, confidence in the corollary of Maine's thesis—that the continued growth of contractual freedom in progressive societies was attributable to an enhanced 'moral consciousness', and that therefore the only classes of persons whose status should be subject to extrinsic control were those that 'do not possess the faculty of forming a judgment on their own interests'[33]—was brought into question by a growing body of knowledge of the actual social conditions under which the vast majority of people, even in the so-called 'progressive' societies, lived. While many millions might have sensed what 'their own interests' were in Victorian England, and in principle were accorded greater 'freedom of contract' than ever before, they were assuredly powerless to do anything much about it. By late in the century, A. V. Dicey and others were pointing to such developments as passage of the Workman's Compensation Act of 1897, as indicative of a reversion in England from contract to status. In our day, that movement has gone a long way towards creation of what seem to be new forms of legal status, made necessary in practical political terms by the recognition of the need to protect the weaker members of society through governmental intervention in the regulation of contracts concerning the conditions of employment, the care of the elderly and the unemployed, and the protection of minorities. In the twentieth century,

54

moreover, the emergence of corporation law and the growing standardization of contract have exercised a profound effect on traditional contractual practices. One authority has gone so far as to suggest that 'It may be that the part which was once played by the family nidus will be played in the future by the syndical nidus',[34] and Professor W. Friedmann, examining the recent trends of contract law in industrialized societies, has concluded that:

> It is clear that contract is becoming increasingly institutionalized. From being the instrument by which millions of individual parties bargain with each other, it has to a large extent become the way by which social and economic policies are expressed in legal form. This is another way of saying that public law now vitally affects and modifies the law of contract.[35]

Aside from the political issues raised by Maine's dictum, the difficulty of assessing its academic validity is enhanced by the fact that he used key terms in special senses that very much limit the range of legal phenomena to which they can be safely applied. In the first place, he was insistent that the movement of law in progressive societies had '*hitherto been*' from status to contract, a qualification that can be said to free Maine from the criticism that he was predicting the continuation of a process that did not take place. Perhaps more importantly, his special definition of 'status' automatically excluded as exceptions to his generalization '*such conditions as are the immediate or remote result of agreement*'. A case can therefore be made that the status to contract thesis is not in the least inconsistent with developments since Maine's day, for the newer forms of legal status have been largely determined, in his sense of the terms, by the will of the contractor, and not vice versa.[36]

Curiously, Maine's unorthodox use of such legal concepts has produced a situation where his views have been more readily accepted by professional sociologists than lawyers. While lawyers, for example, have not agreed that the modern history of marriage reveals any such movement as Maine described, but one, strictly speaking, involving a growing equalization of legal status,[37] the sociologist nonetheless admires Maine's prescience in sensing the important general truth that the social conditions of modern society, in contrast with those of traditional society, have tended to produce a wider range of individual choice in the determination of personal status.[38] Thus, one prominent American social scientist, the late Robert Redfield, applied such broad criteria for sympathetically assessing the status to contract theory, when he claimed that 'On the whole, the broad history of humanity, the narrower history of Europe, and the transformation of tribal society under the influence of contact with other societies fulfil the generalization'.[39] The received view among legal scholars who have tended to apply more strictly technical categories to their appraisal of Maine's work, seems to be, as R. H. Graveson has more cautiously concluded, that:

> On the one hand, the movement in domestic status is away from dependence on the head of the family, with its corollary of vicarious liability, towards full individual legal capacity; on the other, State interference in the terms and conditions of employment in industry has given rise to a new type of personal legal condition which bears many of the features of a status.[40]

Whatever the view one ultimately forms of the continued validity of Maine's famous generalization, however, there can be no doubt that it formed the core concept of his analysis of legal history. His theory of the movement from status to contract, indeed, may aptly be called the manifesto of his lifework.

It is hardly surprising that few of the further details of *Ancient Law* are any longer accepted without qualification. Julius Stone has observed, indeed, that 'scarcely any of Maine's hypotheses have come unscathed through the ordeal of later research'.[41] His materials, after all, consisted of little more than a good grounding in general classical literature, an appreciation of the clues to ancient legal usages contained in Biblical sources, such as Deuteronomy, acquaintance with the travel memoirs of adventuring Victorian contemporaries, and brilliant powers of synthesis and generalization.[42] The remarkable thing is that so little of Maine's speculation can be rejected outright. Yet what are some of the further specific criticisms that have been made of *Ancient Law* by later scholars? In the first place, they have stressed that Maine's sources were not really primitive. Without question, the discovery since his day of the Code of Hammurabi, dating from 2000 B.C., and later still of the Hittite, Assyrian and Eshnunna laws, do make his primarily Roman sources look comparatively modern. One result is that his assumption that codification came much later in the East than in the West has been called into question. One of Maine's most persistent recent critics, and a leading expositor of these early codes, Professor A. S. Diamond, claims to have found little concrete support for Maine's ambitious general theory of the stages of legal development in his own researches, and while admiring Maine's pioneering brilliance, has suggested that the growing mass of evidence reveals an infinitely more complex array of institutional patterns than the author of *Ancient Law* supposed to exist in early legal history.[43]

Specialists too are nowadays in disagreement over Maine's view that in primitive societies legal pronouncements are primarily legitimized by their supposed religious basis. The work of Frazer and Malinowski does seem to demonstrate that, if anything, it is sympathetic magic rather than religion in Maine's highly general sense, that enters into the processes of law-making and law enforcement in early society.[44] Moreover, further field work, as Professor A. E. Hoebel points out, has shown that Maine may have exaggerated the extent to which primitive law is essentially rigid and inflexible,[45] while there is continuing controversy among legal anthropologists as to his generalization that primitive criminal law is largely the law of torts, rather than crimes. Maine's theory of primitive patriarchalism, perhaps the most controversial of the theses of *Ancient Law* in his lifetime, has led to the separate criticism that he had pursued a question that could not really be answered, and still other later critics have concluded that he harboured a rather romantic view of the influence of Roman law in modern European institutions.[46] Finally, like many of his historically-minded contemporaries, Maine found it an easy transition from the philological notion of the 'Aryan' or Indo-European family of languages, to the idea of a continuous Aryan stock, now separated into branches at various levels of social advance, but all alike derived from a common historical community in which there had once flourished uniform social and legal institutions. A great deal of scholarly ingenuity subsequently went into the futile attempt to discover the absolute origins of the Aryans—first in Asia, then in Northern and Eastern Europe, and finally in Africa. That enterprise, and evolutionary theories of social development in general (of which Maine's work was a comparatively mild Victorian type), had become unfashionable by the beginning of the present century, and with some recent exceptions,[47] have remained so.

Yet it would be a great misunderstanding of Maine's contributions to dwell for too long over the details of his work, or to confine our appreciation of his scholarship to the field of jurisprudence alone. One admiring historian of ideas has written:

> The impressive thing in the works of Maine is that they were not purely historical; they are not even specialized history. Here . . . we can see an author beginning to compare, to lift the objects with which he is concerned out of the realm of events, and treat them as things with a somewhat stable and persistent nature. Maine's work on the history of legal and political institutions represents a step in the shift of method and objectives from history in the direction of sociology.[48]

Maine's new *methods* certainly exercised a considerable influence. Among his English contemporaries, his enterprising scholarship was much admired by men of letters with an interest in the study of society, including J. S. Mill, Walter Bagehot, Lord Acton, Henry Sidgwick, and Herbert Spencer, and his books were soon well known in legal and historical circles in America.[49] When the Hungarian legal historian Augustus Pulszky, who spent several years studying under Maine at Oxford during the 1870s, later introduced a translated version of *Ancient Law* to Germany, continental European scholars also became familiar with his work. Indeed, Frederic Maitland once commented that Maine's methods seemed to attract a greater following in Europe than in England.[50] Ferdinand Toënnies, the German author of *Community and Association*, a seminal work in modern European sociological literature, spoke of Maine as 'my teacher',[51] and Talcott Parsons has more recently noted the influence of Maine as well on the work of the French sociologist Emile Durkheim.[52] Another authority has suggested that his forceful demonstrations of the close historical tie between legal and social institutions, and his penchant for constructing general theoretical statements out of widely scattered source materials, makes his work the single most important contribution of nineteenth-century jurisprudence to the early literature of the social sciences.[53] There are then strong grounds for regarding Maine, through the publication of his *Ancient Law* in 1861, as an important forerunner of modern sociology.[54]

Maine's *Ancient Law* also had important implications for its author's political thought. Its historical and anthropological setting, and its treatment of such specific topics as the history of contract and property, provide the book with a certain conservatism of tone that sharply contrasted with Bentham's reformist jurisprudence, for Maine's researches in comparative law had convinced him of the essential fragility of progress in western history. 'It is indisputable', he wrote, 'that much the greatest part of mankind has never shown a particle of desire that its civil institutions should be improved', and elsewhere, 'the truth is, that the stable part of our mental, moral and physical constitution is the largest part of it,' an argument he reproduced in his later polemic against democracy, *Popular Government*.[55] A close reading of *Ancient Law*, in fact, confirms the impression that such anthropological conclusions as these closely parallel Maine's political belief that historically, only a small minority of mankind had demonstrated the ability or inclination to benefit from the actual exercise of freedom of contract, though others had benefitted from the freedom afforded that minority.

Maine included in *Ancient Law* a lengthy and highly conjectural analysis of the modern history of the law of nature, a doctrine he thought 'still the greatest antagonist' of scientific method as it applied to the study of society. Rousseau, by his advocacy of universal equality, and Bentham, through his applications of the greatest happiness principle to legal reform, represent in Maine's discussion the two leading modern claimants to the role performed in the ancient world by those who championed the use of natural law as a universal standard for assisting the continued progress of legal institutions. Yet while the Graeco-Roman doctrine, according to Maine, had been strictly confined to legal usage, he deplored the fact that the ostensibly juridical postulates of these modern philosophers were being used as practical guides to political action. Rousseau's political doctrine of universal equality, in his view, resulted from a misapplication of a Roman legal axiom (*omnes homines natura aequales sunt*) that in its new form, unfortunately encouraged 'disdain of positive law, impatience of experience, and the preference of *a priori* to all other reasoning'.[56] Maine, in other words, drew a distinction between the use that could be made of certain principles by jurists for the reform of the internal machinery of the legal system, and the inadequacies of these same principles when applied by politicians to the task of general constitutional reform. The distinction stems from his concern that such catch-phrases as 'all men are equal', and 'the greatest happiness of the greatest number', might serve to unite the authority of legislatures, which had only risen to dominance as sources of legal and constitutional change in relatively recent history, with the political will of the even more recently emergent prospective inheritors of these legislatures, popular majorities.

Clearly, in his close scrutiny of the slim historical foundations of Rousseau's 'politicized' notion of universal equality, Maine offers evidence that, while as a juridical scholar he viewed the removal of ascriptive legal status as a necessary condition of past European historical progress, politically he would not welcome the unrestrained continuation of that process. As his *Saturday Review* articles written during this same period make clear, Maine was concerned that most men in the conditions of modern society would probably be willing to throw aside a wide range of newly acquired freedoms based on contractual agreement, for the security of renewed status in the state, a choice he foresaw as ultimately culminating in the denial of the privilege of individuated contract to everyone alike.

While Maine directs these *Ancient Law* criticisms primarily at Rousseau, it is clear from his later writings that they were intended equally as a warning against attempts to apply Bentham's juridical principles to systematic constitutional reform in England. In a close restatement of the whole theme in his *Popular Government* essay on 'The Age of Progress', Maine changed his emphasis to concentrate at some length on the dangerous theories that he feared were by that date daily gaining greater prominence through the partisan advocacy of misguided admirers of Bentham:

That because you can successfully reform jurisprudence on certain principles, you can successfully reform constitutions on the same principles, is not a safe inference . . . the simplification of civil law . . . can scarcely lead to danger. It is however, idle to conceal from oneself that the simplification of political institutions leads straight to absolutism, the absolutism not of an expert Judge, but of a single man or of a multitude striving to act as if it were a single man. . . . Again, a mistake in law-reform is of small importance. . . . If committed, it can be corrected with com-

60

Plate 1 Frederic Harrison (1831–1923). A caricature by Walter Sickert dated 'Jan. 5, 1912' and autographed in Harrison's hand.

Plate 2 Sir Henry Maine's godfather, John Bird Sumner, Archbishop of Canterbury, 1848–1862. Oil painting by Margaret Carpenter.

Plate 4 Sir James Fitzjames Stephen (1829–1894). Photographed from life for *Men of Mark*, London, 1882.

Plate 3 Sir M. E. Grant Duff (1829–1906). Engraving by William Roffe from a drawing by H. J. Wells, R.A.

parative ease. But a mistake in constitutional innovation . . . may be frought with calamity or ruin, public or private. And correction is virtually impossible.[57]

Maine honoured Bentham for his gift to the nation of a 'clear rule of reform' that would save the common law system from decay. Nonetheless, he questioned the wisdom of an unqualified application to practical politics of the greatest happiness principle. His sceptical view of the human capacity for improvement is in part traceable to, and was in part reinforced by, the legal researches undertaken by Maine in the preparation of his *Ancient Law*.

Maine's health continued to cause him difficulty during the months following the publication of *Ancient Law*, and in the late Spring of 1861 he went to the countryside to stay with relatives and to rest. He apparently received a great deal of mail, and steady sales suggested that the book would need a second edition almost immediately. In June, he wrote to Mr Murray from Effingham:

> I am sure one of the troubles of your life must consist in impatient authors asking you questions about their books. Perhaps it will therefore be only an old story when I ask you to let me know how *Anct. Law* is going on.
>
> I should like to know, first, because Mr. Cook said something about a new edition being wanted in the autumn, and next because since I have been ill, I have been receiving a really prodigious number of letters and messages about it, to which I am curious to know what weight ought to be attached.
>
> I am slowly coming round. A fortnight ago, I thought I was well, but I have had something of a relapse.[58]

While recuperating in the countryside, Maine seems to have lost no time in bringing his recent literary successes to bear on the advancement of his professional career. Commentators on Maine have long assumed there to be some connection between his *Ancient Law* and his recruitment shortly after its publication as an Anglo-Indian administrator. An unpublished early letter of the historian Lord Acton, who was at the time a twenty-seven-year-old Whig M.P. for Carlow, throws a more precise light on the relationship of Maine's first book and his beginnings as a public servant. The letter was written confidentially to Maine's friend Grant Duff:[59]

Aldenham,
Easter Monday, 1861

My dear Sir,

I did not receive your letter for several days, as it was sent down here whilst I was on a visit in Berkshire. It happened that I arrived at the Oxford station so long before my train was due that I had time to go to Parker's shop, and the first book I saw and bought was Maine's. I read it in the train with extreme delight, so that when I reached home I was entirely disposed and qualified to support in the strongest way the recommendation of your letter. I put it into Lord Granville's hands, who was here, and he went away without returning it to me, which is my reason for directing my answer to the Athenaeum.

I earnestly desire that out efforts will contribute to the result he desires and so highly deserves.

Clearly, at Maine's prompting, Grant Duff had asked Acton to use his political influence to secure a government position for the author of *Ancient Law*. The 'result he desires' was apparently an opportunity in Indian administration, and Lord Granville, Lord President of the Council in Palmerston's second Cabinet, saw to it that the post of Legal Member to the Viceroy's Indian Council was offered to Maine, shortly afterwards. While little known to the general public, the office was one of great prestige among English lawyers. Its most distinguished previous occupant had been Macaulay, who during the 1830s had devised a brilliant plan for codifying the penal law of India. Maine must have been delighted at the thought of a quite new and challenging line of work as he approached his fortieth birthday, and must have been equally enthusiastic over the prospect of the handsome salary that accompanied the Legal Membership. No sooner had the offer unofficially been made to Maine by Sir Charles Wood, the Secretary of State for India, however, than he suffered a renewed bout of illnesses. In the circumstances, his physician strongly advised him that the demanding climate of India would almost certainly further impair his already poor health. Disappointed, he wrote to Sir Charles Wood from his chambers:

Sir,

I have received the opinion of Sir Ranald Martin, and another medical gentleman, to which I referred in my conversation with you yesterday. I regret to say it is in the form of an intimation that 'no consideration whatever ought to induce me to face the climate of India, and least of all, of Bengal.' It only remains for me, therefore . . . to express my sense of the great honour you have done me by your selection, and to assure you of the severe disappointment I feel in declining an office which has greater attractions for me than almost any other known to me.

The fact that you have thus distinguished me renders it perhaps less presumptuous in me than otherwise might be to express a hope that, if any work has to be done at home in connection with Indian legislation or law, I may be employed on it. My studies and lines of inquiry have led me to pay much attention not only to the principles of general jurisprudence, but to the native Indian systems.[60]

In the early spring of the following year, the untimely death of Mr William Ritchie, a relative of Thackeray's who had accepted the Indian appointment when Maine first declined it, led to the offer once again being made to him. Maine's health had apparently improved during the interval, for he was now able to accept. On April 12 1862 he wrote to Sir Charles Wood:

After an interview with my medical attendant, I am happy to be able to accept the office which you have done me the honour of offering to me.

The gentleman in question is much consulted by persons proceeding to India. He has expressed an opinion that in my case it would be especially desirable that I should arrive at Calcutta at a period of the year less unfavourable than that which I should have to encounter were I go to out immediately or after no more than the usual delay.

I mention this opinion without supposing that it can outweigh considerations of the public service. I am, however, under the impression that under any circumstances, the session of the Legislative Council would be over before I could reach India, and further that there would be some advantage in the Legal Member of Council having time to acquaint himself thoroughly with the views of the Home Government on the various legislative measures which are in contemplation.[61]

During the Spring of 1862 Maine was honoured by his election to membership in the exclusive Athenaeum Club. For the present, as he wrote to John Murray, he feared the temptation to become one 'who wastes his time idling about society and his clubs'. In the same letter he noted that 'I daresay you have heard that I have got my posting for October'.[62] Maine left 'Newstead', his temporary home in Wimbledon, in the early summer and passed the next several months travelling on the continent. He occupied his time by collecting information on contract law, 'particularly with reference to the peasantry of southern Europe', which he thought would be useful in India. In September he returned to London, to make final arrangements for his departure in the following month. Jane Maine, apparently because of her poor health, was left with the children in England. To the Right Honourable Henry Maine, newest Member of the Governor-General's Council and acclaimed author of *Ancient Law*, the 'extended field-trip' was to confirm his belief that India was a living monument to the past, where the student of antiquities with an eye for detail could reconstruct the rudiments of the earliest Aryan social and legal institutions, among 'A people which for every century that we reckon can count a thousand years of isolated existence. . . . A people whose religion was archaic when Greek paganism was in its infancy, and whose civilization was already at its decrepitude when Alexander the Great marched upon the Indus.'[63]

6

Calcutta Impressions

Maine apparently left London so quickly upon his return from the Continent that he overlooked calling in at the India Office to bid farewell to his new political head, Sir Charles Wood. Thus, when he reached Calcutta early in November 1862, he found a letter from the Secretary of State awaiting his arrival. 'I am very sorry indeed that I did not see you before you went', Wood wrote with his characteristic dedication to Indian affairs, 'not for the purpose of exchanging civilities, but because I wished to speak to you on one or two important matters of Indian policy.' On such a note of mild reprimand from the higher reaches of Whitehall officialdom, the public records of Maine's long career in Indian administration commence.[1]

The new Legal Member's oversight may well have stemmed from a preoccupation with the prospect of finally seeing India at first hand. He had long been a close student of Indian subjects, though from a distance. Quite aside from the influence of Indian legal antiquities on the composition of his *Ancient Law*, Maine's family on his mother's side had had commercial interests in the East Indies, and there is a strong likelihood that his father had eventually gone to live there. He thus came early to an awareness of the contribution to British overseas greatness of that generally unappreciated class of Indian mercantilist statesman, 'whose field of operation', he wrote admiringly, 'has been practically wider than that of European diplomacy'.[2] As a leader writer on the *Saturday Review*, Maine had frequently employed his biting pen to deplore the 'crass ignorance' of the British public about India. During the heated debate over the future of the East India Company that followed the Sepoy Mutiny of 1857, Maine, in a lengthy series of articles, took a sentimental stand against proposals for abolishing the Company's historic hegemony over the Indian possessions. He feared that by replacing the

65

time-honoured dual system of Indian government, whose roots extended backwards to the Elizabethan era, with an experimental political regime directly controlled from Westminster, the temptation would be often great for politicians to follow 'English prejudice and English half-knowledge' rather than the counsels of persons actually cognizant of Indian affairs.[3] Now, in 1862, that debate had long since been settled by an Act of the British Parliament. In a majestic durbar held at Allahabad on 1 November 1858 Lord Canning had proclaimed the passage of India from the Company to the Crown.

Under the terms of the Indian Councils Act of 1861, the dual system of Indian government established by the East India Company was retained in principle. In India, a Governor-General, appointed for five years, was to be assisted in the formulation of general administrative policy by an executive council of five members, raised in 1874 to six. Among these would be distributed responsibility for the various government portfolios, including Finance, Home, Public Works, Foreign Affairs, Legal and Military, and to their number was added the Commander in Chief, who served as an extraordinary member. Three of the councillors were required to be covenanted civil servants with no less than ten years of Indian experience. When the Viceroy was in residence at the capital, his executive met weekly with him as a sort of loose cabinet. For strictly legislative purposes, the Governor-General was empowered under the Act to appoint six to twelve additional councillors, one half of whom must be non-official Europeans and Indians. Full legislative sittings, which included these special councillors, the Viceroy and his executive, were held periodically at Calcutta, but while publicized, they were strictly managed. The potential influence of the legislative members was diminished not only by the shortness of their two-year terms, but because the Viceroy controlled procedure, and retained the power of veto.[4] Moreover, the consideration of financial matters was reserved to the Viceroy and his executive.

Below the central government, Governorships were established for Bombay and Madras, Lieutenant-Governorships were instituted at Bengal (the seat of the central authority), the North-West Provinces and the Punjab, Commissionerships were created in the Central Provinces, Burma and Mysore, and Representatives of the Governor-General were assigned to the several Native States. In London, representing the supreme authority of the Crown, sat a

Secretary of State for India, who was a member of the British Cabinet, and his fifteen-man Council of India, composed primarily of Anglo-Indians who had been in India a total of at least ten years out of the twenty preceding their appointment.[5] The various elements of this sprawling institutional structure, as Maine wrote, made up 'one of the most colossal Governments in the world', whose task it was to regulate the affairs of a people 'whose view of sovereignty is that view of the sovereign as "king-proprietor" which has scarcely died out a hundred years in Europe', and among whom there was 'no notion of a trusteeship for the people'.[6]

Almost from the day of his arrival to take up residence at Calcutta, first at 15 London Street, then in Council House Street and at 10 Carnac Steet, and finally in Park Street, near Government House, Maine's enthusiasm for India was tempered by his dislike of the capital. There was, he felt, something quite unrepresentative of India about Calcutta and surrounding Bengal province. 'It is not too much to say', he wrote impatiently to the Secretary of State:

> that there is hardly a single idea, general belief, or popular feeling which has any counterpart elsewhere. The natives are totally unlike the natives of other parts and only serve to give a needlessly low opinion of native morality and vigour. The civilians are not the least like civilians of the rest of the country, for their influence for good is much diminished by a sort of hereditary exclusiveness and by the bureaucratic conditions of the secretariat. The Europeans are not like the Europeans of Bombay and still less like Englishmen in England, for they are debauched by perpetual agitation and discontent. So far as learning anything of India from the special character and surroundings of this place, one might as well be in a capital placed at Singapore or Rangoon.[7]

He added, in a later letter to Lord Cranborne: 'The normal state of sentiment in Calcutta . . . is a feeling of the profoundest discontent with the whole system of government, and especially with that feature of the system which assimilates natives to Europeans'.[8]

Maine's first experience of a trying Calcutta legislative sitting during 1863 only served to strengthen him in his conviction that, while the intention of the Indian Councils Act in creating a legislative council had been to give the executive the benefit of 'a greater number of phases of opinion' on pending measures, the

67

constant friction between its official and non-official elements, which seemed to be positively encouraged by the Calcutta press, threatened to bring urgent government business completely to a halt. He complained that:

> The newspapers here have found out that the fear of being supposed to be mere instruments of government is very strong on the legislative members, and they play constantly on this string. It is difficult for you to realise the influence of the Calcutta press; to one who reads the newspapers at a distance, their tone seems too contemptible for them to be powerful: it is not, however, by their arguments but by their *personalities* that they exercise influence. For in a society like this, which, though large for India, is very closely packed together, personal attacks vibrate, if I may so put it, with a force difficult to comprehend in England.[9]

Quite aside from the tendency of Bengal's closely knit European community to stir mischief among the non-official legislative members, Maine believed that Calcutta's infamous weather and unsanitary state had an equally undesirable effect on the pattern of viceregal rule. When, in 1864, Sir John Lawrence pressed for the creation of a commission to investigate health conditions in the capital, Maine wrote to Sir Charles Wood:

> He has paid much attention to the sanitary state of Calcutta, and has already brought out much that explains the unhealthiness of the city. It is strange that, except for a few doctors, the native town has always been *terra incognita* among Europeans. People are now penetrating it on all sides, and the result is amazing. I did not venture beyond the outskirts, but I can describe what came across me by simply saying that, except during two months of rain, three-fourths of Calcutta is permanently in the state in which the Thames was during those two famous years. The Govr. Gen. went further, but declares that his horses became sick, and so he had to return. We are in fact living on the brink of a huge, fermenting cess-pool.[10]

Maine had several times to flee his living quarters for the security of the viceregal bungalows at Barrackpore, because of outbreaks of cholera. Even the Indian members of the new legislative council, according to the Legal Member, abhorred Calcutta. 'Sir Dinkar

Rao', Maine wrote home, 'though constantly quibbling, manages to keep his health by living mainly in European fashion', while the Nawab of Rampur 'got into such a frenzy of terror at the effects of the climate on his health that he implored the Viceroy to let him go away, and on permission being refused, he sent him a medical certificate, and fairly ran away'. The suite of the Maharaja of Patiala were 'fully persuaded that the father was killed by his service on Council at Calcutta, and cite in support of their opinion the case of the Raja of Jessore, who was at Calcutta last year and [who was] attacked with dysentery'. The only Indian dignitary present at one legislative session, Maine noted, was 'the Maharaja of Burdwan, a Bengali, who however makes a point of never sleeping in Calcutta, taking a long journey twice on Council days to and from Burdwan'.[11]

Faced with Calcutta's oppressive living conditions, successive Viceroys had taken to the practice of quitting the capital for extended periods of travel, leaving the executive councillors behind to carry on with the mundane affairs of state. Maine thought the wide discretionary powers assumed by the Viceroy during his absences meant that the councillors were 'systematically kept . . . in ignorance of the most important part of Indian affairs'.[12] Imperfect communications with the executive, the Legal Member felt, encouraged embarrassments in policy, and produced serious lags in the despatch of official business. An illness brought on by the rainy season during Maine's first year at Calcutta resulted in a much desired invitation for him to join Lord Elgin at Simla, the fashionable hill station retreat for high Indian military and governmental officials. Maine later recalled that when he joined the Governor-General, who had been absent from Calcutta for some weeks, 'the Oudh papers alone almost reached from the floor to the top of the table'.[13] His stay at Simla further convinced him of the advantages of removing the executive councillors entirely from Calcutta for at least a part of the year. The building of new railway lines was eliminating the problems of shipping the necessary papers, and Maine was certain that, freed from the inhibiting European community and ill weather of Calcutta, full Council meetings convened periodically in the hills would serve 'as a means of giving energy, accuracy and promptitude to Indian Government',[14] and would bring the British raj into closer touch with its subjects. In 1864, when Sir John Lawrence introduced the experiment of holding a full legislative sitting away from the capital, the innovation was warmly welcomed by his Legal Member. 'It seems to me', he wrote home enthusiastically after the Council had been several weeks at Simla:

> that so far as the machinery of government is concerned, no experiment could be more successful. Of course, our evidence is suspicious, partly in a year in which, from the unnatural delay in the rains, even Simla is as hot as Naples in June, but still I think that men like Grey, who (in the face, I think, of facts as proveable as the rotation of the earth) maintain that the climate of Calcutta has been exaggerated, would not nevertheless deny the smoothness with which everything has gone on at Simla. It seems to me that the papers have reached us readily & have been disposed of much more promptly and with infinitely clearer heads than at Calcutta. I feel sure that the aggregate of work done is very much higher than the Calcutta average. The C. in Chief is troublesome, but much more satisfactorily dealt with, to my mind, in Council than on paper at a distance . . . Simla is not perhaps the place one would have chosen as a probable point of resort for native chiefs, yet I have seen more here in a fortnight than in Calcutta in a year. All over the Punjab, Rajputana & Central Ind. the feeling seems to prevail that we are much nearer them here than in Bengal. Then too there is not the same horror of the climate . . . A native of the higher ranks no more likes excessive heat than an Englishman likes excessive cold, & everyone's Bengalee & Madrasee servants, whose interest is to establish a grievance as a reason for higher wages, admit that they enjoy a Simla summer.[15]

He felt there was much to be said for the view that the government of India should be 'a more or less peripatetic government', travelling to centres of native power like Lahore, Delhi, Lucknow or Benares to legislate on subjects of general native interest.[16] While a permanent capital would always be necessary for the routine administration of finances and the major government departments, Maine, at one stage of his Indian period, favoured abandoning Calcutta altogether and agreed with George Campbell, a Bengal High Court Judge, that the right locality for a new capital was 'Nasik, i.e., the country above the Ghants on the Northern line of the G.I.P. Railway. It is impossible to see the Bombay side without perceiving that it unites most of the moral and social requirements of a place fit to

70

govern India from, & I believe it contains the physical and political recommendations also.'[17] Within a year of Maine's arrival in India his criticisms of Calcutta seemed to find support in tragic events. Weakened by the drain of his energies exacted during a long stay at the capital, Lord Elgin collapsed while crossing a rope bridge on the Gheriah River, and died shortly afterwards at Dharamsala.[18]

Since most of Maine's tenure of the Legal Membership was served after Elgin's death, his Indian career is more closely associated with the policies of the Whig Secretary of State, Sir Charles Wood,[19] and with Elgin's viceregal successor, Sir John (later Lord) Lawrence,[20] colourful hero of the Indian Mutiny and paternalist adherent of the 'Punjab School' of Anglo-Indian administration. On Lawrence's appointment in December 1863 the Secretary of State wrote confidentially to Maine:

> You will be of great use to the new Gov. Gen., Sir John Lawrence: and you must, forgive me for saying so, take pains to be so. He is admirable in an emergency or a crisis. I should have little doubt of his admirable fitness for suppressing a mutiny or ordering a campaign—but he has had no experience of a quasi-constitutional Govt. such as that of India has become. In general, the Gov. Gen. has been an English nobleman who took out with him correct notions enough on this point, and he had to look to the Indian members of his Council for Indian knowledge and experience. Lawrence has all this in himself and the case is exactly reversed.[21]

If Elgin's shortcoming had been his excessive timidity when faced with the complex problems posed by Indian institutions,[22] Maine soon found that Lawrence's fault lay rather in his total distrust of modern administration, and in the negative, simplistic view he held that the proper role of the British raj should be that of a benevolent despot, guarding the traditional virtues of the local peasant societies from the disruptive machinations of the European innovator. 'You wrote to me frankly about him when he first came out', the Legal Member reported to Wood after the new Viceroy had been several months at Calcutta:

> and my experience of him has borne out all you said. I really believe that all India outside Bengal proper would be as safe in his simple hands as in those of any one human being. But his deficiencies are imperfect appreciation of European character—that

71

colonial English character which poor Lord Elgin understood so thoroughly—and impatience of law and legal control. As to the first point, the very worst way of dealing with the Europeans of India is to tell them to their faces that they are all natural oppressors: the proper course is to do them the justice which you mean to compel them to show to others, and to appeal to principles which they are ashamed to gainsay. As to the other point, I quite admit that India as a whole is abnormally lawridden; but when the constitution is spoiled by overdoses of law, the remedy is not to defy law, but to administer the poison more scientifically.[23]

Maine's reflections on Lawrence touched on points that were sometimes to separate him not only from the Viceroy's policies but also from those of the Secretary of State. For while the Whiggish Wood shared Maine's criticisms of the paternalist school of administrative philosophers, and like him believed in the need to wield the positive power of the legislature in the services of progressive government, he was a more cautious reformer than the author of *Ancient Law*. In the first place, Maine's many ambitious proposals for combating 'overdoses of law' by 'administer[ing] the poison more scientifically' seemed to Wood likely to add enormously to the technical element in Anglo-Indian law. He was concerned that the academic jurist's comprehensive legislative plans would outpace the ability of a still largely traditional society to grasp the notion that simple principles of justice lay behind their external complexity:

> I think that in a country under such rule as India has been placed under [Wood suggested] there is every presumption in favour of *custom*. It is the safeguard of the weaker party in absolute government; when you come to more civilised Govts., you come to Laws, & in these matters India is in the transition state. Probably between Natives, if Englishmen & English notions had not intervened, custom would have sufficed—and it is the attempt to make precise law, instead of somewhat loose and indefinite custom, which has led to much of your present difficulty.[24]

Moreover, to a far greater extent than Maine, the Secretary of State had 'a serious distrust of laws made by white men to regulate matters between white masters and black servants' and felt that 'such a state of things calls for more than usual caution on the part of the law makers'.[25] The theme of Anglo-Indian race relations was a constant one in Wood's correspondence with Maine, and when he finally left office in February 1866, he wrote to his Legal Member with his 'parting legacy', urging him to 'see that a succession of a few transitory masters does not irritate the permanent millions'.[26] While Maine shared Wood's moral concern in principle, he nonetheless felt his political head was 'rather too much influenced by general considerations as to the antagonism of races'.[27] Reflecting a sentiment which had grown steadily in strength in the years since the Mutiny, Maine thought that as Europeans seemed bound to come out to India in growing numbers it was 'quite idle to ignore or lament their influence: the only thing is to be prepared for it and to guide it, if we are to compel them to be just to the weaker race—and this no doubt will be the great task of the Indian Government'.[28]

The direction of his planning for the achievement of that goal had already been evident when Maine had sent Lord Elgin an author's copy of his *Ancient Law*,[29] one of a batch of extra copies he had ordered to be forwarded to him at Calcutta. The British administrators of India in the years immediately ahead, he was convinced, could learn much from absorbing its text. If, as he later suggested to the Secretary of State, the chief past obstacle to Anglo-Indian progress had been the narrowly short-sighted pursuit by both branches of the Aryan peoples of their separate interests, then 'the best relations which can be established between the Europeans and the Natives is surely one of contract, provided only that the contracts are fair ones'.[30] Participating in his first major debate in the legislative council, he had emphasized that the 'progress of society seemed to be intimately connected with the completest freedom of contract, and in some ways, was almost mysteriously dependent on it'.[31] During the remainder of his stay in India, he attempted to translate the juridical postulate into a practical reality. As an expert adviser serving the government of India in its massive sociological experiment of transferring a framework of western law to an archaic civilization where social relations had previously been characterized by uniform conditions of predetermined personal status, Maine strove to make of the major theses of his *Ancient Law* a self-fulfilling prophecy.[32]

73

7

European Interests

Maine arrived in India at the beginnings of a particularly important phase of British rule. Under the government of the East India Company, it had been the usual practice to avoid interference with local usages whenever these had not seriously hampered the conduct of European mercantilism. In administrative circles, the most valued Company servant had been the district officer, an amateur judge, tax collector and general counsellor, who combined judicial and executive functions. Often learned in the vernacular languages of the areas he served, the district officer's close personal knowledge of local tradition was heavily relied on in arbitration involving European and Indian interests. With the transfer of authority from the Company to the Crown, and continued European commercial and territorial expansion, the wide range of discretionary powers previously lodged with the district officers gradually gave way to growing uniformity of administrative usages, greater centralization of political control, clearer lines of demarcation between executive and judicial functions, and the increased displacement of indigenous practices by those of the British. At first a largely piecemeal process, the systematic consolidation of Indian legal and administrative machinery occupied the energies of the imperial government for the quarter century following the passage of the Indian Councils Act of 1861.

When the British conquered India they quickly learned that the task of creating and maintaining viable Anglo-Indian civil institutions presented challenges equal in every respect to those of the battlefield. In the field of jurisprudence, for example, the Indian clung to notions, largely inexplicable to the westerner, which since time immemorial, as Maine was led to comment, had been represented in hard customs defining 'relations of castes, and sects, and religions, and races'.[1] The indigenous Hindu legal system was based

74

on *dharmasastra,* or the 'science of righteousness', a loose literature of several thousand years of accumulated wisdom, interpreted by Brahmin priest-scholars learned in its intricacies. Although regarded by Hindus as a general body of legal dictates, the *dharma* were not conceived in any western sense as a body of legal pronouncements that could be enforced by courts. There was in Indian legal practice no easily discernible hierarchy of tribunals, nor any uniformly acknowledged system of judicial procedure. The native 'judiciary' in the countryside consisted of dispersed *panchayats* adjudicating over-lapping disputes at the village, caste and association level. Enforcement of the customary judgements rendered by the *panchayat* was not a specialized function, but one carried out by the general community acting as a corporate unit.

Moreover, there was a separate and equally complex body of Muslim usage, *shari'ah,* coexisting with Hindu law in areas of former Mogul conquest. In response to the basic divergences of such indigenous Indian legal practices from those of the European, there gradually grew up during the long period of Company rule two separate systems of courts. In the *mofussil,* there were the Company's *Sadr* Courts, presided over by officials who had little formal legal training. Codified versions of Hindu and Muslim law formed the staple of these, but were modified at the discretion of Company servants who interpreted them to fit the circumstances of their locale. In the Presidency Towns, there were instituted separate King's or Supreme Courts in addition to the Company's courts, which dealt with cases involving Europeans, and enforced the common and statute law of England as well as Regulations passed by the Governor-General in Council. Not only was the law administered by the Supreme Courts different from that of the Company courts, but it took on characteristics different from those of the common law at home, and underwent further regional modifications at Madras, Bombay and Calcutta. Under the High Courts Act of 1861, provision was made for assimilating the Company's *Sadr* Courts in the Presidency Towns to the High Courts, and a start was made in rationalizing the structure of the subordinate court system. Between 1859 and 1861, a uniform Penal Code, and Codes of Civil and Criminal Procedure were enacted for use in the branches of the Anglo-Indian legal system spread throughout the country. Aside from the task of providing amendments to these as the need arose, the government of

India was left with the corollary goal of enacting a substantive civil code in order to complete this set of far-reaching legal reforms. After 1861, the planning of further measures was vested in a Law Commission and the Secretary of State and his Council in London, working in close collaboration with the Legislative Department at Calcutta.[2]

Maine surmised shortly after taking over the duties of the Legal Membership that the Indian political system was shifting steadily 'from a state in which good government depended on the energy of individuals, into a state in which it depends on adherence to well-considered rules'.[3] He realized this meant the continued demise of the personal discretion of local officials.[4] He also saw that the process must be accompanied by 'a growing intricacy and technicality of Indian law'. As a jurist, Maine welcomed these developments as indicative of the beginnings of a new era of Indian progress, yet he was nonetheless concerned that it had become increasingly difficult to distil the current leading principles of the Anglo-Indian civil law out of the mass of overlapping pronouncements rendered by lawyers, judges and legislators. While eschewing any hopes for the eventual enactment of identical laws for all of India,[5] Maine urged upon his colleagues the advantages that a uniform civil code would have in directing the energies of India's new courts. 'Here in India', he reflected in a memorandum on the legal education of civil servants:

> we have rigid systems in abundance of fixed and arbitrary law, but there is no basis in first principles; and therefore we hope the Commission will give us a simple Code. . . . What we need above all things is a clear statement of fundamental rules. . . . Here the legal classes, the Native Judges and Pleaders and to some extent the Europeans, seem to me to be characterized by infinite subtlety and no common sense. Nothing would more tend to correct these faults than simplicity and clearness in the fundamental rules of the proposed Code, which is sure to have a vast influence indirectly, and to operate as a sort of model.[6]

He believed that in blending European and Indian interests under a comprehensive civil code, the modern Briton would proffer services not unlike those of the Roman during an earlier epoch of Aryan history, when, coming into contact with the customs of less developed

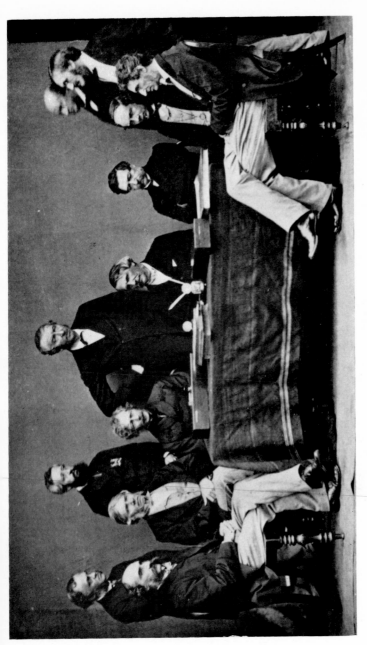

Plate 5 Viceroy's Council at Calcutta, 1864.

Standing: (left to right) Mr S. Lushington (Fin. Sec.), Colonel H. Norman (Mil. Sec. to Viceroy), Sir H. Durand (Foreign Sec.), Mr E. C. Bayley (Home Sec.), Colonel R. Strachey (D.P. Works Sec.).

Seated: (left to right) The Hon. Noble Taylor (Madras), Sir C. Trevelyan (Fin. Member), Sir Hugh Rose (C.-in-C.), Sir John Lawrence (Viceroy), Sir R. Napier (Military Member), Maine (Legal Member), Sir W. Grey (Bengal).

Plate 6 (Above left) The earliest extant photograph from life of Maine, taken at Calcutta in 1863 when he was forty-one years old.

Plate 7 (Above) A photograph of Maine taken by T. R. Williams of Regent Street, London, during Maine's European leave of 1865.

Plate 8 Sir Charles Wood, later 1st Viscount Halifax (1800-1885).

branches of the race, his law had encouraged the swift enforcement of justice and the fuller establishment of free contract.

While planning the consolidation of the remaining departments of Anglo-Indian law into simple codes occupied much of Maine's time as Legal Member, he also strove to provide more efficient procedures for use in the lower courts, as well as new judicial machinery for inculcating a fuller sense of mutual legal advantage among India's contracting classes.[7] Maine realized that for any new measure to gain a foothold in Indian legal practice it must take into account the existence of racial friction, and accept the fact that, left to their own devices, both sides would continue to act out of narrow self-interest. While he had been dismayed on arrival in India to learn of 'that widespread immorality which arises from the comparative inability of the Natives to associate legal claims with moral rights',[8] he had also soon become aware that European merchants had not infrequently set up 'private jurisdictions' in their businesses and factories, while wealthy white planters had intimidated Indian tenants through their ability to enhance land rents with impunity.[9] Maine was convinced that the piecemeal introduction of western legal institutions had actually abetted the prevailing atmosphere of distrust. The extension of European jurisdiction into the fabric of Indian society had seriously displaced the customary legal authority of the *panchayat*, while simultaneously creating a constantly enlarging flow of litigation involving Europeans and Indians to the newer tribunals. Overworked and deficient in staff, it had become a commonplace that the existing lower courts dispensed a poor quality of justice. This, Maine submitted, was because they lacked 'the means of concentrating judicial power at particular points, when the mass of cases becomes . . . suddenly enormous'.[10]

To help remedy a situation which made of the judicial process 'a mockery and a delusion', Maine, working with H. B. Harington, a member of the Viceroy's Council who had had experience as a *Sadr* Judge, drew up a comprehensive plan for the introduction of new Small Cause Courts specially adapted to Indian conditions. While Bentham's judicial schemes had expressly opposed such special courts, Maine felt they provided a more efficient remedy than the existing *Munsif* and *Sadr Amin* Courts for dealing with certain classes of suits relating to questions of fact. Under the prevailing system, *Munsif* Judges with little legal expertise were often at the mercy of unreliable written evidence submitted by native pleaders and *Muktirs*, and subsequently appeals to superior *Zillah* or district courts had become standard procedure, as had the practice in these further tribunals of freely substituting their own theory of facts for those transmitted from below.[11] This meant that the scope for judicial abuse was greatly increased, and supported the complaint of most Anglo-Indians that they suffered unnecessarily from the remoteness and complexity of their legal institutions:

> When I have seen a *Zillah* Judge [Maine wrote] starting some ingenious theory over the head of the Principal *Sadr Amin*, and the *Sadr* Court showing itself still more ingenious than the *Zillah* Judge, and the Privy Council perhaps showing itself more ingenious than all—it has often struck me . . . that the process might after all be like a long mathematical problem in which, if you make a mistake in the first stage, the error only becomes worse, and vitiates the conclusion more hopelessly in proportion as the calculation mounts up and becomes more intricate.[12]

Maine's new system aimed at establishing a great number of Small Cause Courts in the various districts of the *mofussil*. Only in the towns would there be resident Judges. In the country, full-time Registrars were to be assigned to each court to receive suits, conduct all the court's formal business, and exercise jurisdiction in petty matters. The actual Judge would be an itinerating figure, like an English County Court Judge, who would make periodical circuits to the courts under his jurisdiction. A trained lawyer, he would be assisted during periods when there were accumulations of pending suits by a barrister Judge Extraordinary, invested for limited periods by the local authorities. While appeals were to be allowed from the Registrar to the Judge, there would be no further appeal to the High Court unless he expressly allowed it. Maine believed the measure was consistent with the view that legal reforms 'should be directed to one end—the improvement of our Judges of First Instance', and thus saw it as 'contain[ing] the germ of an important revolution in the Indian Judicial system'.[13] Sir Charles Wood's first reaction to Maine's plans was one of concern that they would deprive Indians of the chance for employment in the lower courts, by requiring that the Small Cause Court Judges be barristers practising before the High Court in the Presidency Towns. He wrote to Maine, on 27 July 1863:

Now as to your Courts . . . it seems to me that there is a point for consideration of considerable importance, perhaps of a political rather than a legal view. If I understand your scheme the effect would be to displace a large number of the Native Judges, Moonsiffs, etc., substituting for them English barristers. . . . It would be a very serious matter to displace the Natives of India from so large a share in the administration of matters, and deprive them of public employment. It is difficult to employ them in high executive office & therefore the judicial line was a good career for them & with an appeal to an English superior, which gave security against jobbing, I believe there was little harm in their doing this sort of work—But how will it do to substitute English Judges in all these cases: I cannot help fearing that it will create a great feeling against us that we are going to rule the country *without* them.[14]

Maine had, in fact, originally felt his new courts would have to draw heavily upon the bar at home for qualified personnel, and concluded that the less well trained Indians would have to seek judicial employment among the ranks of the deputy magistrates and collectors. Under pressure from the Secretary of State and Mr Cecil Beadon, Lieutenant-Governor-elect of Bengal, however, he abandoned this view and reframed his measure, as he wrote to Wood on 30 August 1863, 'so as to exclude any notion of bringing Barristers from England, at all events for the present'.[15] While maintaining that the Judges should be English-trained lawyers, he accepted that Indians and legally unskilled civilians could offer useful services in the new capacity of Small Cause Court Registrars, at least until lawyers in sufficient numbers became available. Relieved at the Legal Member's moderation, Wood wrote from London to assure him that:

I quite agree with you that we must look to Englishmen to decide in important cases where English parties are concerned. I have no faith in the moral courage or firmness of the Hindoos; & I have no doubt of the English settlers despairing and bullying the Hindoo Judge as far as he can. Their confidence in the administration of justice requires the acknowledged independence of the English character when the Judge sits alone. We hope to train the Native to this by degrees—& this can only be done by

79

his going through the inferior positions & acquiring this & showing that he has acquired the necessary character for firmness. Your Registrarships may do this as well as other appointments— for I do feel strongly the political advantage of employing Natives as largely as we can in the administration of India.[16]

Maine's bill for reforming the Small Cause Courts, which he was certain would substitute for the incompetence of the *Munsif* Courts 'a regular, fair-dealing, and incorrupt *Panchayat*',[17] became law as Act XI of 1865.

Maine's scheme almost ran aground, when, in an earlier version of the bill, he had proposed revising the Code of Civil Procedure to allow his Small Cause Courts to order the specific performance of contracts.[18] The author of *Ancient Law* felt that one of the most pervasive features of the Indian legal system was the shallowness of the roots of that great institutional expression of public fidelity, trustworthy contractual relations, and indeed, recognized immediately on arrival at Calcutta that the conduct of Anglo-Indian commerce and agriculture had been seriously impeded by the lack of adequate judicial machinery for maintaining legal promises.

Maine's first task as Legal Member had been, under instructions from the Secretary of State, to see to the withdrawal of a bill prepared by his predecessor to remedy breaches of contract 'committed in bad faith'.[19] Believing that legal progress depended 'almost mysteriously' on the civil enforcement of contract, Maine opposed Ritchie's bill in Council on the ground that it confused civil and criminal law, just as the notorious Act XI passed by Lord Canning's Council in 1860, which enabled European planters to force *ryots* to grow indigo in exchange for cash advances, had revealed itself in the Indigo Commission's later evidence as an instrument for encouraging racial oppression. While Maine could not support any other than a civil contract law, however, neither could he accept that ordinary damages were a sufficient deterrent or an adequate protection against irresponsible contractors in current Indian circumstances. For a successful plaintiff in a breach of contract suit to be able to 'seize the *ryot's* bullocks, his plow, and his brass pans' solved nothing, since they were useless to him and totally crippling to the errant peasant. Maine's scheme, on the other hand, would enable the courts to order the actual performance of a previous legal promise where it could be clearly ascertained that the defendant could do so, and had not initially contracted under false impressions. He believed the imposition of 'this kindest, and fairest, as well as one of the most efficient remedies known to civil justice' would assist the processes of Indian legal advance, while furthering the trust of the commercial classes in regular contracts.[20]

Neither Wood nor the Governor-General shared Maine's faith in the efficacy of his proposed specific performance clauses. Both the representatives of an earlier generation of Anglo-Indian statesman-ship, they were quick to remind their Legal Member of the potential for abuse where racial friction was involved:

I cannot help fearing [Wood wrote] that such a power might be used as an instrument for bullying the *ryot* awfully. They contract to plough at a certain time, to sow ditto, to weed ditto, reap ditto, deliver & so forth—I do not say that they ought not to do all these things, but look at the way in which contracts were imposed on the *ryots* who hardly could exercise any free will in the matter.

He was especially concerned over Maine's intention to give his judges 'the power to make an order on a *ex parte* statement *without even requiring proof* of notice to defendant'.[21] Sir John Lawrence sided with the Secretary of State, urging upon Maine that: 'I am very much afraid that the days of the abuses described by the Indigo Commission have not passed away. . . . I think there is much truth in what Sir C. Wood says of the antagonism of races & of the disposition of the stronger & bolder & more energetic man to oppress the weaker. I think that this is history of the whole world.'[22]

Maine's reaction to the criticisms of his superiors was to conclude that they had been blinded to the beneficial efficiency of his proposals by a form of sentimental equalitarianism that ignored recent social trends in India. As he submitted in a letter to the Viceroy of April 1864:

I can see little use in dwelling . . . on the oppression which results from the contact of the weaker & the stronger race. That the Bengalees have been an oppressed race one might be quite sure, even apart from the evidence of the Indigo Commission. But the oppression resulted 1) from actual violence on the part of the planters, 2) from a fear of it when it was not present, 3) from a vague idea that the Govt. was on the side of the planter.

But all this is now changed. There is no violence now perpetrated or apprehended in any part of Bengal, and the natives thoroughly understood that the authorities lean, if anything, to their side rather than to that of the European. . . . What the India Office clearly does not understand is that the state of things indicated by the Indigo Report has quite passed away.[23]

He admitted that his progressive legal measures set standards of discrimination, but these were rational standards that transcended considerations of race. 'When you have once provided for the application of civil tests to contracts', he judged, 'you have done all you can for improvident contractors.'[24] Such was the price of progress:

If a man has promised to do a thing, is demonstrably intending not to do so, and can be proven able to do so, why in the world should he not be compelled by civil penalties to do so? When the principle is so simple, the difficulty of carrying it out can only arise from faults of the system, and the objections to it must be the fruit of prejudice, sophistry, or bad faith.[25]

If he seemed to lean too strongly to the European side on the contract question, he explained to Wood, it was because of 'the extreme onesidedness of views now prevalent'. Maine thought it was 'almost ridiculous to cite great general propositions about the antagonism of race'. If it was a fact that one of the chief burdens of the Indian legal reformer arose from the 'systematic character of European *exploitation*', it was equally true that 'litigation on the side of the *ryot* almost universally arises from widespread concert and combination', and that 'the *ryots* have a high idea of their own force'.[26]

Yet if the reformed legal system must favour some values over others, Maine, as a good Victorian, entertained no doubt as to the appropriate course. With Europeans coming to India in great numbers, their commercial interests must be protected. If a choice must be made between the adoption of measures designed to satisfy the European's contractual expectations and those that protected the status relationships of the old society, he had no doubt that 'it is the party of the Europeans which must win in the end'.[27] While Maine produced successive redrafts of his specific performance clauses in an attempt at overcoming the reservations of his senior colleagues, however, his plans were destined ultimately to be shelved. The Secretary of State was never able to overcome his fears that Maine's suggestions required for their proper working the sophisticated judgement of a type of court official seldom found in India. Shortly before leaving office in 1866, Wood confessed in a letter to Maine: 'I shall not grieve if the clauses turn out to be a dead letter.'[28] The proposals were referred to the Law Commission, and, in view of their attitude that further consideration of the matter should be dealt with under the head of substantive rather than procedural law, they were never revived during the remainder of Maine's stay in India. The final position of the Home Government was summed up in a letter written to Maine by Sir Erskine Perry, a member of the Indian Council and for long a close confidant of Wood:

> With respect to your doctrines on specific performance I cannot divest myself of the profound conviction that it is our duty to protect the humbler and weaker classes from the tendency of the dominant race to exploit them. I see this tendency in every country under the sun, in Java as well as India, in England as well as elsewhere. But in England we are adopting juster views as to the claims of the working people & we are expunging from our statute book those acts which seemed to have been planned solely in the interests of the rich. I do not like to see such acts made the model for colonial and Indian legislation.[29]

While Maine's chief interests as an Indian legal reformer lay in the domain of civil law, he also contributed to the growing body of Anglo-Indian criminal law. He was the author of the Whipping Act of 1864,[30] a measure which had been opposed by the original Indian Law Commission, but which Maine had reluctantly drafted in response to the continuous prodding of the local governments, who argued that the substitution of flogging for imprisonment in certain classes of criminal offence would have the effect of relieving pressures on India's overcrowded prisons. More importantly, he drafted a series of measures designed to bring all Europeans in India under the general criminal law. For minor European offences in the *mofussil*, Maine proposed creating a Court of Quarter Sessions with the existing Sessions Judge as Chairman, assisted by a panel of civilians and several Justices of the Peace appointed from among the ranks of prominent local settlers. Maine thought the plan would 'give Europeans a greater sympathy with justice by their being associated with its administration'.[31] In cases of disagreement, there would be provision for appeal to the High Court from the ruling of the Chairman, and more serious crimes would be reserved for trial by a Judge of the High Court going on circuit. Maine also urged the creation of a new High Court in the North-West, with 'little High Courts' or Legal Commissionerships exercising control over all appellate jurisdiction and all original jurisdiction in cases involving Europeans in the Punjab and Oudh.[32] He expressly opposed uniformity of trial for natives and Europeans.[33]

Maine's most significant reform in the field of criminal law, however, was his sponsorship of a measure to abolish grand juries in India, substituting for them trial by petty jury. No other practice had contributed so greatly as grand juries, in his estimation, to European impunity for crimes committed against Indians. Outside the Presidency Towns, he wrote, European offenders had in the past been in a position 'so exceptional that . . . they are scarcely within the reach of the law at all', and had come to look on impunity as an hereditary right, since the grand juries that met in the larger centres to try their cases invariably took their side.[34] Secret tribunals not open to the wholesome curb of publicity, their procedures did not permit guidance by the judge, nor the cross-examination of witnesses. They were large bodies, 'coming dangerously near the point', as Maine protested, 'at which the instincts of a crowd take the place of deliberation'.[35] By way of contrast, the methods by which petty juries obtained evidence, and their open and broadly based composition, Maine reckoned to be among the most respectable features of British law. Indeed, he once suggested that 'trial by the petty jury has affected English character more than any institution, even more, I am inclined to say, than representative institutions'.[36]

While Maine felt the case against grand juries was 'extraordinarily strong', his proposals caused an outbreak of 'Black Act' sentiment seldom rivalled since Macaulay's famous Act XI of 1836 had brought Europeans resident outside Calcutta under the civil jurisdiction of the company's Courts and deprived them of their rights of appeal to the Supreme Court. A public meeting was organized at the Town Hall of Calcutta to protest against Maine's plans for abolishing 'a

84

cherished institutional sentinel of the public safety'. Maine wrote to the Secretary of State:

> I do not know whether I am right, but I have an idea that the G. General is rather disturbed by this European agitation; which is of course unlike anything he has seen upcountry. I hope he will not give way. If we yield here, it seems to me that we may as well consult the pleasure of the Europeans on every matter which in any way affects them . . .
>
> We are packed very closely together at Calcutta & this meeting will take place at the Town Hall, which is only a stone's throw from Govt. House & our Council Room.[37]

Wood wrote hurriedly in return to urge Maine 'on no account to give up the Grand Jury bill. It would be ignominious in the last degree & most injurious to the Govt. of India & the public good to do so.'[38] By the date of that letter's composition Maine had already been able to report brighter news to the Secretary of State:

> The Public Meeting about the Grand Jury Bill . . . is generally acknowledged to have failed as a popular demonstration. None of the more respectable merchants attended & the attendance generally was thin. I do not pretend that the Bill is liked in this part of the country but I do think that the best of the settlers are convinced that the Gd. Jury is an institution indefensible even in England if it uses its powers seriously (which it never does) and quite unnecessary in India with a scanty & constantly occupied population . . .
>
> The language of the speakers at the meeting was rather super-abundantly civil to myself, but the lower class of newspapers continue to pour frantic personal abuse on me.[39]

With the strong support of the Viceroy, Harington, Grey, and Trevelyan, and the sole opposition of the Military Member, Sir Robert Napier,[40] Maine's measure for abolishing grand juries in India was enacted as Act XIII of 1865.

Though Maine perhaps 'leaned strongly to the European side', then, he was nonetheless not an unmitigated champion of the interests of the stronger race. There were less civilized elements among their number, including those most likely to accuse him of 'Black Act sentiments', who posed a threat to enlightened segments of the

European and Indian communities alike. 'It is impossible to observe the class of Europeans employed on the railway', he wrote to Wood, 'or to see (as I did, as we had 50 of them in the steamer coming out) the sort of men sent by joint-stock companies to India, without feeling that something must be done to make them amenable to justice.'[41] His reformed courts and plans for guaranteeing the fair enforcement of contracts, he was confident, would contribute to maintaining India on the path towards social progress, while corollary measures for minimizing European crimes, which were harmful to both English and Indian interests, would ensure the stability of that course.

8

Indian Interests

To refashion the Anglo-Indian legal system into a framework within which the encouragement and growth of progressive law could take place meant more than simply meeting the special demands of the conquering race. It required that equally careful attention be bestowed on the needs of the indigenous Indian population. Maine, as an accomplished historical scholar, believed that reforms based on scientific principles of jurisprudence would allow for the gradual introduction into traditional India of western practices that would encourage the transformation of law, without involving too abrupt a dislocation of the underlying Indian social fabric. Just as there were segments of the European population more perceptive of the benefits of institutionalized public fidelity, so too there were, in his estimation, elements of the Indian community sufficiently adaptable as to be more readily persuaded of the blessings of the imported civil law. Visiting Bombay while on leave in 1865, Maine was struck by the evidently happier state of relations between the races there, as compared to Calcutta. Though allowing that this racial cooperation might be partly attributed to 'the common pursuit of wealth' in cotton, which was then being grown in great quantities to fill the demand created by the wartime exclusion of the Confederate American states from international markets, he believed the community spirit of Bombay equally due to 'there being such an excellent bridge from race to race as the Parsees'.[1] He thought that carefully constructed legislation might gradually widen that bridge linking the more 'advanced' Indians, such as the Parsees, with the Europeans, and would allow for the assimilation of rigid traditional forms of Hindu legal usage to new and more flexible legal institutions.

Thus, in defending the virtues of the new Indian Law of Succession sent out from London by the Indian law commissioners, Maine lectured his colleagues on the general principles that govern the evolution of legal systems. He emphasized that the major provision of the codifying instrument then before the Council—the abolition of the distinction between real and personal property, and the adoption of the principle that no interest in a spouse's property would under its terms be automatically guaranteed by marriage—represented no small incentive to the development of modernity and free contract in British India, just as a similar set of reforms in the classical world had loosened the rigidity of Roman family law, and eventually infused these into the evolving usages of the barbarian hordes. He expressed the view that while the new code governing succession must at first apply only to the legally advanced Europeans, it might one day be extended to the more sophisticated portions of the Indian community, and eventually even to 'certain wild tribes' of Hindus and Muslims. Indeed, among the vast indigenous populations of India, Maine reflected, the new law could be applied at first only 'in proportion to the barbarism of a tribe' and receptivity to its benefits would be the lowest in those areas burdened by 'the faintness of the notion of individual rights as distinguished from family right'.[2] Nonetheless, there were Indian communities whose inventiveness and adaptability, he was confident, suggested more immediate prospects for assimilation. These, he conjectured, were engaged at the present moment in 'perhaps the last great struggle of barbarism—I do not use the term offensively but as a term of degree—[the Parsees] are ahead of the other races in allowing to women a definite share of property, and in permitting them to enjoy it independently.'[3] Maine, in other words, in applying a further thesis of his *Ancient Law*, submitted that the rigidity ascriptive status relationships of traditional Indian society had had their foundation in the inner life of the extended family group. One key to legal modernization lay therefore, as the new Law of Succession proposed, in devising techniques for creating individual legal personality for the parties to marriage, for at present, as his comparison of the Parsees with other Indian groups suggested:

> If there exists any test of the degree in which society approximates to that condition which we call civilization, it is the degree in which it approaches the admission of a right between the sexes. In this respect, I am sure that by simply applying that criteria, you

88

could construct a scale of barbarism and civilization which would commend itself to every man's perceptions.[4]

If Maine's principle arguments for Indian progress necessitated the creation of individual personality and property rights which had been traditionally monopolized by the family, they extended as well to include the removal of ascriptive status based on indigenous religious practices. Thus, Maine committed himself as Legal Member to a measure allowing the remarriage of native converts to Christianity who were subsequently deserted or repudiated by their families. 'The great majority of Hindus', he argued in Council, 'were married before they reached the age of reason', while converts to Christianity had been 'brought over by the operation of reason'. It was therefore, he believed, the duty of the imperial government to guarantee a freedom of choice otherwise denied by unprogressive social taboos and superstition. For Maine the question was less one of religious sentiment than of secular morality. Freeing the more mobile segments of Indian society from archaic practices was, in his judgement, 'an act of liberty' that was in keeping both with the motives underlying his general principles of legal reform, and with his assured Indian bureaucrat's view that the proposal involved 'the exhibition of the most eminent ingredient of [English] civilization'.[5] Maine allowed the 'clear rule' that great caution was assuredly necessary before undertaking such wide reaching reforms, yet denied that the admission meant making practices repugnant to the westerner 'a basis for further legislation'. The inescapable obligation of the responsible Indian administrator, he was convinced, was 'the necessity of declaring what *ought* to be'.[6]

In his role as Vice-Chancellor of Calcutta University, to which post he was appointed by Lord Elgin in 1863, Maine found further confirmation of the potential progressiveness of the 'enlightened classes' of India. Although the University had only recently been created, Maine was struck by the rapidity with which the Bengalee intellectual community had responded to its westernizing benefits. 'The interest and anxiety of the students', he reported enthusiastically to Wood, demonstrated to his satisfaction the sincerity of their desire to learn from the westerner:

We had 1500 the other day for matriculation and about 500 more for what corresponds to Literary Society. This year, the examination was held in the shell of the new Post Office, a place without flooring and with half a roof. Next year, to all appearances, we must encamp in the Meadow . . . Meanwhile, the number of candidates increases in a geometrical ratio.[7]

Maine seems to have been genuinely enthusiastic about the prospect of an educated Indian middle class, learned in western ways, and leading the Asian subcontinent out of the darkness of static civilization into the clear light of progressive law. The emergence of indigenous professional classes, possessing specialized skills, struck his academic fancy as analogous to the early period of the Roman Republic, or that of the revival of classical learning in medieval Europe. His vision, however, did not extend to embrace the logical conclusion of that process—the demand by Indians imbued of English ideas for control of their own country. To proposals for the creation of a college in the Punjab which would emphasize the study of India's indigenous literature rendered in native languages, Maine had strong reservations. The real future of India's intellectual leadership, in his estimation, lay rather in the role they might play in the adaptation of western ideas, and in the emulation of British virtues. 'To be the astrologer or the poet', he assured the Calcutta University graduating class of 1866:

> . . . or the chronicler of the most heroic of mythical Indian princes (even if we could suppose him existing), would be intolerable even to a comparatively humble graduate of this University. They may be safely persuaded that, in spite of discouragements which do not all come from themselves or their countrymen, their real affinities are with Europe and the Future, not with India and the Past.[8]

The true purpose of higher education in India, the Vice-Chancellor believed, was to bring the advanced segments of Indian society to an appreciation of British values, thus to an understanding of the benefits of western legal and political institutions, and in time, to bring this new-found knowledge home to the vast masses of their countrymen.

Though Maine's long-range reform proposals emphasized the role of the more enlightened classes in assisting the westernization of

90

India, he had also as Legal Member to deal with the pressing practical problems of the unenlightened masses living in their millions in the countryside, and dependent for their meagre livelihood on the land. Like Wood and Lawrence, Maine was sensitive to the relative helplessness of these *ryots* or agricultural peasants, in comparison both with the more adaptable and better placed Indian, and with the commercially inventive European. He saw much wisdom in Wood's reflection that in India as elsewhere in the Empire, 'land is the general cause of quarrel'.[9] Sharing that view, he was thus emphatic in asserting the need for the fullest implementation of fair and uniform contractual rights for all races and classes alike, for otherwise:

> The relation of landlord and tenant which is being rapidly established over Bengal . . . seems to me about the very worst relation which can be set up between rich and poor in India, where there are not hereditary and semi-feudal attachments to modify the natural harshness of the relation . . . if it once becomes understood that buying land for the sake of the mere rent is a profitable investment, the land will at once pass into the ownership of Europeans, who will live at home and exact the utmost farthing from their tenants through Erasian or native gentlemen.[10]

During Maine's years in India, events in Bengal, Oudh, and the Punjab brought his theoretical concern with problems of regulating property rights to the level of practical politics. British land settlements in newly conquered territories, on which colonial tax revenues were based, had literally created individual property rights in India, where previously there had been elaborate co-proprietorships in which *ryot*, *zemindar*, and the local state shared in the proceeds of agricultural production. With the prosperity and growth of population that followed the imposition by the British of political stability in the first half of the nineteenth century, the value of Indian land grew immensely in the prime agricultural areas, and *ryots* who were unable to pay higher rents were commonly evicted, or intimidated by threats of enhancement of their rents into producing crops in which their European planter-landlords had commercial interests. Act X of 1859 was expressly designed to guarantee rights to tenure that would eradicate such coercion in Bengal province. The Act

91

declared that *ryots* who had held land for a period of twelve consecutive years had a 'right' of occupancy in the land they cultivated.

The fees charged of such occupancy tenants were, under the terms of the Act, to accord with the principle of 'fair and equitable rates', and could only be enhanced if it could be demonstrated that they were below others in the same vicinity (the device of '*pergunnah* rates'), or that the value of the landlord's property or its produce had dramatically increased irrespective of the *ryot's* efforts. The intention of the Act, thus, was to confer beneficial proprietary rights on those who had held their land for twelve years, while those unable to prove such proprietorship were relegated to the status of mere tenants at will, whose rents could be settled at the going price in the open market.

British planters in the Bengal *mofussil*, encouraged by the vague criteria governing the 'fair rental 'rates, had in the years after the Sepoy Mutiny followed the practice of threatening enhancement of the rents of their *ryots* as a means of forcing the reluctant peasants to grow indigo. Holding that their beneficial rights of occupancy guaranteed by Act X had been violated, a group or *ryots* took their case in 1863 to the High Court at Calcutta, where Sir Barnes Peacock, who ironically earlier, as Legal Member of the Governor-General's Council had strongly opposed passage of the Act in 1858–9, sat now as Chief Justice. In a decision well received by the English community at Calcutta, Peacock rejected the appeal of the *ryots* of Kishnaghur and Jessore districts, holding that the 'fair and equitable' provisions of Act X meant simply that twelve year *ryots* were to be afforded 'preferential rights' of tenure, and that their rents were thus not in principle intended to be removed from the fluctuations of the open market.[11] In effect, Maine wrote home to Wood, the Chief Justice had laid down that the framers of Act X had meant by 'fair and equitable' simply a rack-rent,[12] and added that Peacock, 'in interpreting this section of Act X . . . entirely refused, and refuses, to take into account the ancient historical relations of *zemindar* and *ryot*'. He was certain that, in a further appeal pending as he wrote, the Chief Justice would be 'forced to attend to ancient rights and customs'. Not even the authority of the author of *Ancient Law*, however, could shake Peacock from his position. Mr Montriou, the *ryots'* legal counsel in the further appeals case, urged upon the Court that, according to Professor Maine's well-known theory that primitive societies dealt with relationships of status and not of contract, it followed that 'what is fair and equitable depends upon the *status* of the *ryot*, and not upon the value of the produce and costs of production' as the English planters contended. Peacock, who found different principles of political economy in Maine's treatise, held however that 'the condition and rights of these *ryots*, at least those whose tenures commenced since the date of the permanent settlement, depend not upon *status*, but upon *contract*', and thus reaffirmed his earlier decision.[13]

The final outcome of the elaborate court proceedings, Maine wrote in protest to the Secretary of State, was that 'the planter has got all he asked', and the *ryots'* proprietary rights, which had under Act X been ceded by the British authorities as a workable political compromise, had been ignored. Late in 1864, however, two High Court Justices overruled Peacock's decisions in a similar case, creating the conditions for a test hearing before the full Court.[14] In March 1865 the Bengal High Court voted 14 to 1 to reverse Peacock's decisions, and substituted the standard of 'proportionate enhancement' as the measure with which to judge future disputes involving questions of 'fair and equitable' rates.[15] The Court, Maine was relieved to hear, had at last upheld 'every single old right', and in assisting the *ryot*, had vindicated the political importance of prescriptive usage.[16]

The Oudh tenure controversy overlapped chronologically with the Bengal rent cases. As early as 28 August 1863 Maine noted in a letter that 'Lord Elgin and I are working on the Oudh question, that of the subordinate tenures and that of the rights of the *taluqdars*.' The position of the landholding Oudh *taluqdars* of the north-central interior was infinitely stronger than that of the landlords of Bengal. Indeed, in 1858, alarmed by the extent of disloyalty among the Oudh peasantry during the Mutiny of the previous year, Lord Canning had instituted a policy of outright support of the *taluqdars* in disputes involving them with the *ryots*, on the assumption that, firmly installed as a landed aristocracy by their British rulers, they would be dependable allies in the north of India. Canning rescinded previous Oudh agreements governing the conditions of proprietorship, and redistributed land among *taluqdars* who had been faithful to the government during the Mutiny. The immediate effect of the measure was to deprive many peasant tenants of proprietary rights

93

which had been granted them under a previous Oudh land settlement in 1856.

The full implications of the fundamental shift in policy, however, only became evident after 1859, when a report submitted by the Chief Commissioner of Oudh, Charles Wingfield, claimed that any restriction of the proprietary rights of the aristocratic *taluqdars*, whose ancestors had controlled the land of Oudh for centuries, was unheard of before the British introduced their Regulation VII of 1822, the instrument which had originally created western style property 'rights' in the North-West. Quite aside from the historical argument, moreover, Wingfield was convinced that the British would be acting on the soundest political principles in affording continued support for the *taluqdar* cause. 'The majority of our *taluqdars*', the Chief Commissioner submitted, 'share the feelings of English landlords.' Through education he would incorporate Lord Canning's plan to 'raise the character of the rising generation of the *taluqdars*', and mould them into an hereditary landed aristocracy on the English model. Not until 1862 did official opposition begin to consolidate against Wingfield's ambitious schemes. The Judicial Commissioner of Oudh, George Campbell, who shortly thereafter, on his appointment to the Bengal High Court, also led the opposition to Sir Barnes Peacock's rent decisions, challenged Wingfield's tenure theories in a separate report on Oudh landholding submitted to the central government.[17]

Lord Lawrence's paternalist impulse was to employ the full legislative power of his Council to counter the proposals of the landlord faction which had so evidently gained a dominant position in the formulation of Oudh policy. Maine, however, with the Secretary of State's support, in this instance counselled caution, on the ground that 'sudden revolutions of principle terribly shake native confidence in the stability of our rule', and moreover, because he felt that 'in the face of the positive assertions of Wingfield . . . that "hereditary tenants" do not exist in Oudh, we ought not to assume that they do exist'.[18] He persuaded Lawrence to reflect further on the matter, while conducting an inquiry under the supervision of Mr R. H. Davies, a Punjab official sympathetic to the Governor's *ryot* views. Maine seems to have experienced much personal uneasiness over the Oudh controversy. In principle, he was no supporter of Wingfield's landlord sentiments, for he believed that objective historical

94

inquiry would show 'occupancy rights' to have existed equally on both sides before the British came to India. Anyone familiar with his studies in legal development knew that:

> occupancy tenures are very old in the history of the world, open markets for land are comparatively new. It is much easier for me to believe that hereditary tenants never existed at all in India or parts of India, than to believe that they always existed but were always liable to rack-rent . . . I have advanced the proposition that in the ancient stages of society the distribution of the produce of land between owner and cultivator is never regulated by contract. The opposite view involves in truth an anachronism, tenure being much more ancient than contract.[19]

Yet Maine realized the Oudh question must finally be settled by political considerations. The imperial lawgiver was obliged to further civilization, and no one, Maine thought, could objectively deny that separate ownership was a fundamental element in social progress. Wood agreed with his view that at such a developed stage of the Oudh debate they should 'modify and improve, not reverse or upset, Lord Canning's policy'.[20] For the Legal Member, the answer in this case lay not in the recreation of the historical past for its own sake, but in discovering some principle of continuity which had its basis in the most recent settlement, and upon which the rights of each side to the dispute could be equitably ascertained.

Davies's eventual report on Oudh tenure illustrated in great detail the hardships that Wingfield's landlord theories had unquestionably imposed on the cultivating classes, and recommended the extension of Act X from Bengal into Oudh as a means of reinstituting *ryot* proprietorship in twelve-year holdings. Although Lawrence was anxious to implement this plan, Maine and his supporters on the Council argued that whereas they had supported a '*ryot* interpretation' of Act X against Peacock's judgement in the Bengal rent cases, they did not believe such to be an enforceable course of action in the present political context. For Maine, Davies's proposals simply 'opposed one assumption to another', and in 're-reversing' Lord Canning's plan, would only add to the dangerously advanced state of friction already existing between the claimants. Government, he believed, must try to improve what had gone before, once its legislative power had been called extensively into service. It must not engage in constant meddling with existing precedents, for he was certain that doing so must lead ultimately to a decline in the authority of the law. Davies's recommendations were in fact eventually dropped, and, in view of the undeniable strength of the *taluqdars*, a face-saving compromise was devised by the Council in 1866 and incorporated in Act XIX of 1868. Under the new regulations the Oudh landlords agreed to concede tenure to those ex-proprietary *ryots* who could prove that they had cultivated their land continuously for thirty years, a stringent requirement that the Council felt itself helpless to oppose. The number of *ryots* thus reinstated with beneficial tenures included little more than one per cent of the total cultivating population, a dismally low figure on which the central government was apparently afforded very poor intelligence. The result of the Oudh land controversies was, in practical terms, an undoubted victory for the landlord school of Wingfield and the *taluqdars*.[21]

So strong had landlord sentiment become in the 1860s that it penetrated even into the realm of Sir John Lawrence's earlier administrative career in northern India, the Punjab, where Lawrence's romantic 'paternalist' ideal of a peaceful nation of small peasant holders, loyally tilling their land under the benevolent approval of the European ruler, had had its fullest application. With the expiration of the original land settlement in Amritsar Division of the Punjab in 1864, the local Settlement Commissioner, Edward Prinsep, created a Commission to carry out a 'routine' review of the records of the earlier settlement. Maine feared the outcome from the start, for as he surmised, Prinsep's land theories approximated to 'the views which have recently become prevalent, which have the support of the great European interests in lower Bengal, and which have been advanced of late with so much tenacity and vigour by Sir C. Wingfield of Oudh'.[22] True to Maine's analysis, Prinsep's inquiries 'discovered' a great number of irregularities in the original settlement of Punjab rights. The Amritsar lists were subsequently revised, so that out of some 60,000 *ryots* who had been recorded as entitled to beneficial rights of occupancy at the first settlement eighteen years earlier, some 36,000 were now relegated to the status of mere tenants at will. For Maine, the lines drawn in the Punjab, where *ryots* had enjoyed unquestioned rights of proprietorship for some years, involved a totally opposite set of political circumstances

96

from those of Oudh, where there had been lacking in the claims of both sides any such clear foundations in prescriptive authority. He now rallied to the support of the dismayed Governor-General. 'I feel so strongly on the subject', he assured Lawrence, 'that I could scarcely with a safe conscience hold my tongue.'[23] If Prinsep's revisions were allowed to stand and extended in the same proportions throughout all divisions of the Punjab, Maine predicted, an agrarian revolution would be unleashed that would sweep the British from the North-West.

In Council debate Maine supported his argument on behalf of the claims of the Punjab *ryot* with principles derived from his studies in historical jurisprudence. In the total view of comparative civilizations, he pointed out, all 'rights' over land or other valuable commodities must be based either on contractual or proprietary practices. Since Punjab tenure had never, so far as the historical records revealed, been based on contractual arrangements in any technical legal sense, he surmised that 'in strictness of language, the occupancy-tenant is a co-proprietor with the landlord'.[24] The academic fact of historical co-proprietorship in Punjab tenancy was not, however, in the estimation of the Legal Member, the only argument against Prinsep's position, nor indeed necessarily his most important objection. Maine suggested that an even more compelling political case could be made on behalf of the principle of upholding social institutions which had an undeniable foundation in usage. Frankly, he submitted:

> even if British rule created the property, I cannot see that it has deeply sinned if it decided somewhat arbitrarily who was to have it . . . we should commit an injustice far more deeply felt if we took it away from those who have enjoyed it for fifteen or twenty years.

It was preferable, he thought, 'to stand even by our mistakes. It is better than perpetual meddling.[25]

The Punjab Rent Act of 1868 reversed Prinsep's findings, and tenants who had been previously recorded as entitled to beneficial rights of occupancy were reinstated, unless a landlord could disprove specific claims in the courts.[26] John Stuart Mill, who had followed the course of the Punjab land question with some interest, wrote to Maine to congratulate him on his part in having temporarily stemmed the tide in India of what seemed to observers in London 'a reaction towards landlordism of the present English type'.[27] For Maine, however, as the course of these several Indian tenure controversies illustrate, his positions were less inspired by any abstract moral sentiment that he might wish to see applied universally throughout India to alleviate the *ryot's* condition, than by his conviction that it was the Law Member's paramount duty to uphold the claims of prescription over those of change as the basic ingredient of wise public policy.[28]

Maine's period of office in the Viceroy's Council coincided with the beginnings of a new era in the philosophy of Anglo-Indian administration, and nowhere was this more evident than in his own department of law. In the years immediately before his arrival in India, the Penal Code of the first Indian Law Commission, as well as Codes of Civil and Criminal Procedure drafted by a later Commission, had been enacted. In the years immediately after his departure from India, an Indian Evidence Act, a revised Code of Criminal Procedure, and a new Contract Act prepared under the aegis of J. F. Stephen,[29] were to be added to this basic corpus of codifying instruments. In the intervening years, while only one major codifying measure, the Succession Act of 1865, was passed into law, it is clear that much of the adjustment of the detail of the earlier codes to the actual working conditions of Indian law, as well as the preparations for the later additions under Stephen in 1872, were only made possible through the energetic draughtsmanship of Maine and the Indian Legislative Department he created and developed almost singlehandedly during the 1860s.[30]

Even before going to India, Maine believed, as he had written in *Ancient Law*, that an era of codification was an unavoidable stage in the transition of traditional or 'customary' legal systems into modern. As Law Member, he followed that belief to its practical conclusions in supervising the drafting and enactment of upwards of 200 Acts[31] that were, in his estimation, the necessary preliminary step towards the goal of an overall consolidation of the burgeoning and largely unclassified judicial and administrative rules of British India. From the time of his arrival at Calcutta, he held to the seemingly paradoxical view that, in order to eliminate the need for legislation in the future, it was necessary to legislate in quantity in the present. To the district officer accustomed to a large degree of personal discretion in the exercise of both judicial and executive func-

98

tions in his locale, Maine's views were bound to appear dangerous, and suspicion of the directions of Maine's thinking was shared by a wide element of 'paternalist' administrators. Alarmed by the rigorous pace of Maine's legislative programme, the Secretary of State wrote a firm note[32] to his Legal Member during 1865:

Let me beg of you not to be in such a hurry in publishing your bills. If there is no great pressure, let us see them first . . . By a little care anything unpleasant can be avoided, but it would be disagreeable to be asked in Parliament if I had seen a bill published by you, and whether I approved it: supposing that I had not, it would bring the workings of the two Governments into discredit.

You have been running a little *too much ahead*, and I don't wish to have to pull you up. You must remember that Parliament calls upon me to answer for your proceedings, and you must avoid putting me into difficulties if you can help it.

In a similar vein, Sir Erskine Perry chided Maine in a note sent out from the India Office in London, reflecting that:

I confess that for myself, I view as an *evil* the tendency to rapid and over-law-making, which our new system of legislative councils produces. It is the fault of all representative governments, that when the legislative chamber is got together, with so much tumult and expense, its chief function is *supposed to be* to create new laws. And I think this tendency is rather greater in India, where the checks on individual theories and crotchets are so much fewer.[33]

Maine, however, did not allow the admonitions of his seniors in London to sway him from his legislative plans. He acknowledged the concern of the India Office but, as he wrote to Sir Charles Wood, he could not see that the programme of his Legislative Department would be anything but beneficial:

You have strongly stated your fear of over-legislation, and you seem to think I have a proclivity toward it. This is not so at all . . . I must ask you . . . not to be mislead by an *apparent* increase. India is gradually being brought under regular law, but some functionaries have been too much used to do as they pleased to mend their ways immediately. Hence, a remarkably large portion of our bills are either bills of indemnity or some such bills in disguise.[34]

In a speech prepared for delivery before the Viceroy's Council in 1866, Maine further defended the Legislative Department, in pointing out that the interaction of western legal institutions with those of traditional India could only find enlightened leadership through the positive exertions of the central government. More legislation rather than less would wrest the flow of Indian legal development from the choking rigidity imposed by uncontrolled and haphazard grants of 'particular legislation', but it must be legislation set to a plan. In the course of his speech, Maine set out four general categories of law that required to be dealt with in India—the special legal provisions that governed the civil and religious customs of the native population, legislation drawn up on behalf of provinces without their own councils, enactments designed to harmonize the special law of the European community with that of England, and general measures of codification.[35] While he believed that each of these categories must expand as India changed over 'from an administrative to a legal condition', Maine stressed in a letter to the Viceroy that: 'I am satisfied that the codification or consolidation, i.e., the reduction of the law into well managed compendia with ample indices, is one of the most useful works ever undertaken in this country, far more useful than legislation.'[36]

Maine's casual definition of codification as synonymous with 'consolidation' casts a revealing light on the difference between Maine's approach to Indian legal reform and that of a previous generation of East Indian administrators who came to their task fresh from the teachings of Jeremy Bentham. By the time of Maine's tenure of the Legal Membership, the radical Benthamite concept of codification as involving the complete rebuilding of the legal system in accordance with abstract rules of reason was no longer as potent a force in administrative circles.[37] Rather, codification had come increasingly to denote the adaptation and simplification of existing law, an approach that necessarily placed high value on thorough knowledge and understanding of the customary practices of Indian law and society. Accordingly, while encouraging change, the new attitude was one favouring modification over radical reconstruction, and Maine's importance as an Indian lawgiver in this

100

transitional period was closely bound to his tireless efforts to replace the ambitious administrative reformism of the analytical jurists with a more moderate view of the potentials for reforming society through legal codification. His aim, which was in principle shared by his successor J. F. Stephen, was to combine the legal anthropologist's awareness of the needs of local diversification with the organization of law into general categories of simplified rules.[38]

These attitudes brought Maine into direct conflict with the Indian law commissioners sitting in London. Chaired by Sir John Romilly, the son of the leading law reformer, the third Law Commission included in its membership several eminent lawyers whose formative years had been passed while Bentham's reputation was at its height. By the end of Maine's tenure of the Indian Law Membership, the Commission had seen the Succession Act of 1865 through to completion, and was largely finished work on a proposed Contract Act and an Evidence Act for India. Maine's grievance with the Commission arose from their practice of drafting measures without consultation with the Viceroy's Government. This the Law Member thought was bound to result in academic exercises in legal reform that lacked the moderating influence of the very officials who had first hand knowledge of India. Maine hoped for the introduction of a new procedure under which the commissioners would pass their preliminary drafts on to the Secretary of State at the India Office, who would in turn forward them to the Viceroy for the comments of a committee of councillors having the power to alter them on points which, in their opinion, were manifestly unsuited to Indian conditions.[39] Disagreement had become critical by 1868, when Maine and the Commission reached a standstill over proposals concerning the new Contract Act and a draft law of negotiable instruments.[40] Maine renewed his criticisms of the Law Commission in a lengthy letter[41] to M. E. Grant Duff, who had only a few days before been appointed Under-Secretary for India in Gladstone's first Cabinet:

Private

29 Charolinghee Rd.,
Calcutta,
Dec. 22, 1868

My dear Grant Duff,

Among many other reasons for rejoicing at your appt. to the Undersecretaryship for India, I feel it a great advantage to have somebody at the India Office to whom I can write with some freedom on matters of business. I am especially anxious just now to unburden my mind on the subject of the relations of this Govt. (or as some people chose to put it, *my* relations) to the Indian law commissioners. I have reason to think that the commissioners believe me to be obstructing the enactment of their drafts, either out of pique at their having differed from me on an important question, or from jealousy and a wish to get the preparation of the Codes entirely into my own hands. At your office, the matter is probably regarded with impatience as something which a little tact ought to settle, or at all events as one in which the opinion of the commissioners ought to prevail.

But the general question which has arisen is one of great seriousness, though I am not sure that I have hitherto found anybody who fully appreciated its importance, except perhaps Lord Salisbury. The question is whether the decision of certain grave points of policy shall or shall not be shifted from the Indian government to the Indian law commissioners, a perfectly irresponsible body, sitting once a week for two hours and including only two gentlemen who have ever been in India, both of those two having been 30 years out of the country, and neither of them having any experience to speak of beyond the Presidency Towns.

Maine accused the commissioners of placing considerations of abstract judicial principle before those of concrete government policy. He contended that while India might have been *carte blanche* for Benthamite experimentation at the time of the first Law Commission, the stage had since been reached where the imposition of radical new legal values from outside the system was neither desirable nor practicable:

I am greatly afraid [he wrote further] that the law commissioners have formed a radically false notion of the India of the present day. I admit that in the various papers written by Macaulay and his colleagues on the subject of the first Code, the Penal Code, there is much to countenance an impression that India is a field for the application of a diluted Benthamism. It is also true that the Codes and parts of Codes framed hitherto by the various Commissions have quite succeeded. But the explanation is to be sought in their subject matter. As to the Penal Code, nobody cares

102

about criminal law except theorists and habitual criminals. The Codes of Civil & Criminal Procedure affected only functionaries and lawyers, & the first chapter of the Civil Code, the Indian Succession Act, merely applied to Europeans. But a substantive Civil Law, applying to everybody and cutting across every transaction of everyday life, is a very different matter.

If ever India was a perfectly ductile & plastic body under the hand of the Legislator, it has ceased to be so now. We may have untaught the natives much, but we have also taught them that any custom, not immoral or dangerous to the public peace, which they chose to make a stand for, cannot be easily invaded. Where thirty years ago there was unhesitating submission to an order of Government, there is now an appeal to the Courts or to a dangerous agitation.

While Maine allowed that preliminary chapters of the proposed codes could be drawn as well in the comparatively calm atmosphere of London as elsewhere, he feared that any final legislative programme would remain sadly lacking in wisdom so long as the suggestions of Indian civil servants with recent experience in the field were ignored.

Maine's controversy with the Law Commission continued throughout his final years in India. Sir Erskine Perry, in an unsuccessful attempt at mediation, counselled caution in numerous letters and dispatches sent out to Maine from the India Office, on one occasion[42] bluntly warning him that 'looking at the constitution of the Law Commission, with its unpaid elements, the value which we obtain from their authoritative names, and their great tendency to take offence, it is impossible not to see that the course proposed by you would lead to a resignation of their posts'. Maine retorted in a later letter that the fact the commissioners were unpaid simply encouraged them in their 'pretention to independence', adding: 'I have always observed that unpaid public bodies remunerate themselves by pretentiousness'.[43] So strongly did Maine feel that, during 1868, he offered to resign his membership of Council, but Sir Stafford Northcote predictably dismissed the suggestion out of hand. In 1870, however, in the face of continued friction between the Law Commission, Maine, and his successor J. F. Stephen, the commissioners themselves abruptly disbanded, and for the time being the fundamental work of Indian codification came to a halt.

Maine's Indian policies reaffirmed a leading theme of both his *Saturday Review* articles and his *Ancient Law*, that while he much admired Bentham's theories of jurisprudence *quā* theories for the internal or 'judge-made' reform of the juridical and court systems, he had little patience with Bentham as a universal reformer in politics. Thus, in the strict context of judicial reform, Maine readily acknowledged the primary importance of Bentham's teachings in preparing the groundwork for codification in India, even while striving during his tenure of the Legal Membership to modify radical elements in the earlier codes prepared under the direct influence of Bentham. Close examination of the total pattern of Maine's Indian views reveals significant further elements of his thought that derived from what Professor Eric Stokes has described[44] as the 'Cornwallis-Whig' tradition of Anglo-Indian administration, rather than from the separate stream of intellectual development which, according to Professor Stokes, gradually led paternalist elements in the Madras system devised by Sir Thomas Munro in the eighteenth century to join with authoritarian aspects of nineteenth-century Benthamism. Thus, his persistent opposition to Lawrence's paternalist, arbitrary and authoritarian approach to Indian administration, and his subsequent support for a more responsible advisory role for the executive members of Council as a countervailing power to offset the unrestrained exercise of executive authority in the Governor-General's hands; his characteristic dislike of publicity in Indian politics; the scepticism he expressed about the supposed universality of Ricardo's utilitarian theory of high rents and *laissez-faire* political economy in the tenure controversies of Bengal, Oudh and the Punjab; his hopes for strengthening rather than eliminating the separations between the judicial and other government departments; his persistent opposition to the consolidation of working control over all administrative functions in the central government, and his counterproposals for the gradual introduction of local executive councils exercising a wide degree of discretion in the day-to-day operation of government in the various parts of India—on such questions as these Maine consistently concerned himself more with the problem of controlling concentrations of political and administrative power than had been usual among the legatees of Benthamite principles previously influential in Anglo-Indian circles.

Moreover, as compared with the Benthamites, there was ultimately an important difference of spirit in Maine's approach to Indian administration. Looking back over his years in India, Maine was assuredly satisfied that through his reforming efforts some small advances might have been made in assisting the progress of Indian society towards modernity. In keeping with the lessons of his *Ancient Law*, he had tried to promote the growing influence of efficient courts of justice functioning under rational legal procedures. He had tried to encourage an increase in the professionally trained indigenous legal personnel, and had striven to achieve the marked proliferation of codified law, settled by the most positive instrument of legal adaption, guiding legislation. Yet there remained other lessons of *Ancient Law*, equally confirmed by his Indian experience, that cautioned Maine against being over-confident of the final results of his efforts at creating a more progressive society out of the complex traditional civilization of the East. The Legal Member had travelled far enough in the vast interior, and wrestled long enough with seemingly insuperable obstacles to western reason, to have seen in the sub-continent endless examples of the conservatism of institutions. He felt in the end that his toils had barely skimmed the surface of the remarkable variety to be found in Indian life. As his Indian tenure drew to its close, he experienced a growing preoccupation with just how awesome were the tasks of the imperial lawgiver. 'We require', he reflected earnestly in a speech warning of the dangers of centralization of administrative power:

> to know what view of tax will be taken by a half-reclaimed Pathan marauder on the other side of the Indus; what will be the effect on Marwari traders of Guzerat of a change in the law of negotiable instruments; what difficulties will arise from altering the received rule of 'market overt' among the cattle stealing populations of the border of the Native States. We need the aid of authorities on the intricate land-revenue law of the temporarily settled provinces, on the heterogenous land tenures of the Punjab and North-West, and on the multitudinous family and clan customs characteristic of all North-West India. [45]

In such circumstances, Maine stressed, efficiency of government must be combined with reliable knowledge of the local differences that flourished throughout India. The transition from the conditions of traditional society to modern constitutional forms, if it was ever to come at all, would never in his view be accomplished with the academic facility suggested by the optimistic reformism of the Anglo-Indian Benthamites, or through the anglicizing radicalism of Tory Evangelicists.

Sir John Lawrence completed his viceroyalty on 12 January 1869 and was succeeded by Lord Mayo. Maine planned to leave office as well during 1869, in keeping with an informal agreement made with the retiring Governor-General at the time his Legal Membership was renewed in 1867.[46] He wrote to Grant Duff from Simla on 3 May:

> I write to the Duke of Argyll by this mail to the effect that I wish to vacate my office on or about October 9th. The Govt. here appear to be very desirous that I should have an opportunity of conferring with my successor before he takes his seat in Council. Now a new man cannot fairly be asked to make the passage to India earlier in the autumn than the last three weeks of September. The Red Sea at the end of August is simply awful, as I can personally testify. But in the third week of September it has got pretty much into its normal state, and in the fourth week the monsoon outside has nearly always come to an end. Consequently, my successor might reasonably be asked to make his arrangments for landing at Bombay on October 1st or 2nd. I should remain there about a week with him, & on or about the 9th I should sail for England and he proceed to Calcutta, which he would make just about the time when the Council settled down to work.[47]

Maine meantime had been pressing his friend and former student James Fitzjames Stephen to accept the Legal Membership as his successor. Sir Erskine Perry wrote from London later that same month, noting that 'I trust that we shall have Stephen as your successor, but our Duke does not seek counsel from us on these matters'.[48] In the early summer of 1869 the Legal Membership was formally offered to Stephen.[49] He hesitated at first, concerned for the welfare of his large family should any disaster befall him in the East, but finally accepted. There was some confusion in arranging a mutually convenient time for the Bombay rendezvous Maine had

106

suggested in his letter to Grant Duff, but the two Law Members did manage to meet there in early October, and spent a week together. Whatever passed between them during that time, meeting at the crossroads of the eastern Empire, remains a mystery. It would be valuable to have had some record of their talks, for they were themselves both at personal crossroads in the development of their philosophical convictions as 1869 drew to a close. Maine, after seven years exposure to Indian custom, was more convinced than ever of the essential conservatism of society. Stephen was at the beginnings of the short experience of imperial government that finally dashed the glamour which the utilitarian philosophy had held for him in his youth, and launched him on his polemical career as a sort of Victorian Hobbes.

Maine had held office as Legal Member longer than any other incumbent in the nineteenth century. His service extended over the administrations of three Governors-General. In recognition of his Indian contributions, the Council, shortly after his resignation, unanimously passed a motion to the effect that:

> This Council, entertaining a high sense of the conspicuous ability displayed by Mr H. S. Maine during the time that he held office as Law Member of the Council of the Governor-General, hereby expresses to him its cordial thanks for his long, faithful and valuable service, its deep regret at his departure, and hearty wishes for his future welfare and happiness.

Lord Mayo, in moving the Resolution, added that: 'I am sure I only express the unanimous opinion of this Council in saying that, whether it be in the Senate, the Council or on the Judicial Bench at Home, the Indian public will still hope for a continuance of those services from which it has already so much benefited.'[50] Maine was much moved by the thoughtfulness of the Council in passing the Resolution. On learning of the Council's action after his arrival in London, he wrote, in his usual formal manner, to the Governor-General:

Private
           The Athenaeum,
           London, Dec. 15, 1869

Dear Lord Mayo,
  I have not forgotten my promise to write to your Excellency, but I have been deferring it until I had something definite to say

on the subjects in which you are interested. The last mail has, however, brought me the Report of the discussion in Council on the Resolution relating to myself which your Excellency initiated, and I feel I ought not to delay my sincere thanks to you for the observations which you made. If I disclaim a good deal of the merit attributed to me, it is chiefly for the pleasure of putting down the language of your Excellency and several of my colleagues to the personal kindness which I have had the good fortune to experience from almost everybody which whom I was associated in India. I trust you will allow me to ask you to express my acknowledgements both to those who spoke and to those who voted on the occasion . . .

If I can at any time be of service to your Excellency by making inquiry or collecting information of any sort, it will give me great pleasure to do this. Any letter will find me whether sent without address to the India Office or directed to 27, Cornwall Gardens, Queen's Gate.

I trust you will give my very kind regards to Lady Mayo.

I am dear Lord Mayo,

Very truly yours,

H. S. Maine[51]

Maine was deprived of the Governor-General's friendship two years after writing this letter, when Mayo was cut down by an assassin while visiting a convict settlement in the Andaman Islands.

Maine left Bombay for Marseilles on 9 October 1869. *The Times*, acknowledging the termination of his connection with the Viceroy's Council, reported soberly that he had completed 'seven years of noble work done for Indian progress'. Herman Merivale had written earlier from the India Office:

You will see a great deal of work either fairly left behind you or in fair process of settlement, and you will leave no inconsiderable 'mark' in our domestic Indian annals—nor do I think you need be afraid of the judgement of posterity as an 'over-legislator'.[52]

In a lighter vein he mentioned in a separate note sent from his home in Cornwall Gardens:

Your wife and my near neighbour dined with us last week—she appeared very well & enjoying her location in our quiet wilderness: to which by the way Lawrence has also betaken himself.[53]

Among the papers Maine took with him on his homeward journey was the manuscript of a series of historical lectures on the general theme of the growth of international law, that he had prepared while considering standing[54] for the recently created Whewell Professorship of International Law at Cambridge, as well as extensive notes he had taken in his spare time on the organization of the village communities of northern India. He intended in the years immediately ahead to apply these first hand observations of a living traditional society to the further elucidation of points of his *Ancient Law*. In doing so, he hoped to throw a finer focus on the historical progress of western man to final civilization.

Village Communities

Maine returned to London during the first week of November 1869, and was reunited with his wife and family at 27 Cornwall Gardens, South Kensington. During the seven years of his Indian service, he had seen his family less than a total of six months. An earlier plan of Lord Lawrence's, which would have brought Maine's wife out with Lady Lawrence in the Viceroy's yacht, *The Feroze*, had disintegrated in the face of learned protest from the Maine family physician, who warned in 1865 that a passage on the Red Sea might prove too much for Jane Maine's delicate constitution, and that 'under no circumstances' should it be attempted. Maine, who was normally equally fragile, apparently held up well during his final trip home from Asia. Grant Duff, if we are to rely on the testimony of his voluminous diaries of Victoriana, called in at Cornwall Gardens the day following Maine's arrival, and found him 'as fit as an English drover'.[1] And a few days later, the retiring Legal Member was observed to be in unusually excellent humour at a dinner party given for James Fitzjames Stephen, who was soon afterwards to leave for India as his successor.

As early as his second leave in 1867 Maine had turned his thoughts to his professional future. There had been some informal correspondence with Cambridge University, sounding him out as a possible candidate for the newly created Whewell Professorship of International Law. There were rumours that if the Life Peerages Bill, then before Parliament, was passed, Maine's name was among those most prominently mentioned for appointment to the Lords. He was, with the advantages of his Indian service, considered as a possible Clerk of Commons, and the Foreign Office apparently offered him their Law Under-Secretaryship.[2] But Maine's chief interest was in an academic position, and fortunately for British legal studies, he was soon able to secure a new post. While in the midst of preparing the fourth edition of *Ancient Law* he wrote[3] to John Murray on 11 December 1869:

> When the Spottiswoode's have completed the title page of the new edition of my book, I think my designation had better be:
> 'H.S.M.,
> Corpus Professor of Jurisprudence in the University of Oxford, and formerly Reader in Jurisprudence and Civil law at the Middle Temple.'
> I daresay you saw that I had been elected to the Professorship—without residence I am happy to say.

During his tenure of the newly created Oxford Professorship of Jurisprudence, from 1871, Maine composed three major volumes elaborating the theses of *Ancient Law*, delivered his important Rede Lecture of 1875, and published several articles based on other lectures.

Oxford was the scene of considerable intellectual innovation for the student of comparative society when Maine took up his chair. William Stubbs the historian, E. B. Tylor the anthropologist, Andrew Lang in mythology and Max Müller in comparative philology had already brought, in self-conscious imitation of scientific achievement in the physical and natural sciences, a new vitality and inventiveness to historical studies. From the varying perspectives of their separate disciplines, these pioneering scholars propagated the leading theme of social investigation in the post-Darwinian decade, that, in order to understand society as it is, we must examine it as it was. Man, they emphasized, is an historical animal, found in different civilizations at various levels of development. The fact of this historical dimension made it important to understand the evolutionary and comparative perspectives of human institutions. The cumulative persuasiveness of such arguments was reflected in the fact that, by the 1870s, the study of early societies had attained a degree of scientific respectability unknown when Maine first set out to compose *Ancient Law*. He reflected on the changes that had occurred, specifically in the domain of legal studies, when he wrote to thank James Bryce for a copy of his Inaugural Lecture on 'The Academic Study of the Roman Law' in March of 1871:

My dear Bryce,

Many thanks for a copy of your Inaugural Lecture. I have read it with very great interest and pleasure and with much general agreement in the arguments and statements. I trust you have not as much ignorance and prejudice to contend against as I had when I said some of the things you have said fourteen or fifteen years ago. I see the signs of an increased attention to Roman Law . . . All who are interested . . . have reason to be thankful for a very powerful effort of advocacy.[4]

Maine and James Bryce, one of England's foremost institutional scholars and later British ambassador to the United States, became close associates at Oxford, united by their common interest in the future of British academical legal studies. They worked together for the creation of a Board of Legal Studies that would co-ordinate and oversee the study of law in Oxford and Cambridge, supervised arrangements for the new Oxford Honours School of Jurisprudence, which came into being in 1872, and shared, during this early phase of Bryce's career, a mutual enthusiasm for the study of Roman law. As Maine wrote characteristically to the Prime Minister in the period, it seemed to him urgent:

to connect legal studies with other academical studies, and . . . I myself have not doubted for years that the proper bridge to join these studies is Roman Law. Indeed, the want of all instruction in the subject leaves a great gap in English classical learning; there is to me at any rate, some ludicrousness in insisting on an acquaintance with the literature of the Romans, but in leaving out of it the only branch of knowledge in which the Romans themselves took a very strong interest.[5]

In the Bryce papers at the Bodleian Library, Oxford, there are preserved several letters that passed between Bryce and Maine during this period, ranging in subject matter from serious discussions of the academic curriculum to personal recommendations and light scholarly gossip:

The Athenaeum,
April 5, 1871

My dear Bryce,

I merely write to say that I have received your letter of the 3rd, for which I am much obliged to you. Do not therefore give your-self the trouble of replying to my letter of yesterday.

I noted Dicey's name among the candidates for the Juris-prudence Examinership. There is a prodigiously long list of them, but the best of them are Dicey, F. Harrison and E. C. Clark (of Cambridge).

I shall be very glad to hear about the Fasting Saint; but all sorts of strange facts are communicated to me, most of them, I am glad to say, corroborative of my views.

Did you know that all action in the Bishop's Court of the County Palatine of Durham began down to 1836 with a distress on the goods of the defendant?

Very sincerely yours,
H. S. Maine[6]

J. Bryce, Esq.

On another occasion Maine wrote from Cornwall Gardens to effect an agreement with his colleague concerning their lecture plans for the Hilary Term of 1871:

My dear Bryce,
I have sent the *University Gazette* a notice to the effect that I shall continue next Term the Lectures of this, but I have said that further notice will be given of the day of commencement. If by any chance it would suit you (as at least I imagine you thought it would) to begin lecturing comparatively late in Term, it would certainly suit me to begin early and give a rather short course. I do not suppose we should clash, but still there seem to me some inconveniences attending two parallel courses on Roman Law.

Will you pardon my mentioning that several persons at Oxford have expressed to me a wish that you would repeat your lectures on the Law of Obligations? The reason is that we have now quite a new set of men at Lectures, men who are aiming at the New School of Jurisprudence and who practically depend on the Professors for tutorial instruction. I myself get on so slowly that I should hardly under any circumstances reach Obligations.

In a further letter of 13 December 1871 we learn something more of Maine's course of lectures:

Doubtless if you lecture on the History of Roman Law you will not conflict with me very much. If, however, you take up Obligation, there would be advantage in your beginning late of a useful sort. My last Term's course and a short course next Term would about take my class to the point at which Obligations are most naturally discussed. Though I begin with the Law of Things, I have not yet nearly finished with Rights in Remise so much have I indulged in Austinian digressions. My idea was to hand the men over to you for Rights in Persons.

I think you are wrong in assuming that the men have few lectures in law. To all appearances precisely the same men (about 30) were attending Bernard's lectures, Digby's, and mine.

My days of lecturing have been Monday and Saturday at noon.

Since Maine's lecturing duties were relatively light, he was free to pursue his London interests, and was apparently engaged soon after his return from India as an occasional contributor to the *Pall Mall Gazette*,[7] and as an unofficial adviser at the India Office.

Maine delivered his first series of Oxford lectures in the Hilary Term of 1870. In his years in the East he had been an academic as well as a practical observer of the customs of the village communities of northern India, and an investigation of their traditional characteristics formed the core of the lecture series. The following summer he reworked the essays, making emendations in small leather work-books,[8] adding a lecture on the growth of European feudalism, and another on the historical evolution of the concept of rent. John Murray was persuaded to undertake their publication as a companion volume to *Ancient Law*. Maine wrote to Murray late in the year:

How long must you keep the MSS for the purpose of estimating the size of the book? There is a notice of my lectures in the new number of the *Academy*. I thought of calling them 'Village Communities in the East and West', six lectures delivered at Oxford by HSM. Would that do?[9]

The book appeared under that title late in March of 1871.

Maine's *Village Communities* turned from a concentration on Roman materials to compare the findings of recent studies in the history of European property with the first-hand knowledge of Indian practices he had gained in the years since the publication of

Ancient Law. He hoped as a result to shed further light on the evolution of modern forms of individual ownership. The researches of von Maurer and Nasse into Teutonic customs demonstrated that the pre-feudal German and English agricultural communities had consisted of a number of families organized into districts comprising three sectors or 'marks': one was the village itself, another was shared by all members of the community, and a third was divided into lots for cultivation by particular families.[10] As Maine had earlier suggested in *Ancient Law* there was at this stage of European historical development no notion of individual 'rights', or of individual property in any modern sense. While lots cultivated by particular families in the arable mark were originally redistributed periodically, in order to ensure absolute equality among members of the local community, the practice eventually declined in western Europe—an important step, in Maine's estimation, in the growth of institutional foundations that were basic to later European culture:

> One stage in the transition from collective to individual property was reached when the part of the domain under cultivation was allotted . . . to the several families of the Township; another was gained when the system of shifting severalties came to an end, and each family was confirmed for a perpetuity in the enjoyment of its several lots of land.[11]

Maine surmised that even in their earliest history the Teutonic tribes, while organized into theoretically equal families, had had 'an abiding tradition that in some one family, or in some families, the blood which ran in the veins of all the freemen was purest'. From these their leaders, at first combining military, political and judicial functions, were chosen. In the circumstances, Maine suggested, the originally 'democratic' mode of appointment eventually became simply 'acquiescence in the direction of the eldest male agnate of the family which held the primacy of the township'. These leaders would tend to receive a larger share of the lands appropriated by conquest, and thus everything which led to the disintegration of the traditional communal village led to their aggrandizement. One power in particular the leader acquired in this manner was of immense historical significance:

> He became powerful enough in his own township to sever his own plot of land from the rest, and if he thought fit, to enclose it;

115

and thus, to break up and enfeeble that system of common cultivation under rules of obligatory custom which depended mainly on the concurrence of all the villagers.[12]

In Maine's reconstruction, thus was created on the ruins of the European village community what he termed 'the manorial group'. The waste of common land gradually became the lord's waste, and legal writers began to speak of the lord's 'rights' as superior to and of greater antiquity than the commoner's.[13] The grasslands fell under varying degrees of control by the lord, and a new class of holders of tenemental land in the manorial group emerged, who Maine rather romantically suggested correspond to the free heads of households in the older village group. All other tenures came eventually to be regarded as [being] '. . . in their origin, servile'. Later, powerful Teutonic monarchies were formed, with sufficient authority to distribute grants in the new 'national' waste land brought by their conquests. In western Europe, where this emerging pattern of feudalization became most completely established, the result was that 'it gave precision to relations which under purely Teutonic social conditions may have been in a high degree vague and indefinite'. Further, Maine would not allow that these historical developments toward the new status system of medieval European feudalism were inconsistent with his well-known view that the overall legal movement in progressive Aryan societies had been one in which the sphere of contract gradually gained at the expense of ascribed legal status. As he submitted: 'If . . . some free village societies fell during the process into the predial conditions of villeinage, . . . a compensating process began at some unknown date, under which the base tenant made a steady approach to the level of the freeholder.'[14]

Maine was emphatic in his *Village Communities* that in those parts of India where indigenous social patterns had not been seriously disturbed by the European conqueror, the traditional modes of landholding remained largely those of joint cultivation organized at the village level. The eastern communities he had observed while an Indian civil servant had thus struck him as reminiscent of von Maurer's accounts of the pre-feudal western township, with its separate households dominated by despotic male family chiefs, and 'Authority, Custom and Chance . . . the great sources of law, . . . not Contract'.[15] The *ryot* of northern India, he pointed out, while

116

cultivating the 'arable mark' allotted to him by the village council, knew nothing whatever of individual ownership. Instead, throughout the interior of India, elaborate communal traditions still bound all persons equally to a system of complex 'public' arrangements which aimed at achieving 'the interdependence and responsibility' of all members of the village. Applying his 'historical and comparative' methods, Maine concluded that Indian society had never progressed independently to the 'manorial stage'. While she would presumably have remained a static pre-feudal society indefinitely on her own, the western innovator, in introducing the novel relationship of landlord and tenant into Indian agricultural, had in recent years been laying the foundations for fundamental change in the East. The indigenous version of the practice of 'periodical redistribution of lots in the arable mark', Maine thus noted, was being replaced in those parts of India under the direct influence of European customs, by new kinds of tenure, which steadily substituted the regimen of contract for that of status. The result was bound to be the gradual dissolution of traditional Indian society:

> The sense of personal right growing everywhere into greater strength, and the ambition which points to wider spheres of action than can be found within the community, are both destructive of the authority of its internal values. Even more fatal is the increasing feeling of the sacredness of personal obligation arising out of contract . . . The brotherhood of the larger group may still cohere, but the brethren of some one family are always wishing to have their shares separately.[16]

Maine clearly viewed his latest researches as having a practical application. Close examination of the western history of property, in his estimation, would certainly bring light to the problem of the reformer in the East, for 'these primitive European tenures and this primitive European tillage constitute the actual working system of the Indian village communities'. What separated Indian development from European, in Maine's judgment, was simply that in the East 'the village group [is] either unmodified or has not yet nearly passed into the manorial group'.[17] Thus, Maine was led in his *Village Communities* to a defence of feudalism as an important, indeed a necessary catalyst, for transforming pre-modern societies. While popularly regarded as a technique for organized oppression, he

117

argued that from the standpoint of the evolution of property, feudalism actually encouraged important economic and social innovations. While the restless European feudal lord had reclaimed the waste land for expanding cultivation and habitation at a crucial stage of western history, the communal villagers he had observed in the East were typically 'grudging and improvident owners of their waste land', highly intolerant of new agricultural methods developed in the progressive societies. The scholarly inferences of the historical jurist thus came close to the views of the middle-class Victorian civil servant. The march of individualism in the western world, which Maine believed to be the special genius of nineteenth-century European civilization, had been positively bound up with the freeing of the land for private ownership under the historical aegis of the feudal lord. Prior to that transitional stage: 'The land was free only in the sense of being free from feudal services, but it was enslaved to custom. An intricate net of usage bound down the allodial owner, as it now binds the Indian peasant, to a fixed routine of cultivation.'[18]

In presenting his latest lectures on early law, Maine expressed the hope that they might not only bring the current researches of comparative studies to a wider audience, but that some of his students might be persuaded by them to form a new generation of pioneering scholars in the field of comparative legal history. The plea was not to go unheeded, for among those who sat through Maine's Oxford lectures, several, including Sir Frederick Pollock, Sir Paul Vinogradoff, and Frederic Seebohm,[19] later attained great academic eminence as legal antiquarians. For those of his students less inclined to persist with formal scholarship, Maine's new volume of lectures implied an equally important practical message. Man was confirmed as a creature of history inextricably bound up with his past. Maine would be content if he could create in the minds of the young lawyers beyond his lectern a lasting appreciation of the slowly evolved historical wisdom of the institutions that joined the generations, and safeguarded individualism in the modern world.

Later studies in the history of comparative types of proprietorship have shown that many of the views Maine elaborated in his *Village Communities* were oversimplified. In the first place, most of his detailed conclusions as regards the supposed developmental movement of the Teutonic communal organization into the manorial group were unwarranted by the limited evidence at his disposal. Moreover, he frequently generalized too widely from the isolated examples of Indian joint ownership with which he was familiar. The more detailed researches of B. H. Baden-Powell, published in his *The Indian Village Community* (1896), and *The Origin and Growth of Village Communities in India* (1899), revealed a great diversity of different modes of ownership in land throughout the Indian sub-continent. A. S. Diamond has further suggested that while 'ownership' in the modern sense is absent from extant fragments of the early legal codes, certain forms of family ownership were certainly not unknown, and these suggest the need for a modification of Maine's theory that, so far as property is concerned, the earliest historical usages had been those of outright primitive communism. Finally, later anthropological field work has led to the discovery that many primitive societies, while knowing no concept of individual ownership in land, do have clearly defined notions of ownership of personal chattels. Yet while *Village Communities* requires these important qualifications, it must also be allowed that Maine saw, as did few of his contemporaries, that the great gulf separating modern from traditional societies was largely traceable to the radically different views of ownership and tenure found in the two. This general thesis of *Village Communities* certainly still has as much validity as when Maine first enunciated it nearly a century ago, as the experiences of latter day western social scientists and administrators in the 'underdeveloped countries' have amply confirmed.

Maine's new book was well received in London, to the apparent relief of both the author and his publisher.[20] Maine noted buoyantly in a letter of 12 April 1871: 'I hope it is doing pretty well. That very handsome stuff in the *Saturday Review* ought to have been of use.'[21] The same day he wrote Grant Duff: 'You will be glad to hear my book is doing pretty well. I am agreeably surprised to find it thought interesting. I dined with J. S. Mill, Miss H. Taylor and Cairnes, the Political Economist, on Sunday. It was a curious experience.'[22] He wrote further to Murray later that same month:

I have just received a letter from J. S. Mill, speaking of the book in much handsomer language than I care to repeat. I mention this because considering the character of the book, this testimony more than outweighs any hesitation of the book-sellers. He is to review it with his name in the *Fortnightly*. He expresses his

119

opinion that the European and English part of the discussion will more than float the Indian part. I am therefore hopeful.[23]

Though Maine's new book was much reviewed and commended, it soon became clear that many reviewers found lessons between its covers not intended by the author. Maine was shortly complaining to Murray that the *Daily News* as well as the *Examiner* had proclaimed him 'a prophet of agrarian radicalism', finding in *Village Communities* a clear demonstration of the natural justification of communism in property. Maine, whose political sentiments ran in quite the opposite channels, flatly rejected the unsolicited compliment as 'quite groundless'.[24]

With the publication of Mill's review in the May *Fortnightly Review*, Maine learned that the Liberal philosopher was on the side of the radicals. Dissenting from Maine's implied critique of Benthamite approaches to jurisprudence, while allowing that his latest historical studies had made important further contributions to academic inquiry, Mill saw the most significant aspect of Maine's work in its application to current political life: 'Though assuredly not written with a view to any such purpose, his *Ancient Law* is a most powerful solvent of a large class of conservative prejudices, by pointing out the historical origin not only of institutions, but also of ideas.'[25] Mill believed Maine's most recent researches into property brought into even clearer focus the question:

> whether the older or the later ideas are best suited to rule the future, and if the change from the one to the other was brought about by circumstances which the world has since outgrown— still more if it appears to have been in great part the result of usurpation—it may well be that the principle, at least, of the older institutions, is fitter to be chosen than that of the more modern, as the basis of a better and more advanced constitution of society . . . The system under which nearly the whole soil of Great Britain has come to be appropriated by about thirty thousand families—the far greater part of it by a few thousand of these—is neither the only nor the oldest form of landed property and . . . there is no national necessity for its being preferred to all other forms.[26]

Mill submitted that if the British people were to resolve to change

120

the system, they would by no means be overstepping their 'natural' rights. Indeed, he felt positively that 'if the nation thought proper to reverse the process and move in the direction of reconverting property into some new and better form of collective [property] . . . it would be making a legitimate use of an unquestionable moral right.'[27]

Mill's arguments were met on Maine's behalf by the authoritative pen of the anthropologist E. B. Tylor, whose monumental *Primitive Culture* was in the press when he published a lengthy review of *Village Communities* in the *Quarterly Review* for July 1871. While expressing reservations as to whether sufficient information was yet available to support all of Maine's more ambitious generalizations,[28] the review was highly complimentary. Like Mill, Tylor believed Maine's new volume had an important bearing on present political controversy, since there were abroad 'certain modern projects of a communistic possession and cultivation of land, schemes confidently advocated as a cure for the evils of our present social system'.[29] Tylor however, drew different lessons than Mill and the radicals from Maine's latest researches. Granting that early communistic organization had been a useful and perhaps essential feature of the European past, he judged that although 'its virtues are great, its practical defects seem insurmountable'. Drawing the findings of nineteenth-century anthropology to Maine's defence, Tylor held confidently to the view that:

a peasant village, governed by old men whose supreme authority is ancestoral custom, is not a society with progressive tendencies. Socialistic cultivation of land is an institution which village communities have existed long enough to condemn as practically objectionable . . . . Even the weaker remains of the community-system is likely to disappear altogether, in countries where they come into competition with the larger capital and superior management which belongs to individual ownership.

As he concluded, finding a happy convergence of anthropological evidence with accepted Victorian opinion:

On the whole, it may be laid down as a conclusion, that so far as regards the problem of feeding the greatest number of mouths from a given district, the decision of history, after a trial lasting

121

through many ages, is being given for individual as against communistic possession of land.[30]

Maine found Tylor's appraisal of *Village Communities* more to his liking. As he confided to Murray in a letter of 12 July: 'Many thanks for the *Quarterly*. The article on my book seems to me very good and just in the right tone.'[31] According to Frederic Harrison, however, who wrote to John Morley shortly after a perusal of Mill's *Fortnightly* article, all the leading participants in this curious anthropological controversy seemed in grave danger of taking themselves too seriously: 'I must say Mill is rather dull on Maine. I suppose he cooks up Maine on the principle of "cane my Master and I cane thee." The whole controversy is a lot of antiquarian moonshine: how did the pair of breeches develop out of the fanciful back side?!!'[32] Yet while Harrison found too much high seriousness for his tastes in the disputations of the 'political embryologists', general interest in Maine's newest book remained high in London literary circles. Sir M. E. Grant Duff records in his *Diary* that Sir Henry Thring had soon renamed South Kensington 'Maine's Village Community', since so many India Office officials lived in that 'newly developed' area of London.[33]

Since Maine's new university appointment required his presence in Oxford only two days a week, he soon found himself more involved in London affairs than ever before. Even while still in India, Sir Erskine Perry had written him from the India Office that 'I trust . . . we shall have you among us soon after your return'.[34] Maine was indeed a frequent visitor to the India Office in the months after his arrival home, where he served as an unofficial legal adviser to the London based Indian Council. Early in 1870 he was appointed a Member of the Commission for Digesting Law,[35] and moreover hoped that if the work of the Indian Law Commission was to continue, he would be offered a position on it. The life of the London public servant, in which Maine now increasingly moved, was one where days were spent between the committee rooms of Whitehall and the elegant clubs of St James's. It was a routine that required financial resources, and Maine, who had very little private income, was soon once more enlisting the support of the amiable Grant Duff, now a prominent Liberal statesman with a decidedly clearer channel to patronage than his former teacher. Maine wrote him from his residence on 10 June 1870:

Private

My dear Grant Duff,

I have just returned from Cambridge and found your card. I understand it to mean that nothing has yet been done at the India Office about paying members of the Judicial Committee except talking about it.

This being so, let me ask you whether the Duke could be moved to bring about my being placed on the Privy Council, independently of what may be done about paying the Judicial Committee. I have had several hints given me about the intention of the legal part of the government to offer me employment of a new kind, and it would greatly affect my own disposition to accept, if the employment were joined to the definite status of Privy Councillor. Not only that, but I believe the arrangement I have indicated to be the best for doing the work and most in the interest of the public.

I do not however suppose that the Duke knows anything of this, and indeed I imagine that the etiquette of the Cabinet would prevent his asking that this status should be conferred on me except as an honour consequent on my seven years of Indian service.[36]

Whatever the reason, Maine was not named a Privy Councillor. Before the year was out, moreover, the possibility of an appointment to the Indian Law Commission was removed by the resignation of the existing body. Maine, who seemed to feel there was a connection between his failure to make the Privy Council and the longstanding animosity between himself and prominent members of the Indian Law Commission, complained in a further letter: 'I gather that Ld. Romilly is avenging on me the wrongs of the Indian Law Commissioners, even going the length of saying he will not sit if I am put there.'[37]

Maine was only temporarily discouraged by his abortive attempt at a Privy Councillorship. Early in the New Year, he wrote further to Grant Duff with an alternative plan for advancing his professional interests. I reproduce the lengthy letter intact as it reveals the usually circumspect Maine in an unusually frank frame of mind:

27 Cornwall Gds., S.W.
                                            April 8, 1871

My dear Grant Duff,

   I am half afraid that the subject of this letter will make you
laugh, but for that very reason I hope you will keep it scrupulously
to yourself. You will remember my asking you to move the Duke
of Argyll in respect of a particular distinction which I coveted.
From many things I have heard, I am satisfied that it is quite out
of my reach, and that the honours to which (if any) I am destined
are much more modest. It is a humble wish which I am now
expressing and of which I am asking you to make yourself in
some informal way the channel. If you do not like the business, I
have strong reasons for thinking that another man (Lord Halifax)
would manage it for me, but I should prefer its being in your
hands.

   First, I have this story to tell. When the second class of the
Star of India was established, an intimation (which I rightly or
wrongly took to be official), was made to me that I was to be
asked whether I wished to be included in it. Before I could answer
'yes' or 'no'—and my answer would almost certainly have been
'no'—I got another intimation that there would be an inconvenience in distinguishing one Member of Council from another,
and that the case of each Member of Council would be considered
on his return. Some such intimation was also made to Durand
who was deeply offended by it, and by putting all his English
interest into action, succeeded in getting the rule set aside in his
own case.

   When I did return, there had been too many changes at the
India Office for this transaction to be recollected, and indeed there
are few distinctions which until recently I should have coveted as
little as the K.C.S.I. But I have latterly come to think otherwise.
In the first place, I am getting impatient of being again designated
"Professor". Besides the absurdity of the appellation for a man
living in London, I think it helps to make people associate me
exclusively with the class of purely speculative thinkers, out of
which I am taken by 7 years service in a government so important
as that of India. Then again, useless as the title is in London
society, I am not at all sure that it would not add to my influence
at Oxford.

Maine went on to offer reasons other than those of possible university advancement for wanting the K.C.S.I.:

Moreover, I am still made just a little angry by certain things in India. The newspapers which used to attack me do not fail to remind their readers from time to time that I have found my true level in England, and indeed, if they knew of some omissions of the India Office, this would not be a very unreasonable conclusion. Then again, some former Indian associates of mine have got it into their heads that Stephen scrupulously and pointedly avoids all reference to me and never gives me credit for any share in legislation. Even supposing the fact to be so, I attach no importance to it, as I attribute it to Stephen's unconscious egotism, occasioned by extreme concentrations of mind on his own work and doings. But, supposing it to be remarked in India, it certainly adds to the impression that I have been thrown aside.

I think the distinction of K.C.S.I. would put an end to these ideas; nor, considering some of the persons on whom it has been conferred, do I suppose there is anything outrageous in my aspiring to it. If you think that you could help me to it in not too formal or direct a way, I should be obliged to you; but, as I said before, there is always Lord H. as a *pis aller*.

Very sincerely yours,
H. S. Maine[38]

Grant Duff did intercede on Maine's behalf, and on 15 May 1871 the Duke of Argyll wrote to inform Maine of his appointment as a Knight Commander of the Star of India. Maine wrote to his old friend to thank him for his role in arranging the knighthood, adding that having 'once made up my mind to go in for the thing, I have grown rather hot upon it'. Later the same year Maine's good fortune was enhanced still further when the usual seniority requirements were waived, and later ratified by special Act of Parliament, to allow his appointment as a permanent paid member of the Indian Council in London.[39] Though unquestionably pleased, Maine found that certain problems accompanied his latest achievements. Sir Henry lectured his publisher in a business letter:

One of the misfortunes of this new title of mine is that the letters constantly go wrong. In the advertisement of my book (*VC*) you print there 'B.S.C.I.' The proper letters are 'K.C.S.I.' It is of no importance, but perhaps you will have the letters right on the title page of the remaining copies (those to be struck off) of *Village Communities*.[40]

Maine was puzzled, as he wrote in a further half-serious letter, that 'some people do not seem to identify me, as now named, with my old self.'[41]

In 1871 Maine sat for a photographic portrait at Elliot & Fry, who were at that time located in Baker Street, London, and the result is a pleasing likeness. The fine detail of the daguerreotype shows Sir Henry in decidedly more robust health than in other photographs of him which are extant. He was forty-nine years of age, and somewhat heavier in the face and chest than in his youth. There is evidence of decided greyness in his peculiar Dundreary whiskers, and a receding hair line seems to exaggerate the largeness of his forehead. The penetrating eyes, beneath rather heavy eyelids, and the unusually delicate lips, seem in actual photographic reproduction much as they are represented in the written recollections of contemporaries. To my mind, the sharp detail of the black and white portrait captures the quality of softness in his features even more successfully than does his painting in oils by Lowes Dickinson. There are no fewer than four versions extant of the Dickinson rendition of Maine. The original, in the possession of Trinity Hall, Cambridge, was used by Grant Duff as the frontispiece of his *Memoir of Sir Henry Maine* (1892). There is another version at Maine's undergraduate College, Pembroke, and two others are still in the possession of the Maine family. One of these hangs in Bina Gardens, London, the other at Clavering, Essex. Maine, who suffered under the sort of nervous impatience characteristic of those who are constantly ill, seems not to have enjoyed the tedious procedure of sitting to an artist. At the time Lowes Dickinson was beginning work on Maine's oil portrait, or perhaps when Maine was being sketched for the admirable Blake Wigram etching of him addressing the Indian Council, Sir Henry wrote to Lord Lytton:

My dear Lord Lytton,   India Office
    After I had left Cartwrights on Saturday evening, I recollected that I had promised to submit myself this week to the disagreeable process of sitting to a painter in my spare hours. This is an engage-

ment which I shall not have the smallest difficulty in breaking on any given day, but it makes it all the more necessary that I should again ask you to be kind enough to leave word here on what day you wish to have some conversation with me. The only impossible days of the week are Thursday and Saturday, on the first of which I am occupied all day with Committees, while on the second I lecture at Oxford. Tuesday is Council day, but the later part of the afternoon is generally free.

Today I propose to go to my sitting in the afternoon.[42]

While Maine disliked sitting to a portrait painter, the many photographic portraits of him that I have been able to discover in preparing this study suggest that he had a rather more kindly attitude to the photographer's studio. As a proper Victorian man of science, Sir Henry was apparently disposed to the claims of the newly invented camera as a rapid and accurate means of preserving likenesses.

The English Patriarch

From the relatively lowly status of a classics exhibitioner to Pembroke College, Cambridge, Maine had risen by the date of the publication of *Village Communities* to a position of great esteem in the world of letters. *Ancient Law*, his *magnum opus*, was in its fourth edition, and widely used in the law schools of America and Europe. It was favourably compared with the works of Blackstone, Bentham and Austin as a fitting addition to the great books written by British legalists. Moreover, because Maine stressed the 'historical and comparative' approach, his reputation extended wider than the community of legal scholars to encompass the admiration of other students of society who viewed him as one of the creators of a new discipline devoted to human history. Sir Donald Mackenzie Wallace, for example, busy with the preparation of a volume on communal settlements in Russia, wrote effusively to thank Maine for advising him on a preliminary portion of the draft:

> Let me assure you that I feel very grateful to you for the suggestions which you kindly made regarding my article and still more for the explanations I have just received. We young authors are very apt to use our virgin swords with more ardour than discretion, unless we have at our elbow an experienced, cool-headed Mentor, willing to whisper to us sage counsels . . . In any case I shall considerably modify the conclusion of the article when I publish it in my book, but before that time I hope you will kindly allow me to have some small talk with you on the subject. And in any conversations which we may have, you must look on me as a mere novice in the science of 'political embryology'—possessed of very imperfect knowledge and always grateful for hints and suggestions when they come from one who may be called the

English Patriarch of that Science. At present I feel that I am on the threshold of that great subject and am conscious of that enthusiasm and buoyancy—not unmixed with solemnity—which the traveller feels when entering on a great unexplored tract of country.[1]

At least, Maine could muse by the early 1870s, his English admirers were paying for their explorations of his work. There was no doubt, as a letter which he wrote to his publisher while vacationing at Heathcroft, Weybridge, shows, that Maine's books were selling widely abroad as well, and were especially admired in the United States. Yet he was realizing no income from the American sales:

I happened to dine the other day with a large party of Americans, who told me that my book on 'Ancient Law' had been sold in the United States to the extent of many thousands. One of them, an eminent lawyer and U.S. Minister at Constantinople, told me he thought almost every attorney in the States had a copy, and they all seemed much surprised that no part of the profit had reached you or me. One gentleman, whose name I did not catch, but who said that his firm (bookselling or publishing) had branches in London and New York, assured me that the system of press piracy had no existence now with respectable publishers and with regard to that class of books, and I understood him to say distinctly that the American publisher, if the point were brought to his attention, would certainly answer the claims of the author, especially if, in the event of further editions, advantages were promised him in the form of advance sheets.

The American edition is very handsome and the publisher is Scribners.

It is not a matter on which I could well move, but it has struck me that you might see your way to doing something, though I would not ask you to take any step if you disapproved or saw no use in it . . .

It is evident, from letters I receive, that the Americans are a good deal interested in the book.[2]

He wrote to Murray further that *Ancient Law* had obtained 'a quasi-educational and professional footing, and though it is not more immoral, it is rather more imprudent to pirate a book having a restricted sale'.[3] Henry Holt, setting out on a brilliant publishing career in New York, agreed with Sir Henry's assessment, and bought the plates from Scribner's in 1874, on the understanding that he would have sole rights to future American editions of Maine's works. As he confided to Sir Henry, his 'enthusiastic admiration' of *Ancient Law* 'makes the publication of it a pleasure for which I am willing to pay something'.[4]

Enthusiastic admiration of Maine's writings was not uncommon among Americans. The unprecedented historical progress of the United States seemed to represent the unfolding in practical political terms of his theory of status to contract. Reciprocally, Maine held high hope that the universities of this relatively new civilization of advanced freedom of contract might provide needed recruits for the arduous task of building his new science of society. As he wrote encouragingly to Theodore Dwight Woolsey of Yale, whose books on comparative political institutions had experimented with the 'historical and comparative' method:

> Hitherto, the speculations of your countrymen on politics have had too much, it seems to me, of a local tinge, and yet an American has many advantages over a Western European in forming a comprehensive theory of political science. Many of the problems which your countrymen have had to solve, have no doubt been perfectly novel, but nevertheless there is much in your institutions and political practise which should make you more intelligent and sympathizing students than we are of the ancient and even of the medieval world. I have always thought that great results might be expected from American political sagacity, when joined to sufficient learning.[5]

We now know that over the years Maine had made the acquaintance of many well-known Americans during trips they made to London. Apparently the first of note was young Oliver Wendell Holmes Jr., who met Maine briefly while passing through London in the 1860s. Harold Laski remembered[6] Holmes recalling many years later that in his first meeting with Maine the two had breakfast with Frederick Pollock, who was then a young law student, and afterwards walked to Blackheath to visit John Stuart Mill in the late morning. As a law student at Harvard, Holmes read *Ancient Law* before it became required reading, and had re-read it again in 1867.[7]

In 1871 he was again in London, and called on Maine early in June of that year. Sir Henry, who was not at home when he called, wrote to him at his hotel in Piccadilly, and the note is especially interesting as it describes what seems to have been his typical daily routine:

27 Cornwall Gds., S.W.

My dear Sir,

I was at a meeting of the Royal Society yesterday evening and was very sorry not to have been at home when you called. Perhaps I may mention that frequently in the morning and almost invariably in the afternoon I am at the India Office, which is only a short walk from Bolton Street, across the Green Park and St James's Park. Thence I usually go to the Athenaeum Club which is also close at hand, and thence homewards. If I could make sure of finding you at any particular time, I would call in Bolton Street.

All Sunday afternoon I am pretty sure to be found there, at least 'till 4 or 5 o'clock.'

O. W. Holmes, Esq[re.]

Very truly yours,
H. S. Maine.[8]

Young Holmes, half the age of the author of *Ancient Law*, persisted in his attempt, and Maine wrote again after several days asking him to dinner in Pall Mall:

My dear Mr Holmes:

Will you give me the pleasure of your company at dinner on either July 2nd or July 3rd (whichever day suits you best) at the Oxford and Cambridge Club in Pall Mall at 8 o'clock? I am half ashamed to do a thing which has so inhospitable a look as asking you to dine out at a club, but the fact is that my wife and I are (to our sorrow) engaged every evening during the remainder of the month, and at the beginning of July Lady Maine goes out of town to some people whose arrangements (as it turns out) will not admit of her postponing her visit.[9]

From their initial meeting, the two legal scholars formed a lasting bond of casual friendship. Justice Holmes, as he was later known, eventually modified his enthusiasm for Maine's historical studies, but there is no doubt that Maine's innovating scholarship had a significant early influence upon his own juridical ideas. Professor

Theodore Dwight, in an Introduction to the 1864 American edition of *Ancient Law*, had early expressed the hope that a scholar as competent as Maine would apply historical techniques similar to those of *Ancient Law* to the study of the English common law itself. Holmes's classic *The Common Law* (1891) was to be an impressive answer to the plea. Among the influences that led to the writing of the volume, he later explained to Harold Laski, the example of Maine's pioneering studies provided 'the philosophic passion'.[10] The few further extant letters that were written between the two scholars indicate that Maine shared an equally high appreciation of Holmes's early writings, declaring several papers sent from Massachusetts to be 'both ingenious and original', and expressing the opinion, on learning of Holmes's decision to leave the Harvard law faculty for 'practical work'[11] several years later, that his going would be a great loss to theoretical inquiry.

In a letter to Holmes of 30 June 1873 Maine mentioned the 'very great pleasure' he had recently had 'in making the acquaintance of a colleague of yours and of his wife, Mr and Mrs Adams'. Henry Adams, the brilliant and erratic American educator and man of letters, was in fact honeymooning in Europe when he first met Maine at Oxford. 'We have been very busy at Oxford and were received there uncommon well', Adams wrote to C. M. Gaskell early in June of 1873, 'I saw all the men I expected to see—Stubbs, Burrows, etc.—and a number I did not expect to see—as Sir H. Mayne and Laing of Corpus.'[12] Adams was appointed Assistant Professor of History at Harvard in 1870, and is credited with having introduced into Harvard the 'seminar method' of teaching. His seminar on medieval institutions, which was open only to juniors and seniors, became famous in the New England academic community. The recent discovery at Western Reserve University, Ohio, of a notebook owned by Charles Thring, who as a student was a member of the seminar in 1874–5, provides evidence that Maine's *Ancient Law* and *Village Communities* then formed the basis of the course. The marbled cardboard notebook is crammed full of references to Maine. William H. Jordy, after careful examination of the notebook, concluded[13] that: 'The class crawled through Maine from cover to cover, stopping first at one page, then another further on, for questioning, elaboration, criticism and perhaps discussion.' Adams, whose life was a strenuous, and ultimately disillusioning

132

intellectual crusade in quest of meaning in history, found a certain fascination in Maine's suggestive generalizations, though he was impatient at the thought of the enormous efforts of historical scholarship that would be required to demonstrate their accuracy. As he wrote of *Ancient Law* to one of his former pupils, Henry Cabot Lodge: 'Sir Henry Maine's book is precisely such a one as I like to give to students to admire and to criticize. I know of no writer who generalizes more brilliantly. But every one of his generalizations requires a lifetime of work to prove it.'[14] Several years later Adams supervised a collection of essays prepared by his first Harvard PH.D. students, later published as *Essays on Anglo-Saxon Law*, which were highly critical of Maine's patriarchal theory of early family organization. Yet if he was critical of the detail of Sir Henry's work, it had nonetheless been the chief influence leading him to a fascination with 'the science of archaic jurisprudence', which seemed to him at this stage of his career capable of supplying some of 'the most needed links in the chain of human development'.[15]

During the same period, Maine first made the acquaintance of the American scholar of antiquities, Lewis H. Morgan, who has been acclaimed by his latest biographer as the founder of modern anthropology. Morgan was no mere arm-chair philosopher by the time of his arrival in London in 1871. As a young lawyer, he had founded an unusual fraternity, 'The Grand Order of the Iroquois', whose purpose it was to encourage a wider appreciation of the traditional customs of the Indian societies of the Finger Lake district of New York State, where he passed his childhood. He later defended these same Indians in the federal courts against attempts by unscrupulous land agents to force them off their lands, and was adopted into the Hawk Clan of the Tonawanda in gratitude. Through wise investments in railway stocks, Morgan amassed a sizeable fortune, and became a member both of the legislature and of the senate of New York.[16] His financial successes enabled him to devote his time increasingly to the study of his beloved Indian tribes, and during the year previous to his visit to London he published a curious monograph, entitled *Systems of Consanguinity of the Human Family* (1870), that made his name well known among students of society both in America and abroad. Morgan had been struck by the peculiar custom practiced among the Iroquois of always tracing their family descent through the female line. On a trip to the western United States, he noticed

133

that the Chippewa Indians, while culturally autonomous and speaking a separate tongue, had a similar method of tracing kinship. When a missionary told Morgan of a hill tribe of India, the Tamils, whose practices were similar to those of these American Indian tribes, he was led to the view that matriarchal kinship ties may once have been universal. Using the facilities of the U.S. State Department, Morgan set about drafting elaborate questionnaires, to be sent to government officials, scientists and missionaries around the world with the intention of establishing definitively that the development of human society had followed a general pattern of evolution through definite steps, ranging from outright promiscuous intercourse, to forms of matriarchy and patriarchy, to its culmination in 'final civilization'.

Since Morgan's researches were to form the rallying point for later criticisms of Maine's theories of patriarchalism in early society, it is an interesting fact that the two scholars met personally as early as 1871. Morgan's travel journal, dated 27 July 1871, included the entry:

> *London*: In the afternoon I called upon Mr McLennan by appointment and we went down to the Athenaeum Club to meet Sir Henry S. Maine, author of Maine's *Ancient Law*. McLennan had previously written to him of our intended call. He is a member of this famous London Club, and spends most of his time at the Club House in Pall Mall. Sir Henry is a good sized and handsome man about fifty and perhaps over, of fine personal appearance and manners. We had a half hour's talk, mostly on Indian matters, and the ages of barbarism, and I left quite well pleased. I told him he and Lubbock should write and put McLennan in a professorship at Cambridge so as to free his time and enable him to follow his ethnological work.[17]

Maine seems not to have read Morgan's *Systems of Consanguinity* when the two first met, for shortly before leaving London, the American sent Sir Henry author's copies of some of his recent papers, and Maine wrote to thank him:

> I am extremely obliged to you for your paper on 'Stone and Bone Implements', which I have just found at the Athenaeum. I will read it at once. I think it must be the same paper which Sir John

134

Lubbock told me he was reading with great interest. I am just on the point of writing to Professor Henry for your larger work.[18]

It was not long, however, before Maine was thoroughly familiar with Morgan's publications. By the time of their meeting in 1871, working independently, Morgan had reached conclusions similar to those of Maine's *Ancient Law*, in holding that there were two broadly distinct ways of organizing societies in human history, one preceding the other in point of time. The more ancient form of government and society, they both believed, had been based on the immediate blood tie of family, clan or tribe. The second form of social and political organization rested on territorial sovereignty and individual property. On the more specific question of the kinship *type* of the 'earlier' social organization, however, the two held quite different views. Indeed, in the midst of the great Victorian age of historical synthesis and evolutionary social thought,[19] the fundamental question of 'which came first: patriarchs, matriarchs, or promiscuous hordes?', was to leave very little room for scholarly fellowship.

Critics

While Sir Donald Mackenzie Wallace might proclaim Maine 'the English Patriarch' of the new science of archaic jurisprudence, not all shared that view. As time passed, critics of Sir Henry's theories were more frequently heard. Some felt philosophically ill at ease in the presence of the 'historical and comparative method' and others, like the *Athenaeum* reviewer of *Village Communities*,[1] had further reservations about the soundness of the factual basis of Maine's grand designs of legal development. James Fitzjames Stephen, an otherwise close friend, former student and admirer, was typical of the first kind of critic. As a practical lawyer and Indian administrator, he doubted that Maine's scholarship had any real application to contemporary affairs. As he wrote to Lord Lytton:

> Maine always appears to me to have a mind as powerful as it is transparently clear and ingenious. I wish his powers ran in a more human channel than the odd one he has dug out for himself in the study of ancient law and early institutions. He and I have the queerest friendly battles on the subject of the proper method of theorizing about law. He always appears to me to be satisfied when he understands as a matter of historical fact how the law came to be what it is on a certain point. The work I care about is ascertaining specifically what the law on a given subject *actually is*, and then throwing it into as plain and systematic a form as I can.[2]

Others, like John Stuart Mill, although impressed with Maine's mastery of historical narrative, feared that exaggerated devotion to the past might lead to a dangerous conservatism of judgement in the present. He complained, in a letter to the economist J. E. Cairnes of August 1872, that the historical school had become too fascinated by the irrational and customary elements that underlay social morality:

Their error is, as is so often the case, a half truth giving itself out for the whole, for they are quite right in thinking that a good . . . institution is more likely to take a deep root when it has been called for by a felt want of the people, than when it has been set up by a king or a revolutionary on the strength of its general merits. But this truth is continually perverted into an attack on the use of reason in matters of politics and social arrangements.[3]

John Morley, Mill's protégé, who was at the time editor of the *Fortnightly Review*, concurred. He wrote to Mill, apparently with Mill's review of *Village Communities* in mind:

It appears to me that the popularity of this method is becoming excessive, and tending to substitute semi-antiquarian research after origins of laws, ideas, etc., for energetic endeavour to test their expediency and truth. A hundred years ago people used to ask whether a thing was true; now they only want to know how it came to pass for true. I gather from one or two expressions in your most recent criticisms that you would be likely to encourage one in inveighing this peril from the abuse of a method which in the hands of Maine and others has been producing such dazzling results.[4]

The impetuous Frederic Harrison had an equally critical, if somewhat more light-hearted, explanation of how the historical school had become so fashionable. He was firmly convinced, as he confided to Morley, that they 'actually make themselves by a sort of joint-stock-mutual-puff-and-admiration society'.[5]

Maine's *Village Communities* had shown that as early as 1870 he was aware of dissenters from his methods of pursuing the study of legal history,[6] yet he was apparently reluctant to engage openly in polemics. He was nonetheless fully capable of scholarly indignation, as was clear from some very heated words he wrote on the occasion of a blistering attack on *Ancient Law*, made in an article by an unknown Irish solicitor, a Mr O'Connell, in the *Law Magazine* for October 1862. Maine wrote to Murray from the Athenaeum:

Will you take an opportunity of looking at the October number of the *Law Magazine*, published by Butterworth and, I am told, edited by the publisher. It contains an article on my *Ancient Law*, signed by a man named O'Connell, which, though prefaced by

137

some compliments, is a violent attack on the book. The writer is obviously an impudent and ignorant Irishman, without a shade of a title to an opinion on such a subject, and his paper is only remarkable as illustrating the curious dislike which, as I perceive from several signs and especially from a queer book by Lord Arundell of Wardour, the ultramontane Papists have shown of *Ancient Law*.[7]

O'Connell's critique did provide grounds for Maine's annoyance. The spirited Irish solicitor refused to address Maine as 'Sir', on the grounds that the title was 'a feudal incongruity', and chided him as being 'as little at home in Homer's language and mythology, as he is in the genesis of general jurisprudence'.[8] Finding 'a mass of errors' in *Ancient Law*, O'Connell wondered aloud why:

> . . . all this crudity should have for years back lain conspicuously and authoritatively before the British Empire, throughout capital and country, and colonies as in America, and should have reached a new edition without a syllable of reprehension. I defy language and evidence to say or show more thoroughly the state of jurisprudence and its profession in the English language.[9]

Maine was deeply incensed by O'Connell's charges, and wrote further to Murray after several days:

> As I felt that a man is no very good judge of an attack on himself written with such an ardour, I asked a friend of mine to look at Mr O'C's paper, and see whether Mr O'C had hit on any errors or defects in my book—the friend in question being Mr Cliffe Leslie who has very critically examined 'Ancient Law', which as a Professor of Jurisprudence, he uses constantly as a textbook with his class . . . All that is necessary is to gauge Mr O'Connell's capacity by pointing out that he has . . . claimed as erroneous Roman law passages literally translated from the greatest Roman lawyers.[10]

Leslie, political economist and authority on Irish land tenure, wrote a leader on Maine's behalf for the December number of the *Law Magazine*. Praising his friend's widely recognized abilities as a classical scholar as well as a jurist, Leslie scolded O'Connell for his rudeness, and submitted that Maine's eminence was justifiably un-

138

questioned. 'Count Moltke', he concluded, 'has been said to be silent in seven languages. There are four in which, for a different reason, Mr O'Connell would do well to observe silence—Greek, Latin, French and English.'[11]

There were, however, more formidable critics than Mr O'Connell —critics whose painstaking researches represented a more telling challenge to the factual validity of Maine's theories. The *Law Magazine* complaint that *Ancient Law* had 'for years back lain conspicuously and authoritatively without a syllable of reprehension', was in fact somewhat misleading. In the very year that *Ancient Law* was published, the Swiss jurist Johann Bachofen, who apparently was unaware of Maine's own investigations, brought out in Stuttgart his *Das Mutterecht* (1861), the first serious attempt at demonstrating that the historical antecedents of modern kinship systems lay in matrilineal rather than patrilineal methods for tracing descent. And while Maine was vacationing in Europe and preparing the third edition of *Ancient Law* in 1865, J. F. McLennan published his *Primitive Marriage* in London. Both writers emphasized aspects of primitive social usage that called into question the very foundations of Maine's work, and especially his belief that the embryonic social group had been the patriarchally dominated family.

There is a small well-detailed photograph of Johann Bachofen, reproduced in the *Schweizer Lexicon*, that suggests more of the successful man of commerce than the esoteric scholar of antiquities. Double chinned and balding, with a decidedly distinguished crop of white whiskers, he was forty-six years old and Professor of Roman Law at Basle when his most important work was published in 1861.[12] Bachofen had studied law at Berlin and Göttingen while the influence of von Savigny and the German historical school of jurisprudence was at its peak, and the impressive achievements of the new and largely Germanic science of comparative philology were widely acclaimed. Against this background of intellectual influences, his complicated, romantic style was formed. *Das Mutterecht*, Bachofen's treatise on 'the *gynaicocracy* of the ancient world in its connections with religion and law', was an almost mystical literary vehicle for his influential thesis that 'mother-right', and kinship through the female line, had historically preceded patriarchal authority and kinship traced through the male line.

Bachofen was convinced that in prehistoric times human groups

139

must not have recognized any kinship ties whatsoever, and had lived in promiscuous societies devoid of developed notions of marital loyalty. Under the influence of 'crude religious impulses', according to the author of *Das Mutterecht*, the exploited females in the early reaches of history eventually revolted from a situation they abhorred, and Bachofen, interpreting reports of isolated Amazonian communities as modern remnants of more widespread past historical practices, suggested that they must have literally forced the institution of monogamous marriage upon the male of the species. Success in establishing 'mother-right' meant that women became the heads of families through whom descent was traced, and the new fact of this female social ascendancy became incorporated in the literature of classical times. Thus, in Greek mythology, Bachofen felt, the material symbols of 'mother earth', Demeter and Hera, embodied the supposed divine character of motherhood in the earliest recorded periods of Greek history, while the transition of Athene from a goddess of war protective of acropolises to one who first taught the womens' arts of cooking, weaving and spinning symbolized the gradual demise of *gynaicocracy*, and heralded the ascent of the newer notion of male supremacy. In the mythological conquests of Dionysius, who overcame the complex schemes of Hera to subdue him, Bachofen thought fatherhood had been symbolically recast as divine, and the mother relegated in this new literary imagery to the role of a less important deity. The Appollonian or solar symbols of masculine power thereafter increasingly replaced the lunar symbols of female divinity associated with Diana as the literary reflection of actual social and political authority. The emergence of male power thus traced in classical mythology, Bachofen concluded, was eventually given its most systematic institutional expression in the Roman legal practice of *patria potestas*.[13]

The Scottish lawyer John Fergusson McLennan, while sympathetic in general with Bachofen's matriarchal thesis, had serious reservations about his heavy Germanic prose and questionable method of scholarship, which, he later complained, was 'of so mystic a nature that it is difficult to obtain from it distinct propositions'.[14] Moreover, in his *Primitive Marriage*, he rejected Bachofen's Amazonian theory as naïve and unconvincing. Like Bachofen, McLennan believed that in the earliest western communities there had been no notions of separate kinship, and that undifferentiated human hordes

140

must have practised promiscuity. Only eventually had men become aware of common roots in the mothers who reared them, and later still, first learned to grasp the idea of belonging permanently to an identifiable 'stock'. McLennan felt Maine's notion of primeval patrilineal authority was in these circumstances unthinkable, for at first there was no way of establishing systematically who their fathers were, as there were literally no families, no 'appropriation of a partner'. Adding a different emphasis from that provided by Bachofen's *Das Mutterecht*, he noted that the struggle for survival in early human history made hunters and braves highly valued, and it had thus been in the interests of the horde to rear its healthy males, while killing off the female young.[15] Such practices eventually led to the formation of what McLennan called 'exogamous tribes'. Where female genocide caused a scarcity of mature women within the group, McLennan thought it probable that 'wives were actually obtained by theft or force'. These social features increased the sexual importance of females, for each woman, as he delicately put it, would normally have 'several wooers'. While friction existed among larger groups of males so long as the capture of women continued, within smaller groups necessity forced the practice of limited promiscuity.

In these emerging internal groups, women, like other forms of property, were held in common, and children, while at first only vaguely attached to the mother, came to be regarded as regular members of the group. In time, totally indiscriminate promiscuity waned, while the notion of kinship, still only partially grasped, first established itself in human consciousness.[16] Eventually, these smaller groups became systematically organized on the principle of polyandry. In a ruder form, McLennan surmised, husbands of a wife were not necessarily viewed as relatives, while a higher form, the 'Nair polyandry', required that all husbands be brothers. McLennan, an unabashed evolutionist who believed universal history consisted of a gradual progression upwards by stages, viewed the emergence of Nair polyandry as an important advance on the road of human progress toward modern systems of kinship. In passing through the stages of Nair polyandry, he suggested, the wife and children initially lived in their mother's house, later in a house with their husbands while remaining technically attached to the mother's, and later still passed entirely into the house of their husbands. The eventual result was to 'create a community of blood and interest in the husband',

141

the appropriation of offspring to the father's line, and their subsequent disqualification as heirs to property in the mother's line.[17] Only relatively late in western history, according to this analysis, could the practice of monogamous marriage and patrilineal methods for tracing descent have emerged. Of Maine's patriarchal theories of kinship organization, McLennan concluded that: 'The learned and ingenious writer must be held to have taken up the threads of legal history where they began to unwind themselves anew, after the completion of a social revolution.'[18]

While acknowledging Maine's ingenuity in setting apart the most important historical categories of human social organization as those based on kinship and on territory, McLennan's *Primitive Marriage* (1865) further disputed Sir Henry's explanation of the actual process by which smaller social units had gradually grown larger in early times. As he contended, it was through the practice of *exogamy* that initially homogenous and undifferentiated human societies had become heterogenous, for within loose tribes, those bound together by the notion of stock tended to form interlocking *'gentes'* or houses within the larger unit. He supposed that other tribes in the locale must increasingly come into contact with these, 'under the influence of kinship, similarity of elements of structure, contiguity and convenience'.[19] At the same time, *gentes* of similar stock deriving from these different tribes would eventually unite to form large *tribes of descent*, the important forerunner in McLennan's view of a notion of familial social and political community recognizable to the modern. Thus, McLennan's version of the historical process governing the stages of social and political aggregation required standing Maine's on its head. 'The order of social development in our view', he concluded, 'is that the tribe stands first, the *gens* or house next, and last of all the family'.[20]

In the winter of 1872 Maine delivered a series of lectures on the history of the legal status of women to his Oxford law students, and noted that there had recently been considerable discussion 'among writers belonging to the school of so-called prehistoric inquiry', concerning 'the place in the history of human society to which this peculiar group, the Patriarchal Family, is entitled'.[21] The general thesis of Maine's lectures was that so far as the surviving Indo-European legal records indicated, women had had no individual personality whatever in early times, and that while similar conditions

142

continued to prevail in contemporary India, where the wife remained bound to the legal personality of her husband, in the western progressive societies there had been a constant widening of the personal and proprietary liberty of women. In implicit opposition to the Bachofen-McLennan thesis of early matriarchal ascendancy, Maine thus held that the degree of female freedom taken for granted by his critics depended on legal rules for curbing the 'natural' instincts of male dominance that had only relatively recently made their appearance in the most advanced European societies. As Sir Henry thought:

> inasmuch as no class of similar importance and extent was, in the infancy of society, placed in a position of such absolute dependency on the other sex . . . the degree in which this dependence has step by step been voluntarily modified and relaxed serves undoubtedly as a rough measure of tribal, social and national capacity for self-control. . . . The assertion, then, that there is a relation between civilization and the proprietary capacities of women is only a form of the truth that every one of these conquests, the sum of which we call civilization, is the result of curbing some one of the strongest, because the primary, impulses of human nature.[22]

Though Maine's lectures were no direct answer to his critics, the quiet defence of his theories did not go unnoticed. T. E. C. Leslie, in an article written for the *Athenaeum*, was quick to see their relation to the researches of Bachofen and McLennan. Short of the introduction of new materials that offered conclusive proof of the superiority of their matrilineal argument, Leslie suggested, the competing theories were neither inconsistent with nor invalidated Maine's views.[23]

One of McLennan's complaints about Maine's legal anthropology was that while its generalizations were based almost exclusively on Roman materials, it claimed to fit the general legal history of western civilization.[24] Mr O'Connell, in his *Law Magazine* attack on *Ancient Law*, had similarly taken Sir Henry to task for ignoring Irish sources, vaguely hinting that they might reveal archaic Aryan legal practices inconsistent with the major hypotheses of *Ancient Law*. Although presumably not influenced by the disrespectful Irishman's advice, Maine vacationed in Ireland during the summer of 1873, partly in

143

order to examine the Celtic law books housed at Trinity College, Dublin. While there he worked with materials that appeared the following year in published form as the third volume of an ambitious government-sponsored translation.[25] He was lecturing on Irish law, and had formed a general outline for a book on the subject as early as the autumn term of 1873, as *The Times* carried a notice on 13 October that 'a new work may shortly be expected from the pen of Sir Henry Maine. It is called the *Early History of Institutions*, illustrated by the Irish Brehon law, and will be published by Mr Murray.' According to a letter Maine wrote to Murray at the time, however, he was at that date still far from having finished his manuscript:

> The appearance in *The Times* of a paragraph about my Brehon book from the *Athenaeum* reminds me I ought to tell you that I fear I cannot enable you to make a positive announcement concerning it at your bookseller's meeting. A great deal of new material turned up while I was in Ireland; still, I hope to have it completed early next year. I think it will be about as large as *Ancient Law*.[26]

His estimate of time proved optimistic. It was not until 10 September 1874 that he could tell Murray that 'I think all my *MS* will be ready for the printer in a fortnight, or thereabouts'.[27]

Sir Henry's purpose in the *Early History of Institutions* was to examine the commentaries of a professional class of Irish jurists, the Brehons, whose code had been used, until its abolition by James I, in Ireland. He thought the Brehon tracts revealed fragments of a stage of Aryan legal development that spread from Ireland to India at one time, long before the promulgation of the Twelve Tables of Rome in the fifth century B.C. By comparing this early Irish law with the contemporary legal systems of India and eastern Europe, both branches of the Aryan societies that were never fertilized with the seed of Roman notions of legal progress, and by contrasting these with features of the later Roman law, he hoped to further illuminate the historical patterns of legal evolution he had first outlined in *Ancient Law*. His goal was to hold up a corner of the curtain of western history, to see what had existed as universal practice before the legal inventiveness of the Romans transformed customary law. As he believed:

144

the great difference between the Roman Empire and all other sovereignties of the ancient world lay in the activity of its legislation . . . For many races, it actually repealed their customs and replaced them by new ones. For others, the results of its legislation mixed themselves indistinguishably with their law. With others, it introduced or immensely stimulated the habit of legislation. . . . But, wherever the institutions of any Aryan race have been untouched by it, or slightly touched by it, the common basis of Aryan usage is perfectly discernible; and thus it is that these Brehon law-tracts enable us to connect the races at the eastern and western extremities of a later Aryan world, the Hindoos and the Irish.[28]

Maine's latest researches satisfied him that the Irish law of the Brehon Code contained features similar to many of those of the Indian Code of Manu, and many which tended to be on the wane in later Roman jurisprudence. Community was largely determined by kinship rather than contiguity, and legal concepts were notable for the absence of notions of individualism. Land in Irish law was originally held in common by family groups. There was little distinction, according to the Brehon sources, between the offices of lawgiver and priest in early Irish law. *Patria potestas* was the brutally basic fact of social and political existence. The major findings of his Irish studies thus served to vindicate the general outlines of legal development first traced by Sir Henry in *Ancient Law*.[29]

Maine's book met with a generally cordial reception in a country which by the date of its publication was devoting much of its intellectual strength to the ambitious task of discovering laws of natural evolution in all fields of social studies. Enthusiastically reviewing the book in the *Athenaeum*, Cliffe Leslie saw Maine's Irish researches as 'a contribution of the highest value and interest both to comparative jurisprudence and to the history of human society and civilization', and in a further review in the *Fortnightly*, he ventured the prediction that 'one of the results of his works on the history of law will be the application of the historical method to political economy'.[30] J. E. Cairnes found more interest in Maine's emphasis on the fundamentally static conditions of early society, and believed his work for that reason more scientifically plausible than Herbert Spencer's, whose sociology placed great stress on constant social change.[31] For J. F. Stephen, Maine's latest book was 'wonderfully ingenious' and the author 'nearly, if not quite, the cleverest, most dexterous man I ever knew',[32] while the historian E. A. Freeman wrote to Maine with unabashed enthusiasm:

I have been up into Montenegro, seen the prince, walked about unhurt among pistols and yataghans, and mourned only that they were idle, while there was so much Turk-slaying to be done within a stones-throw . . . what brought you into my head while I was up there was that I had heard that, besides state-lands and private-lands, there are communal-lands, both pasture and forest, but, I understand, no tillage. So pray turn your mind to Montenegro. I have no books to refer you to, but one may be sure that some German professor has taken that in hand, like everything else. Also, is there not such a thing as a common Aryan, perhaps a common human, dress? The dresses in these parts, the Roman military dress, the Highland dress before army tailors took it in hand, and the dress which our own fore-fathers are shown in in the tapestry, all seem variations of one type. And the kind of shawl or blanket which the Montenegrin uses is very like a toga.[33]

Sir Henry was no different from historian colleagues like Freeman in diligently seeking after 'survivals' with which to illustrate his writings. Writing to Grant Duff, who was about to leave for India to take up the Governorship of Madras at the time Maine was preparing the draft of *Early History of Institutions*, Sir Henry advised him to:

make the acquaintance of Phear, the Calcutta Judge. He is a prig, but has really much knowledge of the ways and life of Bengalees. His name reminds me that you must really read his article on 'Rustic Bengal' in the new number of the *Calcutta Review*. And when you are at Calcutta, try to get a view of one of the swell native houses inhabited by a *Joint Family*. The institution is a very curious one and Phear could tell you what to observe in its way of conducting itself. And, when you are at Allahabad, get Strachey or some of his people to point out to you the most perfect village-community in that neighbourhood![34]

Shortly after the appearance of Maine's new book he received letters from two American friends. The first of these, from his American publisher Henry Holt, assured him that:

The sale here is steady but continuous. The first fact is due to the timid attitude of retailers—and buyers as well, owing to our great financial depression: the second fact is due to the book being so necessary to a certain class of minds that they at length screw their courage up to buying it, in spite of hard times. Many of them had failed to screw their courage up, though, so the book did not start off to a rush.[35]

Maine's other letter, from Henry Adams, suggested that the *Early History of Institutions* was decidedly better received in London than in Adam's senior seminar at Harvard. While admitting the ingenuity of Maine's latest work, the American historian had greater reservations than ever about the grandiose hopes of the new generation of political anthropologists, who seemed to feel that somewhere in the mists of the historical past lay the source of ultimate meaning in human civilization:

My dear Sir Henry,   22 February, 1875

I was delighted to receive your book, not only for the book's sake, but to feel you had not forgotten me. I have read it through with great interest and pleasure and shall write a notice of it for the April *North American*. Of course, I shall attack it ferociously. There is a delightful want of responsibility in writing in this country on such subjects, a feeling that no one will read it, or care for what is said if they do, and this stimulates the writer to the most reckless *tours de force* by way of criticism. . . . So I shall attack all your opinions on the principle that it is better to be thorough about it. As it amuses me, and won't hurt you, I suppose there can be no just ground of objection. I only wish I could ever do anything myself that was half as good.

The truth is, the more I study this subject, the less practical and positive are the results. I have again this year taken a class through your 'Ancient Law', encouraging them to dispute, and overthrow if they could, every individual proposition in it. Then we read the 'Germania', and are now half way through the '*Lex Salica*', translating and commenting on every sentence. They have had to read your 'Village Communities', McLennan's book, Nasse, and everything else they could lay their hands on, including much Roman law and other stuff. They are deep in theses on numerous

147

abstruse points, and argue in the lecture room by the hour. But I regret to say that except as an intellectual exercise I cannot see that there is any great result. I believe they do learn a better method of investigation than they might in a simpler study, and I hope they will make better lawyers for the training, but they have not yet solved the riddles of archaic law. Nor have I, in spite of having read more dreadful German lawbooks than a Christian community ought to tolerate . . .

My friend Wendell Holmes told me he had seen you in London, which I was delighted to hear, as he has long been one of your warmest admirers here. My own life is of the calmest kind. My wife and I jog on as peacefully in this remote corner of the Arctic Circle as though we had half a century behind us. We hope you will still pay us a visit one of these days. For a summer excursion, to one who can tolerate the sea, America is not altogether a bad resort. My wife wishes to be remembered to you & Lady Maine. She is still at times a little homesick for London, but I doubt whether we shall ever get the energy to cross the ocean again, unless we become dyspeptic or otherwise imbecile enough to be driven by physicians. As Europe is the only pleasant remedy in the whole *materia medica*, the doctors prescribe it for everything from a toothache to apoplexy.

Thanks again for the book. I hope you find Holt a satisfactory publisher. He wrote me some months ago that you were a most satisfactory 'client', and if he patronizes you as few of his class do with us poor scribblers, you must indeed feel an increased degree of pride.

Ever very truly yours,

95 Marlborough Street, Boston   Henry Adams[36]

Although Maine's answer to Adams has not survived, we can only assume he must have found the letter a curious one, for his experiences as a jurist had run absolutely counter to those of his American correspondent. The more Sir Henry studied the law the more clearly practical did the endeavour seem to him, and, as he was shortly to demonstrate in his Rede Lecture, the more he refined his techniques of historical investigation, the more immediate did he feel the need to point out the lessons of the remote past for the political present.

Scientific Conservatism:
The Rede Lecture of 1875

In 1875 Maine was chosen for the great academic honour of delivering the annual Rede Lecture at Cambridge University. He journeyed by train to Cambridge on 25 May for the special occasion in the Senate House, where, many years before, he had gone with less confidence than now to recite his undergraduate prize poems. Sir Henry had chosen to lecture on 'The Effects of Observation of India on Modern European Thought'. One young man present later wrote of the Rede lecturer that: 'His features could scarcely be called handsome, but they bore the impress of his robust and vigorous intellect; and the interest of his subject, and of his treatment, lost nothing from an elocution which was both virile and refined.'[1] The lecture was immediately acclaimed as among Maine's most important papers. *The Times* reprinted the entire text on its outer sheet. In an accompanying editorial, Maine was seen as boldly cutting a path to be followed by a new generation of students of comparative society:

> Just as the successful study of the structure and functions of the human brain were possible only through the careful examination of brains less complex than that of man—just as the origin of language had to be sought after, not from the rich development of civilized human speech, but from the imperfect utterances of the savage, so too, we must look for the key to the origin of our institutions in something more simple and more primitive than themselves, something of which we have lost the trace among ourselves, and which we can regain only from less advanced nations, which have preserved what we have destroyed, or rather, if the Americanism be permitted, have 'improved away'.[2]

A more recent assessment by an American social scientist considers the now largely 'forgotten' Rede Lecture as a major landmark in the early literature of sociology.[3]

Maine's purpose was to crystallize into manageable proportions the implications for British historians of his previous researches into early society, and especially of his analyses of Indian legal institutions. The British presence in India, he felt, provided an almost unique laboratory for the nineteenth-century scholar with an interest in the historical study of man. Shut off geographically by the Himalayas, so vast territorially that its social institutions had remained largely impervious to the innovating customs of previous foreign invaders, India awaited the investigations of European students who wished to know more of their own past. For while contact with western customs had already largely corrupted the indigenous practices of the coastal areas, to proceed inland into the interior of India was to discover a new world, or rather, the old Aryan world unaffected by the new:

> No doubt the social state there to be observed can only be called Barbarism, if we could only get rid of unfavourable associations with the word; but it is the barbarism either of the very family of mankind to which we belong, or of races which have accepted its chief and most characteristic institutions. It is a barbarism which contains a good part of our own civilization, with its elements as yet inseparable and not yet unfolded.[4]

The longevity of the Indian state of 'Barbarism' had been continued through the operation of the caste system, and further encouraged by the conservative teachings of the Brahmins. The conditions for examining pure Aryan survivals then, remained still intact, although Maine felt they would probably vanish within the lifetime of his audience. Sir Henry urged the transfer of the spirit of Vico, Montesquieu and Tocqueville, of Hugo and von Savigny, from the European and American stages to the Asian.

Granted that India contained remnants of a primitive Aryan social condition, Maine asked, what additions to our knowledge might we expect from its study? He illustrated by referring to the light his observations of Indian practice had thrown on the evolution of notions of property, for the fact of private property was of such importance to western man that 'in our own day . . . its existence

150

has been taken as the basis of a great deductive science, "Political Economy".' It was indeed a commonplace among influential political economists that separate property and economic competition were natural, and had existed from time immemorial to answer the basic needs of acquisitive human nature. In fact, Sir Henry reminded his audience, his continuing investigations since the publication of *Ancient Law* confirmed the view expressed in that work that there were large portions of the human race with vastly different notions than those of the western European on the subject of property. In India, as he had learned during the land tenure controversies, one might find the idea of ownership, but ownership in common rather than by individuals; there would be found a kind of rental and profit-taking, but it was accompanied by a fixity of tenure curiously controlled by local custom in a manner quite unfamiliar to European ideas; and there competition flourished, but among large social aggregates, and not between individuals or groups of kinsmen.[5]

Maine believed, as he had argued in his *Village Communities*, that the real importance of such Indian observations lay, not in their isolated analysis alongside the most modern western ideas on the subject of property, but rather in the results that would follow from bringing together these researches with other studies into the early landholding practices of western Europe, and comparing them with the development of notions of property in societies historically unaffected either by Roman civilization or by the legal and political institutions of Hinduism. Maine advocated the application of such 'historical and comparative' techniques not only to the evolution of property, but to the further study of all Aryan institutions. The very least result, he was certain, would be a growing awareness that unfamiliar social institutions were 'equally natural, equally respectable, equally interesting, equally worthy of scientific observation, with those of western Europe'.[6] The most important result, Maine wrote eloquently, might be the foundation of a new evolutionary science of man:

India has given to the world Comparative Philology and Comparative Mythology; it may yet give us a new science not less valuable than the sciences of language and of folk-lore. I hesitate to call it Comparative Jurisprudence because, if it ever exists, its area will be so much wider than the field of law. For India . . . includes

151

a whole world of Aryan institutions, Aryan customs, Aryan laws, Aryan ideas, Aryan beliefs, and at a far earlier stage of growth and development than any which survive beyond its borders. There are undoubtedly in it the materials for a new science, possibly including many branches. To create it, indeed to give it more than a beginning, will require many volumes to be written and many workers to lend their aid.[7]

Maine's new methods, then, would have the effect of softening the prejudices that often blocked the appreciation of institutions foreign to the Englishman. Holding that all human social organization had an intrinsic interest to the student of the 'historical and comparative' method, he suggested that: 'It is not the business of the scientific inquirer to assert good or evil of any particular institution. He deals with its existence and development, not with its expediency.'[8] Yet, as Maine's discussion of property makes clear, when questions of 'expediency' *were* involved, he was quick to draw his own conclusions from legal history. 'Nobody is at liberty to attack several property', he intoned, 'and to say at the same time that he values civilization. The history of the two cannot be disentangled.' Maine's historical studies, as he made clear in the advancing arguments of his Rede Lecture, lent themselves to service in behalf of a new type of 'scientific' or academic conservatism, whose authority derived from the application of comparative methods to the study of the past. By the adoption of his approach, Maine submitted:

> [as one result] we of western Europe might come to understand ourselves better. We are perhaps too apt to consider ourselves as exclusively children of the age of free trade and scientific discovery. But most of the elements of human society, like most of that which goes to make an individual man, comes by inheritance. It is true that the old order changes, yielding place to new, but the new does not wholly consist of positive additions to the old; much of it is merely the old very slightly modified, very slightly displaced, and very superficially recombined.[9]

In the course of his lecture Maine rejected the Benthamite principle of the 'greatest happiness of the greater number' as an 'unscientific' standard for gauging the desirability of new legislation. Instead, he looked forward to the time when legislators would look

'far less to discussions on moral philosophy as it is presently understood, than to some such application of the comparative method to
custom, idea and motive as I have tried to recommend'.[10] Since
Britain was obliged to make laws for societies scattered across the face
of the earth, Maine thought it undeniable that his approach offered
the advantage of flexibility. Roman law, and later Roman imperial
greatness, had been built firmly on the wisdom of recognizing local
custom. In contrast, he felt, the dogmatic teachings of the British
political economists:

> generalize to the whole world from a part of it . . . they are apt
> to speak of their propositions as true *a priori* and for all time . . .
> they greatly underrate the value, power and interest of that great
> body of custom and inherited idea which, according to the meta-
> phor which they have borrowed from the mechanicians, they
> throw aside as friction.[11]

Maine's Rede Lecture, then, represents the conviction of an
Indian policy-maker as much as the credo of an academic historian.
His paper was written as much at the India Office as in the British
Museum. Indeed, not since the Mills had frequented the 'India
House' had there been such a combination of renowned academic
philosopher and practical counsellor in the higher realms of Anglo-
Indian government. Progress, Sir Henry reminded his listeners, was
not a natural attribute of human society, but rather a specifically
Greek notion whose seed had fertilized the institutions of a few progressive societies of Western Europe. It now fell upon the Briton to
carry that revolutionary creed to India, yet Maine was convinced
that the transfer of the energizing spirit of social progress would fail
without the utmost care being bestowed on mingling the old with
the new. Maine's discussion of property left no doubt that he thought
advantages lay in the break-up of communal holdings, yet he differed from militant advocates of *laissez-faire* in being more sensitive
to the cruel disruption of familiar routine involved in that transition:

> Though it be virtually impossible to reconcile the great majority
> of the natives of India to the triumph of western ideas, maxims
> and practices, which is nevertheless inevitable, we may at all
> events say to the best and most intelligent of them that we do not
> innovate or destroy in mere arrogance. We rather change because
> we cannot help it.[12]

Quite aside from Maine's preachments on Indian administration, his Rede Lecture emphasis on the relationship between private property and progressive civilization barely conceals that his message was intended as much for British as for Indian ears. Maine was concerned at the growing influence in Liberal party circles of the radical Manchester school of political economists. On such domestic party issues as Irish land reform, the free circulation of property they would encourage by guaranteeing tenants certain rights in relation to their landlords struck Maine as introducing a dangerous principle into the British body politic. As we shall see, he eventually came to join forces with the aristocratic Whigs in arguing that the break-up of established property that would result from such measures would only be achieved at the expense of free contract, and would thus be a throw-back to an earlier condition of the western branch of Aryan society.

While London journalists praised Maine's latest speculative journeys into the future of social studies, two Americans were already more concerned with the political implications of Maine's lecture. Chauncey Wright, reviewing his Rede Lecture for *The Nation*, took Sir Henry to task for his off-hand criticisms of Bentham, holding that Maine had been unfair to Bentham by attacking a logical system with an historical argument.[13] Maine's American publisher, Henry Holt, writing to suggest arrangements for the publication of the essay in America, urged him to add another paper expanding his criticisms of Benthamism:

Oct. 18, 1875

My dear Sir Henry,

A thousand causes—illness and travel among them, have delayed my telling you that I read the miscellaneous pieces you were kind enough to send, with great interest and benefit.

Your appreciation of the physical sciences explains very clearly where you found your original path in historical, or rather archeological jurisprudence. It is strange and most edifying to find a worker in your field so well realizing what it can gain from the other.

Should it not be well to print these papers in a volume with *Village Communities*, thus making a third vol. uniform with *Anc. Law* and *E.H.I.*, instead of two thin volumes looking a little sparse and chill beside the others?

We begin to hope for some relief from our desperate commercial stagnation here, and when we get it, I would gladly make such a volume, embodying your latest amendments to V.C., if Murray would agree to take duplicate plates of it, or of the V.C. part, as soon as his edition of V.C. shall be exhausted.

As Holt continued:

In this collection of essays ought to be included one to be speedily contributed by you to, say, the contemporary, explaining that remark in the Rede Lecture about the evidence of Comparative Jurisprudence being against Utilitarianism. It is pretty hard for anybody to tell what anybody else means by Utilitarianism, but I take it for granted that you meant something more than that legislators have not universally been influenced by the Utilitarian standard, and that probably you have evidence not yet applied in the discussion against the U. theory of the genesis of morals. In any other respect, the theory seems to me (if I've any right to have any say about it) hardly worth attacking; but in this one it seems so impregnable that anything much affecting it must be of gigantic importance.[14]

The American publisher pursued the question further in a letter of the following month:

I will with pleasure join Murray in bringing out the new volume to contain *Village Communities* and pieces heretofore uncollected. Let me again express my hope that it will contain your say about Utilitarianism. I incline to suppose that an exposition of your views would more distinctly than has yet been done define the limits on which alone the doctrine is worth supporting, and tend to stop a good deal of loose (though sometimes bloody) skirmishing in territory over which its wisest supporters would not attempt to assert control.[15]

Maine, however, never responded to Holt's suggestion. Underlining the relevant passages in Holt's latest letter before sending it to John Murray in Albemarle Street, Piccadilly, he noted that 'what follows about Utilitarianism turns on some crotchet of his own. He wants me to add to the volume a paper on the subject, but it does not enter into my plans to put into the book anything new or quite un-Indian. Probably I shall lecture on Holt's subject at Oxford, and this would come into a new volume.'[16] When the third edition of *Village Communities*, with the Rede Lecture and other appended material, appeared in London and New York bookshops in 1876, there was no essay on Bentham.

Had Holt looked closely at the *Early History of Institutions*, he would have found at least a partial answer to his request for an elucidation of Sir Henry's position on utilitarianism. In two essays on the subject of sovereignty that he added after his lectures on early Irish law, Maine provided a rather more extensive exposition than in any of his previous writings of his philosophical differences with Benthamite jurisprudence.[17] Maine began these lectures where he had concluded in one of his earliest publications—the paper on territorial sovereignty which he had first read before the Juridical Society of London in 1855. While acknowledging the great contributions to British legal studies of the analytical jurists, Sir Henry felt that the Austinian theory of sovereignty exaggerated the influence of specific acts of the sovereign on the acceptance by the average citizen of legal obligations. While Austin's view rested on his assumption that in every society an individual or group sovereign was invested with the authority to issue commands or enforce sanctions that were obeyed out of fear of coercion, Maine now stressed other, and in his view equally important factors, that lay behind the legitimation of particular views of law and society:

First of all . . . the history, the whole historical antecedents of each society by which it has been determined where, in what person or group the power of using the social force is to reside. . . . Next, it is . . . the entire mass of its historical antecedents, which in each community determines how the sovereign shall exercise or forbear from exercising his irresistible coercive power. All that constitutes this . . . the whole enormous aggregate of opinions, sentiments, beliefs, superstitions, and prejudices, of ideas of all kinds, hereditary and acquired, some produced by institutions and some by the constitution of human nature—is rejected by the Analytical Jurists.[18]

Maine here restated his analytical distinction between two principle types of political society, an older variety, remnants of which still survived in the modern world, where men lived by the custom-

156

ary rules of their family and locality and only occasionally felt the arbitrary dictates of a remote absolute despot, and a newer type, where a centralized authority provided uniform legislation to regulate the affairs of a relatively well-integrated population that shared a sense of political community transcending local custom.[19] In the older type, Maine thought, stability largely depended on the unquestioned acceptance of the tried and customary, strengthened by the conserving power of myth and superstition. Only in the newer variety were the Austinian categories of legal analysis appropriate, for only there did political and legal authority tend to become associated with the notion of a territorial monopoly of physical coercion. The historical process was strewn with relics left in the advance from the older to the newer type—the village council or Indian *panchayat*, the Greek *ecclesia*, the Roman *comitia* and senate, the British parliament—and Maine suggests that the steady emergence of centrifugal over peripheral characteristics in these institutional patterns reflects a real movement of the lines of social control towards the centre. Now Maine believed there were still many societies of the older variety flourishing in the world. In these, the teachings of Bentham and Austin could have little practical meaning, since the habitual use of positive legislative enactments as a primary source of political and social innovation was unknown. As Sir Henry was led to comment:

> The capital fact in the mechanism of modern states is the energy of legislatures. . . . Until that fact existed, I do not . . . believe that the system of Hobbes, Bentham and Austin could have been conceived; wherever it exhibits itself imperfectly, I think that the system is never properly appreciated.[20]

Thus, had Henry Holt consulted Maine's *Early History of Institutions* he would have found that, while both Bentham and Maine hoped for the creation of a 'science of society', each began with strikingly different assumptions. For Bentham, social science had been conceived as a rational instrument for reordering the corrupt and inefficient institutions of contemporary British government by the enlightened employment of legislative power to 'maximize happiness, minimize expense'. Since Maine's historical studies had led him to believe that legislatures had seldom been the chief agents of social change, his goal was in a sense less ambitious. Maine would be

157

satisfied if his 'historical and comparative' method provided occasional insights into the common substratum of human nature underlying widely divergent institutional usages. Sir Henry had little doubt that such inferences would confirm his view of the human species as basically cautious and conservative, and indeed, this position added a further contrast to the more optimistic view of the Benthamites. The rulers of Austin's model, Maine had suggested, 'command because, being by the assumption possessed of uncontrollable force, they could *innovate without limit at any moment*'.[21] History, however, had taught Maine different lessons, and his years in India had introduced him to:

> independent political communities . . . in which the Sovereign, though possessed of irresistible power, *never dreams of innovation*, and believes the persons or groups by whom laws are declared and applied, to be as much part of the necessary constitution of society as he is himself.[22]

The analytical jurists, Maine concluded, succeeded in producing a systematic theory of law only by 'throwing aside all the characteristics and attributes of Government and Society except one'.[23] He had introduced a theme to be more fully explored for its political implications in his later work on *Popular Government*.

158

Patriarchs—or Matriarchs?

In January 1876, while J. F. McLennan was recuperating from a serious illness at Algiers in North Africa, a revised edition of his *Primitive Marriage* appeared in London, under the title *Studies in Ancient History*. After the passage of more than a decade, he was impatient at the little response he had received from those whose positions he had chiefly intended to disturb in first publishing his matriarchal theories. As he wrote in prefacing his new volume:

> I think myself that the case is made out to such an order of probability as to demand an answer . . . Sir Henry Maine and others who agree with him are no longer entitled to say that the proposition that kinship through mothers only preceded kinship through fathers rests upon the observation of scattered savage communities of other than Aryan races.[1]

McLennan, indeed, felt that primitive patriarchalism as Maine conceived it was a uniquely Roman institution, not even common among other branches of the so-called Aryan peoples. He included a paper on 'Divisions of the Ancient Irish Family' in his new edition, intended as a closely argued rebuttal of Maine's contention, in the *Early History of Institutions*, that the Brehon lawbooks illustrated conclusively a type of early Irish family similar in all essentials to the Roman notion of *patria potestas*. For all Maine's elaborate efforts, he contended, Sir Henry had left the subject of Irish kinship patterns as 'mysterious as he found them', and sarcastically marvelled: 'what a wonderful instrument of research comparative jurisprudence is, compared with direct historical inquiry by means of records and documents.'[2] Sir Henry, apparently undisturbed by these latest polemics from McLennan, continued quietly filling his notebooks with what he thought was new evidence in support of his patriarchal theories, listing elaborate bibliographical references on folio sheets under 'German *patria potestas* and agnation', 'Slavonian *patria potestas* and agnation', 'Celtic *patria potestas* and agnation', 'Greek *patria potestas* and agnation', presumably for future deployment in the academic battles of the anthropologists.[3]

Several months after the publication of McLennan's revised edition of *Primitive Marriage*, the American anthropologist L. H. Morgan wrote Maine a lengthy letter on the delicate subject of the deepening disagreements over method that were becoming evident among practitioners of the new science of man. Sir Henry's reply is preserved in the Morgan Collection at the University of Rochester, and in it, he reflects on the differences between Morgan's and his own approach to the study of early society:

> I have carefully followed all your investigations so far as they are known to me, and in my last book I have spoken of the value of your *Systems of Consanguinity and Affinity*. I hear with much pleasure that you have a volume in the press.
>
> As you truly say, we have attacked the same subject from opposite sides. I understand you to have begun with observations of the customs of savages, whereas I began as a Professor of Jurisprudence and should very probably have never interested myself in primitive usage, if I had not been profoundly discontented with the modes of explaining legal rules which were in fashion when I began to write. I am still apt to limit my enquiries to ancient institutions which I can more or less distinctly connect with modern ideas and ways of thought.
>
> No doubt the two lines of enquiry promise more and more to connect themselves together, and if I am not yet prepared to say that the connection has been established, I am quite ready to be convinced whenever the evidence is sufficient. Your work on *Systems of Consanguinity*, etc., carried the evidence much farther than before, and I shall look forward with great curiosity to your new publication. No doubt the history of property is greatly bound up with that of social development, and I suspect that physiology and biology must be called in before all is clear. I myself stumble a little at the unquestioning acceptance by anthropologists of the theological assumption of the descent of mankind from one single pair which seems to pervade a good deal of present investigations of savage customs.[4]

160

Maine's 'curiosity' over his American friend's recent researches was satisfied in March 1877 with the publication simultaneously in New York and London of Morgan's *Ancient Society*. Karl Resek has described the volume as an heroic attempt to bring together the laws that governed man's advancement from earliest history to the threshold of modern civilization.[5] It was an ambitious book, and although characterized by the unilateral evolutionary emphasis of much nineteenth-century historical scholarship, it guaranteed Morgan an important position among the modern founders of anthropology.[6] The American scholar set out to delineate the three broad stages through which he believed mankind had progressed in its long journey towards modernity: savagery, barbarism, and civilization. In each period of social advancement, human notions of government, the structure of the family, and of property, had assumed definite characteristics, and Morgan saw it as his task to describe in some detail the processes of change. Like Maine, Morgan distinguished two apparently distinct methods of organization in the history of human society. The first and older form, he suggested, was 'a *social* organization, founded upon gentes, phrateries and tribes', in which government was personal and dealt with members 'through their relation to a gens or tribe', and from which we derive the Latin notion of '*societas*'. The second type, which Morgan felt coincided with complex civilization, was 'a *political* organization, founded upon territory and upon property', in which government dealt with persons 'through their relations to territory—e.g., the township, the county and the state', and from which we have the Latin idea of '*civitas*'.[7] Both forms, he emphasized, were distinct, but related in an evolutionary train of development.

While Maine had exhorted his fellow students of society to turn to India for examples of the living past, Morgan in the pages of his *Ancient Society* summoned his fellow Americans[8] to learn of mankind's collective past from the North American Indian living around him and still partly in the stage of barbarism. He believed that their social organization represented a fairly complete example of the growth of institutions in his first and earlier sense of government. There, before the observant American's eyes, could be seen the development of the Iroquois gens into *phratries*, tribes and confederations. For the Indian to attain an even higher stage of civilization, it was necessary only 'to supercede the *gentes* by townships and city

161

wards, the gentile by a territorial system. The going down of the *gentes* and the uprising of organized townships mark the dividing line, pretty nearly, between the barbarian and the civilized worlds, between ancient and modern society.'[9] Moreover, Morgan believed the essentials of gentile organization observable in the American Iroquois were universal among all societies of the more ancient variety.[10]

It was in his detailed discussion of the 'growth of the idea of the family' that Morgan first provided grounds for serious academic conflict with his English colleague. Morgan believed the notion of the family had passed historically through a series of successive phases, and, in contrast with Maine's conclusions regarding the extent of the practice of *patria potestas* in primitive societies, that 'neither the monogamian nor the patriarchal can be traced back of the later period of barbarism'.[11] Long before the appearance of these stages, he contended, there had evolved three other forms of family, the *Consanguine*, the *Punaluan*, and the *Syndyasmian* or 'pairing family', in all of which descent had been traced through the female line. Even earlier, Morgan was convinced, at the very 'lowest conceivable stage of savagery . . . the bottom of the scale', humans, like the lower animals, had practised promiscuous intercourse.[12]

There was a further difference separating the two scholars. The American apparently found other lessons for contemporary politics in his historical studies than did Maine. As Morgan wrote towards the end of *Ancient Society*:

> Since the advent of civilization, the outgrowth of property has been so immense . . . that it has become on the part of the people, an unmanageable power . . . The time will come, nevertheless, when, human intelligence will rise to the mastery over property, and define the relations of the state to the property it protects, as well as the obligations and limits of the rights of its owners. The interests of society are paramount to individual interests, and the two must be brought into just and harmonious relations. A mere property career is not the final destiny of mankind, if progress is to be the law of the future as it has been of the past . . . Democracy in government, brotherhood in society, equality in rights and privileges, and universal education, foreshadow the next higher plane of society to which experience,

162

intelligence and knowledge are steadily tending. It will be a revival, in a higher form, of the liberty, equality and fraternity of the ancient *gentes*.[13]

For Maine, who had so shortly before written in his Rede Lecture that 'Nobody is at liberty to attack several property and to say at the same time that he values civilization', Morgan's heady assertions presented a disturbing contradiction of his views.

Morgan sent Maine an author's copy of his book shortly after it appeared, but it was some weeks before Maine, who was apparently ill at the time,[14] even acknowledged receiving it. When he did write, there was decided reserve in his tone:

> Many weeks have passed since I received your volume on *Ancient Society*, but I have not acknowledged it simply because I have been reading it very carefully, though slowly, through. Now that I have finished it, I feel that it would be a bad compliment to pass any concise or summary judgement upon it, and I will only say that I have read it with the strongest interest, and that there is hardly a chapter which does not present some new materials for thought. What opinions I am destined to form on the many new theories which it suggests, I do not know; but I intend to give them that full attention which is deserved by the conscientiousness and laboriousness evident in every part of your work and by the novelty and ingenuity of your inferences . . .[15]

For once the British anthropologists agreed among themselves. 'In the school of Tylor and Sir Henry Maine', Sir John Lubbock reflected uncharitably in a London review of the book, 'a writer needs more than industry and good will'.[16]

Maine was diligent in keeping his promise to write to Morgan after further assimilating his ideas. Not until the following Spring did he do so, however, noting:

> Possibly you may remember that when I thanked you for kindly sending me your work on *Ancient Society*, I told you that I intended to read it with much care. I am now studying it with great attention and with great interest and profit, and have no doubt that I shall have occasion to express my opinion of it in print. Not indeed that I am likely to trespass on what is strictly

163

your ground. The field of inquiry into the early history of institutions is now so extensive that it may be usefully mapped out into different parts occupying different tendencies.[17]

Observing that 'investigators like yourself, who work by actual observations of group customs and those who, like me, are chiefly busy with ancient records and bodies of written law' had much common interest in comparing their findings, Maine proceeded in a lengthy review of technical points to question the underlying assumptions of Morgan's theories of matrilineal descent. Morgan, who was recovering from a nervous breakdown brought on in the concluding stages of his researches for *Ancient Society*, showed remarkable stamina in replying with an even more lengthy letter the very next day. Protesting that 'I claim no exclusive field in the gentile organization and should be glad to see you enter it in good earnest', he suggested politely that the unusual tendency of Maine's mind 'to definition' made him an especially formidable critic. Drawing on his knowledge of the Iroquois, Morgan firmly defended his matrilineal views, and concluded by inviting Maine to America, where he promised, he would take him 'to one of our Reserves, and show you members of the different *gentes*, and see what they have to say about them'.[18] Morgan's spirited rebuttal met with an unkindly reception by Sir Henry, as a letter he wrote to E. B. Tylor from the Athenaeum, recently discovered at Oxford pasted inside the cover of Tylor's copy of *Ancient Society*, reveals:

> I look forward with much interest to the paper on Morgan. His book is certainly most curious, but there is something unsatisfactory about the man. I wrote to him at his own invitation the other day and put to him a very simple and definite question, and now I have a letter of four quarto pages complaining of the . . . 'tendency of (my) mind to definiteness' and of the difficulty of answering it after all. Perhaps, as I fear is now the case with McLennan, he lives in fear lest anybody should get scent of his supposed discoveries.[19]

Despite their scholarly differences, Maine and Morgan did continue to correspond sporadically. The last letter Maine sent him was written several years after the appearance of *Ancient Society*, to express thanks for a collection of recent American anthropological studies that Morgan had forwarded to him:

164

I have now found your own paper on the Stone Pueblo on the Arimas River, and two pamphlets by Mr Bandelier on Mexican tenures and social organization. All of these look in the highest degree interesting, and I will make no delay in studying them.

I am sorry to have such an indifferent account of your health. I have had myself a return of Indian fever, but the waters of Spa took the remains of it away. Perhaps you have heard that J. F. McLennan is dangerously ill, and I fear hopelessly. I am sorry to say that (as I am told) illness has much increased his acerbity of temper, and he is described as employing himself as well as he can, on a book which is to annihilate his old adversaries, including myself.

If the books which you have sent me suggest any questions which require an answer, I may venture to write to you again. Meantime, allow me to assure you of the deep interest with which I have read everything you have published, even when on some points I do not wholly agree with you.[20]

Maine's source of information about J. F. McLennan's failing health was doubtless Francis Galton, whom he saw regularly at the Athenaeum. Apparently Sir Henry had proposed a visit to see his old rival, with Galton acting as intermediary. The overture brought forth McLennan's final letter to Maine, so far as I have been able to learn:

My dear Sir Henry,

Since Mr Francis Galton was here I have been really ill with many hours of fever daily and much cough and asthma. I should be truly delighted to see you but, for reasons that are easily explained, I doubt whether at present I could venture to do so.

I have felt it absolutely necessary to devote the first part of the work upon which I have long been engaged to a refutation of the proposition contained in your 'Ancient Law' that a family of the Roman type, with its features of *patria potestas*, agnation, etc., is primordial and universal, and after a minute study of the evidence you have produced, I think I can show that there is no proof for it in any case but the Roman. I was working on this when I broke down, twenty months ago, with fever. This summer I got it nearly completed before being compelled to cease work again.

I should have liked beyond anything to have a talk with you on the subject, but in my present weak state everything excites me, and exposes me to attacks of high fever and you will readily understand that I could not possibly keep off the subject. Much, therefore, as I should like to see you, I fear I must put off the pleasure till I am a little stronger.[21]

Within a year of these letters, both of Maine's chief academic adversaries were dead. McLennan died of consumption at Hayes Common on 16 June 1881 following a long, tragic illness, and was never able to complete his final critique of Maine's *Ancient Law*. L. H. Morgan died at Rochester, N.Y., in December 1881.

Maine did eventually publish an extended answer to their criticisms of his patriarchal thesis, in an essay on 'Theories of Primitive Society', which formed a chapter of the final volume in his *Ancient Law* series, entitled *Early Law and Custom* (1883). The book was otherwise largely devoted to exploring in greater detail than he had elsewhere the relationships between early legal practices and religious institutions, and in preparing it Maine relied heavily on recent translations by Max Müller of eastern religious manuscripts. If there was any excuse to be offered for waiting so long to defend his views, Maine submitted, it was that he was 'not satisfied that the investigation has advanced far enough to admit of a very careful opinion'.[22] Sir Henry contended that it had never been his object to determine the 'absolute origin of human society', and indeed, that he had always felt 'a certain distaste for inquiries which, when I have attempted to push them far, have always landed me in mudbanks and fog'.[23] Rather, it had been his intention to investigate 'real' historical events whose existence was beyond dispute, and thus to create 'theory giving an account upon rational evidence of a primitive or very ancient social order'. Using these criteria, he wondered anew 'of what races of mankind it was not allowable to lay down that the society in which they were united was originally organized on the patriarchal model'. Maine acknowledged that matriarchal societies such as Morgan and McLennan described were known to exist, but held that these were easily explainable as a later development which must have occurred 'when man has advanced in his intellectual power and retrogressed in his instincts'. Beginning with the patriarchal model, he suggested, it was possible to account for the

166

occurrence of matriarchy, but he believed that Morgan and McLennan had been unable convincingly to show how patriarchalism might have been derived from matriarchalism. 'Morgan', he noted in a light-hearted jibe at the American's politics, 'seems almost to suppose that it was introduced by popular vote.'[24]

Maine felt the matriarchal model repugnant to basic facts of human nature. Calling on the authority of Darwin, as well as the writings of recent Continental sociologists trained in modern biology, he held that the matriarchal theory overlooked the sheer physical superiority of the male of the species, a power which was necessarily in the earliest reaches of human history 'the principle formative cause of the groups within which the conception of kinship first grew up'. Moreover, it overlooked the instinct of sexual jealousy in man, 'the most uncontrollable of his instincts when he had most of the animal in him'.[25] Sir Henry further criticized both Morgan and McLennan for the apparent rigidity of their evolutionary methods, which stipulated set 'stages' from promiscuity to modernity through which man must pass on the road to civilization. He reflected:

So far as I am aware, there is nothing in the recorded history of society to justify the belief that during that vast chapter of its growth which is wholly unwritten, the same transformations of social constitution succeeded one another everywhere, uniformly if not simultaneously. A strong force lying deep in human nature . . . might no doubt in the long run produce a uniform result, in spite of the vast varieties of circumstances accompanying the stern struggle for existence; but it is in the highest degree incredible that the action of this force would be uniform from beginning to end.[26]

Finally, Maine defended his position on the ground that, while he worked with the actual *written* records of the past, and confined his attention to the Aryan societies, his opponents speculated on a much grander scale. The difficulties that must be attendant on their attempts to describe the remote past in this manner, he believed, were readily apparent when one merely reflected on the 'innumerable delusions . . . current in England . . . of a country so near to us in situation and civilization as France'.[27]

Sir Henry's latest exposition of his patriarchal theories met with a reserved reception in London literary circles. *The Athenaeum* concluded, in a cautious assessment of the *Early Law and Custom* essays, that 'as he himself admits, there is much to be said before the subject can be considered settled'.[28] The mythologist Andrew Lang, in writing to thank Sir Henry for a complimentary copy of his new book, felt that Maine had in particular underestimated the importance of many of J. F. McLennan's insights:

> I am reading with great pleasure the book you have been so good as to send me. If I can get leave to review it somewhere, I will be able to say what occurs to me about various points. As to McLennan, his writing may have given the impression described on p. 201 of the 'clock-bell tolling the hour', but that was not I think his own best opinion. I remember him saying that 'all sorts of arrangements were going on in all sorts of places, simultaneously', or words to that effect, though these arrangements tended on the whole, he thought, to assume the forms of the processes and stages you enumerate in his terms.
>
> It is a shame that his remains are not published as, whether one agrees with him or not, they include a large collection of notes which it would be hard to bring together again.
>
> P.S.—I think Morgan was all at sea. He was no scholar and had not the head for argument. As for jealousy (p. 205) it *is* practically in abeyance among the races who present their wives to visitors as a piece of hospitality. I'm afraid all this can hardly be discussed in our modest monthlies, especially the *Saturday Review*![29]

To L. H. Morgan's defence came Friedrich Engels. *The Origin of the Family, Private Property and the State* (1884) was, indeed, full of praise for Morgan's discussion of the matriarchal social tie, and of his stirring thoughts on the probable future demise of private property. Maine's only significant contribution to the study of society, according to Engels, had been his discussion of the emergence of contract in progressive societies, an analysis which 'insofar as it is correct', Engels added, 'was contained long ago in the *Communist Manifesto*.'[30]

Maine was not without his own warm supporters. His old friend Lord Lytton wrote reassuringly that: 'The controversy which occupies your Seventh Chapter is quite new to me. I had hitherto accepted the patriarchal theory as an undisputed hypothesis, as well established as natural selection, and I have read with the interest of novelty your impartial statement of the counter-theory—against which the case seems to me conclusive.'[31] Other voices bore the credentials of academic authority. E. B. Tylor, writing in the *Nineteenth Century*, concluded that 'The claim of the patriarchal system to have belonged to primitive human life has not merely long acceptance in its favour, but I venture to think that those who uphold it have the weight of evidence on their side, provided that they do not insist on its fully developed form having at first appeared.'[32] Writing to Edward Westermarck, who was at the time engaged in preparing his classic *History of Human Marriage*, Tylor suggested that his friend acquaint himself with Maine's recent rebuttal of the matriarchal thesis.[33]

There was of course no victor in the curious controversy that engaged the energies of the patriarchal and matriarchal schools of nineteenth century political anthropology, each of which sought detailed evidence to support their particular version of the absolute historical origins of the family with the kind of fervour an earlier generation of social philosophers had bestowed on the quest for a clearer view of the state of nature. Anthropologists today recognize the existence of both types of kinship structure, frequently co-existing in the same social system. Maine and his contemporaries, in attempting to build their new discipline upon historical rather than analytic foundations, were never able to surmount a fundamental difficulty of that approach: the inevitable tendency for their inquiries to degenerate into antiquarian free-for-alls in the bottomless historical store-house of 'facts'.[34] Yet while these early evolutionary founders of modern social anthropology did not succeed in their undertaking, their vigorous pioneering efforts helped to create a sustained interest in the investigation and typology of kinship forms that was a necessary first step on the road to whatever current understanding we have of an important aspect of human social organization. As for the heated pitch of their inquiries, the matters which exercised their imaginations were, after all, burning issues in an age struggling to come to terms with emerging sentiments of social equality. For a scholar to assert that women had once universally been the politically and socially dominant sex required no inconsiderable amount of intellectual courage in a civilization dominated by males. Conversely, while Sir Henry may never had intended that such inferences be drawn from his scholarship, his researches seemed to 'naturalist' foes of female emancipation a clear illustration that the earliest Aryan social unit was but a somewhat harsher form of the type of household dominance exercised by the Victorian *paterfamilias*.

In recognition of the services he had rendered to scientific historical studies, the French Institute, in May, 1883, elected Sir Henry to Associate Membership in the *Academie des Sciences Morales et Politiques*, in the place left vacant by the death of the American man of letters, Frank Waldo Emerson. Maine had already accumulated his fair share of honours by the time of his election to the *Academie*. In 1866, the American Academy had been the first learned society to honour him with membership. In 1876 he became a Member of the Dutch Institute, and in 1877, of the *Accademia dei Lincei*. To these were added the Madrid Academy in 1878, the Royal Irish Academy in 1882, the Washington Anthropological Society in 1883, and the Juridical Society of Moscow in 1884. He had by that date attained membership in the Royal Society.[35] In choosing Maine for Associate Membership in the *Academie*, the French academicians apparently passed over the claims of Herbert Spencer. Bitterly disappointed, the renowned sociologist wrote a friend of his decision to decline an offer of the lower position of Corresponding Member, on the ground that 'I am by implication recognizing the propriety of this estimate of relative claims. Sir Henry Maine is my junior by two years, and he is in his standing as an author my junior by ten years, so that no plea of seniority can be alleged.'[36] It seemed that even in the awarding of honours there could be no peace among the 'political embryologists'.[37]

Return to Cambridge

In 1878 Maine resigned his Oxford law professorship, after delivering his final series of lectures on the Roman 'Law of Things' and 'Law of Persons' at Corpus Christi College.[1] The Oxford chair, which had been more or less made to fit the circumstances of Sir Henry's professional life in London, was thereafter to be held by a resident professor engaged fulltime in the life of the University. With Maine's strong support, Frederick Pollock was appointed as his successor.[2] Maine's years at Oxford had been the most productive of his scholarly life. His *Village Communities, Early History of Institutions,* and *Early Law and Custom* are little more than revised versions of Oxford lectures he prepared during this period. Sir Henry had usually journeyed to Oxford by train for his weekly afternoon lectures, and stayed overnight at the University in temporary lodgings. He had thus been able to enjoy a regular Oxford social life, as an amusing letter written by the historian John Richard Green to E. A. Freeman on 11 November 1875 suggests:

I met Maine and has a long chat with him about you and many things. Likewise Fitzjames Stephen, Henry Sidgwick, Venn, Dicey, Lushington, and other nice folk—all members of an *Ad Eundem* Club on to which I have been chosen. We dined at Christ Church and strove after dinner to get out of 'the House' by Canterbury Gate. But we were withstood by a proud young porter who would not open save that we produced the card of Harcourt with whom we had dined. So we put three Professors to the front, Maine, Bryce and Henry Smith; but the proud young porter put to flight the three professors. Then we set in array the Cambridge men, with Fitzjames Stephen at their head; but the proud young porter drove the Cambridge men back. Then we held a *Gemot*, and I proposed that we should camp out for the night in the midst of Canterbury Meadow, and renew the fight on the morrow. But Bryce, the wily one, stole from the *Gemot* and privately entreated the proud young porter, sending him 'Compliments of the Dean', and other wileness and so being tangled in his talk, the warder let us go free. But see how great a thing it is to get out of the House![3]

For all the pleasures of the Oxford appointment, it had seemed inevitable that Maine would eventually leave. His combination of academic and administrative skills, and his ambition, lead him as we have already seen to be constantly on the look-out for new professional openings that would enhance his status and income while allowing him freedom to pursue his literary interests. It is an interesting historical footnote that when Lord Lytton was named Viceroy of India in Disraeli's second Government, he sounded Maine out on the possibility of giving up his Oxford chair to return to India. Maine wrote to him from Marienbad, where he had gone to take the waters, on 26 August 1876:

I have waited for a holiday—a holiday which I am spending at this very stupid place—before replying to a short letter which I received from you some months ago. I am much honoured by your hint about returning to India, but I really think that I have settled down into the groove in which I shall continue for the rest of my life. Now that the formerly absurd tenure of my seat in Council has been changed by a short Act of Parliament passed this session, I am reasonably contented with my position, which I refused to give up when tempted the other day by an offer of the new Under-Secretaryship at the Foreign Office, with further prospects held out. The fact is, I am rather loath to resign perhaps the only post in the public service which admits of my continuing my literary work.[4]

When Maine wrote that he had been tempted 'the other day' by the Foreign Office Under-Secretaryship, he really meant several months before, as a letter to Maine from the Foreign Secretary, Lord Derby, reveals:

> Foreign Office,
> 23 St James's Square,
> April 24, 1876

Dear Maine,

I need not say that I regret your decision, though I have neither the right nor the wish to question it. You are undoubtedly doing valuable public work in your present post, and you are a better judge that any one else can be as to the suitableness of one or other of the positions between which you have had to choose, as regards your own inclination.

F.O. has no conceivable claim upon you; but I am sorry for the F.O.—and sorry for myself.

> V. truly yours,
> Derby[5]

There is more than a hint in Derby's note that Maine was still actively entertaining other possibilities, and by early the following year, the 'one or other of the positions' had been definitely narrowed to one. Dr Thomas Geldart, Master of Trinity Hall, Cambridge, died in September 1877 following a lengthy illness. He had headed the Cambridge law college since 1852, when Maine taught there as an unknown young don. Two Trinity Hall men, the Senior Tutor, R. H. Latham, and Professor Henry Fawcett, were known to want the Mastership. Neither of them, however, could muster sufficient backing among their colleagues, and Maine was instead eventually offered the post. As Sir Henry explained to Lord Salisbury, in a letter written to assure the Secretary for India that acceptance of the Mastership would not interfere with his duties at the India Office, he owed his stroke of good fortune to a peculiar political deadlock within the College:

My dear Lord Salisbury,

It is just possible that your eye may have been caught by an announcement in the newspapers that I have been elected to the Mastership of Trinity Hall at Cambridge, and you may wonder how the duties of the position are reconcilable with those of a Member of Council. I ought then to explain that the Mastership is a virtually honorary office, which, till the last incumbency, was held always (or nearly always) by the Dean of the Arches and Judge of the Prerogative Court. I hope it will interfere with my functions at the India Office even less than did my Oxford Professorship, which I resign at midsummer.

The Fellows of Trinity Hall have been engaged for nearly six months in a struggle to elect one of two candidates out of their own number. They were divided six against six, and the man who should have given the casting vote is a lunatic in confinement. They therefore put strong pressure on me to accept the office before the nomination lapsed.

Very faithfully yours,
H. S. Maine[6]

James Fitzjames Stephen thought the circumstances surrounding Maine's selection were simply the latest in a seemingly endless line of examples of Sir Henry's characteristic ability to further his career without having to make great sacrifices. He wrote[7] peevishly to Grant Duff's wife on learning of the appointment that Maine:

always seemed to me, in an invalid sort of way, no doubt, to bear a great deal of quiet cheerfulness and courage under troubles which are by no means specially easily to bear. He has, however, been better provided than most men with comfortable means and paddings which have fallen on him most opportunely. The gods really are good to a man who after being obliged to refuse a great office by an untraceable illness, has another offer of it upon the death of the incumbent as soon as that offer can be accepted, and who gets in these days a sinecure of £600 a year and a good house for life, because of two rivals, either of whom would have beaten him in a dead heat for it—each party preferred him to either of his rivals.

Maine was installed as Master of Trinity Hall in a simple ceremony held in the College Chapel on Christmas Day 1877. Among the guests at a banquet honouring the new Master following his installation were the Master of Pembroke, Maine's undergraduate college, and Dr William Guillemard, Maine's first classics tutor, and himself a Christ's Hospital 'Blue Coat Boy'.

Sir Henry's new position was primarily an administrative one, and he did little lecturing in the law college. He continued the tradition of holding periodic reunions of law graduates of Trinity Hall, and his Christmas celebrations at the Master's Lodge became especially well known among prominent members of the legal profession. J. F. Stephen usually attended and stayed with the Maines in college. In a decidedly more charitable mood, he described one such occasion in a letter to Lady Grant Duff:

> When your letter came I was away from home at Trinity Hall as the guest of H. S. Maine. They have Christmas feasts there every year and for several years past I have gone down and sat in the seat of honour, for it is a law college and makes a point of always having a Judge seated by the Master . . . We ate a good deal up, but still we went on far too long. I was pleased to see Maine, however, and he had in his house three Indians, with by no means untutored minds—namely, Sir A. Lyall, a charming person independently of his poetry—Colonel Alan Johnson, also a special friend of mine, and General Strachey, the brother of John who is a great ally of mine. So we were very jolly and merry.[8]

The annual banquet began with a sherry party from five until eight in the evening, when the guests adjourned to the Combination Room for tea and roast apples. There was card playing until ten, when those who had stayed on sat down to a heavy meal of boar's head and milk punch. Stephen confessed in another letter to Lady Grant Duff that although nothing made him feel 'quite as old as going back to Cambridge', he always looked forward to the Master's banquets, with their 'specially legal character', as 'a pleasant little dot in the year'.[9]

Maine had a deep admiration for Cambridge and its classical tradition, and in the light of political developments after his return there from Oxford, it is apparent that his academic colleagues felt certain reciprocal affections. In November 1882 Spencer Walpole, who had represented Cambridge University as a Conservative M.P. for twenty-six years, informed the University Senate that he intended to apply for the Stewardship of the Chiltern Hundreds. His decision to retire was greeted with mixed feelings of regret and curiosity as to who would succeed him. *The Times*, noting editorially that Cambridge University members had traditionally been earnest Churchmen and sound Conservatives, proposed that the ideal successor to Walpole would be one who 'could unite moderate political convictions with strong literary or scientific leanings'.[10] Cambridge would do well, the newspaper suggested, to follow the

175

example of the voters of the University of London, who had recently selected the eminent student of early society, Sir John Lubbock, as their Member of Parliament.

Cambridge men, who took their *Times* seriously, saw much merit in the editorial arguments. Many apparently felt privately that Maine, measured by these criteria, would be the ideal candidate. He was an accomplished man of letters, as well as an experienced public servant, and moreover, was known not to have strong party feelings. The Conservative Party held their nomination meeting at the Red Lion Hotel, Cambridge, during the afternoon of 9 November 1882. It was only the day before that W. H. Thompson, Cambridge Professor of Greek, who had known Maine from undergraduate days, discovered that Sir Henry's position at the India Office would definitely not bar him from standing. He immediately sent telegrams to Maine in London, urging him to allow his name to be brought forward. He wrote to Sir Henry at greater length from Trinity College:

My dear Maine,

You will have received my telegrams, just now despatched. The Conservative Party holds a meeting tomorrow to fix upon a candidate. From what I have heard they are not unlikely to select Raikes. He is disapproved of in this college, I can say nothing of any other, and a strong desire has been expressed by men of various opinions that you would consent to be put forward—if on no other grounds, on that of academical and literary attainment, which are lacking in the other case. I have heard that this is the feeling even of professed Radicals like Jackson and also of reputed Conservatives.

I have not had time to communicate with the men of the College or even with Latham; for until an hour ago I was under the impression that your official position would be a bar to your sitting in Parliament. But I am now told that probably your tenure has expired, or could do so shortly. I need hardly say that it would be a gratification to me personally if your saw your way to allowing yourself to be brought forward.

Walpole's letter is given in the *Times* and you will have probably seen it there. You will write I hope by return as the matter presses.[11]

176

When the Conservatives met the following day, however, Maine's name was not put forward. It is probable that a distaste for partisan politics was an important factor in his decision not to stand. At the time of the general elections of 1885, he reputedly told a friend who inquired after his political affiliation that if there was an ideal Toryism he would probably be a Tory, but since in his estimation, modern party politics entailed a compromising of principles, he preferred not to be stigmatized by a party label. As things turned out, Henry Raikes was selected to stand for the Conservatives, and in the subsequent polling he drubbed his hapless Liberal rival, Professor Stuart. The *Spectator*, speaking for the defeated side, commented that the result merely confirmed its suspicion that Cambridge cared little for learning as compared to its passion for Toryism, and even seemed to prefer its Toryism rather rank.[12]

In 1881 Maine delivered a paper on 'The King and His Relation to Early Civil Justice' before the Royal Institution, which suggested that while he continued to shun the market-place of practical politics, his academic studies themselves seemed to contain growing elements of political sentiment. Maine's paper provided an analysis of some of the oldest known portions of the Teutonic codes, contained in the so-called Salic Law, a body of legal rules of the fifth century A.D. which governed the activities of the pre-feudal Germanic 'Courts of the Hundred'. Sir Henry was interested that the eventual demise of the popularly selected Teutonic court president, the '*Thingman*', and his replacement by the '*Graf*' or king's representative, seemed only the most conspicuous event in a general historical movement among the Salian Franks away from popularly controlled legal institutions, in the direction of a new system of courts administering justice exclusively in the king's name. Maine was certain that such trends were no accident, for it was his thesis that, as social pressures among progressive peoples led to demands for more flexible procedures, kingship had had inherent advantages over popular courts or assemblies of freemen. In the case of the Franks, Maine suggested, so long as the courts remained in the control of the popular element, the accused was literally 'judged by one's peers', and too many people were involved in the administration of justice. Moreover, there was, according to Maine, the greatest practical difficulty in 'bringing up the people to the discharge of their public duties'. Thus, as he contended, 'much of ancient freedom was . . . lost

177

through the vastness of the payment in person which it demanded.'[13] In contrast, the superior military power gradually concentrated in the king's hands gave royal legal pronouncements binding force. The further ability of a mobile court retinue to take justice into the countryside created the more efficient situation in which 'It was not the litigant who went to the king, but the king who went to the litigant'. Such had, in fact, remained the case until relatively late in western legal history, when the growing complexity of the law eventually led, as in England by the time of Magna Carta, to the compulsory replacement of the mobile Common Pleas by centralized courts with permanent judicial establishments. Maine concluded that from the standpoint of the legal historian, the Salic Law served to demonstrate that monarchical institutions had for long been 'the most valuable and indeed the most indispensable of all reforming agencies'[14], an achievement that was often erroneously assumed by modern Europeans to belong to legislatures alone.

In a second paper prepared for delivery at the London Institute several months later, Maine turned to explore the implications of the view that 'a great deal of the progressive civilization of the human race has consisted in the discovery of remedies against violence', especially as concerned the problem of regulating succession to political power. While at an early historical period succession was presumably secured by simple recourse to 'natural selection', Maine thought the special service to modern European civilization of the Germanic *lex Salica* was the invention of primogeniture, 'to which, as a political institution', he wrote, 'I may observe that the human race has been deeply indebted'.[15] Bringing his latest legal researches to the support of Burke's analysis of French society after 1789, Maine suggested that whereas democratic partisans of the French Revolution claimed that the overthrow of the old class structure created for the first time a comprehensive sense of unity and national spirit among Frenchmen, the underlying features of France's most significant national characteristics had been forged during the great age of monarchy, indeed, 'may be traced in great part to the Salic rule of royal succession'.[16]

Maine asked Lord Acton to read a draft of this second paper, and upon doing so, the Liberal historian did not hesitate to make his reservations clear. Maine had emphasized the great political service to western historical progress of the practice of primogeniture, and

178

while partly agreeing, Acton suggested there was more to be learned from its history than that alone. For primogeniture, Acton felt, may once have been politically useful, but he feared it embodied a serious conflict between succession to property and claims to political authority that in more recent times had acted as a hindrance to the continued evolution of free institutions. He urged Maine to point this out in his paper, or his historical inferences would be left with 'a Tory tinge'. To his suggestion, Maine stubbornly retorted that 'you seem to use Tory as a term of reproach'. Acton was astonished at Maine's response, and was still distressed when he wrote to his close confidante Mary Gladstone from Cannes, upon his return there from London:

> I was much struck by this answer—much struck to find a philosopher, entirely outside party politics, who does not think Toryism a term of reproach, and still more to find a friend of mine ignorant of my sentiments about it. And I am much tempted to have it out with him, and discover what he really means.[17]

Acton, with whom Maine more frequently came in contact after 1875, apparently found Sir Henry's personality an intriguing combination of intellectual and authoritarian elements. He wrote further to Mary Gladstone from Tegernsee after learning that she had asked Sir Henry to tea, assuring her that she would find Maine a most stimulating guest. His nature was to exercise power, and to find good reasons for adopted policy. Augustus or Napoleon, in Acton's estimation, would have been wise to make a man like Maine their prime minister. Maine had no strong party feelings, he continued, but at heart he was not a modern Liberal in the great age of Liberalism, for he was convinced that 'Manchesterism' must eventually lead to the loss of India. He was intensely nervous and sensitive, but Mary Gladstone would probably find that the fragility of his body stood in sharp contrast to his powerful, masculine mind. 'When I feel sure of some conclusion', Acton reflected, 'I go to Maine, and he always knocks it to pieces.' He concluded that, in his view, Sir Henry was one of the finest intellects of his generation.[18] By 8 August 1880 Acton, who was curious to learn of Mary's reaction to Maine, wrote again, inquiring 'whether he showed you the luminous side of his mind, whether you saw why he always disagrees with me, and

179

why some people are more afraid than fond of him'.[19] But we unfortunately are left with no record of Mary Gladstone's impressions of Maine, as fragments of her diary which are in the British Museum contain no mention of their meeting.

While Acton moved steadily to the view that the history of human liberty could be described as the continual widening of the base of active political participation in Church and State, Maine in his later years became more firmly convinced than ever before of the dangers posed to civilized institutions by that movement. With our knowledge of the circumstances of his personal and public career, it is possible to draw up a tentative catalogue of the probable causes that lay behind his concern. A middle-class gentleman whose comfortably privileged position had only been realized after a prolonged effort over the years to accumulate a modest fortune in property,[20] Sir Henry found the awakening of democratic sentiment among influential English politicians a disturbing challenge to his accustomed way of life. A sickly man, Maine's perpetual ill health led him in middle age, so it seemed, to an almost predictable intolerance of new and untried routine. A lawyer increasingly imbued by the natural conservatism of his profession, his instincts had been reinforced by his first-hand experience of the vast complexity of government and administration in the non-western world. An acclaimed historical scholar, Sir Henry had become firmly convinced that the real cement of social life was custom and habit, and that although human reason had led some societies to an awareness of the benefits of a wide exercise of freedom of contract, few had been capable of the political discipline necessary for its continuance. And, as a Member of the Indian Council in London, with the professional's pride in the high intelligence of the Anglo-Indian civil service *corps d'élite*, he believed the growing exposure of the Indian masses to radical western ideas invited disaster to overtake the gradual adaptation of the Asian sub-continent to the more advanced position of its Aryan kin. As Indian politics moved into the arena of British domestic affairs in the decade after Maine's return from Asia, and control of Indian administrative policy fell increasingly under the purview of the political parties of Westminster, his thoughts turned more and more to defending the historical authority of the institutions of the British Empire. As he wrote in an Indian Office dispatch reminiscent of Burke that he prepared during this period:

180

I claim for the Indian Constitution the ordinary presumption against change, which throws the burden of explicit proof upon the advocates of change; and I assert that there is the strongest presumption against sweeping change, when the institutions in question are so unexampled in the political history of mankind as those of British India.[21]

It was in India that Acton would find the foundations of Maine's 'Tory tinge'. Indeed, it was a growing concern over the dilemma of the British exercise of power in the Empire that chiefly lay behind Maine's uneasiness at trends in domestic politics in the years preceding the publication of his attack on democracy in *Popular Government*. In order to grasp the connection between the two, it is necessary to turn to a consideration of certain developments in Anglo-Indian political thought in the interval that had elapsed since Sir Henry's return from India in 1869.

Imperium et Libertas

In April 1872, having personally supervised the passage of a number of important measures of Indian legislation, James Fitzjames Stephen had abruptly resigned his position on the Governor-General's Council, and sailed from Bombay for England. Although he served as Legal Member for only a little over two years, the legislative record compiled during that time guaranteed his reputation as one of the most significant Anglo-Indian lawgivers of the nineteenth century. As he later recalled, comparing his incumbency with that of his successor, Arthur Hobhouse:

> I felt that for family reasons my time in India must be short (I had not been there two months before I suspected that I should have to leave before my time was up). I determined to make the most of my opportunity. I worked night & day, cut up . . . drafts & redrew them after my own devices, & by ways & means & in particular by incessant labour, passed so many Acts that Hobhouse & Lord Northbrook looked on me as a sort of revolutionist & did little or nothing in that direction.[1]

With the close of Stephen's period of office, the high-water mark of Indian codification had been reached.

Before going to India, Stephen had moved his family to a new residence at 24 Cornwall Gardens, only a matter of yards from Maine's house. The proximity of their households enabled the two Indian administrators to enjoy each others company with a minimum of inconvenience during the 1870s. They met almost immediately upon Stephen's return to London. As the historian J. A. Froude recalled, they seemed at their reunion 'like two schoolboys'. At the annual dinner of the Cambridge Apostles' held shortly afterwards at the Star and Garter Inn, Richmond, Maine was in the chair, and

Stephen, in proposing his health, suggested lightheartedly that 'the legislation passed in India during the rule of his friend and himself should henceforth be called the "Acts of the Apostles".'[2] In different circumstances Fitzjames might have been willing to reiterate the claim in perfect seriousness. For as his political writings during this period suggest, he did indeed view the efforts of Maine and himself as 'Acts of Apostles'—apostles in the service of a new religious faith, the cause of the British Empire.

As early as 25 April 1872, while still on the high seas en route to Suez, Fitzjames had written to Emily Cunningham noting that: 'I have two books of John Mill's: his book on *Liberty* and a book called *Utilitarianism*, on each of which I have much to say & when they are properly read they will do instead of articles, but I want to get well into practice for the P.M.G. by the time I get home.'[3] A week later, when he had completed a preliminary reading of Mill's essays, he wrote further[4] to the same correspondent:

> I returned to my Mill today and fired some shots into him. It is curious that after being . . . a devoted disciple and partisan of him up to a certain point I should have found it at last impossible to go on with him, but his politics & his morals are not mine at all, though I believe in & admire his logic and his general outlines of philosophy. I recollect—about three or four years ago—I had a battle royal on these points with my brother Leslie; & we at last came to the conclusion that the real difference between us was that he thought better of mankind than I do. It is a long story to think how this difference colours not only one's politics but one's morals and one's religion too. But it does, and I am rather taken by the idea of making Mill's later works the peg on which to hang the statement of a variety of doctrines on this subject which I have been forming for many years.

Stephen made good his intention by publishing a lengthy series of 'letters' which appeared in Frederick Greenwood's *Pall Mall Gazette* during the final months of 1872, and January 1873. In the form of an elaborate critique of Mill, the essays, as Stephen later wrote to Lord Lytton, were 'full of Indian impressions . . . little more than the turning of an Indian lantern on European problems'.[5] They were brought out in book form by Smith, Elder and Co. during April 1873 under the title *Liberty, Equality, Fraternity*.

Stephen claimed to be 'in a certain sense . . . a utilitarian', yet there were several points on which he felt his views could not be easily reconciled with the 'common utilitarianism' of the younger Mill. Thus, he rejected the famous doctrine of Mill's *On Liberty* that 'the sole end for which mankind are warranted, individually or collectively, in interfering with the liberty of action of any of their number, is self-protection', on the ground that its application to practical politics would result in chaos. While Mill had held that merely 'self-regarding' actions were the concern of individuals and not governments, Stephen suggested that compulsion must always be employed, even by benevolent régimes pursuing beneficial goals, in cases other than those covered by Mill's criteria.[6] He followed Hobbes in holding that it is the use or threat of sanctions, rather than the exercise of reason and persuasion in Mill's sense, that ultimately guarantees the acceptance of political obligations.

While Mill had further taught that liberty was endangered whenever politics and religion were united, Stephen rejected this view as equally untenable in principle. Organized society would be unthinkable without the belief in a future state. Contrary to Mill's argument he asserted that all political morality, like religious faith, must draw heavily on community-wide acceptance of some notion of 'heaven and hell', as a means of managing mankind's natural selfishness:

> The real leading motives of the mass of mankind are personal prudence and passion. Their centre is self; and every religion which means to govern men must recognise this fact and appeal to personal motives. It does not become a spiritual power in the true sense of the word power—it cannot, that is to say, impose itself *in invitos* until it has practically solved this problem. How Christianity, Mahommedanism and Brahminism solved it we all know. Even Buddhism had, after a time, to set up its hell.[7]

The individualistic rationalism of Mill's writings did not, in Stephen's estimation, ring true to the conditions of actual political life. While the theories of *On Liberty* seemed fully plausible to parlour-room Liberal intellectuals in London, where the established traditions of politics largely removed the necessity of recourse to violence and coercion as instruments for effecting public policy, he felt they were sadly lacking in the context of Anglo-Indian government, where the cruder exercise of brute force was of necessity always close to the surface. Any doctrine that failed to recognize such facts of political reality was unfit to advise statesmen, for 'a power which can be defied with impunity is no power, and [as for you], you will never be anything more than a Ritualistic Social Science Association'.[8] Governments, then, in Stephen's analysis, must always act *as if there were* a God. When they ceased doing so, it signalled the demise of the previously dominant creed. Such a period seemed to him near in England, yet he was concerned that the emerging creed, with its god 'Democracy', and its dogma of 'Liberty, Equality, Fraternity', based itself upon a dangerous rationalism that ignored the cruel necessities of the exercise of power in controlling the short-comings of human nature. In fact, as he argued in a lengthy review of the doctrinal trinity of democracy, 'whichever rule is applied, there are a vast number of matters in respect of which men ought not to be free; they are fundamentally unequal, and they are not brothers at all, or only under qualifications which make the assertions of their fraternity unimportant'.[9]

Stephen's book was intended to form a contribution to current political and theological discussion in England, but it derived its chief impetus from his reflections on the British role in India. He was disturbed by the arguments of a new generation of British radicals, professing to find their philosophical views in Mill and their political leadership in John Bright and the Manchester Liberals, who seemed intent on applying the doctrines of democracy not only in England but throughout the Empire. He had little patience with their sentimental humanitarianism, and their dogma of 'Fre-quality'.[10] Human history was directed by a succession of imperial powers, and the mantle of power had lately been cast on England. The real need was to *act*, firmly but benevolently, to ensure that British beliefs compatible with the requirements of power politics and the imperfections of human nature would be transformed into beneficial effects. Stephen submitted that it was undeniable that the exercise of British hegemony in Asia had afforded peace and uniform conditions of justice throughout territories even more vast than those of Imperial Rome. One thus need not make apologies for the blessings of the autocratic *pax Brittanica*. In what seemed to be the twilight of European Christianity, he expressed the passionate new faith of Victorians who found relief in serving the church of Empire, whose

185

gospel, Stephen wrote, was British law and order. Maine had reflected in an earlier conversation with his friend: 'It is a great shock to find that the world was not made for man.'[11] Stephen now answered as an apostle of Empire:

> We stand on a mountain pass in the midst of whirling snow and blinding mist, through which we get glimpses now and then of paths that may be deceptive. If we stand still, we shall be frozen to death. If we take the wrong road, we shall be dashed to pieces. We do not certainly know whether there is any right one. What must we do? 'Be strong and of good courage.' Act for the best, hope for the best, and take what comes. Above all, let us dream no dreams, and tell no lies, but go our way, wherever it may lead, with our eyes open and our heads erect. If death ends all, we cannot meet it better. If not, let us enter whatever may be our next scene like honest men, with no sophistry in our mouths and no masks on our faces.[12]

While *Liberty, Equality, Fraternity* was by no means the first critique of Mill that had appeared by 1873,[13] Stephen's polemical style made him the central figure in a heated controversy. Like everything else since his return from India, he commented, it was 'to a large extent a personal question'. While he greatly admired Carlyle,[14] the argumentative author of *Liberty, Equality, Fraternity* openly admitted that he found Mill and his followers, by comparison, intellectually 'cold as ice'. The best of Mill's writings, he allowed, had the precision of a surgeon's knife, but he confided to Emily Cunningham that he found Mill's general tone devoid of humanity:

> Goethe was worth fifty Mills. He was a man & a vigorous one, and for my part I always felt about Mill that he was as somebody said of somebody, a book in breeches. Everything I ever knew or heard of his actual personal life was petty and narrow. I have no doubt he had in a very narrow circle all the eager feelings of a family, but outside of that he was as narrow as it was possible for a man to be and as cold as ice. I knew him for years and wrote to him often on various subjects, & he never got beyond 'Dear Sir' with me; never so far as 'My Dear Sir' even. Talking to him was like reading his books, as you can imagine.[15]

Mill was never able to answer Stephen's critique, as he was

seriously ill at Avignon, and died only a month after his book was published. His cause was taken up by Frederic Harrison in the June 1873 *Fortnightly Review*. The brilliant *Fortnightly* had become the leading intellectual spokesman for 'advanced liberalism' in the years after John Morley took up its editorship in 1867 at the early age of twenty-nine, and it was Morley who persuaded Harrison to undertake a review of Stephen's book, to follow immediately after a short leader written by himself noticing Mill's death. Harrison's paper,[16] holding to the authority of Comte and Mill, advanced the argument that it was spiritual and moral force, rather than sheer physical power, that underlay the lasting institutions of civilization. He suggested that *Liberty, Equality, Fraternity* amounted to little more than 'Calvinism *minus* Christianity'.[17] Only a philosopher whose judgement had been warped by exposure to Indian affairs could have displayed such a singular lack of 'Humanity':

> Mr Stephen forgets how dangerous are the analogies of the East. He is too ready to decide questions of liberty, of the sphere of government, and of social sentiment, by the inexhaustible mine of Indian experience. It is the custom nowadays, but a custom a little overdone . . . Indian society is not ours, its civilization is not ours, nor its moral atmosphere the same . . . it is an Empire founded on conquest, maintained by the sword, and but lately cemented amid a deluge of blood and passion. The absolute power of its rulers, the iron grip they must maintain, are apt to fill men's minds with something like the fumes of power as they used to infect Roman Emperors, and now infect Russian Czars.[18]

Morley himself added a further critical notice of Stephen's book in the August *Fortnightly*,[19] pointing out that whereas Mill's 'self-protection' principle afforded the minority a shelter against coercion by the majority, Stephen's emphatic justification of force would leave them constantly exposed to that danger.

Harrison and Morley, however, were by no means as uniformly critical of the *Liberty, Equality, Fraternity* essays as their published reviews would suggest. When Morley first asked Harrison to undertake a defence of Mill, the leading British exponent of Comtist positivism found after a preliminary reading of Stephen's book that he agreed with much of its contents, and while he could not forgive the author's 'bludgeoning Philistinism', neither could he in conscience deny the general validity of Stephen's argument. Harrison therefore agreed to do the review only if he could confine his comments to the bearing of Stephen's chapter on 'Fraternity' to Comtean teachings. As he wrote in a lengthy letter to Morley setting out his position:

> I think he is in the main right, and he has done a good work. I do not say that he has not done it with a bludgeoning Philistinism which is a little trying, and that he has not made some bold fallacies—but I don't wish to detract from a really good and useful argument, in which he is successful. I think—although I dislike his way of putting it & see how much he leaves out—as against Mill he is successful & even triumphant.
>
> 1. What he says of *Liberty* is right. Mill has talked about abstract and absolute right, & has idealised the individual in a way that is metaphysical nonsense and also extremely anarchical. Stephen fairly demolishes all this. Mill's plea for the sacredness of individual liberty is a dangerous sophism . . . Stephen does not quite hit the true ground that society is a natural thing & you can only ask what is good for it and its members & not the whirligig of *rights*—but practically he hits the right line in asking. He is as near the truth as a politician or lawyer need be, though not as clear as a philosopher or critic should be.
>
> 2. What he says about *Equality* is admirable. His argument as to the equality of the sexes is a little brutal but *so far as it goes* is unanswerable. It leaves out the finer positive argument for women's superiorities, but it does justice and no more than justice for men's. And there again he is as right as a mere legislator or lawyer need be—far more right then Mill's subversive paradoxes.
>
> 3. As to *Fraternity*, I am not quite sure, but I think Stephen is fairly right. I don't know what becomes of his Christianity, but that is his affair. Of course he utterly misunderstands Comte's Humanity which he imagines to be all men including W. E. G. This of course is ridiculous. And I am not sure that Comte would not agree with Stephen as to the hollowness of the democratic bluster about 'a man is a brother'.[20]

'Every true positivist', Harrison confessed, 'is a real conservative, & I am wishing for the time when as conservatives our time will come to defend the immortal institutions of men against sentimental

188

sophists, noble or ignoble.' The goal of modern politics, indeed the 'leading problem of our age', as Harrison had writtten separately in a January 1873 article on 'The Revival of Authority', was 'to found Authority without oppression, upon a Public Opinion without Democracy'.[21]

Morley, however, had sensed danger in letting Stephen's analysis of 'Liberty, Equality, Fraternity' stand unanswered. True Liberals, he retorted, owed their dying Master the duty of 'mak[ing] old Stephen's big ribs resound with thwacks, the monstrous Goliath as he is'.[22] It would be allowing the uncontested entry into the arena of British and Indian affairs of an unnecessarily harsh tone if Stephen was not challenged. 'I see Stephen's merits perfectly well', Morley wrote:

> but they are not at all likely to escape notice, for they fit in with the most marked qualities of our countrymen. His merits are exactly the thing which make it most desirable to point out his demerits; otherwise, the one will help to disguise and pass off the other. If there were any danger of the truth of his contentions being passed over, I wld. not for the world press on his errors . . . But there is no such danger: because what is true in his book is only after all a sort of long-winded and pompous *Amen* to a number of propositions wh. Englishmen have accepted for hundreds of years and acted on—we have to prove that we are as fond of order & good government & as firm for it as Stephen is— and yet without bluster, swagger, bounce, brutality; that we recognise as clearly as he does the hard facts of the world, and know as well as he that they cannot be evaded by fine phrases and soft-sawder; but that it is one thing to face them with the dignity and calm of a man like Marcus Aurelius and another thing to go at them like Bill Sikes.[23]

When the second edition of his *Liberty, Equality, Fraternity* appeared in 1874 Stephen acknowledged that in the interval since the first printing, its arguments had been 'very generally criticized'. He had thus decided to preface the new version with some comments on the 'representative' criticisms of Messrs Morley and Harrison. His answer to Morley's *Fortnightly Review* critique was that 'the wise minority are the rightful masters of the foolish majority, and that it is mean and cowardly in them to deny the right to coerce altogether for fear of its being misapplied as against themselves'.[24]

Harrison's defence of the Comtist separation of 'Thought' and 'Force', and his emphatic assertion of the organic and spiritual basis of society in opposition of Stephen's 'mechanistic authoritarianism', struck the author of *Liberty, Equality, Fraternity* as a mere 'bag of words which means anything, everything, or nothing, just as you choose'.[25] Harrison, who found Stephen's 'literary brutality' almost unbearable, was thus confirmed in a view he had expressed in an earlier letter to Morley. 'It seems to me', he had written, 'that Stephen's Indian experiences have not worked him *good*. He is grown brutal, domineering, & noisy. There is a sense of '300,000,000 niggers' to be kept quiet about his ideas of religion, & he writes like a man who has been touched with "Punjab-Heat"—if you know what that is.'[26]

Stephen's *Liberty, Equality, Fraternity* must be taken into account as an important influence in the development of Maine's later political thought. In *Popular Government*, Maine refers to the work as 'admirable',[27] and certain portions of Stephen's book, especially his lengthy chapter on 'Equality', have a clear bearing on specific points of Maine's own later analysis of democracy. It had been the object of Stephen's book 'to examine the doctrines which are rather hinted at than expressed by the phrase "Liberty, Equality, Fraternity",' for he believed it to be 'something more than a motto. It is the creed of a religion, less definite than any one of the forms of Christianity, which are in part its rivals, in part its antagonists, and in part its associates, but not on that account the less powerful.'[28] Maine's *Popular Government* essays, written ten years later on the eve of the Third Reform Bill, provided a companion study to Stephen's *Liberty, Equality, Fraternity* in substituting for his friend's analysis of each of these three ideological subdivisions of the emerging democratic creed clearly related discourses on what seemed to him the three most likely practical defects of the new type of rule: the fragility of its constitutional form, the difficulties that arose from managing its complex institutions as compared with those of other regimes, and the antiprogressive tendencies that had revealed themselves during past attempts at attaining 'popular government'. Stephen had concentrated on the logical and practical problems associated with the *creed* of democracy, and Maine was soon to add to these certain reservations concerning its *institutions*, reservations whose authority derived, as he contended, from the findings of the 'historical and comparative' method. Moreover, both were agreed on the need to combat the arguments of the new type of utilitarian radicalism with others derived from earlier, more authoritarian strains, of that same doctrine.

While Maine found much to admire in Stephen's political views, however, he did not always share the opinions of his colleague and former pupil. In a review essay of Fitzjames's recently published *Introduction to the Indian Evidence Act*, which appeared in the *Fortnightly* for January 1873, Maine provided some significant clues to the major similarities and differences in their outlooks as philosophers of Anglo-Indian administration. Like Stephen, Maine had little patience with the *laissez-faire* or 'do-nothing' school of Indian policy-makers, and he praised Stephen's adaptation of the English rules for determining the admissibility of evidence for use in Indian courts of law as an enterprising addition to Indian law reform. The conservative Whigs, the Manchester Liberals, and the Tory paternalists who opposed the transformation of Indian institutions by means of positive acts of legislation seemed to Maine altogether naïve on the facts of political life in the British Empire. The exercise of power could be ignored but its consequences never avoided, and as Maine contended,[29] if it was not administered by the positive legislative action of the Government of India, then initiative would only come to rest elsewhere:

> If the Indian legislature were abolished, legislation would not be arrested. It is not a gratuitous, but an inevitable and never-ceasing process. If, (to employ Austin's phraseology) the commands of the Sovereign are not issued through the special organ called the Legislature, another set of commands will be issued through Courts of Justice; and so far as regards India, these last commands will, from the nature of the case, scarcely ever even make a pretence of being adjusted to equity or expediency. The obscurity with which what is really a simple truth appears to be apprehended is probably due to our habit of assuming that the common distinction between executive, legislative, and judicial power is absolutely accurate and exhaustive.

He shared Stephen's view that it was literally a waste of valuable time to deplore the British corruption of Indian customary practices, for whether or not Calcutta or the India Office acted directly, he had

191

long since urged in his juridical studies that 'the indirect effect of English government was, from the first, enormously to quicken the springs of social activity, principally by breaking up that common life of families and communities by which they have been retarded'.[30] Change in India, as in all traditional societies in contact with the progressive West, was thus inevitable, and the only relevant question in the circumstances was what philosophy of change was to be pursued.

It was on precisely this point that Maine and Stephen differed. The author of *Ancient Law* believed the scientific historian was in a position to discern clues as to the processes governing historical change, and indeed Maine prided himself that his professional career had been largely devoted to an effort at making such information freely available to the rulers of British India. Yet there pervaded his India Office dispatches a constant element of caution in the face of schemes that, in his estimation, were designed to effect too rapid a dislocation of customary practices. Thus, while he thought Stephen's proposed Indian Evidence Act a worthy attempt to transplant in India the best experience of English efforts to devise wise rules governing the admission of legal evidence, he was nonetheless certain that the reform would need further modifications after a period of exposure to the actual conditions of Indian society. As he submitted:

It may be suspected that, after more experience of its working has been gained by the servants of the Indian Government, who will henceforward be universally familiar with it, a certain number of its rules will be found, so far as India is concerned, to require modification. The reasons for this opinion may be thus stated. The rules of evidence are founded on propositions concerning human nature and conduct which are approximately true. When, however, we are transferring a system from England to a country so far removed from it, morally and mentally, as India, we cannot be quite sure that all the propositions which are roughly true of one people and one state of society are in the same degree true of another people and another social state. Still less can we be sure that the relative truth of rules founded on propositions of this sort is the same in the two countries.[31]

Maine had always believed that when traditional institutions clashed with modern, it was the old that must give way, but he never quite succeeded in concealing in his Indian utterances a note of

192

nostalgia, a melancholy recognition that much that was tried and familiar must be sacrificed in the exchange. In contrast, Stephen held an almost aggressive preference for British institutions. As he wrote characteristically of the Indian village community, in a chapter dealing with his Indian legislation that he contributed to Sir William Hunter's *Life of Lord Mayo:*

> The historical interest of these institutions and their durability speak for themselves; but the merits of an institution are not to be measured either by its durability or by its historical interest. The fact that the institutions of a village community throw light on the institutions of modern Europe, and the fact that village communities have altered but little for many centuries, prove only that society in India has remained for a great number of centuries in a stagnant condition, unfavourable to the growth of wealth, intelligence, political experience, and the moral and intellectual changes which are implied in these processes. The condition of India for centuries past shows what the village communities are really worth. Nothing that deserves the name of a political institution at all can be ruder or less satisfactory in its results. They are in fact a crude form of socialism, paralyzing the growth of individual energy and all its consequences.[32]

The author of *Liberty, Equality, Fraternity* entertained no doubt as to the agency that was chiefly responsible for the 'growth of individual energy' in the British Empire. His support was unreservedly on the side of the imperial soldier-administrator class who, like Hobbes's *Leviathan,* need not apologize for achieving peace and order through compulsion, who need have no qualms over their replacement of the brutish oppression of the Indian 'state of nature' with British law backed up by the enlightened restraint of British military power. Stephen regarded Maine's guiding theory of 'status to contract' as merely another way of saying that 'force changes its form' as societies grow to maturity, and thus as a vindication of his belief that compulsion underlay progress.[33] For Maine however, with his finer feel for institutions, force taken alone was never an adequate means for maintaining society, just as for him the Austinian 'command theory' of sovereignty was never able to provide a comprehensive view of law. He must have viewed Fitzjames's exuberant admiration of the conquests of the British military

193

as embarrassingly simplified, and his adulation of the benefits of British force as unnecessarily overdrawn. Leslie Stephen, in his *Life* of Fitzjames, summarized his brother's correspondence with Lord Lytton at the time of the Delhi durbar in January 1877 when Queen Victoria was proclaimed Empress of India. It is marvellously full of his idealistic enthusiasm:

'I am no poet' he says, 'as you are, but Delhi made my soul burn within me, and I never heard "God save the Queen" or saw the Union Jack flying in the heart of India without feeling the tears in my eyes, which are not much used to tears.' He becomes poetical for once; he applies the lines of 'that feeble poem *Maud*' to the Englishmen who are lying beneath the Cashmire Gate, and fancies that we could say of Hastings and Clive, and many another hero, that their hearts must 'start and tremble under our feet, though they have lain for a century dead.' Then he turns to his favourite 'Christmas Hymn,' and shows how, with certain easy emendations, Milton's announcement of the universal peace, when the 'Kings sate still with awful eye,' might be applied to the *pax Britannicus* in India.[34]

One cannot easily imagine Maine uttering such acts of faith on behalf of any government. If he erred, indeed, it was rather on the side of unquestioned acceptance of another creed. As he had written in *Ancient Law*, Sir Henry believed that the historical process could only be plausibly explained if one assumed the existence of an unequal distribution of moral genius. Such a quality could, he thought, be encouraged in unprogressive societies by a general reform of their civil law, but its appearance could never be predicted with certainty. And while he held that compulsion was an inescapable burden of world power, he felt strongly that the British were not on that account relieved of the obligation to assist the subjects of their conquests in their gradual transition from the unprogressive social arrangments of traditional society to more flexible institutions regulated by the modern regimen of contract. If the attempt failed, the long-term result would only serve to illustrate a truth Sir Henry had long tried to propagate, that societies capable of the disciplined self-interest necessary for the spread of freedom of contract have appeared but seldom on the stage of world history.

J. F. Stephen's Indian thought, in the opinion of Professor Eric

Stokes, represents 'the blending of the Utilitarian zeal for efficiency in government with the Evangelical sense of mission and race'.[35] For Maine, whose historical scholarship had lead him to the view that it was wise to avoid a wholesale acceptance of the judgement of either of these traditions of Anglo-Indian administration, the dilemma of the imperial ruler was not so easily resolved. The Englishman in India, whatever his political persuasion, was forced into the role of teacher, just as in the specific realm of law, the imperial legal reformer could not avoid the fundamental questions of the jurist. The realization led Maine constantly back to an attempt to effect some sort of plausible compromise between British, Hindu and, Muslim usage, for while he had not a moment's doubt of the superiority of British institutions, yet neither could he in good conscience dismiss the Indian customary law, with its timeless pedigree, as entirely without its usefulness. If nothing else, it served for the time being as at least as effective an instrument for maintaining law and order as British garrisons and Sepoy guns. Maine thus pursued a path of Indian policy different in significant details from that of his old friend. In Maine and Stephen, indeed, whose careers as jurists, Indian administrators, journalists and critics of democracy were otherwise remarkably similar, one detects during this period the embryo of the two leading streams of later nineteenth-century British imperialism:[36] the assertive, evangelical and militaristic variety that found its earliest champion in Stephen's *Liberty, Equality, Fraternity*, and the more subtle and moderate line reflected in Maine's hopes of gradually infusing into the indigenous institutions of the Englishman's unprogressive Aryan kin the necessary catalysts of social progress. Maine's attitudes thus often seem closer to the cautious Burkean element in nineteenth-century intellectual liberalism as it affected imperial doctrine than do those of Stephen. In neither view, of course, would one expect to find an exponent of the argument that the inevitable goal of British rule in India must be self-government. When such a sentiment first came to be widely expressed by the Manchester Liberals, and during the 1870s became influential among other Gladstonian Liberals, then Maine found more that united than divided him philosophically with Stephen, and much that repelled him in party 'Liberalism'. Thereafter, he increasingly banded together with him to do battle with the adherents of the new heresy.

195

16

India and Party Politics

While Maine and Stephen are often cited as leading Victorian spokesmen of intellectual liberalism, neither of them was a supporter of the policies that attracted the dominant element to the British Liberal party after 1867. Upon returning from India they shared the view that there was little to commend the domestic politics of either the Liberals or Conservatives. Disraeli's leadership of the Second Reform Act and his new ideological slogan of 'Tory Democracy' simply confirmed their view of him as a cynical political opportunist willing to expound any plausible doctrine for its Conservative party advantage. Gladstone seemed equally dangerous in pursuing a steady policy of removing control of the Liberal party machinery from the moderating hand of its aristocratic Whiggish elements. Maine would thus have sympathized with Stephen's bitter comment, in a letter of March 1875: 'The truth is that I am neither Tory nor Liberal. I simply hate English politics & do not concern myself with them at all.'[1] Isolated by choice from participation in active politics at home, the two jurists found consolation in addressing their administrative energies during the period to the furtherance of their Indian goals. There is some evidence that they found the leadership of one of the British political parties definitely more enlightened in this sphere. Especially after the Conservative victory in the general election of 1874, there was much that drew them to support the Indian policies of Tory Imperialism over those of Gladstonian Liberalism.

While Maine and Stephen shared a common interest in a wide range of Indian policy questions, they worked together most closely as Indian colleagues during the 1870s in pressing the cause of codification and general legal reform. From the resignation of the third Law Commission in 1870, until the appointment of Lord

Salisbury in early 1874 as Secretary for India in Disraeli's second Cabinet, plans for codifying further departments of Indian law lay largely dormant. Stephen's own extensive additions to the codified law had been based on revised drafts originally drawn up by the defunct Commission. When these were enacted, the supply of pending measures was depleted. Both of the former Legal Members agreed in laying blame for this state of affairs on the new Whig Viceroy, Lord Northbrook, who had been named by Gladstone to succeed the assassinated Lord Mayo in May 1872. 'I do not know', Maine wrote confidentially to Lord Lytton about Northbrook's Legal Member, Arthur Hobhouse:

> whether you have observed that the codification & consolidation of the law of India have been virtually arrested, though the Law Member was created mainly for the purpose of carrying it on. Hobhouse has really done nothing whatever to advance it . . . he is opposed to codification on the same principles that were dear to English lawyers 50 years ago.[2]

The tone of complaint in dispatches coming home from Northbrook's government in India, he wrote to Lord Salisbury, was in danger of establishing itself as a regular feature of the transactions involving the two branches of Indian government. He was impatient that under Hobhouse's incumbency, 'of the branches of Indian government which is growing most in importance, legislation, we [are] allowed to know less than the humblest Baboo in Calcutta'.[3]

When Salisbury succeeded Lord Argyll at the India Office in 1874, Maine immediately began a campaign for the revival of the work of Indian codification. He persuaded the Secretary of State to hire Stephen to prepare a consolidation of all the English statute law affecting India. The measure was subsequently drawn, and further reworked by Maine and Stephen to incorporate various criticisms, but disagreement between the Indian and home governments led to its eventual abandonment.[4] Shortly thereafter, Maine urged upon the Secretary of State the desirability of an entirely new Law Commission composed of Stephen, F. S. Reilly, and himself. Sitting in London, their task would be to carry to the final stages those sections of the proposed substantive civil code still outstanding.[5] While Salisbury was sympathetic to Maine's cause, Northbrook's Government was not co-operative. Arthur Hobhouse complained that: 'The

197

India Office is insisting on codification . . . on purely abstract grounds, with an English Commission to find out laws in India'. He regarded Maine's plan as 'a fine specimen of the *a priori*, abstract, transcendental mode of treating practical subjects which prevails in high quarters just now'.[6] Maine, who thought the charge merely indicative of the real difference of approach between himself and the 'naturalist' school of Whiggish rulers, retorted that Northbrook's 'do-nothing' Council 'perhaps . . . takes too readily for granted that there is insufficient "practical acquaintance with the details of Indian law" in the India Office'.[7] The truth was, Maine wrote to Lord Lytton, that while cautious administrators like Northbrook and Hobhouse complained of the manner in which western reformers meddled in the customary usages of Indian law, whole departments of law were lacking in India. Maine had advanced the proposition in his legal writings that a basic feature of customary law was the dominance of cumbersome procedures over substantive law. The transition of customary law involved a process in which 'substantive law has the look of being gradually secreted in the interstices of procedure'.[8] Since earlier Law Commissions had completed the Penal Code, and Codes of Criminal and Civil Procedure, Sir Henry urged that the next great task of the imperial law reformer was to complete the Civil Code. In order to do so, it would be necessary literally to create the missing departments of civil law:

As to codification in general [he wrote], I fully admit the general truth of your observations on the multiplicity of Indian customs. Yet I venture to assert that any man accustomed to look at legal systems as a whole will agree with me that the great characteristic of Indian customary law is its poverty. The usages, obstinately adhered to, of which you speak, cluster round a comparatively small number of the branches of law; there are great provinces of jurisprudence wholly unrepresented in legislation or custom, and the body of Indian legal rules as a whole is very much like the map of Africa before Livingstone's discoveries.[9]

Northbrook, Maine asserted, was quite wrong to think that by witholding the support of the government of India from his schemes for legal reform he was protecting customary Indian law. 'If these great blanks are not filled by the legislature', he emphasized, 'they will be filled by the Courts of Justice, and the natives will suffer the deep wrong of having a foreign system imposed on them by a process which necessarily has nothing to do with policy or expediency.' The Viceroy's Council, however, were not persuaded to accept the India Office plan for reconvening the Law Commission during Northbrook's tenure of office. Relations between the two governments were decidedly cool throughout the duration of the simultaneous incumbencies of a Whig Viceroy and a Tory Secretary for India.[10] By March 1876 Stephen could note despondently in a letter: 'The government of India throw more or less cold water on the scheme [of codification] & it is at present indefinitely suspended.'[11]

In April 1876 Northbrook resigned, and Disraeli was at last enabled to appoint a Tory, Lord Lytton, to succeed him. Relations between the India Office and Calcutta immediately improved. Maine wrote directly to Lytton shortly after the new Viceroy arrived in India, expressing the hope that Whitley Stokes would be chosen to follow Hobhouse as Legal Member. He was known to Maine to favour codification, and indeed Stokes and Maine had worked closely together in projecting further legislative plans when the Irish philologist went out to head the Legislative Department at Calcutta in 1867. With his friend in the Legal Membership, Sir Henry was confident that 'the scandal of allowing a great undertaking to fall through will be fully recognized and . . . no part of the necessary machinery will be allowed to remain in abeyance'.[12] Characteristically, he also lost no time in forwarding the new Viceroy a copy of the latest edition of *Ancient Law* for his general edification.

As Maine had hoped, the government of India was now decidedly more amenable to proceeding with codification. A dispatch sent home on 10 May 1877 agreed with the Secretary of State that the time was ripe for pressing on with the codification of the substantive law in terms similar to those outlined by Salisbury in an earlier dispatch to Northbrook's Government, dated 20 January 1876. Yet Lytton held to the view that codification should be undertaken in India by a select committee of the Viceroy's Council under the direction of Stokes. On 9 August 1877 Salisbury sanctioned this course, and Stokes immediately set to work on drafting bills covering various departments of the substantive civil law, including Private Trusts, Easements, Alluvion, and Master and Servant. The Transfer of Property Bill and the Negotiable Instruments Bill, earlier drafted by the third Law Commission, were completely redone at the same time.[13] Maine, who had hoped for a full English Commission as a means of overcoming the opposition of the Indian Judges, accepted the procedures adopted by the Viceroy as preferable to a continuation of the complete stalemate in codification. Yet by February 1878 Sir Henry was writing to Salisbury pointing out that obstruction to the work of Stokes had reached serious proportions in India:

> the Government and the Law Member of Council are encountering, in the matter of codification, exactly the same opposition from the Judges and lawyers of the Indian Presidency Towns, which prevented the enactment of the Penal Code for nearly twenty years after its preparation by Lord Macaulay and his colleagues. I always thought that it would be so, and for that reason I greatly preferred the revival of the Law Commission to the system now adopted in India. The old Law Commission was very inconvenient in many respects, but it answered the objects of its authors in enabling the government of India to point out that its codes were in the first instance framed by Judges far more eminent than any Indian judicial functionaries. The Indian Judges are permanent opponents of codification, for the obvious reason that its absence practically permits them to legislate for India; and now there is no Commission to take the edge off their attacks, and the Law Member of Council, though an able and skilful man, is a local lawyer, whose promotion has excited every sort of jealousy.[14]

Faced with these difficulties, the committee approach was eventually abandoned. A new plan originating with the Viceroy called for the creation of a fourth Law Commission which, unlike its immediate predecessor, would be constituted in India rather than in London. While Maine, as a loyal member of Lord Salisbury's Indian Council, naturally preferred the idea of a Commission meeting in England, he nonetheless accepted the Viceroy's formula as, in the circumstances, 'an extremely good one'.[15] He was anxious to placate Stokes whose most recent letters, he wrote to the Viceroy, 'complained bitterly of my want of interest in his labours & seemed to treat any doubts about his Bills as disloyalty to the Great Cause of Codification'.[16] In February 1879 a new Law Commission was announced in accordance with Lytton's scheme, and included Stokes, Sir Charles Turner, the Chief Justice of Madras, and Mr Raymond West of the High Court at Bombay. In a Minute prepared shortly after the Commission was named, Sir Henry urged the commissioners to get on with the task of creating a codified law of tort or civil wrong. 'The absence of a measure on the subject', he wrote, 'is the one great gap in the body of Indian codified law, and one hardly understands the spirit in which a system of this kind could be framed, with a law of contract enacted but a law of tort omitted.'[17]

It was a plea Maine had first pressed on the law commissioners as early as 1864, and during his own tenure of the Legal Membership, had tried to meet with his plan for enacting a measure providing for the specific performance of contract. For one with such faith in the benefits of the widest possible exercise of contract, it seemed a high priority indeed to have codified a department of civil law with the clearest bearing on the encouragement of notions of legal obligation in a society still largely without them. The Commission did appoint Frederick Pollock to draft such a measure, but the emotions surrounding the subject were as much a barrier as they had been in Maine's time in India, and Pollock's drafts were indefinitely suspended. In other areas, the labours of the fourth Law Commission resulted in positive additions being made to the body of existing codified law. In 1881 a Code of Negotiable Instruments was enacted, and in 1882 Codes were added covering Trusts, the Transfer of Property, Easements, as well as revised Codes of Criminal and Civil Procedure. The latest upsurge in the momentum of law reform slowed to a halt in the mid 1880s, and the goal of a completely codified substantive civil law for India remained incomplete. Stokes commented in 1887:

> To all appearances, the Indian Government has at last yielded to influences resembling those which in India pigeon-holed the Penal Code for more than twenty years, and which here in England deprive the nation of the priceless boon of a body of substantive law not only wise, but clear, compact, and easily ascertainable.[18]

In recognition of Maine's strenuous efforts on behalf of Indian codification, Stokes dedicated his large two-volume compendium of *The Anglo-Indian Codes* (1887–8) to him, 'In Gratitude for Wise Teaching, Friendly Encouragement, and Official Support'.

While Maine's primary interest in Indian policy centred in the business of the Legal Department, he found that his attitudes on a wide range of Indian topics increasingly coincided with the spirit of

Salisbury Toryism. Lord Northbrook's cautious Whig outlook, while possessing undeniable virtues in the context of domestic British affairs, seemed to him quite inadequate not only for the needs of Indian legal reform, but for the conduct of most other departments of Indian administration as well. Writing to Lord Lytton about Maine's views of Northbrook's financial policy, for example, J. F. Stephen recalled: 'He spoke as strongly as I wrote about the policy of doing nothing, and having faith in god (a very little "g" this time), as revealed in the laws of political economy.'[19] Another illustration of the differences Maine felt with Northbrook's Liberalism can be seen in Sir Henry's opposition to his plan to raise the minimum and maximum ages of candidates for the Indian Civil Service from the existing 17–21 age limits to the ages of 19–22, a reform which, if carried, would have tended in its operation to dilute the influence of the English public schools in the Service. Maine wrote a lengthy Minute on the question, holding that he would leave the minimum at 17, and 'lower the maximum . . . to 19, if I had my way'.[20] Once candidates had been selected, he favoured their being sent for two years of university residence, a scheme opposed by Northbrook on the grounds that it favoured the retention of close links between Oxford, Cambridge, and the I.C.S. Maine's plan was in fact acted on by Lord Salisbury in 1876, and had the effect of encouraging the creation of an intellectually superior English civil service *corps d'elite* functioning as an exclusive class of Indian administrative guardians.

Maine's opposition to much of Northbrook's policy stood in sharp contrast with his support for most of that of his Tory successor. Thus, Maine wrote to Lord Lytton on 7 June 1878 declaring his full support of Lytton's financial policy as well as his aggressive North-West frontier policy.[21] Earlier that same year he had backed[22] Lytton's controversial Vernacular Press Act, a measure giving the Indian authorities wide powers of censorship over newspapers printed in the Oriental languages that was strongly criticized by Gladstonian Liberals. Maine, like Stephen, was much attracted it seems by the decisive quality of Lytton's Indian policies, as against the cautious Liberalism of his Whig predecessor. As he wrote to the Tory Viceroy: 'Your friends and your enemies alike would call you a very progressive Viceroy . . . it is possible that some men in the Council are just a little scared of you; but even among these I doubt whether there are not some who have the strongest sympathy for parts of your administration.'[23] Sir Henry's flirtation with Tory Imperialism[24] during the incumbencies of Salisbury and Lytton was, moreover, set against a backdrop of growing anti-imperialist sentiment among the ranks of advanced or radical Liberals at home. Gladstone, influenced by the economics of the Manchester Liberals and the moderates' view that Lytton's domestic policies were bound to incite the emerging classes of politically conscious Indians to extremism, worked after 1876 to consolidate British public opinion firmly against a continuation of the Conservative course. When he won a decisive victory at the polls in 1880, it is not surprising that he appointed as his new Viceroy a Liberal statesman capable of radical action to arrest the trends of the previous four years. Lord Ripon's tenure of the viceroyalty,[25] indeed, marks an important turning point in the history of British India, and coincided with a new shift to the left in the internal politics of the Liberal party. When Ripon went to India, he did so with the avowed intention of confronting Toryism as well as Whiggery wherever they presented themselves in the domestic policies of the Indian Government; when he left, it was a matter of months before the Indian National Congress came into being.

Ripon's internal policies consisted, firstly, of attempts to undo the effects of Lytton's previous legislative programme, and secondly, of totally new measures designed to reduce the level of friction between the European and Indian, by affording the indigenous population some greater share in the administration of Indian affairs. With both these goals Maine had little sympathy. Thus, when Ripon pressed for the abolition of the Vernacular Press Act, Maine and General Strachey alone dissented out of the total membership of fifteen on the Indian Council.[26] When the Viceroy urged the election of Indian members to the Imperial Council as a means of attaining accurate intelligence of public opinion in India, Maine advised the Secretary of State, Lord Hartington, against allowing the proposal to stand.[27] When Ripon tried to raise the question of increasing the maximum age for I.C.S. candidates again in 1884, Maine seems to have been 'the secret spring of the opposition' on the Indian Council.[28] If we are to accept the authority of J. F. Stephen, writing to Lord Lytton confidentially in 1882, Maine had in fact early formed an opinion of Ripon as a dangerous advocate of 'sentimental Liberalism' in Indian circles:

I have seen Maine several times lately & hear from him that Ripon, whom he profanely calls 'that bloody little fool', is behaving like the very devil in India—commiting the abominable sin of nigger-worshipping to an accursed degree. I think you might make a most effective assault upon him in the House of Lords, in which I would be delighted to help. I really think you might do your party, your ex-Empire, and your land a service by blowing up the way in which a British Marquis who hates his God may come to worship his nigger. Maine's point is that Ripon's policy is six times more rash and dangerous than anything you were ever accused of.[29]

The end of Ripon's plans for transplanting radical European sentiment to Indian legislation seemed to Maine foreshadowed by such measures as the Bengal Tenancy Bill of 1883. Based on Gladstone's Irish Land Bill of 1881, the legislation aimed to secure fixity of tenure, fair rents, free sales and compensation for disturbance for *ryots* who had held land for twelve years, by curtailing the exercise of freedom of contract by landlords.[30]

It was, however, two further innovations of Ripon's viceroyalty that chiefly aroused Maine's concern for the future of Indian political development at the hands of doctrinaire English Liberalism. The first was Ripon's famous resolution of May 1882 on local self-government.[31] While Sir Henry had supported Lord Mayo's efforts at increasing the amount of financial and administrative decentralization in Indian affairs, the priority which Ripon gave to extending that process threw Maine into a defensive stance. Like a majority of ex-Indian officials at the India Office, Maine was sceptical of the political wisdom of Ripon's scheme for shifting the internal control of his new local boards, wherever possible, from official to elected non-official Indians. He was numbered among those Indian councillors referred to by Sir Richard Cross in a note discussing the Viceroy's resolution, written during March 1883:

Many old Indians are certainly very nervous, and they seem to change their minds along with commonplace utterances coming from almost any quarter. I have noticed this tendency in the Indian Council here, though those who have left India within the last few years are not so affected by their fears as the older men.[32]

The older men on the Council feared that the principle of wider popular participation in Indian government, introduced with such a tone of immediacy by the Viceroy, provided a precedent that would be used by extreme elements of the Indian community to the serious embarrassment of the imperial authorities. Maine himself wrote to Ripon's Legal Member, Courtenay Ilbert, pointing out the uneasiness the Viceroy's plans had aroused in London, 'to some extent owing', he reflected, 'to some expressions which strike me as to be regretted in the Resolution of May, and which seem to hint that the Government of India underrates administration as compared with "political education".'[33]

While Sir Henry was sceptical of the political sagacity of Ripon's local government policy, he was downright alarmed at the recklessness of the Indian government in introducing a measure, on 2 February 1883, that would enable qualified Indians to try European criminals in the *mofussil*. The controversial 'Ilbert Bill',[34] whose fate was to form a basic article of propaganda in the arsenal of Indian nationalists for years to come, was drawn by the Legal Member as a routine measure to cover an anomaly in the application of the principal of equal justice in British India. Since 1877 Indian magistrates had exercised criminal jurisdiction over Europeans in the Presidency Towns, and Ilbert, believing that he had the support of the India Office, proposed to extend that regulation to courts in the countryside, while allowing Europeans rights of appeal and reserving cases involving capital offences for the jurisdiction of the High Courts. In fact, when preliminary papers on Ilbert's Criminal Jurisdiction Bill were forwarded from the India Office to Maine in Paris, where he was on holiday, Sir Henry wrote immediately to the Secretary of State, Lord Hartington, warning him that the measure would almost certainly result in an explosion of racialist protest among European planters. He urged him to write straight away to the Viceroy, pointing out that 'the game [is] not worth the candle'.[35] Hartington, however, through a strange blunder, failed to warn Ripon.[36] The Bill was published, and an agitation against the measure was launched almost immediately. Sir Henry, who in the circumstances assumed that the Viceroy had merely ignored his advice, wrote to his friend Alfred Lyall, who was at the time Lieutenant-Governor of the North-West Provinces, that 'Lord R., not very patient of advice at best, especially detests it when it comes from a retired

Indian, & so he put his hand deep into this hornet's nest'.[37]

The 'Ilbert Bill' produced strong reaction not only in Calcutta, but among those in London who were already suspicious of Ripon. J. F. Stephen wrote several angry letters to *The Times*, denouncing the measure as evidence that Ripon's administration seemed intent on destroying British power in India: 'If we were to remove all anomalies from India', he protested, 'our first step should be to remove ourselves.'[38] Grant Duff wrote to assure Ripon of the support of loyal Liberals, noting that Stephen was 'frantic', and that 'the same tone in your speeches and other authorized documents which has made you so boundlessly popular with the Natives is not agreeable to the "Bismarkian" kind of Briton'.[39] Maine seemed closer to Stephen under the pressures of the agitation, complaining in a note to Ilbert of 'the weak-kneed'ness of people high in office with you'. He thought that 'nothing could be worse than that the Governor-General should use the mechanism of Indian government to produce a particular result, and that then the mechanism should not work in the way intended'.[40] As the controversy continued unabated Sir Henry urged that the Bill be referred to a Commission, 'and a hint might be given to the Commissioners not to report in a hurry'.[41] The home authorities, however, felt that vacillation at this stage would be politically harmful, and pressed the Viceroy's Council for speedy action on a modified version of the Ilbert Bill. By late in 1883 Maine too was of that opinion,[42] and a compromise measure, allowing Indian magistrates to try Europeans in the *mofussil*, while reserving the right to trial by jury with a panel of whom half should be European, was finally enacted.

The controversies of Ripon's viceroyalty brought home to Maine the growing relationship between imperial policy and party politics in England. He was dismayed at the amount of popular sentiment aroused by the recent actions of the Viceroy's Council. He wrote to Arthur Lyall, describing the reaction in London to Ilbert's Criminal Jurisdiction Bill:

> I cannot quite confidently answer your question as to the real temper of public opinion here about Criminal Jurisdiction over Europeans, but my impression is that the feeling is genuine and strong. It is not less so on account of the artificiality of the news by which it was raised. The *Times* Correspondent telegraphs to

Madras a probably exaggerated account of the indignation of the Europeans in India; then *The Times* backs him up mildly; then the article and telegraph are re-telegraphed to Calcutta, producing still stronger statements from the Correspondent, till at last, as the process continues, there is real excitement on both sides.[43]

The point had first been raised by Maine in his *Saturday Review* denunciations of newspaper agitation for army reform during the Crimean War, and it was now revived by his fear of the consequences of the growing intrusion of sentimental British party slogans into Indian affairs.

When the controversy over the Criminal Jurisdiction Bill was at its height, Sir Henry had complained in a letter to Ilbert: 'The members of the present Government of India do not much care to communicate on matters of policy with anybody at the India Office except the Secretary of State.'[44] Two weeks earlier, he had written to Lyall in a similar vein: 'There is reason to believe that [Ripon] has no really confidential correspondence with anybody in this country except Bright.'[45] Given the trends of British party politics, it seemed increasingly likely to Maine that the day was not far off when India might have a Secretary for India and a Viceroy sharing party sentiments even more radical than those of the Manchester Liberals. He was concerned that safeguards should be available to breathe caution into the institutional machinery of imperial government when that time arrived. One potential defence was the Viceroy's Executive Council, but Maine thought the blunders of Ripon's recent policies pointed up serious shortcomings in that body. He wrote to Ilbert, after the outbreak of agitations against the government over the Ilbert Bill:

If you and your colleagues were not prepared for this, it only illustrates what to my mind is a dangerous weakness inseparable from all Governments of India, namely, owing to each member of government having five years at most to serve, and owing to every member retiring practically into private life when he leaves the government, there is no such continuity of knowledge and tradition as other governments possess, though one would say *a priori* that no government needed it more.[46]

In the circumstances, some further check was required, and the framers of the Indian constitution had recognized this in providing for an Indian Council in London. Maine placed great importance on the value to Indian administration of the advisory opinions of the ex-Indians comprising that body, and during the 1870s strove to lengthen the tenure of certain of its members as a means of adding to their effective say in the policy-making process.[47] As he wrote to Lord Lytton in 1878: 'The Council is a highly Conservative body, as a whole. Conservatism is the reason for its existence, for it was expressly created to maintain the stability of Indian Government.'[48] Yet by the early 1880s, the Indian Council itself seemed in danger of falling victim to party politics. Maine at least felt this to be the case in reflecting in a letter to Arthur Lyall that 'Radicals do not like the notion of any authority interposed between India and a probably Radical Parliament, and Lord Ripon is said to support this view, though his dislike of the Council really rests on other grounds.'[49] During the viceroyalty of Ripon's successor, Lord Dufferin, various plans for a parliamentary inquiry into Indian government were in fact widely entertained. Maine felt certain that if the question of continuing the Council were ever raised while the House was dominated by Gladstonian Liberals, its future would be short-lived, and indeed, by 1885 he was unwilling to predict the likelihood of its continuation. He wrote confidentially to Arthur Lyall: 'I may possibly have elected to stick to the Indian Council just when it is to be abolished . . . Ripon of course does his level best against it, professedly because it obstructs the flow of British benevolence into India, really because we are suspected of imperfect sympathy with Manchesterism.'[50] When Lord Randolph Churchill became Secretary for India in Salisbury's brief 1885 Conservative Government, and at first seemed as amenable as the Liberals to a parliamentary inquiry, Maine urged him to confine the scope of any such enquiry 'to the forms and mediums of government and not . . . the question how particular classes of men have discharged their duties',[51] a request he presumably felt would discourage emotional partisanship. In the event, Churchill changed his mind about the political wisdom of proceeding with an investigation, Gladstone became preoccupied with Ireland after the return of the Liberals in early 1886, and the question was indefinitely set aside.

Maine was a man of his age in supporting the exercise of British power in India. While he was not blind to the shortcomings of Anglo-

Indian administration, he believed the certain alternative to it was anarchy. Sir Henry was by no means a racialist. Indeed, his historical studies did much to show the common racial origins of Englishmen, Indians and Irish, at a time when such a suggestion was bound to raise eyebrows. Yet Maine accepted on faith that the Indian was morally backward as compared with the best examples of European civilization, and believed that gap could only be closed through the long-term operation of European institutions upon the static society of the East. Such a goal required conditions of political stability, and Maine in later life became less prone to deny that British military power since the Mutiny was, in the final analysis, the arbiter of Indian peace. While he was never so preoccupied with this fact as his friend Stephen, it is an interesting aside that Sir Henry's last act of importance at the India Office during this period was the preparation of documents 'legitimizing' the British annexation of Upper Burma on 1 January 1886.[52] In pursuit of the necessary conditions for the realization of his goals of domestic Indian reform, Maine was drawn into the vortex of imperialism.

It was largely this development in Maine's Indian thought that led him to accept the view that the institutions of Anglo-Indian government did not in themselves provide sufficient assurance against the spread of radical sentiment in India. If anything, he had become concerned with the extent to which people associated with those institutions seemed amenable to those views. Thus, when Sir William Wedderburn, a radical Bombay Civilian who later served as President of the Indian National Congress, made known his desire to obtain a post at the India Office, Sir Henry wrote in protest to the Secretary of State, noting: 'I have always understood Wedderburn's "great desire" to be to set up in England as a permanent Indian agitator, and his desire is probably now stimulated by the prospect of a series of Parliamentary Committees.'[53] Alfred Lyall, with his more recent first-hand knowledge of the movement of ideas in India, wrote that the result of the efforts of such well-meaning Englishmen was that 'the rising generation of educated natives is displaying much jealousy of the English officials in India; it may culminate in a struggle for official emoluments and political power that will force on some vital issues, since if the ambitious native gets power he will certainly use it'.[54] Maine, who had all along felt that one of the most unfortunate results of the controversy surrounding the 'infernal

209

Ilbert Bill' was 'to produce a disposition in high places to regard political partisanship as the first qualification even for Judgeships',[55] responded that Lyall's observations simply confirmed a fear he had long harboured. He noted despondently that 'the native cavils I have seen appear to be mere echoes of supposed British opinion, and are mostly founded on the grossest ignorance'.[56] Maine, with the impatience characteristic of the bureaucratic expert, accepted the argument of his friend Stephen, that Gladstonian Liberal slogans about self-government and political equality were merely hollow words in Indian conditions. Concerned for the future of British imperial hegomony in an age of emerging radical sentiment, he turned in later life to meet the challenge of these new ideas in their British breeding ground, by examining them in the light of his 'historical and comparative' method.

The *St James's Gazette*

Analysing the election results of 1880 in the May *Fortnightly Review*, John Morley concluded that the impressive Liberal victory of that year represented 'the first occasion . . . on which, after a long campaign in one great pitched battle, the party of justice, moderation and peace, have routed the party of aggression, intrigue, and lawless national vanity'.[1] Viewing the political struggle of 1880 with such clear notions of right and wrong, the radical Morley, though he lost his own seat in the parliamentary constituency of Westminster, had good reason to be happy with the returns, which gave Gladstone's Liberals 347 seats, the Conservatives 240, and the Irish Nationalists 65. Sir Stafford Northcote, House leader of the defeated Tories, complained that there were no fewer than 113 'extreme or unclassed Radicals' in the new Parliament, and it was indeed certain that the efforts of Joseph Chamberlain's radical 'Birmingham caucus' had played a significant role in Gladstone's victory. The National Liberal Federation, under Chamberlain's leadership, had won sixty of the sixty-seven seats it contested, thus laying the foundation for the uneasy Liberal alliance of Whigs and radical reformers that characterized Gladstonian politics during the early 1880s.[2]

Morley well realized that the new House, with a membership that included besides Chamberlain and Sir Charles Dilke such radicals as G. B. Firth, Thorold Rogers, Jesse Collings and Henry Broadhurst, would interpret 'justice, moderation and peace' as meaning the elimination of privilege and the sweeping reform of social abuses. Frederic Harrison likewise sensed an historic watershed in British politics, and urged Sir Charles Dilke, who had seconded Trevelyan's 1879 Resolution calling for the extension of the franchise to agricultural labourers, to abandon the old '*stick-in-the-mud* Radicals' and form an altogether new party on the strength of the emerging parliamentary pattern of forces. There was an air of historical immediacy in his tone, for as the positivist philosopher believed: 'Unless this is done, there will be a swaying back again some day and in 1886 the old trick of 1874 will be played over again. The Tory is only stunned. He must be killed. And not only killed—but put in his coffin and not only put in his coffin, but screwed down with a brass plate nailed on the top.'[3]

Maine was a close enough observer of British domestic politics to be alarmed by the widespread acceptance of such professions of radicalism after the election of 1880. Influential public figures, like Dilke, were known as professed republicans, increasingly outspoken in their view that the trappings of monarchy were inconsistent with popular government. The House of Lords was almost casually ridiculed in radical literature as an outmoded anachronism that blocked the pure expression of the majority will. Men whom Maine had long regarded as responsible politicians now calmly conceded in growing numbers that the logical sequence of Disraeli's Reform Bill of 1867 was yet a third extension of the franchise that would admit the uneducated and propertyless agricultural labourer to the voting lists. Others among the leadership of the swollen Liberal ranks, Sir Henry was convinced, had had no sincere wish to see British institutions democratized at all, and like Faust, would soon pay heavily for their acceptance of the radical support that guaranteed Gladstone's electoral majority. 'The moment for redeeming the pledge has come as rapidly as the term of compact with the devil,'[4] he wrote bitterly soon after the announcement that Chamberlain and Bright had been included in the Cabinet. Like his friend Stephen, he felt 'every day more & more disgusted with English public affairs. In them, as it seems to me, there is no salvation & in another generation, I am inclined to think politics will be a trade which no gentleman & no one who really respects himself or herself (for I suppose it will be open to women) ought to follow.'[5] Thus, as the years passed, Sir Henry, preoccupied with the revelation of his historical studies that most of mankind abhorred change, was clearly among those John Morley had in mind when he wrote to Gladstone:

For myself, I have always felt that the scientific specialist is the most likely of all to lose the social and humane point of view. His mind is inevitably narrowed, I fear, by the narrowness and inti-

212

mateness of the specialist's conception of Truth, and this narrow view of Truth chokes his care for Freedom and Humanity.[6]

Anxious to put on record his fundamental opposition to the teachings of the 'New Radicalism', Sir Henry turned to a means of political expression he had made frequent use of in the past: the unsigned newspaper article.

During the 1870s we know that Sir Henry had continued his connections in London journalism, contributing leaders fairly frequently to Frederick Greenwood's brilliantly edited *Pall Mall Gazette*.[7] Greenwood's editorial policy at the time was built on firm support of the Conservatives, although officially the newspaper insisted that its political line amounted to 'strong but independent support' of the Government. Yet Greenwood's political party sentiment was scarcely concealed: when Maine returned from India, for example, he is reported to have asked George Smith 'if the *Pall Mall* had been sold to the Conservatives',[8] so strong was the bias. And it is an interesting aside that, as J. W. Robertson Scott convincingly shows in his history of the *Pall Mall Gazette*, Greenwood played an important part in the purchase by the British government of the Khedive's Suez Canal shares in 1875. No other single act of statesmanship did so much to advance the cause of imperial sentiment, firstly by bringing India and surrounding territories over 4,000 miles closer to direct British control, and secondly by opening up Africa to the further expansion of British influence. When the Liberals won the 1880 election, the newspaper changed hands, and the new proprietor, Henry Yates Thompson, brought strong pressure on Greenwood to support Gladstone's anti-imperialist domestic and foreign policy. Greenwood flatly refused, and resigned from the paper early in May 1880. John Morley, who was closer to Thompson's advanced Liberal views, immediately was named editor. Within a month, however, Greenwood had organized a new evening newspaper, the *St James's Gazette, an Evening Review and Record of News*, which was intended to continue the representation of the Conservative point of view. The Gladstonian Liberal, Lord Acton, wrote in a letter of 23 May 1880 to the Prime Minister's daughter: 'The animosity of the defeated party is natural, manifest, and invincible. They have offered Greenwood £110,000 for his newspaper,

213

besides general offers of indefinite sums—enough to start it four or five times over.'[9]

Most of Greenwood's *Pall Mall* writers, including Maine, left with him to join the staff of the new *St James's*, which, as J. W. Robertson Scott commented, 'Although professedly independent . . . preached almost the full Tory faith'. While we do not have a record of Maine's articles for the *Pall Mall*, we are fortunate enough to know something of his journalistic activity on the *St James's*. Indeed, when the first number of the new Greenwood paper appeared on 31 May 1880 it is significant that the unsigned leader, 'The Future of Political Ignorance', which heavily criticized the Liberals for their widely rumoured plan to enfranchise the agricultural labourer, was from Maine's pen. In one of the notebooks of the *Maine Collection* at the British Library of Political and Economic Science, there is interspersed on loose foolscap sheets a list acknowledging his contributions for the period 31 May 1880 to 31 December 1881, which identifies upwards of 130 of his lengthy articles on current political trends.[10] The topics of these anonymous essays—criticisms of Gladstone's Irish land policies, advocacy of protectionist tariffs, support of an imperialist foreign policy, opposition to further measures of political enfranchisement—show clearly the extent of Sir Henry's profound disillusionment with the goals of Gladstonian Liberalism.

Few measures introduced during Gladstone's second administration angered Sir Henry more than his proposals for Irish land reform, for they represented to him the latest example of a dangerous trend he had been watching during his adult lifetime. He had found little to complain of in the original Landlord and Tenant (Ireland) Act of 1860, for it had specifically recognized that the relationship of Irish landlord and tenant should be based on freedom of contract and not on tenure or service. Prepared only a few months before the publication of *Ancient Law*, the Act thus seemed to vindicate the major thesis of that book. In 1870, however, in hopes of curbing the continued practice of rack-renting and arbitrary eviction in Ireland, Gladstone had enacted a further measure which introduced the precedent of regulating the landlord's absolute right of disposal, by granting the peasant tenant's rights of compensation in certain cases of eviction. The legislation proved at best partially effective in fixing tenures and stabilizing rents, and when poor harvests in 1879–80

214

again brought landlord and tenant to the verge of a land war in Ireland, Gladstone committed his new Government to a fresh attempt at solving their differences. The cornerstone of his latest plan was the controversial Irish Land Act of 1881 under which a land court was to be charged with fixing judicious rents in Ireland. Once the three Commissioners had fixed a rate of rental, it would remain at that level for fifteen years, and tenants would only be removed if the court could be persuaded that a serious infringement of tenancy had taken place. In order to resume possession of the land after a further fifteen years, the landlord must receive the prior permission of the court, and moreover, tenants were to be encouraged to purchase their holdings outright with government loans of up to three-quarters of their cost.[11]

Maine's *St James's Gazette* articles illustrate that he viewed these developments as a serious reversal of the trend away from status towards free contract. Writing in an age when government intervention in the regulation of economic affairs was still largely unknown, Sir Henry joined forces with aristocratic Whigs and Salisbury Tories in arguing that to tamper with private property and free contract was to open the floodgates 'to those who hold the land of every country to the common patrimony of all born on it'.[12] He agreed with the Whiggish Argyll (who resigned from the Liberal Government over the Land Act) as he seldom did on Indian matters, that the logical conclusion of such meddling in British economic affairs was 'a Communistic attack on the legitimacy of property in land'.[13] He also shared Salisbury's grim amusement at the spectacle of a Liberal Prime Minister being pushed to the brink of radical chaos by his acceptance of the support of the Manchester school of political economists, yet utterly overlooking the fundamental laws of political economy in attempting to satisfy their reformist impulses:

> Political economy could not be better described than as the science which establishes and states the results of free contract working on established ownership . . . Property in land, as an institution, has claims to be regarded as the form of property which it is the least safe to violate . . . the recognition of its ownership has become a standard by which advance in civilization can be measured, while dimness of recognition shows a recoil to barbarism. Wherever it is really in peril, we are at the beginning of the end.[14]

215

Gladstone's Land Act of 1881 struck Maine as better suited to the needs of a civilization altogether devoid of notions of separate property than to those of Ireland, and indeed he thought the proposed new courts rather reminiscent of the means that had been employed by the British to guarantee equitable conditions in the communal soil of India. The imposition of such a regimen upon the economic practices of a country already exposed to the revolutionary idea of individual rights would curtail the progressive aspirations of even the more backward of its contracting classes. 'If it be true that the Irish peasantry are incapable of entering into free contracts', he wrote in reflecting on the relevance of his *Ancient Law* to Liberal land policy, then:

> this is the same thing as saying that they are incapable of forming a judgement on their own interests. The propositions are, in fact, identical. In that case somebody else must form a judgement for those who cannot form one on their own. The sociological rule which affirms that the progress of society is from status to contract only expresses one aspect of the truth that societies in time become civilized and free because the individuals contained in them learn to manage their own affairs, instead of requiring other persons to manage for them.[15]

Sir Henry, on this assumption, would revoke Gladstone's 'artificial' restrictions on the economic activity of the Irish contracting classes, for the government's declared policy of 'giving one man's property to another . . . [and] . . . restrict[ing] the liberty of men to make contracts in their own interests' was bound to have the effect of relegating the abler contractor, who was the real catalyst of social change, to stultifying new conditions of proprietary status.[16] In his eagerness to defend established property against radical reformers, Sir Henry was thus doubtless prone to see the virtues of the landlord and to ignore the very real plight of the vast majority of the 'contracting classes'. While the impoverished Irish tenant may very well have understood his own interests, the principles of 'freedom of contract' and 'liberty' were certain to remain mere hollow phrases so long as he was without a reasonable share of political and economic power. It is worth remembering that during the same period that Maine wrote for the *St James's Gazette*, his old Oxford colleague T. H. Green, in a seminal lecture delivered before the Liberal

216

Association of Leicester on 'Liberal Legislation and Freedom of Contract', gave a popular rendition of a philosophical theme he had long urged upon his academic contemporaries—that government action could legitimately be employed to secure new types of 'positive freedom' for all classes of society alike. Maine did not offer a realistic alternative to the use of positive government regulation to achieve a wider distribution of the benefits of free contract in Ireland. Instead, he fell back on the argument he had first developed during the tenure controversies that arose in Bengal, Oudh and the Punjab while he was in India: 'Property is nothing if it be not old.'[17]

Maine's critique of Gladstone's Irish policy was but one facet of a general denunciation of the ominous principles he thought were being introduced by the 'New Radicalism' under the auspices of the Liberal Government. In an early *St James's* article on 'Radicalism Old and New', Sir Henry set out the reasons for his concern. Looking back over his lifetime, he thought the period 1830–80 was unparalleled in British political history as 'the one half-century during which all, or nearly all, English institutions were reconstructed—peacefully and without revolution or serious convulsion'. He acknowledged that it was neither Whig nor Tory who had made this possible, but the radical Benthamite writers on the *Westminster Review*. Yet while Maine had often in the past castigated these radical reformers, he now gave them credit that 'the very originality of their scheme consisted in their proposal to reconstruct society without violence, revolutionary or legislative. Property and contract were not only to be maintained, but were to be made the agencies by which the material existence of the entire community was to be improved.'[18] Nothing, he thought, could be further from the goals of the newer radicalism that had increasingly shown itself in British affairs since 1867, and which had become 'entirely fluid, taking all shape and direction from the accidental and temporary pressure of great masses of ignorant and impulsive men'.[19] While Maine, like J. F. Stephen, thus attempted to turn elements of Benthamite and Millian utilitarianism against a newer generation of radical politicians who claimed them as their intellectual champions, he nonetheless held Bentham ultimately responsible for the current state of affairs. Bentham had believed common people could not misunderstand their own interests, while Maine now insisted that, so far as the majority of mankind was concerned:

217

To speak plainly, he grossly underrated human stupidity; and thus he blinded himself to the probability that the more widely political power was distributed, the larger would be the amount of dullness and ignorance allowed to exercise influence on human affairs.[20]

Around this theme, Sir Henry developed out of the mundane issues of Westminster politics during his *St James's* period—the Ground Game Act, the Compensation for Disturbance Bill, the Bradlaugh case, Parnellite obstruction of parliamentary procedures, the Bribery Commission Reports, the 'Quixotism' of Gladstonian foreign policy, the latest Liberal franchise and redistribution proposals—a thoroughly pessimistic appraisal of the future prospects of British liberty.

Maine's *St James's* view of the nature of political leadership, which chiefly underlay his impatience with the rising generation of democratic partisans, was really an extension of beliefs he had first expressed in the pages of the *Saturday Review* during the 1850s, now deepened by a lifetime's apprenticeship as an historical scholar. As in that earlier period, Sir Henry held firmly to what one might call his 'cyclical theory of political *élitism*', in which the historical process was depicted as the unfolding of a constantly regenerated aristocratic pattern of rule:

> The true authors of human improvement are aristocracies, if the word 'aristocracy' be properly understood. A privileged class arises because it is stronger and wiser than others. Rejoicing in its strength, it instructs and civilizes itself. Very often the knowledge and skill which it has acquired is diffused beyond its limits. It constantly happens that this larger portion thus obtains new strength, at the same time that it becomes conscious of new appetites; and then it excludes its predecessors from their monopoly, or insists on sharing it. But the old process only recommences. Aristocracy rises on the decay of aristocracy, and the world makes progress by one privileged class pushing another from its seat.[21]

While he believed good birth was the single most important criteria of likely succession to positions of political influence in most societies, Maine allowed that: 'Men with great direct capacity for government, or with great capacity for exercising the arts which in these times serve as substitutes for government, do constantly arise

218

from the classes which never, as a whole, give proof of fitness to rule'. Yet he reaffirmed his long-held view that 'These men are really accidents; they belong, as gardeners say of flowers, to the class of "sports".'[22] Long before the appearance of the works of the continental 'political sociologists' Gaetano Mosca and Vilfred Pareto, Robert Michels and M. I. Ostrogorski, Maine had thus established his own pioneering analyses of political *élitism* in a series of articles written in the period 1855–82.

Maine's political writings in the *St James's* differ significantly from those of his *Saturday Review* days in their frequent preoccupation with tracing the implications of a subsidiary theory he had constructed to describe the phenomena of popular revolutions. In a remarkable article on 'Signs of the Times' this second 'cyclical theory' is given its fullest statement. The sentiment behind the following extract from that essay is basic to an understanding of Maine's *Popular Government*:

First, a disorderly minority spreads alarm through society. Alarm is followed by a sense of helplessness. Then a functionary appointed to discharge a definite set of duties breaks through the rules which constitute his office; a *coup d'etat* is struck, and society is saved. Next, except in the minds of the few, there is a general feeling of relief; and from all but a few there is a chorus of applause. What follows is always the same. The community whose rights have been usurped hastens to place the whole of its powers in the hands which saved it from its own hesitations and from the anarchy to which its hesitations had conducted it. A Prince President is empowered to dictate Organic Laws; a Speaker is requested to make and publish rules for Urgent Business. A despotism, orderly, effective, not outwardly oppressive, but fatal to liberty in one case and to the Constitution in the other, has been established, and like all despotisms, tends steadily to draw all branches of affairs within its sphere . . . Saviours of society are often as far as possible from heroes: they have constantly more than their share of the weaknesses of human nature, they are idle and luxurious; they are sometimes visionaries, and occasionally madmen. It looks however, as if in the modern world the true objection to dictatorships as finally solving the political riddle is that human life is so frail. A form of government dependent on a central force which

219

the progress of discovery and invention is always making it more and more easy to annihilate is one with which mankind will never permanently be satisfied . . . It will be strange if, in the absolute governments which seem so likely to rise on the ruins of democracy, short reigns with violent ends are to alternate with the long ascendancy of a secluded maniac.[23]

Maine explicitly links the rise of such dictatorships with the advent of democracy. Without the 'worship of numbers' there would be no scope for demagogues. What concerned Sir Henry was that modern 'speculative Liberalism' seemed to equate the growth of world population with the need for wider participation in the management of political affairs. Yet in the teachings of Thomas Malthus, Maine readily found support for his view that 'there is no virtue in numbers'. Malthus had suggested as a solution to the coming crisis of population growth that mankind should check their own multiplication, but Maine felt that while such a plan might find adherents in the progressive strata of society, it was a sobering reflection that 'the races which tend most to multiply and to elbow out the others under the conditions of modern society are the imperfectly civilized races, and those which have no affection for liberty either in Church or State'.[24] The real lesson of Malthus, he submitted, was that 'the direction of human progress is, after all, towards aristocracy', for the 'chronic difficulty of the human race as it multiplies demands, as one alternative remedy for it, an aristocracy of intellect.' If not, and democracy appeared for its brief moment before falling victim to the demagogic manipulation of popular revolutionary heroes, then 'another aristocracy is inevitable, and this will be an aristocracy of force'.[25]

Maine's exploration of the foundations of democratic government, in a large series of articles ostensibly written on the subject of Gladstone's proposals for enfranchising the argicultural labourer, lead him to cast a sentimental glance backward at the traditional British political system. Before the impact of philosophical radicalism had made itself felt in the first quarter of the nineteenth century, he surmised, British government had been conducted by aristocratic factions and thus, there had been no hypocritical assumption 'that the masses understood the questions to be debated in Parliament'. The old system relied on:

the tendency of a certain part of the community to break away from one faction and vote upon occasion with the other. This 'third party' ought to consist [he continued], and as a fact generally did consist, of the educated portion of the community frightened by the excesses of one side or disgusted by the blindness and obstinacy of the other.[26]

The unfortunate difference with democracy was that in 'first ascertaining the average opinion of all persons whatsoever who in any community are controlled by government or affected by law, and then [of] founding all government and law on this average opinion',[27] it was assumed that every man *has* a political opinion, and that each required a secret ballot to express it. 'It turns out', Maine suggested to the contrary, 'that large numbers of voters have no such opinion; and meantime the Ballot has destroyed the chief moral force which kept this class relatively pure—namely, the disapprobation of their friends and fellows, incurred by disloyalty to their colours.'[28] While Maine was aware that the investigations of the recent Bribery Commission had revealed substantial injustices in the electoral practices of the traditional British political system, he thought it naïve to assume that a simple piece of legislation like the Corrupt Practices Act (1883) would completely remove such corruption from a democratic body politic. Democracy, indeed, would merely substitute its own brand of corruption. Was not, he asked, the invention of 'Liberal Hundreds, Two Hundreds, and Four Hundreds', and the renovation of the Conservative Associations—each of which was to devote sizeable amounts of its time to 'attempts to "organize" an opinion which, among a certain section of the voters, has no existence whatever'—a subtle form of moral corruption?[29] Was not the democratic electoral prospect of 'the gradual debauching of a constituency by "nursing" it, by going to live in it or near it, by spreading your charity far and wide, and by sending your wife to call on everybody else's wife' another example?[30] In an unsigned 1880 article on 'The Whigs', written to commend the aristocratic Whiggish elements of the Liberal party for their blockage of Gladstone's Compensation for Disturbance (Ireland) Bill, Sir Henry showed how far were his own political preferences from recent trends in Liberal party politics. Opposing the widespread suggestion that these Whigs should cross over to the Conservative side and desert the Gladstonian Liberals altogether, he reflected nostalgically:

Those who, like ourselves, would make a stand against the blind hurry of Radicalism, cannot desire that these natural Conservatives should lose their power of restraining its onward rush by planting themselves in front of it.

There was indeed much that Maine, as a man of property and modern science, could not help but admire in their aristocratic outlook:

> Its coolness, its judiciousness, its attachment to the past, not because it is venerable or beautiful, but because it was the cradle of a particular set of political principles and of a certain order of society belonging to them[31]

If he had latterly opposed progressive Liberals and Whigs alike in leaning to the Tories' Indian policy, there was less that divided him from the Whigs in domestic politics. Indeed, had he not already found comfort in Tory Imperialism of the Salisbury variety during the 1870s, he would doubtless have been numbered among the non-party Whigs who drifted towards Toryism over the issues of Irish Home Rule and agricultural enfranchisement in 1880–6.[32]

Maine's *St James's Gazette* articles on democracy often have the rather despondent tone of one writing of a *fait accompli*, and certainly Sir Henry thought the new regime of 'popular government' had been guaranteed by the reforms of 1867. It thus remained only to suggest means of guarding against its excess. Maine thought he saw in recent trends in British politics many similarities with France on the eve of the French Revolution: the growing acceptance of the political dogma of popular sovereignty in place of the divine right of kings; the growing importance of demagogic oratory; a tendency to encourage organized political agitation outside the formal institutions of government, as with the Irish Land League and Mr Chamberlain's Birmingham caucus; and, as Irish examples illustrated abundantly, the toleration of gradually increasing disorder.[33] Holding such views, Maine urged the need for steady checks against the rising tide of radicalism. He stressed the important political role still to be played by the House of Lords, where he thought 'authority comes from the fact of its existence, from its antiquity, from its prescriptive title, from its recognitions, from its actual discharge of important functions'.[34] The findings of the 'historical and comparative' method left no doubt as to the alternative:

As political science, like all science, is based on observation and experience, we have to ask what the world knows of single all-powerful assemblies. It has frequently seen them both in ancient and modern times . . . All the instances of it are in most particulars strikingly alike. Single governing assemblies belong naturally to periods of revolution. They begin with turbulence and end in imbecility. After encouraging anarchy they become hopelessly servile to cliques of their own members. They are always harsh, generally cruel. They beget a longing for strong and orderly government either among themselves or in the country which they rule, and they nearly universally succumb to military despotism. The Long Parliament was gloomily harsh, the Convention bloodily cruel; both experiments resulted first in a series of *coups d'etat*, and lastly in the absolute government of a soldier.[35]

The one hope for popular government, Maine wrote in an article on 'Principles of Parliamentary Procedure', which was prompted by recent suggestions that *clôture* should be introduced into the Commons, was 'the unlimited discussion which is permitted in a certain number of freely governed countries'. There were, he thought, two characteristics of the British House of Commons that above all distinguished it from every other assembly of the same kind in the world: its great size and its usual emptiness. Without the check provided by the Lords, measures could be hastily drawn and passed through the single popular chamber, and thus would be forfeited the major guarantee of British government against despotism—that its institutions compelled the legislature 'to pause before action'.[36]

Apart from their topical interest, Sir Henry's anonymous articles in the *St James's Gazette* provide an interesting perspective on the composition of his *Popular Government* (1885). There are a large number of passages in the articles which reappeared five years later in his volume on the theory and practice of democracy. When Maine published his book, he emphasized that his position was that of an objective observer, appearing as a scientific student of society armed only with the 'historical and comparative' method, and having as his purpose simply to project an unbiased light on some of the probable difficulties inherent in popular government. He mentioned in his preface that the essays comprising the work had originally appeared in the *Quarterly Review*, and Greenwood's newspaper was not mentioned. Yet it is now clear that he drew heavily on his *St James's* articles; in the summer of 1880 and thereafter, Sir Henry was writing anonymously against Gladstone's Liberal administration, while in *Popular Government* he reverted to his professed role as an academic observer of society:

St James's, 8 June 1880:
. . . There is hardly a single epoch in English political and social history at which government by universal suffrage would not have prevented all that has followed. It would have expelled the House of Hanover, and restored the Stuarts. It would have forbidden the power-loom, the spinning-jenny, the threshing-machine, and probably the locomotive.

Popular Government (98):
. . . if for four centuries there had been a very widely extended franchise and a very large electoral body in this country, there would have been no reformation of religion, no change of dynasty, no toleration of Dissent, not even as accurate Calendar. The threshing-machine, the power-loom, the spinning-jenny, and possibly the steam engine, would have been prohibited.

The intensely partisan critiques of 1880 gave way to the 'objective analysis' of 1885:

St James's 14 July 1880:
. . . Mr Gladstone's Government has disclosed itself as a Government of pure Radicalism . . . the state of affairs is not unlike that which would have existed in the First French Revolution if in the celebrated Committee of Public Safety Carnot and Robespierre had been the same person.

Popular Government (126):
. . . We are drifting towards a type of government associated with terrible events—a single Assembly, armed with full powers over the Constitution, which it may exercise at pleasure. It will be a theoretically all-powerful Convention, governed by a practically all-powerful secret Committee of Public Safety, but kept from complete submission to its authority by Obstruction, for which its rulers are always seeking to find a remedy in some kind of moral guillotine.

Among Maine's extant manuscripts, moreover, is a partial draft in his hand of *Popular Government*, which demonstrates conclusively the close relationship of the *St James's* articles to his later extended critique of democracy:

> Inherent difficulties of democracy. Smallness of share of power not worth having. Must go to somebody else. Stephen (at other end). *L.F.E.*
>
> As a fact, power goes to wire-puller. What he is? Does not merely manage. Could do nothing without party spirit. Tendency for mankind to take sides. Guelf and Ghibelline. Other Italian parties. Savages, Irish factions. O. & C. Colours, Whig & Tory. Hume's remarks. It is in name of party that wire-puller succeeds. Future system intended to bind a man to party he has adopted. His party be like blue ribbons of army.
>
> System established what does it come to. Government by average opinion. *Expand St J. G. 8th June, 1880.*
>
> Goal of democratic progress. Inconsistent with history. Darwin and Carlyle.
>
> Inconsistent also with science. Malthus. *Expand. St J. G. 7th July, 1880. Malthusianism and modern process.*
>
> Inconsistent with discussion. Future of plebiscites. *St J. G., 8th Sept., 1880. Age of Plebiscites.*[37]

Maine apparently remained secretive about his association with the *St James's Gazette*. Lord Acton, who read and commented in detail on an early draft of *Popular Government*, knew nothing of Maine's latest newspaper adventure. Although unusually well-informed of London literary gossip, Acton seemed far afield when he commented in a letter to Mary Gladstone in July 1880, that 'Sir Henry Maine, like Stephen, used to write in the *Pall Mall*. I don't know whether he has joined Morley.'[38] Similarly, Leslie Stephen, in his *Life* of his brother Fitzjames, was uncertain of Maine's role on the *St James's*, and he was familiar enough with the details of Sir Henry's life to write his appreciation for the *Dictionary of National Biography*.[39]

New knowledge of the background of the composition of *Popular Government* by no means deprives the volume of its interest for the student of nineteenth-century history and political thought, though

225

it necessarily detracts from the degree of objectivity we must ultimately ascribe to it.[40]

If Sir Henry's analysis of democracy, which we turn to in the following chapter, is approached with the full realization that behind the apparently innocent desire merely to 'examine some of the *a priori* theories associated with Popular Government' there lay a pointed attack on specific legislative measures of Gladstone's second administration, the immediate sources of his pessimistic conclusions are seen to be closer to contemporary political events than to the confines of careful historical scholarship. Maine may be said to have 'used' history to make points against the contemporary advocates of party Liberalism, an approach which was bound to be inadequate since, with the appropriate choice of counter-materials it could always be used with equal persuasiveness by the other side. The major themes of *Popular Government*, then, had already been formulated in Maine's *St James's* reflections on the disturbing political trends he believed were forecast in the radical basis of Gladstone's 1880 electoral victory. By 1885, when the latest Liberal enfranchisement measure had almost doubled the electorate by adding close to two million voters to the registers, when the accompanying redistribution virtually annihilated the county Whigs by abolishing 160 seats and shifting the balance to larger county and borough units, when Gladstone was known to be moving towards Home Rule for Ireland, and seemed in view of his sympathy towards Ripon's viceroyalty to be intent on loosening the reins of British hegemony in the eastern Empire, historical 'fact' and political opinion had become indiscriminately blended for the author of *Ancient Law*.

A Manual of Unacknowledged Conservatism

By the time Maine left the writing staff of the *St James's* at the beginning of 1882, he was a most resolute opponent of British democracy. He shared the attitudes of J. F. Stephen, who wrote to the wife of Maine's biographer, Lady Grant Duff, who was at the time in India: 'I believe when you come back to England both you and M.G.D. will be of the same illiberal creed as I and that you will perceive that if a great country is delivered over to be governed by mechanics and labourers it will not long continue to be a great country.'[1] The 'Prospects of Popular Government', the first of four essays Maine wrote over the next two years for the *Quarterly Review*, which together form the basis of his *Popular Government* (1885), argued at greater length the case of those who, like Maine and Stephen, felt the coming of complete democracy to England would be a tragic mistake. The article appeared, unsigned, as the last piece in the *Quarterly* for April 1883. An autograph manuscript, comprising the final draft of the essay in Sir Henry's hand, is now in the Princeton University Library, a gift of the late Harold Laski.

Democracy was judged in Maine's *Quarterly* articles and condemned. His case rested on exposing what he believed had been the uniform failure of past utopian schemes for realizing rule by the many. His method was to hold democracy up to the mirror of history, and thus to deflate the ambitious theories of its recent champions. Maine regarded the very idea of democracy being a desirable form of government as a modern notion, one which first attracted serious attention through the influential writings of the French rationalists of the eighteenth century. Its subsequent history had not been impressive. Although the theory of popular sovereignty had been practically applied in France, Italy, Spain, Portugal, Holland, Belgium, Greece, the Scandinavian countries and South America, Maine held that the 'sober student of history' must conclude that 'since the century during which the Roman Emperors were at the mercy of the Praetorian soldiery, there has been no such insecurity of government as the world has seen since rulers became delegates of the community.'[2] Maine thus contended that, so far from fulfilling naïve hopes of realizing the millenium, all countries which had experimented with popular government in modern times actually had histories of unstable and insecure governments. Only the United States could be excused from the generalization, but Sir Henry maintained, as he had in his *St James's* articles on America, that progress there was traceable to an *economic* freedom that allowed unequal achievements to be rewarded, and not to the existence of *political* democracy.[3]

Maine noted that increasingly since the beginning of the nine-teenth century, imperialism had come to play a dominant role in the foreign affairs of major powers, necessitating the growth of large military establishments. He thought the spirit of democracy, which encouraged objection to commands felt to be wrong, and thus under-mined constituted authority, was incompatible with militarism, which demanded as the key to efficiency the unquestioned acceptance of decisions. He therefore maintained that it was no coincidence that military insurrections are found to be more common where civil institutions are most popular. For the individual citizen seemed to prefer salvation at the hands of a military despot to indecision, while the individual soldier discovered that the 'share of power which belongs to him as a unit in a regiment is more valuable than his fragment of power as a unit in a constituency'.[4]

Maine followed Stephen's lead in *Liberty, Equality, Fraternity*, in adopting the Hobbesian view of liberty as a literal fragmentation of political power into individual units when he advanced more general criticisms of democracy. In a democracy, he argued, the units of power are in principle equally divided among all citizens, regard-less of their aptitude for politics, but each of the units, because of the very wide distribution of power, must be infinitesimally small.[5] Like the opportunist in the business world who accumulates capital and becomes a monopolist, the unscrupulous party 'wirepuller' tends to gather these unaggregated units of political power into his hands, by

228

making electoral pledges in exchange for votes. Maine, that is, viewed the 'art of the wirepuller' as being not unlike the skills of the Nonconformist preacher or demagogue, who gives seeming importance to a body of commonplace doctrine 'by persuading [it] to wear a uniform and take a military title'.[6] In this demoralizing process, Maine felt, the absolute equality *and* liberty that the democrat naïvely assumed would follow on acceptance of his form of government, were lost. Moreover, the wirepuller operates behind the façade of democratic parties, and because parties are dependent on votes, they naturally tend to become more and more alike, more homogenous, less interested in the principles they supposedly stand for than in the more immediate business of staying in power. What primarily concerned Maine was that more promises would inevitably have to be made though fewer could be kept. He feared that, goaded on by the democratic need to satisfy the demands of the many, parties would eventually have to redistribute wealth and destroy institutions which were previously the preserve of minorities who had earned their right to them. This meant socialism, in other words a revolution, after which the greatest probability, since few men knew what they wanted and there was no practical way of ascertaining the general will, was that democracy would result in dictatorship and stagnancy. Like Tocqueville, Maine felt democratic institutions had a tendency if unchecked to bring innovative legislation to a halt.

Maine's argument led him to an extremely pessimistic position. While the supporters of democracy claimed that universal education would prepare the masses for political power, Maine answered that its potential virtues would probably be offset by its tendency to produce unquestioned commonplaces. An important element in his fear of popular government, indeed, was his doubt that democracy would ever be sympathetic to the claims of scientific truth.[7] The majority of people resist science. He cited hostility towards the theory of evolution long after considerable evidence had been adduced in its favour. In modern conditions, he felt, similar popular distaste for policies which nonetheless were supported by scientific evidence could prove inconsistent with progressive government. Sir Henry believed strongly that as the modern world grew increasingly dependent upon scientific and technological knowledge, only an élite of talents, the aristocrat and the man of science, would be receptive to the new ideas upon which progressive societies would need to be guided. In a democracy, on the other hand, the supposed 'opinion leaders' find themselves 'listening nervously at one end of a speaking tube which receives at its other end the suggestions of a lower intelligence'. Progress, Maine thought, came instead through natural inequalities, as a product of the 'beneficent private war which makes one man strive to climb on the shoulders of another, and remain there through the law of the survival of the fittest'.[8]

The results of Maine's initial analysis of democracy were chiefly negative. He urged its partisans to realize that popular government, as it had been known in modern times, showed no signs of being of infinitely long duration. He appealed to the teaching of history, though his historical inferences suggested the polemicist rather than the academic. If Englishmen chose democracy, he warned, 'the British political system, with the national greatness and material prosperity attendant on it, may yet be launched into space, and find its affinities in silence and cold'.[9]

In his second article, 'The Constitution of the United States', published in the *Quarterly* for January 1884, Maine undertook specifically to illustrate his arguments by correcting European misconceptions about the nature of American democracy. In the reprinted essays, this article came last, and thus may be viewed as forming the prescriptive element of his later political theory. Sir Henry here used the American constitution as the text with which to lecture his countrymen, and argued his case as a constitutional lawyer. His claim was that the American constitution, seen historically, was simply a modified version of the British constitution which was in existence between 1760–87.[10] When the Republic was created, the framers of the constitution, as the *Federalist Papers* make clear, strove to combine the ideal of democracy with a rigid and conservative form of government which would make change difficult. Indeed, Sir Henry saw the greatest virtue of the United States constitution as the manner in which it inhibited rash, unmeditated change. He felt that despite the 'nauseous grandiloquence of the American panegyrical historians', a colourful phrase referring to the nineteenth-century American historian Charles Bancroft, the stability of American government was due in reality to its having a well-defined, conservative constitution with roots in the past, rather than to its reliance on mere emotional commitments to the democratic fashion of the moment. He suggested, as he had in the *St James's,* that the British parliament would do well to heed the lessons to be learned from the study of American political institutions. Whereas the British House of Commons, as Bagehot had seen, was increasingly relegated to an inferior position below the Cabinet, the American Congress normally remained in full control of legislative powers. Moreover, defeated bills in the American Congress did not lead to the defeat of the government, and this lessened the likelihood of instability. Ironically, Maine reflected of current British practice:

> The nation whose constitutional practice suggested to Montesquieu his memorable maxim concerning the Executive, Legislative, and Judicial powers, has in the course of a century falsified it. The formal Executive is the true source of legislation, the formal Legislature is incessantly concerned with Executive Government.[11]

Maine continued his comparison of the two systems by arguing that while there were adequate checks against hasty action in the American legislative process, the method by which the government of the day passed bills through the English House of Commons remained dangerously vague and unchecked:

> An English Bill begins in pretty rivulets or stagnant pools. Then it runs underground for most of its course, withdrawn from the eye to the secrecy of the Cabinet. Emerging into the House of Commons, it can no more escape from its embankments than the water of a canal; but once dismissed from that House, it overcomes all remaining obstacles with the rush of a cataract, and mixes with the trackless ocean of British institutions.[12]

Implicit in his argument, as his *St James's Gazette* articles written in the same period make clear, was a plea for stronger checking powers concentrated in the House of Lords, that would help to offset the uncontrolled ascendancy of the Cabinet over the Commons which he felt must accompany popular government.

When Maine republished the essay after the latest franchise extension had been passed by parliament, he pointed out that if a similar Franchise Bill had been introduced in the American Congress, it would have had a more difficult passage, since it would be regarded as an amendment to the constitution. In England there were no such precautions, and a measure of such momentous occasion as a radical reconstitution of the electorate could be enacted in the same manner as one dealing with sewage disposal. He maintained that some method of restraining the democratic impulse should be encouraged, some constitutional device totally removed from the immediate political process. The effectiveness of the American constitution in this respect could be seen in the very few amendments that had been made to the original document. The sagacity of American political institutions, which Maine believed combined a conservative view of human nature with the myth of political equality, he concluded, 'may well fill the Englishmen who now live in *faece Romuli* with wonder and envy'. [13]

Maine's third article returned to the more general themes of his first paper. Here he was concerned with the precise meaning of democracy, when stripped of its emotional appeal. Sir Henry did not agree that democracy had special claims as a social philosophy or a 'way of life', but insisted that it is simply, in Aristotle's terms, a *technique* of government based upon the majoritarian rule of the many, as opposed to types of régime governed by the few or the 'single person'. Moreover, he viewed democratic government as a form of rule capable of becoming no less extreme than unrestricted kingship, and found support for this in the hypocritical manner in which democratic politicians seemed willing to 'worship' the mass electorate:

> Democracy is Monarchy inverted, and the modes of addressing the multitude are the same as the modes of addressing kings. The more powerful and jealous the sovereign, the more unbounded is the eulogy, the more extravagant is the tribute. 'O King, live for ever,' was the ordinary formula of beginning an address to the Babylonian or Median king, drunk or sober. 'Your ascent to power proceeded as uniformly and majestically as the laws of being and was as certain as the decrees of eternity', says Mr Bancroft to the American people.[14]

For Maine, then, democratic government implied 'monarchy inverted', a new form of despotism created by standing the traditional variety on its head.

In this essay Maine deliberately used the terms 'democracy' and 'popular government' to mean different things, for he believed it was the democratic partisan's error in confusing the two—one a form of government, the other a general term of approval technically applicable to any form of rule—that had led to confused thinking. Emotional terms like 'Freedom', 'The Revolution', 'The Republic', 'The Reign of the People', were, he claimed, in no way logically necessarily related to democracy, though modern British radicals seemed increasingly to think they were. Maine traced the propagation of the myth to the political writings of Rousseau, who in his view had been more responsible than any other for having taught that a golden age of government was attainable *only* in a democracy.[15] On the contrary, Maine submitted, experience demonstrated that not only was democracy unprogressive, it was also the most difficult form of government. He argued that, practically speaking, it was impossible to find out the will of the people. Besides, he doubted whether the will of the people is of any value in the making of statesmanlike decisions. He repeated his belief that all that had made England wealthy and powerful had been the work of enlightened minorities, while the masses, in whom the ultimate power to decide political issues was now to be placed, were ignorant:

> Thus it comes to pass that an audience composed of roughs or clowns, an audience quite ready under very slightly altered conditions to 'eave' many an 'arf-brick' at the platform, is boldly told by an educated man that it has more political information than an equal number of scholars.[16]

If England had experienced the literal rule of the many during the previous three hundred years, Maine believed, the ignorance of the majority of men might well have prevented the reformation of religion, there could have been no change of dynasty, no toleration of dissent, not even an accurate calendar. With a calculus as rigid as Bentham's felicific principle, Maine concluded that if the people's will had prevailed, 'the threshing-machine, the power-loom, the spinning-jenny, and possibly the steam-engine, would have been prevented'.

Maine continued with a short analysis of political parties. While the democratic partisan believed mass-based parties served to offer alternatives in legislation, as well as to perform the more general task of representing the people's will, Sir Henry thought one unversed in contemporary European political styles would find it strange that 'the system of government consisted in half the cleverest men in the country taking the utmost pains to prevent the other half from governing'.[17] In other words, Maine felt, democratically organized parties were obstructive of clear decisions made without regard to partisan considerations. He would have preferred something like a National Government, or a coalition of political experts united in permanent leadership. As for the 'Party Hero', the larger-than-life symbol of the democratic party's supposed virtues, he would be found on closer inspection so bound to the interests of his particular faction, and so indebted for his ascendancy to the organizational wirepuller, as to be usually less than fair to his competitors, and always lacking in independence of judgement. Maine feared, as he had in the *St James's*, that 'democratic' political parties, operating with highly organized efficiency in a large impersonal electorate, would lead inevitably to corruption—a corruption moreover of a special kind. While simple folk believed in their importance as supporters of a particular party, in reality, they would be mere objects to be manipulated by managers operating from behind the façade of those parties.

Maine's last article in the series, 'The Age of Progress', did not appear until April 1885, several months after parliament had actually enacted the Franchise Act. His chief purpose, thus, was to emphasize the even greater need now to recognize the essential conservatism of human society, in the historical and comparative view.[18] It is significant that Maine here drew most heavily on materials from his studies in legal anthropology. He thought the close study of the past revealed clearly that collective man, so far from being wedded, as democrats assumed, to the artificial idea of progress, was if anything downright averse to rapid change. As he had written decades before in his *Ancient Law*, 'the stationary condition of the human race is the rule, the progressive the exception'. The very strata of society that the democrat assumed would gain most from adopting his form of government was not, in Maine's judgement, capable of meeting the enormous demands that type of rule would make on its capacities. When Maine revised the *Popular Government* essays shortly after the passage of the Third Reform Bill, he added one final nostalgic reflection on the passing of the great age of aristocracies of talent:

Whether—and this is the last objection—the age of aristocracies be over, I cannot take upon myself to say. I have sometimes thought it one of the chief drawbacks of modern democracy that, while it gives birth to despotism with the greatest facility, it does not seem to be capable of producing aristocracy, though from that form of political and social ascendancy all improvement has hitherto sprung.[19]

Maine's essays on democracy immediately attracted a good deal of attention. Henry Sidgwick recorded in his diary for 29 October 1884:

I have been reading Maine in the *Quarterly*.—The best anti-democratic writing that we have had. He dined with us this evening: seemed really concerned that we have no proper constitution in England: thinks it would be a real gain to have a constitutional code settled by Parliament.—The genuine alarm that Maine seems to feel at the existing state of things in England impressed me much, since his intellect has always seemed to me a very cool and disengaged one.[20]

Shortly afterwards, Sidgwick noted despondently in a letter to James Bryce: 'I do not see how we can get on without something like a combination or co-operation of English parties,' and advised Bryce that Maine's essays on democracy would have to be taken into account in his projected two-volume study of American democracy.[21] J. F. Stephen, who had read the proofs of Maine's articles, understandably thought them 'one of the very best things he ever wrote'.[22] Matthew Arnold found greatest interest in the essay on the American constitution, yet while acknowledging Sir Henry's undoubtedly 'rare and characteristic qualities of mind and style', felt he had missed something essential about democracy in America. Himself recently returned from a successful lecture tour there, he thought Maine's *Popular Government* argument too legalistic, and suggested that democracy in the United States meant far more than the bare definition Maine had given it, as simply a *form* of government.[23] *The Times*, in an editorial analysis of Sir Henry's *Quarterly* articles, took the more general line: 'However much we may differ from the writer in detail here and there, the articles contain much that no serious political thinker can deem himself entitled to overlook.'[24]

Maine reworked the essays during the early summer of 1885, assisted by a set of the four papers his publisher had pasted inside a folio book that he found 'especially convenient'. As well, he had extensive notes and suggestions made by the indefatigable Lord Acton.[25] Acton wrote to Mary Gladstone at the end of April that: 'Maine, whose series of articles *forms in reality an assault on the Government,* promises to adopt all my remonstrances in the reprinting of them. These filled twenty-six of my pages in all, so I count on a considerable modification of the text.'[26] Acton, now fully aware of why Maine had refused to purge his London Institute article, on kingship, of a 'Tory tinge', was bitterly disappointed with the completed revisions. Maine in fact changed little, even though he continued to insist that he had made major modifications in his essays. As he later wrote unconvincingly to his publisher, in a formal business letter setting out the character of his latest work:

Maine's *Popular Government* is not a mere reprint, or even a revised reprint, of articles published in the *Quarterly Review*. It is described in the Preface, which was submitted to the Editor, as composed (p. xii) of the 'substance' of the articles. When HSM first spoke to Mr Murray on the subject of republishing his contributions, Mr Murray expressed a good deal of doubt, founded on his own experiences, of the probable success of republished articles. This was the principle reason why HSM attempted the reconstruction of the articles with the view of converting them into a substantive work, a task entailing much labour which extended, in all, over not less than three months.

Considerable portions of the book are quite new: for example, the economical arguments towards the end of Essay I, the beginning of Chapter II, and the argument about Hereditary Chambers at the end of Chapter III; and the Preface is virtually a new Chapter. Besides this, every sentence in the articles was separately considered with reference to the fitness of its place in a book, and a number of changes more or less extending over the whole work were made from this point of view.[27]

Maine, in fairness to him, apparently undertook the final stages of the preparation of *Popular Government* in the midst of a recurrence of one of his periodic illnesses. Before leaving London for a long stay at St Leonards-on-Sea in July, he wrote to Murray: 'I have received the proofs of all my four essays. I hope there will be no difficulty in their standing over a little for correction, as I have been very unwell, and am not yet fully recovered.'[28] A photograph taken

236

Plate 9 John Murray (1808–1892), Maine's publisher. Portrait in oils by C. W. Furse ($45\frac{1}{4}'' \times 33\frac{1}{2}''$).

Plate 10 (Below left) Bust of J. F. McLennan (1827–1881), author of *Primitive Marriage* (1865), Trinity College, Cambridge.
Plate 11 (Below) A photographic portrait of Maine taken in London during 1871. (Original size, $4'' \times 2\frac{1}{2}''$.)

Plate 13 Photographic portrait of Lady Maine, by H. S. Mendelssohn, South Kensington, c. 1885.

Plate 12 Sir Henry Maine was sixty-two when this photograph was taken, and his features most closely approximate those of the Lowes Dickinson portrait

by Netherville Briggs of Baker Street seems to confirm that Sir Henry was in poor health at the time. His features were marked by increased sallowness, and his eyes were ringed and watery. He had developed a decided paunch and his sidewhiskers were now clearly grey. Yet the look of determination on his tired face nonetheless bespeaks the conservative polemicist rather than the calm scholar at sixty-two years of age.

The publication of *Popular Government* in early October 1885 was heralded by a lengthy review in *The Times*. The reviewer believed that 'No more important contribution to the philosophy of politics has been made for a long time'. The book's 'scientific impartiality', he felt, was its strength.[29] A disgusted Lord Acton thought the review merely 'a symptom of the change which is so remarkable in *The Times* in the direction of conservatism.[30] As he reflected in a letter to Mary Gladstone, in which he noted the similarity of Maine's personal disillusionment with Liberal party politics to that of many in the Whiggish element of the party:

> It is not the popular movement, but the travelling of the minds of men who sit in the seat of Adam Smith that is really telling and worthy of all attention. Maine tells me that his book, A Manual of Unacknowledged Conservatism, is selling well. It is no doubt meant to help the enemy's cause, and more hostile to us than the author cares to appear. For he requested me not to review it.[31]

The first edition of *Popular Government* was quickly exhausted, yet while Maine was delighted with the extent of its popularity he was dismayed that as the book was more widely noticed, it was primarily by radical journals. He realized, however, that:

> In spite of my declamation of partisanship, I can hardly expect the true progressive Liberals to like my book. But I have no cause to complain. I thought *The Spectator*, if anything, absurdly complimentary. *The Athenaeum* is weak . . . I confess it struck me that Dilke had the first paragraph put in after the rest of the article had been written . . .[32]

He wrote again to Murray on 8 November: 'I rather wonder that no Conservative paper or periodical has noticed the book—the reviewers, though not discourteous, have all been manifestly radical.'

He reflected in a lighter vein, however, that he was not averse to educating the radicals:

> Will you please send copies of my book, from the author, to . . . Mr G. H. Cunningham, Messenger, India Office, Westminster, S.W.
>
> I send this last in response to an application which amused me much: it was from an India Office Messenger, as Secretary to an East End 'Chamberlain's Radical Club'—I hope my book will do them some good.[33]

Maine's complaint that no Conservative paper had noticed his book was shortly allayed by a highly favourable review in the *St James's Gazette*, where Sir Henry was understandably regarded as something of a senior citizen. Interestingly, it was written by J. F. Stephen's son, J. K. Stephen, and its sympathetic treatment of *Popular Government* suggests the deep influence of his father's thought on his own. Maine wrote to thank him on 14 November:

> The few words you sent to me the other day give me an opportunity of thanking you for the excellent notice of my book which appeared in the *St James's Gazette* of Thursday. There was a good review of it in *The Times*, but none other has appeared which is to be compared with yours. I am much gratified by the pains and thought you have evidently bestowed on this volume.
>
> The notices which have appeared, save the two I have mentioned, have been feeble, though generally courteous. I hear that John Morley, who has been haranguing against me in various places, is preparing a literary fulmination, I presume for the *Fortnightly*.
>
> Please tell your father that a copy will be sent to him as soon as possible. If there is any delay, it will be owing to some temporary scarcity of copies.[34]

While *Popular Government* enjoyed a wide circulation in the months following its publication, and continued to be much admired by conservatives like Stephen, it ultimately proved to be harmful to Sir Henry's standing as a scholar. Yet the polemics that have contributed to make *Popular Government* so unattractive to democrats should be seen in their proper historical perspective, and must be balanced against the many important insights of the book. In the first place, we must grant Maine the courtesy of acknowledging that his criticisms of democracy represent a forceful exposition of sentiments that were by no means dead when he wrote his essays. Indeed, while he was busy publishing his *Quarterly Review* articles, the most acclaimed sociologist of the day, Herbert Spencer, was simultaneously bringing out a series of papers in the *Contemporary Review* that argued with intense concern the thesis that the drift of legislation in England in recent years, while productive of an 'increase of freedom in form', had been accompanied by a 'decrease of freedom in fact'.[35] Collected and republished under the famous title *The Man versus The State* (1884), Spencer advanced views not unlike those of Maine, to the effect that while in their 'intrinsic natures' philosophical Toryism was associated with a militant social organization and the régime of status, and Liberalism with an industrial social organization and the régime of contract, these positions were being reversed in the utterances and actions of the major British political parties.[36] Alarmed at these developments, Spencer felt compelled in the face of the continuing Liberal legislative initiatives of the early 1880s to warn of 'the coming slavery'. And of course there were still many Westminster politicians who listened with the greatest seriousness to the warnings of men like Maine and Spencer:[37] in 1885, England was on the threshold of a new political age, in which greater demands for popular political participation seemed to be coinciding with the beginnings of the gradual decline of Britain's unquestioned hegemony in world affairs. Had not even the greatest of Liberal philosophers, John Stuart Mill, made the 'tyranny of the majority' a central concern of his political writings? The heavy weeklies and monthlies were filled with endless numbers of soul-searching articles by M.P.s, students of society, and *littérateurs*, using the leading topics of practical politics as the pegs upon which to hang their reflections on the past greatness and the future uncertainties of British constitutionalism.

There is the somewhat separate question of the long-range validity of leading elements in Maine's political thought. While in the generation immediately following Sir Henry's death his political writings fell into disrepute, and have for the most part remained in obscurity ever since, we are perhaps now in a better position to judge the general worth of those writings. One recent historian of nineteenth-century thought, viewing *Popular Government* in the context of the total range of Maine's literary output, has concluded that:

'Maine's survey of the geographical range of popular government is masterly, still to be read with profit. Seldom has a better survey of an actual situation been penned.'[38] As Professor W. A. Robson[39] and others have further pointed out, Maine's *Popular Government* predicted with remarkable accuracy the powers for evil inherent in modern nationalist movements, and showed great prescience in recognizing that while militarism was incompatible with the goals of democracy, the lack of decisive leadership in 'popular governments' seemed frequently to encourage military rule. Sir Henry's concern over the potentials for political manipulation in an age increasingly preoccupied with the authority of public opinion, which we now know was a central theme of his political journalism, continues to have relevance, as does his critical assessment of the parliamentary form of government as an agency for recruiting and controlling those possessed of scientific and technological knowledge. Moreover, a case can be made that the spirit of the work, in which Maine attempted to get behind the ideological beliefs of his contemporaries to reveal the gulf separating political theory and practice, makes *Popular Government* one of the earliest of the truly modern studies of British political institutions. Certainly we must now allow that he was largely successful in demonstrating the ideological naïvety of the more extreme democratic apologists of his day, for few social scientists would nowadays dispute his assertion that great difficulties surround the creation and maintenance of democratic political systems. In essential agreement with another of Sir Henry's leading views, it is a commonplace among later students of practical politics that too much democracy, and the encouragement of too many political interests, may well lead to abuse and political instability.

Yet when all this is said in favour of *Popular Government*, it remains in other respects an unsatisfactory book. Maine's rather unrealistic insistence that democracy must mean literally 'government by the many', and his deduction that because such a condition was a practical impossibility, a truer picture of the actual political process required instead the adoption of an 'élitist' theory of political leadership, was a major weakness of his argument. Most later analysts of democracy have abandoned the simple numerical definition used by Maine, and regard as 'democratic' only those régimes in which a receptive social climate coincides with certain political practices. Among the latter would be universal suffrage and regular

240

elections for choosing representatives, legally guaranteed boundaries separating the private from the public realm, channels for allowing the access of those politically interested to the decision-making apparatus of the state on a continuing basis, and the persistence of publicly recognized opposition, so organized that it has a real chance of alternating as the legal government. Rather than being a régime in which 'the people govern themselves', democracy, in this view, consists of a system of procedures for attaining 'responsible' government, whereby 'the people' are enabled to freely choose and thereby *periodically control* their political leaders. When its conditions are actually met, many of the countries Maine cites in support of his argument that democracies are inherently unstable are seen not to be 'democracies' at all, just as nowadays we are rightly sceptical about the use of such terms as 'peoples' democracy' when applied to known dictatorships. Moreover, while Maine insisted that democracy was rendered impossible by the inexorable rise of élites, later writers have argued that in principle the élitist thesis is not incompatible with democratic requirements. Even allowing the debatable point that the *internal* management of organizations always tends towards oligarchical control, numerous organizations in the practising democracies (pressure groups, political parties, etc.) must nevertheless *compete among themselves* for shares of influence in a policy-making arena in which there is no permanent monopoly over political rewards.[40]

Perhaps a more fundamental shortcoming of Maine's argument, in the final analysis, was his mixing together of the observation that democracies were scarce, with the conclusion that they were therefore positively undesirable. While he might marshall an impressive array of 'historical and comparative' data to illustrate that democracies *had been* few in number compared with other forms of government, he was not logically entitled to conclude that democracies are therefore not worth striving for in the present. Rousseau made the famous observation in the *Social Contract* that if men were gods, then practising democracy (as Maine used the term) would be truly possible. Accusing Rousseau of naïvety, Sir Henry countered in the pages of his *Popular Government* that if they were wise, they would wish instead for an aristocracy of intellect and taste to govern their affairs. Yet is such a choice ever a concrete possibility in the political marketplace? One dream was surely as noble as the other, and Sir

Henry was never able convincingly to coax from the mute records of the past any final authority for his special vision of the comparative morality of ideal political régimes.

Maine's recurring ill health led him, while he was still preparing the final draft of his *Popular Government* essays, to accept and then reject an offer from Sir Richard Cross to become Permanent Under-Secretary at the Home Office in Lord Salisbury's new Conservative Government, which had been hurriedly formed after the defeat of the Liberals on a budget amendment early in July 1885. Maine wrote to Cross on 9 July, noting that: 'I had a sudden attack of illness yesterday, which led me to consult my medical attendant, who, I am sorry to say, has noticed symptoms which, though removable with rest and care, are in his opinion quite fatal to my undertaking new and important duties in my present condition.' He added: 'I feel . . . it would be neither fair to you nor to the public services if I did not resign the Undersecretaryship to which you have done me the honour of appointing me, but which, fortunately, as it happens—I have not actively taken up.'[41] The Tory Home Secretary, however, pressed Maine to reconsider, and apparently was prepared to make special arrangements in order to retain his services. Several days later, Sir Henry wrote further:

My dear Sir Richard Cross,

I have deferred replying to you for a day or two, partly in deference to your own suggestion and partly because I thought it due to the extreme kindness of a letter in which I could not but see that you offered to sacrifice yourself in order that I might have rest, to take a further opinion of the highest authority on the course proper for me to follow. Accordingly, I made arrangements for consulting Sir Andrew Clark, who has seen me often before and who, I need scarcely say, has a great reputation for sagacity in such cases. I told him expressly that I consulted him on account of your most kind proposal for enabling me to have rest. He went most carefully and minutely into the subject and all the questions connected with it, and I have just received from him the enclosed opinion, signed by my own medical adviser as well as himself. You will see that it is quite distinct, and, I am afraid, leaves nothing more to be said. At the same time S. A. Clark assured me that I should get quite well under favourable conditions.[42]

He enclosed the letter drawn up by his medical attendants:

16 Cavendish Sq., W.

14 July, 1885

We have together examined Sir Henry Maine; and having considered in what manner and to what extent his health would be likely to be influenced by his acceptance of the appointment which he has been offered at the Home Office; we are strongly of opinion that his health would be injuriously affected by the work of that appointment and that he ought not to undertake it—

Andrew Clark, M.D., LL.D., F.R.S.,
Physician to the London Hospital
T. Laurence Read, M.R.C.S.E.[43]

Maine told Cross he thought his illness had been 'brought on by the foolishness of having taken no holiday for three years'; to Lord Salisbury, he wrote separately that 'I have unconsciously overworked myself, partly by neglecting to take the prescribed holiday from my ordinary official work, and partly by preparing a book, of which I have published some introductory portions in the *Quarterly Review*.'[44] In a later letter to Grant Duff, written from Hurst Lea, Albany Heath, where he was then recuperating, he added that after initially accepting the offer he had 'become very seriously ill with all the symptoms of what doctors call a "Break-down". I must have, without knowing it, greatly overworked myself somehow.' Yet further comments in this same letter suggest another reason for his having finally decided against taking up the new post:

It was not an office which I at all coveted [he reflected], and I was not feeling well at the time; but it was pressed on me in a very flattering way and you know I always had an ambition to have an office which (for that is really the attraction), would give me a private secretary . . .

It has been a disappointment in some respects. But innumerable letters from friends console me by telling me I should have found the work intolerable. It appears to involve an infinity of small legal points, of no particular difficulty, but requiring constant attention. Though Lord Salisbury thought otherwise, I think there would have been much difficulty in keeping on the Headship at Trinity Hall; and it actually appears that the H.O. Undersecretary is the only Permanent Undersecretary who has no

Private Secretary. The truth is that that office has been allowed to fall into great disorder.[45]

Maine was apparently anxious to leave the India Office altogether by the date of the publication of *Popular Government*, presumably because of his growing disillusionment at the intrusion of party politics into imperial affairs. 'I am not satisfied with the state of things at the India Office', he confided to Grant Duff:

Randolph Churchill is courtesy itself to the Council and knows better how to use it than men of higher political reputation. But he is almost as full of fads as that imposter Ripon. I look with much misgiving on the open parliamentary inquiry into all Indian administration. There is no point in writing about public affairs. All is in doubt till the new Parliament is elected. And no human being knows what will come of the Election.[46]

Yet as Sir Henry had admitted to the same correspondent, he was not willing to throw off his membership on the Indian Council for the first thing that came his way. Three months later, his health having decidedly improved, Maine's hopes revived at learning of the impending retirement of the great parliamentarian and author of *May's Parliamentary Practice*, Sir Erskine May, as Chief Clerk of the House of Commons. He wrote immediately[47] to the interim Tory Prime Minister from the Master's Lodge, Trinity Hall:

My dear Lord Salisbury,

I must confess that I am tempted to write to you solely by the promptitude and kindness with which some months ago you attempted to gratify my desire to change my appointment at the India Office for another. The attempt was abortive, to my great disappointment, but three months rest has quite restored my health, as my doctors said it would, and with my restoration, my wish to quit the India Office has revived.

What I have to ask you is simply that, if in any capacity you have to consider the successor to the Clerkship of the Parliament now vacant, you will let my name pass before your mind as that of a person who thinks he would not discredit the office. I ought to mention that some years ago, before the tenure of my seat on the India Council was offered, the idea of my becoming Clerk of the Parliaments was entertained by Lord Derby, then Secretary of State for Foreign Affairs in Lord Beaconsfield's Government. But the matter went off through perfectly intelligible causes.

Sir Henry then added:

> With regard to the last letter which I received from you, you may perhaps be interested to hear that, much to my surprise, and (I suspect) to the still greater surprise of my publisher, the first edition of my book on 'Popular Government' has been exhausted in three weeks, and I have at once to prepare another. It cannot have much effect during the present excitement, but it may perhaps do some good hereafter.

His prediction that *Popular Government* 'cannot have much effect' proved for the moment a very accurate one, for in the 'present excitement' of the national polling which began three days after Maine sent his request to Salisbury, the Liberals were returned with a majority of eighty-six. When Gladstone's latest Government was finally completed in February 1886 the offer of the Clerkship was made to Maine by the Liberal Prime Minister, yet citing poor health, he promptly refused.

Sir Henry's abortive attempts to leave the India Office in 1885 raise again the question of his physical frailty, and its almost constant bearing on the course of his later career. Were Maine's dogged illnesses always genuine, or was he a somewhat lazy man, who, according to a letter written by J. F. Stephen to Lady Grant Duff on 15 December 1881, was not above using his 'mysterious' relapses to further his professional interests?[48] Was Stephen merely backbiting when he had observed, in a further letter to Lord Lytton of 1879, that 'all through the Afghan row [Maine] was taking his holidays at Cambridge, in his sinecure Master's Lodge. I asked him if he ever came to the office. "No", he said, "they might ask me to do something." Can genius go farther? Is not this a sight to make a poor sinner pray?'[49] Or are we to accept Stephen's rather different judgement in yet another letter written in this same period: '[Maine] has', he observed, '. . . a weight & force & originality of mind which are an odd contrast to his *excessive physical delicacy and nervous ways*'?[50] These questions have an obvious bearing on our interest in Maine as a biographical subject. They also have a direct relation to our final assessment of his scholarship, for commentators have always forgiven Sir Henry a certain casualness of approach on the grounds that his physical disabilities made painstaking attention to details impracticable. There seems really to be no conclusive evidence one way or the other. Certainly Maine often made patently feeble excuses in order to avoid the tedium of committee meetings,[51] but one suspects knowledge of this must merely strike a sympathetic chord in those having had much experience of committees. As far as his temperament is concerned, there indeed seems little doubt that Sir Henry was most content when the greatest distance separated him physically and emotionally from 'busy occasions', whether professional or social. His preferred pace was the calm shuffle of the Athenaeum Club, with its magnificent first-floor gallery (where he deposited autographed copies of his books) serving as his beloved refuge from the hurly-burly of Whitehall and the streets below.

When we turn to examine what we know of Maine's specific illnesses, there is some evidence that he suffered chiefly from recurrent bouts of nervous and digestive disorder: at least this conclusion is suggested by his frequent trips to 'drink the waters' at continental spas. Even while in India, he had written to the Viceroy during January 1865 of his:

> having to go to Europe for a few months on sick certificate. I have suffered severely of late from nervous debility, entailing great difficulties in sleeping, but latterly the ailment has caused some (though not at the present serious) derangement of the actions of the heart. It is the last symptom which threatens to precipitate matters, & moreover, good as is the climate of Simla, it is not good for weakness in that direction. I have, however, reason to believe that certain Continental waters will do for me what they did before under similar circumstances, and it is to have the benefit of them that I think of going away.[52]

We know, moreover, that Maine suffered from the painful effects of gout. In India he apologized to Sir John Lawrence for his absence from a Ball at Government House 'because my trouble has incapacitated me from getting a dress coat on'.[53] Thirteen years later Stephen noted in a letter 'I am sorry to say Maine seems to me not well. He has had a variety of troubles, said to be different forms of gout from last summer.'[54] In the same period Maine wrote to Sir

Courtenay Ilbert of a further ailment, noting that he had been 'seriously, indeed for a time dangerously, ill at Cambridge, with quinsy'.[55] How did these attacks affect his disposition? The drain of energy exacted by continuous bouts of illness, sometimes serious, at others little more than bad colds or headache, doubtless contributed to make Sir Henry appear to many of his contemporaries a rather brusque and intolerant figure, jealous of any wastage of his physical and emotional reserves on minutiae, whether at the India Office or in the performance of mere social niceties. 'Maine never says or writes anything without good reason', commented his friend Whitley Stokes.[56] His long history of physical frailty led him to adopt an attitude of resigned fatalism about his person that, as Lord Acton felt, struck the casual observer as if he were a man 'without sympathy or throb'.[57] And, since he was always concerned with the immediate prospect of renewed attacks of his illness, he tended to be more preoccupied with them than most people: there is scarcely an extant Maine letter outside those that deal strictly with business matters that is not without some reference to his health. It seems likely that while Maine was unquestionably an unusually sickly man, he was also, like many another Victorian worthy, something of a hypochondriac.

The most significant potential source of information as regards Maine's health, of course, would be the records of his medical attendants. Sir Henry was the patient, at various stages of his career, of a number of distinguished London practitioners in addition to Sir Andrew Clark—including Sir James Ranald Martin, Sir Joseph Fayrer, Dr E. C. Robson Roose, Dr Laurence Read, and Drs Bright, Brodie and Macrae—but because of the extremely correct attitudes of these Victorian gentlemen, any of their case-books likely to be useful to our present inquiries have been destroyed. I have been able to find only one letter purporting to cast light on Maine's medical history, in the extensive collections of the splendid Wellcome Foundation Medical Library in Euston Road, London. It was addressed by Sir Henry to a 'Dr Rost' during the winter of 1877:

India Office,
Dear Dr Rost,   Jan. 26, 1877
    Dr Zacharia's charge would not be too large for a limited number of readings, but, if my experiment succeeds, I think of

continuing it till my eyesight quite recovers, and in that case the payment required is high enough to create a difficulty. Perhaps therefore I had better ask you to name somebody who would not ask more than 5/- a reading.

I ought to explain that I do not require a 'lesson' in the usual English sense of the word—that is, I do not need anybody to *teach* me, but only to read to me.

Very faithfully yrs,
H. S. Maine.[58]

Dr Rost, however, was no medical man at all, but the Librarian of the India Office, a Doctor of Philosophy in oriental studies of Jena University. Sir Henry, who usually wore a monocle rather than regular eye-glasses, was apparently suffering from temporary eye trouble and wished to hire a reader to assist him with his academic studies as well as with his India Office work. It seems that Dr Zacharia's charges were too high for Sir Henry's liking.

During the early 1880s Maine had the pleasure of seeing his eldest son, Charles Sumner Maine, becoming established in his own professional career. Charles had always been Sir Henry's favourite: the earliest extant evidence linking the two is a copy of the *Arabian Nights*, now in my possession, inscribed in Maine's hand: 'Charles Sumner Maine from his papa, on his Ninth Birthday, Mar. 18, 1859.' While a sickly lad, Charles was talented, and seemed likely as the years passed to follow directly in his father's professional footsteps. After graduation from Cambridge, he read for the Bar, and considered for a time going into the Indian service. When Lord Lytton set out to reconvene the Indian Law Commission in 1878, he suggested that Charles become its Secretary, but as Sir Henry wrote to the Viceroy, while his son '*was* thinking of taking his chance at an Indian career at the Indian bar; now, owing to an improvement of his health, he has given that idea up; and, if he went to India at all, it would be to undertake some special duty.'[59] Instead, he was appointed by Lord Granville[60] in 1880 as Secretary to the British Auxiliary Commission for revising the Egyptian mixed tribunal system, and left immediately for Cairo. He later published a paper on his experiences in that post in the August 1885 *Fortnightly*, in which he argued that 'it is against our interests to assist internationality in Egypt in any form', and berated the 'guileless' Liberal

248

Government for its indecisive Egyptian policy.[61] On returning to England Charles was appointed by Fitzjames Stephen to a permanent Clerkship of Assizes on the South Wales circuit.

On 13 September 1884 Charles married Amabel Copeland, the widow of a Mr Ernest O. Copeland, at St Mary Abbott's, Kensington. The ceremony was conducted by Sir Henry's brother, Lewin George Maine, vicar of Sowerby, Yorkshire.[62] 'Bell' brought more to the marriage than her young son Nevill by her previous marriage: she was the recipient of a sizeable private income from consuls and property. In a letter to Lady Campbell-Bannerman dated 2 November 1884, Lady Maine reflected: 'You know I daresay that my son Charlie is married. They are staying here now. She is very elegant and distinguished looking and I think we are quite satisfied although there is a little stepson to put up with . . . They go to Biarritz for the winter in a fortnight. My son seems well since his marriage.'[63]

As the Charles Maines passed the winter months of 1884–5 at Biarritz on the Golfe de Gascogne, Bell was already expecting a child. On the following 1 July she gave birth in London to a baby boy. William Hartwick wrote to the proud new father:

> 12 Leinster Gds.,
> Hyde Park, W.
> 8/7/85

My dear Charlie Maine,

I learned for the first time yesterday afternoon on paying a visit at Cornwall Gardens that you were invested with paternal distinction. You have not lost much time! I heartily congratulate you on Mrs Maine's safety. I hear the most astonishing accounts of the baby from Lady Maine. I never saw her so elated . . . I am assured on the best authority that the form and features of your son and heir leave nothing to be desired, and that his head bears a marvellous resemblance to the head of his grandfather. Of course he will be *another* Henry Sumner Maine. May he grow up worthy of the name.[64]

It seemed only logical to Maine's relatives that the eldest son of Europe's most devoted scholar of *patria potestas* should have been blessed with a male child and heir. A cousin from Scarborough had no doubt, as she assured Charles, that 'Almost as much pleased as the parents will be the grandparents, and I know your mother had set her heart on a son, though she would have welcomed a daughter.'[65] Another relative, a Miss S. M. Searle of St Leonards, wrote to urge 'dear Cha' to name the baby 'Henry II.'[66] The infant was christened 'Henry Cecil Sumner Maine'.

Final Years

As the year 1885 drew to a close *Popular Government* was already well into its second edition. Among the recipients of author's copies of the book was Henry Reeve, who almost exactly fifty years earlier had brought out the first English translation of Tocqueville's *Democracy in America*. His interesting letter of thanks is preserved among the miscellaneous letters of the *Maine Collection*:

> 62 Rutland Gate,
> 13 Nov.

> My dear Sir Henry,
> I really must express to you the pleasure and deep interest with which I am re-reading your Essays on 'Popular Government', now collected in a volume. The novelty of some views on an old subject, and the wisdom of your reflections, render it a most important contribution to political literature. It has the flavour of Burke, but without his passion.
> In the original Preface I wrote to my translation of Tocqueville in 1835 (soon after the First Reform Bill) I expressed opinions very similar to those of your essays. They have not varied. I am still inclined to think that what is called Democracy will devour Civilization. In France this process is already far advanced.

Yet while Reeve was no enthusiast for unqualified democracy, he did not share Sir Henry's alarm at the prospect of far-reaching changes in British constitutional practice:

> In this country [he suggested] there are two barriers. The first is the *form* of the House of Commons, which renders it incapable of doing many things at once. It works in Shackles.
> The second is that the habits and manners of the English people

have not yet undergone any complete or violent change. They retain the impressions of the old society. I think the Radicals over-rate their power. There is a vast mass of *featherbed resistance*.[1]

Reeve's argument found support in Sir Henry's own household. At least that conclusion is suggested in a letter written by 'Lizzie' Maine from Cornwall Gardens to Maine's American publisher, Henry Holt. As she wrote in March 1886:

> 'Popular Government' is selling largely here—the third edition is just ready—Just at this time when we are so unsettled, and as many people will have it, 'on the eve of a revolution', its subjects are interesting; but somehow, as far as a *revolution* here is likely, it seems *impossible* to believe in the steady-going commonplace Englishman going in for any enthusiastic change.[2]

Her remarks captured the sentiment of most of the reviewers of *Popular Government*.

The *Contemporary Review* had already ventured the opinion early in the New Year that Sir Henry's academic reputation would not be enhanced by his latest volume. Nothing would have been more useful than a thorough treatment of modern democracy, the reviewer thought, but nothing could be more worthless than Maine's 'superficial philosophizing' about it.[3] The *Westminster Review*, equally positive in tone, forecast in its January number than Maine would most certainly lower his standing in the scholarly community by publishing a book so bound to contemporary controversy.[4] *The Nation* added an American voice to these unsympathetic assessments, in observing several weeks later that:

> our cordial admiration for Sir Henry Maine's works inspires us with some regret that the rarest powers of expression and of thought should be employed in the partisan warfare of the moment. Hundreds will read *Popular Government* who will not care to study *Ancient Law*. But to students, Maine's greatest work will still remain his *Ancient Law*.[5]

In February 1886 a more extensive critique of *Popular Government* appeared, written by the American editor of *The Nation*, E. L. Godkin. Godkin accused Sir Henry of employing a 'chemical method' of reasoning to impute causal relationships between democratic political institutions and political instability.[6] While Maine advocated

Plate 14 Pen and ink drawing of John Morley and Henry Labouchere, the radical leader, conferring in the Commons, *c.* 1885 (?).

Plate 15 Vanity Fair cartoon of Frederick Greenwood, editor of the *St James's Gazette*, by Pellighrini, 19th June, 1880.

Plate 16 Lord Acton, from *The Illustrated London News*, 1895, CVI, p. 267.

Plate 17 Commemorative medallion of Maine by Sir Edgar Boehm, Westminster Abbey.

Plate 18 (Below) Gravesite of Sir Henry Maine, photographed at Cannes, February 1888.

the use of stricter definitions in political discourse, he had himself been further guilty of an indiscriminate application of the term 'democracy' to such totally different political systems as the South American military dictatorships and American democracy. Moreover, Godkin did not share Maine's view that democratic régimes were necessarily either unsympathetic to scientific truth, or suspicious of intellectual excellence. He wondered why Sir Henry had not consulted American experience on this point, for as he proudly believed, 'there has never been any society in which new discoveries and inventions . . . have been received with so much readiness.'[7] Godkin admitted that in his political rituals the American might seem anti-intellectual, yet insisted that outside of politics the attainments of scientific and literary men were highly valued. As he submitted, 'scientific men, working in their own fields, are nowhere so widely known and respected by the masses'[8] as in America.

Godkin's rebuttal of *Popular Government* was supplemented by a lengthy English review of the book written by John Morley for the February *Fortnightly Review*. The Liberal statesman took a more direct line than Godkin, in arguing that Sir Henry's analysis amounted to little more than 'a rattling Tory pamphlet'. He found it hardly surprising that an Indian bureaucrat should hold such a low opinion of democracy. 'It was said of Tocqueville', he observed, 'that he was an aristocrat who accepted his defeat. Sir Henry Maine in politics is a bureaucrat who cannot bear to think democracy will win.'[9]

Morley thought that in depicting democracy as an infallible and utopian form of government, Maine had drawn a picture that no serious democrat would accept as an accurate representation of its claims. He had undertaken the impossible in trying to 'measure' the performance of democracy against other régimes on matters like stability and progressiveness, for there were no common standards of measurement. Finally, Morley believed that to the extent that modern political life involved a constant struggle between the forces of knowledge and tradition, it was more likely that looking to the future: 'The interests of science and the interests of democracy are one.'[10]

Maine answered his *Popular Government* critics in a signed article in the March 1886 number of the *Nineteenth Century*. While holding firmly to the views expressed in his book, he here shifted his emphasis. He had written his essays on democracy to discredit extreme sentiment in favour of that form of government, yet Sir Henry did not think it 'beyond the powers of the human intellect to mitigate or even to remove the infirmities of popular government'.[11] He agreed with Mill that, since democracy seemed certain to win the day, what was needed as a safeguard against its excesses was 'a centre of resistance'.[12] In *Popular Government*, he had stressed the primary importance of institutional checks as a means to this end. In his *Nineteenth Century* review of his critics, he placed greater emphasis on the need of modern democracies to guarantee social and political privileges to the minority comprising the men of intellect and science.

Maine's defence did little to appease his detractors. Lord Acton assured a reluctant Mary Gladstone that it was:

> quite right to take in Maine's book and to think out his thought. But it is not a new departure and every good Liberal ought to have discounted the argument of that work and more besides, before avowing himself a Liberal. Morley's article seemed to me a failure, and I reproached Maine with preferring Morley to me.[13]

Lord Bryce, whose monumental study of American democracy was in the press, wrote separately to Henry Sidgwick with similar reservations about Maine's *Popular Government*:

> As you refer several times to Maine, I must say that a re-perusal of his book leaves me with a low opinion of everything in it but its style. . . . He doesn't seem to me to come near understanding America: does not even quite understand the U.S. Constitution: and his charges against democracy generally are as self-contradictory as his historical instances are one-sided and flimsy. There is a better case to be made against democracy than he has made. Nevertheless, I admit the charm of his writing to justify the popularity of the book . . .
>
> I am beginning to fear that the subject of political science is not only difficult but also heavy, for which it needs a style like Maine's and an equally unsubstantial treatment to make it readable.[14]

The first reaction of William Cory on reading Sir Henry's critique of democracy, was that Maine had become 'a desperate old Tory'

254

since their undergraduate days together at Cambridge. 'I should guess few men so able have been so remote, unconsciously, from friendships', he wrote to a friend, and added: 'I had rather be what I am than so superior a person as to speak of the extant English people as the *faece Romuli*!'[15] Yet such criticisms notwithstanding, the course of Maine's political beliefs was firmly set. To Humphrey Ward's jubilee history of Queen Victoria's reign, published in 1887, Sir Henry contributed an essay on Anglo-Indian administration which was little more than an appendix to *Popular Government*. 'The tempestuous controversy lately raging in these islands', he reflected soberly in his final assessment of democracy, 'clearly compels us to hesitate before laying down whether England, the parent of popular government, is an example of the success of that government in keeping a numerous community under the same political institutions.'[16]

During 1886 Sir Henry began again to entertain thoughts of abandoning his seat on the Indian Council. He was encouraged in this when he learned that Vernon Harcourt, under pressure of his work as a leading member of Gladstone's new Cabinet, was about to resign the Whewell Professorship of International Law at Cambridge. He wrote confidentially to Henry Sidgwick from London early in December:

Dec. 8, 1886
London

Private

My dear Sidgwick,

I asked you the other day to let me have some conversation with you on a matter which concerned myself, but it has struck me that I should, after all, save you the trouble by writing to you on the subject.

It is this. I happened to ask Vernon Harcourt, at the funeral of the late Minister of Trinity, whether he was going to lecture this Term. He answered that he should very probably lecture in November; but that, if he did not, he should certainly resign. November is now over and Harcourt has not lectured so that I doubt not that he will resign at the end of the year.

It has occurred to me to form a plan of succeeding Harcourt if I can, and of abandoning my seat on the Indian Council, of which I am much tired. It will involve some sacrifice of income, but I have long felt that sooner or later I must make my choice between my Cambridge and my London duties.

I have paid a good deal of attention to International Law. I used to lecture on it at the Middle Temple, and, when I published my *Ancient Law* I had manuscript enough almost for another volume; indeed, some propositions of mine on the subject found their way into *Ancient Law*, and have been generally accepted by modern writers . . .

On the other hand, anybody who remembers that I resigned a Cambridge Professorship 30 years ago may very well think me too old . . . and I feel it would be absurd that I should send in any testimonials.[17]

Maine's candidacy for the Whewell Professorship was apparently opposed by certain dons who felt Sir Henry's preoccupations as Master of Trinity Hall and as a member of the Indian Council would interfere with the duties of the office. Maine thus wrote further to Sidgwick, who was one of the Electors, repeating his assurance that:

On grounds of general propriety, I think it would be extremely wrong that any public servant should hold a seat on the Indian Council and two academical offices: the Mastership of Trinity Hall and the International Professorship; and therefore, if I were elected to the latter, I should resign the Indian Council as soon as the current Indian business permitted. This you are quite at liberty to state to the Electors.[18]

He authorized Sidgwick formally to declare him a candidate if the opportunity presented itself, and added somewhat disingenuously: 'Of course I am not for a moment suggesting that you would necessarily vote for me.' Several days later Maine was named to the Whewell Professorship, but he did not resign from the Indian Council. There were apparently bitter feelings in Cambridge. A lengthy letter Maine sent to Sidgwick late in 1887, defending himself on the grounds that the appointment of the Aitchison Commission to inquire into the recruitment of educated Indians to the I.C.S. had necessitated his remaining at the India Office, is the last extant Maine letter I have found:

The present claim of the India Office for my assistance or services certainly goes beyond the expectation I had [he wrote] and of its strength and duration I am, of course, no very good judge. But out of the business undisposed of there is one part in regard to which my withdrawal might certainly embarrass the Secretary of State seriously. I refer to a group of questions connected with the proposed reorganization of the Public Service in India. The Government of India is a bureaucracy, and the educated Natives of India, who sometimes affect the deepest interest in politics, take a far more genuine interest in the system by which public employment is distributed. This group of subjects, which called urgently for attention early in 1886, has always been a good deal in my hands. I drafted myself the dispatch which directed the formation of a powerful Commission to investigate some of the points involved. I have had much correspondence unofficially with some of the Commissioners, and latterly with Lord Dufferin. The Commissioners are now preparing their report, and this will very shortly be laid before the India Office.

It seems to me that this group of subjects falls fairly within my reservation of current business, though at the time at which I wrote to you the consideration of part of it had just been transferred to India. Do you think that any good would be done if I asked you to mention to the gentlemen to whom you have spoken that I proposed to retain my seat in Council (under the above reservation) until these questions are disposed of? . . . I confess that to me it would be a great advantage, for I have been so taken aback by the opinions which you have reported to me that I require to look at the situation all round and see what ought to be done.[19]

Maine's selection as Whewell Professor, as a result of which he undertook the preparation of his posthumously published lectures on *International Law* (1888), marked the last of his many academic honours, and coincided with a continued decline in his health. He was less able than ever before to summon the energy to engage in sustained academic work. Ambrose Tighe, through the pages of the April 1886 *Nation*, issued a direct challenge to Sir Henry to provide a fuller defence of his patriarchal thesis against recent criticisms,[20] but Maine had already by that date said his final words on the subject. In an unsigned article on 'The Patriarchal Theory', published in the *Quarterly Review* for January 1886, he had reiterated the major

points of his theory of primitive patriarchy, while ostensibly reviewing an edition of J. F. McLennan's collected anthropological papers
which had been seen through the press by his younger brother
Donald McLennan. Finding the volume 'most absurdly controversial', he emphasized that he remained open to conviction that the
matriarchal family had historically preceded families organized on
the principle of *patria potestas*. But until 'the eager disputants who
have already made up their mind' could provide firmer evidence in
support of their views, Sir Henry felt moved to recommend 'a little
more modesty and a little less zeal'.[21]

Maine was a tired and sickly man, and his differences with the
'matriarchal school' were never resolved. Yet he at least had the
consolation in later life of knowing that his advocacy of the 'historical
and comparative' method had guaranteed his place among the leading English jurists of the nineteenth century. One of the last letters
he addressed to his publisher suggests the extent of that success:

> Trinity Hall Lodge,
> Cambridge,
> Nov. 21, 1886
>
> My dear Murray,
>
> I am glad to hear that *Ancient Law* and *Village Communities*
> are requiring new editions. I think they had better be mere re-
> prints. The *V. Communities* must be greatly re-written some day:
> much controversy on its subject is proceeding on the Continent
> but it is at present too soon for me to take up the subject anew.
>
> I think this will be the eleventh edition of my *Ancient Law* and
> the fourth or fifth of *Village Communities*.
>
> Will you kindly send a copy of each of my books (or of such as
> are in print) to A. W. Maine, Esq., Maxwell Place, Kelso,
> Roxburghshire? The parcel should go by rail, and should be
> marked 'From the author for the Kelso Library.'
>
> Very kindly yours,
> H. S. Maine[22]

In an earlier letter he had noted: 'I am inclined on the whole to
think that the favour with which Austin's *Jurisprudence* is regarded
as an educational book is rather declining—I am repeating what I
heard the other day from one of the Oxford Professors . . . He added

that the credit of this book was chiefly kept up through its being prescribed by the University of London.'[23]

By the late autumn of 1887 Maine's health had deteriorated to such an extent that his doctors ordered him to stop work altogether. Sir Henry therefore arranged leaves of absence from the India Office and the university, and resolved to spend a period of recuperation at Cannes in Southern France. A friend who met Maine in the train from Paris found him looking 'deathly ill'. In a letter sent to the Prime Minister from Cannes on 19 January 1888 Lord Acton mentioned that 'Maine is in my hands, laid up with overwork'.[24]

Acton's estate at *la Californie* was a famous gathering place for Victorian intellectuals. Situated high on the olive-coloured hills to the west of the main town of Cannes, the villa commanded a magnificent view of the whitewashed Mediterranean buildings and green sea that stretched below. Maine took up rooms at the Montfleury Hotel nearby, and during the first days of his stay, went to dine with the Actons in the evenings. His host found him 'at times . . . nearly as good as ever, and quite happy about himself; only disinclined to study, and a Tory of the most ordinary and uninteresting type'. When Maine was not inclined to join the Acton's guests at dinner, young Dick Acton was sent around to keep him company, for as Lord Acton later confided to Mary Gladstone, he thought it 'useful to him to hear so able a man, even at second best'.[25]

During the evening of 1 February, Maine suffered a severe stroke, and Lady Maine was immediately summoned from London by telegraph. Sir Henry lay in a coma during the following two days and expired without ever regaining consciousness, on Friday, 3 February. When Lady Maine arrived at the railway station early next morning she was met by Lord Acton, who took it upon himself to tell her that her husband had died while she was *en route* from Paris. Two weeks later Acton wrote a lengthy letter to Charlie Maine outlining the circumstances of his father's death. I recently discovered it, still in its original envelope, among a batch of neglected family papers in the possession of Sir Henry's grandson, Henry Cecil Sumner Maine:

Cannes, Feb. 13.

Dear Mr Maine,

I was glad to see, from your very kind letter, the way in which you look at the great loss you have had. Indeed we cannot regret

259

that none of you were out here, for it was very sad to see your father lying unconscious, and to feel that we were all unable to help. I asked both doctors whether bleeding would not relieve him, but they were afraid of weakness of the heart. But he suffered no pain, and never felt the sorrow of parting. At first it was thought possible that he might become conscious for a time, and that must excuse my mistake of asking Lady Maine to come.

We made out that Dr Robson Roose thought ill of his condition; but it appeared to all of us that he was getting stronger, more active, and more serene. I think that was also Dr Bright's impression. None of those who met him when he dined or lunched out observed that anything was the matter with him. The Isaacsons were his neighbours at dinner, and I think their company and good nature were valuable to him. I believe that Mr Isaacson thought that he was seriously out of sorts.

When Lady Maine proposed to let me see the portion of his lectures which he had with him, I did not think it right to accept the offer, not only because I am no jurist, but because he at one time spoke of showing them to me before sending them to Knowles, and ended by not doing it. I concluded that he had thought it unnecessary, and rightly judged that, if anybody, some legal friend ought to look them over.

Acton then suggested that Maine's mental powers had towards the end shown signs of serious decay:

I should wish to explain to you exactly what I meant in speaking about these lectures to Miss Maine. I believe that your father composed out of his head, verifying here and there, but carrying all his materials in his mind. This is far more trying than work done with the help of notes and extracts. Such an effort must have become more fatiguing and exhausting then ever. Last summer, when he was interested in making out what had suggested to Grotius the idea of his book, I told him that the whole account was given in Grotius's letters, and asked him to come and read the passages in my library. He said "Ha! more books you want me to read." And he never came.

Although the first jet of his thoughts was as clear and as strong as formerly, I am inclined to think that he was less ready to take all the precautions he used to take, and would feel harassed by minutiae. There was that impatience of drudgery which is natural to great minds in their maturity. All the time here he avoided everything like heavy reading, and rather seemed to enjoy a little expedition to Monte Carlo.[26]

Later in the month Acton wrote further: 'I hope to learn before long that Lady Maine has got over the immediate effects of her terribly melancholy journey. A report reached us that she was detained at Lyons; so that we were glad to least to learn from you of her safe return.' He added: 'You are very kind indeed to propose that I should keep one of the books from your father's library in memory of him.'[27] Charlie Maine's careful attention to the details of his father's estate suggest his intention to carry on in his footsteps, perhaps to become his biographer. But his promising career was cut short when he died of a sudden attack only four months after the death of his father. Lady Maine lived on in a world of fading memories for another thirty-two years, until her death in 1920 at the advanced age of ninety-three.

Maine was buried at Cannes on a superb hillside site overlooking the sea. In an *éloge* delivered at his grave, Fustel de Coulanges, the celebrated author of *The Ancient City*, pronounced him the greatest English historian of his day. *The Times*, in a lengthy obituary notice written by Humphrey Ward, thought his pioneering contributions to the scientific study of men had been of the calibre of Montesquieu. On the day of his funeral, 8 February 1888, a special memorial service was held in the small Trinity Hall Chapel, Cambridge, the college where Maine had begun his professorial career as an unknown young classics don in 1844. Among those present to hear the oration by the Vice-Master, Henry Latham, were many undergraduates.[28]

As the outcome of a meeting of friends and admirers of Sir Henry's work, held at the India Office on 20 June 1888, a fund was launched to erect a suitable permanent memorial. Sir Edgar Boehm was commissioned to execute a marble medallion of Maine's features, which was to be placed in Westminster Abbey. Grant Duff, Arthur Russell and Alfred Lyall went to the Abbey and wandered for a long while with Dean Bradley examining the available spaces. They finally decided on a position 'immediately above the bust of Cobden, and near enough to the monument of Warren Hastings to be pronounced in good Indian company'.[29] Months later, during the afternoon of 17 December 1889, the Secretary of State for India, Lord Cross, with Lady Maine at his side, unveiled the tablet while a small gathering of scholars and Anglo-Indians looked on. No speeches were given. The medallion bore a short inscription written by Sir Frederick Pollock, which said:

Sir Henry James Sumner Maine, K.C.S.I.,
(1822–1888)

Member	Master
of the Council	of Trinity Hall
of India	Cambridge

Veterum Prudentiam Indagavit
Indis Leges Novas Condidit
*Suis Antiqui Iuris Fontes Reclusit**

*He investigated the learning of the ancients.
Framed new legislation for India.
Laid open the sources of ancient law for his own people.

Notes

Chapter 1. Origins of a Lawyer

1. Information in J. Mason, *Kelso Records: Being Traditions and Recollections of Kelso*, Edinburgh, Brown 1839; J. Haig, *The History of Kelso*, Edinburgh, Fairbairn, 1825; F. H. Groome, ed., *Ordnance Gazeteer of Scotland*, London, Mackenzie, [n.d.], iv.

2. G. F. Black, *The Surnames of Scotland: Their Origin, Meaning and History*, N.Y., New York Public Library, 1946, p. 574; see also R. A. Main, *The House of Main: Historical, Genealogical and Heraldic Notes Relating to the Mains and Kindred Families*, London, 1939 (privately printed).

3. *Kelso Church of Scotland Baptismal Register, 1813–1810* (italics added), Registrar's Office, Edinburgh; *Kelso Mail,* 27 February 1804. The 'James Main' given as a witness was presumably a brother of Adam Main: *Kelso Mail,* 4 November 1837, records the death of 'Mr James Main, fenar, Kelso, in his 90th year', and on 6 July 1848, of 'Catherine Mitchell, relict of Mr James Main, fenar in Kelso, aged 65'.

4. *Kelso Parish Rolls, 1820–1847*, Registrar's Office, Edinburgh; *Glasgow Herald*, 6 June 1825, p. 2; *Kelso Mail*, 8 September 1836; 25 May 1843; 23 October 1857; *Border Almanac*, 1892. In a letter to his publisher of 8 June 1877, Sir Henry Maine wrote: 'The writer on whose behalf I spoke to you last night at Lord Houghton's is my sister-in-law and cousin, Miss Maine. You very probably have met her, as she lives with us about half of every year. She has published some novels with Smith, Elder & Co., of which the last, "Scarscliff Rocks", has been decidedly successful.' *J. M. Arch.* Eliza's books included *Among Strangers: An Autobiography* (edited by E.S.M.), 1870; *Annie: An Excellent Person*, 1872; *Marchmont of Redlands* (2 vols.), 1872; *Scarscliff Rocks* (3 vols.), 1875; *Angus Grey* (3 vols.), 1878. Reviewing Eliza's first book, *The Athenaeum*, 8 October 1870, thought it 'naturally and pleasantly written . . . should find a place in many a home circle', yet her further works were represented as 'humdrum unromantic' copies of Trollope. See also Chapter 19, n. 2, *supra*.

5. *Records of the Marischal College and University of Aberdeen*, ii, printed for the New Spalding Club, 1898, p. 151.

6. J. A. Venn, *Alumni Cantabrigienses*, ii, vol. 4, p. 292. Sir M. E. Grant Duff says Maine was born 'near Leighton', *Memoir*, p. 2; The Everyman's Library edition of *Ancient Law* describes Maine as a native of India, while P. Drucker, 'The Employee Society', *American Journal of Sociology*, lviii, 1953, p. 358, speaks of 'that great Irishman Sir Henry Maine'.

7. In his Will and Testament, 2 January 1888, Probate Registry, Somerset House, London, Sir Henry bequeathed *'to my brother* the Reverend Lewin George Maine and to my sister-in law Eliza Sophia Maine a legacy of seventy five pounds each'. In a letter to John Murray of 22 May 1874, Maine mentions: *'A brother of mine* [is] settled in New Zealand on the outskirts of civilization. I want to send him a box of books, which he tells me is the most acceptable present he could receive, and adds that any books would be welcome except strictly scientific books. This however, throws me on the whole range of literature and I find it virtually impossible to make a selection. It occurs to me that you have on your shelves copies of as good books as have been published during 15 or 18 years (he has been as long as that out of this country) and that you, or somebody about you, could make up a list of your own books for me enough to form a box-full.' *J. M. Arch.*

8. *Memoir*, p. 2.

9. *Records of the Society of Lincoln's Inn*, ii, Admissions, 1800–93, London, 1896, p. 234: 'James Maine, M.D., of the Province of Hindustan, dec'd.'

10. *J. F. Stephen Papers*, Camb. Univ. Lib., Add. 7349, ff. 38039.

11. Maine did have a French connection, though he probably romanticized its social significance. In the *Maine Collection*, LSE, Volume 13, Item T, there is written not in Maine's hand, 'Anna de Cossette, Roquefort, 1848', and ff. 41.55 show her accounts as residual legatee under the will of Charles Bartlett James Fell, 'late of Calicut in the Malabar Coast': *Register of Deaths*, 1849, 451.197. Somerset House, London. Fell's will was drawn up at Madras, and proved in London, 25 March 1851, and while Anna de Cosette's lawyers were Roumieu, Walters and Co. of Lincoln's Inn, presumably Henry Maine had some role in handling her legal affairs. Anna de Cosette was Charles Fell's aunt, and he was the brother of Eliza Maine (Henry Maine's mother): therefore she was Sir Henry's great-aunt. Charles Fell may well have been the namesake of Sir Henry's first son, 'Charles Sumner Maine'.

12. E. S. Maine, *Marchmont of Redlands*, London, Smith Elder, 1872, i, pp. 17–18.

13. *Memoir*, p. 2. Grant Duff rather amusingly adds: 'As Fate destined him

to have so much to do with the Government of India, it was fortunate
that he retained no grudge against the poppy.'

14. Cited in E. H. Pearce, *Annals of Christ's Hospital*, London, Rees, 1908,
p. 96.

15. *The Times*, 22 September 1838, cited in R. A. Main, *op. cit.*

16. *Census of Kelso*, 1841: Ref. 793/1/22; 1851: Ref. 814/8/19, Registrar's
Office, Edinburgh.

Chapter 2. Pembroke College, Cambridge

1. *Maine Collection*, LSE, i, f. 92; iii. f. 310. Only one of the manuscript
notebooks, from Maine's second year at Cambridge, is extant: there are
some 378 pages of notes on aspects of classical literature, as well as
lengthy lists of towns and cities of the ancient world, complete with
drawings of their location and planning: ii, B.

2. *Ibid*, iii, C. f. 5: in the same section, especially at iii. D. f. 9, Maine
hints that he was already beginning to formulate one of his most
important later theses, that early Roman private law was primarily a
law of status.

3. F. W. Cornish, ed., *Extracts from the Letters of William Cory*, Oxford,
Hart (for subscribers), 1897, pp. 16–17; O. Browning, 'Sir Henry
Maine', *Cambridge Fortnightly*, February 1888, pp. 48–50.

4. Cited in *Memoir*, p. 6.

5. Sir H. J. S. Maine, *Village Communities in East and West*, London,
Murray, 1871 (3rd edn, 1876), p. 328: subsequent entries as *VC*.

6. For discussion of the Apostles', see F. M. Brookfield, *The Cambridge
Apostles'*, London, Pitman, 1906; A. W. Brown, *The Metaphysical
Society*, Columbia University Press, 1947, p. 5 *et seq.*; A. Sidgwick
and E. Sidgwick, *Henry Sidgwick: A Memoir*, London, Macmillan.
1906, pp. 29–31.

7. *Memoir*, p. 10; see also H. Latham, 'Sir Henry Maine', *Cambridge
Review*, February 1888; H. Adams, *The Education of Henry Adams:
An Autobiography*, London, Constable, 1919, p. 368, speaking of
Maine and Rudolph Sohm, recalled that 'convinced that the clue of
religion led to nothing, and that politics led to chaos, one had turned to
the law, as one's scholars turned to the Law School, because one could
see no other path to a profession'. In Maine's *Saturday Review* articles
(see Chapter 4, *supra*) there is ample evidence of his anti-clericalism and
his distrust of radical religious sects: 'Bible Burning', *Saturday Review*,
i, 8 December, 1855, p. 90; 'The Division List on Sabbath Observance',
ibid., i, 1 March 1856, p. 334; 'May Meetings', *ibid.*, ii, 3 May 1856,
p. 2; 'Academical Freedom', *ibid.*, ii, 7 June 1856, p. 118; 'Lord
Ravensworth on "Revealed Religion",' *ibid.*, ii, 15 November 1856,

p. 630. Further references to the *Saturday Review* will be entered as *Sat. R.*

8. H. J. S. Maine, *H. F. Hallam: A Memoir*, London, Spottiswoode and Shaw, 1851 (privately printed), reprinted in A. H. Hallam, *Remains in Verse and Prose*, London, 1863. G. N. Ray, ed., *The Letters and Private Papers of W. M. Thackeray*, Oxford University Press, 1945, ii, p. 525: William Thackeray mentioned in a letter to Mrs Brookfield of 27 April 1849, that 'I saw Harry Hallam—he and the faithful Maine were reading hard'. As for the *Memoir* of Hallam, Mrs Brookfield wrote on 29 January 1851: 'I can't say I much like the *Memoir*, it seems very short and bald, and as if it were intended for the public instead of intimate friends' *ibid.*, ii, p. 746. Years later, Maine was asked to bring out a new revised edition of Henry Hallam Sr's *Constitutional History of England*. He wrote to John Murray on 31 December 1877: 'It would cause me great pride to have my name associated in any way with Mr Hallam's and I should have great pleasure in doing anything for the advantage of his family, but the fact is I have not given special attention to the subjects embraced in the *Constitutional History*, and I frankly say I do not think myself equal to editing it in a thoroughly satisfactory way.' He suggested his friend T. C. Sandars (1825–94), noting that :'His only published work is an edition of Justinian's *Institutes*, but he is a very able man and a very skilful writer and he has been for some time Reader of Constitutional Law and Legal History to the Inns of Court. I am under the impression that he uses Hallam's *Constitutional History* as a text-book in his classes.' *J. M. Arch.*

9. Information in F. Galton, *Memories of My Life*, London, Methuen, 1908, p. 66; O. Browning, *Memories of Sixty Years at Eton, Cambridge and Elsewhere*, London, Lane, 1910, p. 18; Lord Lytton, *Julian Fane: A Memoir*, London, Murray, 1871, pp. 24–5; A. G. Gardiner, *The Life of Sir William Harcourt*, London, Constable, 1923, i, pp. 52–4.

10. L. Stephen, *Life of Sir James Fitzjames Stephen*, London, Smith Elder, 1895, p. 102 *et seq.*: Stephen notes that 'Maine's influence upon my brother was second only to that of my father.' Further information in *J. F. Stephen Papers*, Camb. Univ. Lib., Add. 7349. f. 32.

11. H. J. S. Maine, 'Midsummer Night's Dream', *Edinburgh Review*, lxxxvii, April 1848, pp. 418–29.

12. C. Bristed, *Five Years at an English University*, N.Y., Putnam, 1852, p. 612 *et seq.*

Chapter 3. Law Don

1. In a more serious vein, R. H. Murray, *English Social and Political Thinkers of the Nineteenth Century*, Cambridge, Heffer, 1929, p. 196, has pointed out the parallel between Maine's work and the writings of

Samuel Taylor Coleridge: 'The comparative point of view had been Coleridge's, and his attitude to history prepared the way for the "Ancient Law" and its numerous descendants.'

2. Cited in *Memoir*, p. 9.

3. *Ibid.*, p. 10.

4. *J .F. Stephen Papers*, Camb. Univ. Lib., Add. 7349. f. 38.

5. W. S. Holdsworth, *A History of English Law*, London, Methuen, 1938, xii, p. 77.

6. Discussion based on W. S. Holdsworth, *op. cit.*, xii, pp. 78–101; xv, pp. 231–47, 350–68; and B. Abel-Smith and R. Stevens, *Lawyers and the Courts, 1750–1965*, London, Heinemann, 1967, pp. 53–76. According to the latter study, in England in the twentieth century: 'The law, as a field of academic study' is still 'tolerated rather than encouraged by the legal profession.' p. 349.

7. W. S. Holdsworth, *op. cit.*, xv, pp. 234–7; B. Abel-Smith and R. Stephens, *op. cit.*, p. 64 *et seq.*

8. Parliamentary Papers, *Cambridge University Commission . . . Reports, 1852/53*, xliv, Correspondence and Evidence, p. 77: subsequent entries as '*CUC*'.

9. *CUC*, p. 80. Maine included in his evidence a copy of a notice given out for the perusal of prospective law students in Cambridge.

10. D. A. Winstanley, *Early Victorian Cambridge*, Cambridge University Press, 1940, p. 152.

11. *CUC*, p. 91.

12. *Ibid.*

13. B. Abel-Smith and R. Stephens, *op. cit.*, p. 71.

14. *CUC*, p. 79.

15. *CUC*, pp. 72–3.

16. *Rolls of the Parish of Kelso, 1820–1854*, Registrar's Office, Edinburgh: 'Henry James Sumner Maine of the University of Cambridge and Jane Main of this Parish, after due proclamation banns in the Church of Kelso, were married here on the 20 Dec., 1847, by the Rev. Mr Kell of the Episcopal Chapel here.'

17. Probate Registry, Somerset House, London; *Cambridge Chronicle*, 23 March 1850, p. 2: 'March 18, in Finchley Road, the wife of H. S. Maine, Esq., LL.D., of a son.'

18. *Memoir*, p. 14.

19. F. W. Cornish, *op. cit.*, p. 46. Maine wrote several amusing articles on 'hydropathy' in which he was obviously reflecting on personal

experiences: 'Medical Education', *Sat. R.*, i, 12 April 1856, p. 470, and Bathing Towns', *ibid*, ii, 30 August 1856, p. 391.

20. G. N. Ray, *op. cit.*, ii, p. 508; *CUC*, p. 78. Maine noted: 'The Professor has no residence, but the College of Trinity Hall usually permits him to occupy a set of its rooms on payment of the usual rent.'

21. G. N. Ray, *op. cit.*, ii, p. 508. Maine's interest in general literature apparently continued from his youth to be a favourite diversion. Thus, Oscar Browning, *Memories of Sixty Years at Eton, Cambridge and Elsewhere*, London, Lane, 1910, records that when he met Maine in 1871, he 'called on him at a house near Windsor, and found him, characteristically, reading a novel'.

22. F. Brookfield, *Mrs Brookfield and Her Circle*, London, Pitman, 1905, p. 287: the letter was dated 29 May 1849.

23. W. S. Holdsworth, *op. cit.*, xv, pp. 237–9; B. Abel-Smith and R. Stevens, *op. cit.*, pp. 63–8.

24. H. J. S. Maine, 'The Inns of Court', *Sat. R.*, i, 1 December 1855, p. 76.

25. *J. F. Stephen Papers*, Camb. Univ. Lib., Add. 7349, f. 38.

26. *Memoir*, p. 14.

27. R. I. Best, *Whitley Stokes, 1830–1909: A Memorial Discourse*, Dublin University Press, 1951, p. 3; J. W. Burrow, *Evolution and Society: A Study in Victorian Social Theory*, Cambridge University Press, 1966, pp. 137–78. In reviewing Maine's *Ancient Law*, *Quarterly Review*, cx, July 1861, p. 117, Montague Bernard noted the 'striking resemblance between these inquiries and those which have been pursued of late years into the origin and relations of language . . . as Professor Müller has shown how philology may be made to throw a new and curious light on other departments of literature and science, Mr Maine has done a similar service to law'.

28. F. Harrison, *Autobiographic Memoirs*, London, Macmillan, 1911, i, p. 157.

29. Harrison to Professor Beesly [n.d.], 1858, *Harrison Collection*, LSE, Sect. A.

30. F. Harrison, *op. cit.*, i, p. 152.

31. *Ibid*. Harrison recalled that 'the substance of the problem we studied together', and referred to Maine's Middle Temple lectures as being 'afterwards, his book *Ancient Law*'.

32. H. J. S. Maine, 'The Conception of Sovereignty and Its Importance in International Law', in *Papers Read Before the Juridical Society of London, 1855–58*, i, pp. 26–45. While little can be said with certainty of the intellectual influences exerted on Maine, it is worth noting that the monumental *System des heutigen römischen Rechtes* (9 vols) of Freidrich von Savigny (1779–1861) was published during the period 1840–1851.

33. *Ibid.*, p. 32.

34. H. J. S. Maine, 'Roman Law and Legal Education', *Cambridge Essays*, 1856, reprinted in *VC*, pp. 330–83. The original draft, partly in Maine's and partly in his clerk's hand, is in the *Maine Collection*, LSE, xix, Item I.

35. H. J. S. Maine, 'The Inns of Court', *op. cit.*, p. 76.

Chapter 4. The 'Saturday Review'

1. *J. F. Stephen Papers*, Camb. Univ. Lib., Add. 7349, Box 2, f. 51.

2. M. M. Bevington, *The Saturday Review. 1855–1858*, Columbia University Press, 1941, p. 15. H. Paul. *The Life of Froude*, London, Pitman, 1905, p. 147, recalled that: 'It is difficult for the present generation to understand the influence which that celebrated periodical exercised, or the terror which it inspired, forty years ago.'

3. See Sir M. E. Grant Duff, *Notes From a Diary, 1851–1895*, London, Murray, 1897, i, p. 83. J. W. Robertson Scott, *The Life and Death of a Newspaper*, London, Methuen, 1952, p. 19, noted that 'it was Maine . . . who had suggested the paper's name'. But there are varying accounts of the circumstances of the naming of the *Saturday Review*: see, for example, H. W. Law and I. Law, *The Book of the Beresford Hopes*, London, Cranton, 1925, p. 215, and H. R. Fox Bourne, *English Newspapers*, London, Chatto & Windus, 1887, ii, p. 248.

4. *Maine Collection*, LSE, xviii, Item Y, f. 2r *et seq*. Of Maine as a literary stylist, E. Elton, *A Survey of English Literature, 1830–1880*, London, Arnold, 1920, i, pp. 102–3 wrote: 'There is no better Cambridge prose than that of Sir Henry Maine. By Cambridge prose I mean a prose of which logic, reason and dislike of surplusage form the mental basis, and which is distinguished by the great 18th century virtues of closeness, orderliness, incisive clearness, and freedom from rhetoric.' Maine's journalistic writings, however, are not always free of the last characteristic.

5. M. M. Bevington. *op. cit.*, pp. 331–91.

6. 'Eothen in the South West', *Sat. R.*, iii, 17 January 1857, p. 45.

7. 'Administrative Brahminism', *Sat. R.*, v, 13 March 1858, pp. 259–60.

8. 'Eothen in the South West', *op. cit.*, p. 45.

9. 'Dear at the Money', *Sat. R.*, iii, 14 February 1857, p. 142.

10. 'Our Newspaper Institutions', *Sat. R.*, i, 3 November 1855, pp. 2–3. This leader from Maine headed the first edition of the *Saturday Review*. Maine's fear of the power of the press for irresponsible manipulation of opinion must be seen in light of the Victorian practice of anonymous

journalism. As Maine wrote elsewhere: 'Though we utterly deny that anonymous journalists make statements at their fancy, as victims of their malice may direct, we must add that some kind of change does really seem to come over a man when he is penning a production which is not to bear his signature at its foot', a point of view that has generally been accepted in newspaper practice since his day. See his 'Anonymous Human Nature', *Sat. R.*, ii, 8 November 1856, p. 608. Maine was especially critical of *The Times* as a result of the paper's campaign for army reform during the Crimean war, a campaign which, due to the enterprising efforts of their chief war correspondent, W. H. Russell, attained tremendous influence in the formation of British public opinion. As *The History of the Times*, ii, *The Tradition Established*, London, Printing House Square, 1939, p. 167, asserts of the power of the paper during the 1850s: '*The Times* could make or unmake Generals, Ministers and Governments. Its power became so great that towards the end of the war the *Saturday Review* (of 3 November 1855), founded for the express purpose of combating the power of Printing House Square, declared that "no apology is necessary for assuming that this country is ruled by *The Times*".' The *Saturday Review* quote is in fact taken from Maine's 'Our Newspaper Institutions,' *op. cit.*, p. 2.

11. 'Our Newspaper Institutions', *op. cit.*, p. 3.

12. 'The Language of Party', *Sat. R.*, i, 26 April 1856, p. 511.

13. *Ibid.*

14. 'Political Dalliance', *Sat. R.*, ii, 29 November 1856, pp. 672–3.

15. Cited in *Memoir*, p. 12, from an unsigned *Morning Chronicle* article.

16. 'Eothen in the South West', *op. cit.*, p. 45.

17. 'Dear at the Money', *op. cit.*, p. 142.

18. 'Your Petitioners Will Ever Pray', *Sat. R.*, i, 8 March 1856, p. 358: in Maine's view, 'the members of the House of Commons are not delegates, but representatives', and thus, ostensibly harmless petitioning could in difficult times lead to 'impudent interference with the rights of the legislature.'

19. 'Southwark and Public Opinion', *Sat. R.*, i, 10 November 1855, p. 27.

20. 'Beranger', *Sat. R.*, ii, 12 April 1856, pp. 465–6.

21. 'Mr Thackeray and the Four Georges', *Sat. R.*, i, 15 December 1855, p. 106. In 'The Moral of McNeill', *Sat. R.*, i, 16 February 1856, p. 285, Maine wrote further of American cultural standards that while 'the standard of what is "extraordinary" . . . differs in different minds and in different countries . . . it is low in the United States, where every Jefferson Brick is "one of the most remarkable men in the country".'

22. 'Memoirs of James Gordon Bennett and His Times', *Sat. R.*, i, 3

November 1855, p. 15; 'Leaves of Grass', *Sat. R.*, i, 15 March 1856, p. 393. For Maine, Whitman's work was that of an ideological writer more committed to propagandizing a specific form of political régime, democracy, than to the pursuit of artistic truth.

23. The researches of Joseph Hamburger have shown how the philosophical radicals skilfully pressed their reformist views through the periodical press during this period. Hamburger argues that James Mill, who popularized Bentham's political ideas, was not the champion of the middle class (in Maine's sense) but rather, hoped for the advent of an unrestricted democracy which would derive its strength from a broad coalition of the 'middle rank'. See his 'James Mill on Universal Suffrage and the Middle Class'. *Journal of Politics*, xxiv, 1962, pp. 167–190; *James Mill and the Art of Revolution*, Yale University Press, 1963; *John Stuart Mill and the Philosophical Radicals*, Yale University Press, 1965.

24. J. Bowring, ed., *The Works of Jeremy Bentham*, ix, *Constitutional Code for the Use of All Nations Professing Liberal Opinions*, Edinburgh, Tait, 1843. Maine, later equating the teachings of Bentham with those of Rousseau for their 'revolutionary' overtones, noted of the *Constitutional Code* that 'the ideal political system for which he argued . . . has not a little resemblance to that of Rousseau and Sieyes.' *Popular Government*, London, Murray, 1885, p. 163; subsequent entries as '*PG*'. According to Maine, as Bentham lost faith in the possibility of gradually reforming English institutions, he came to place his trust in 'a sort of legislation *to force men to think and feel, as well as to act in conformity with his standard* . . . It was then that he published his attack on the British Constitution, and published his proposals *for reconstructing it from base to apex. As the classes which it placed in power refused to recognize or promote the greatest happiness of the greatest number, he proposed to displace them and hand over all political authority to the greatest number itself* . . . This reasoning had great effect on some of the most powerful minds of Bentham's day. His disciples—Grote, the two Mills, Molesworth, the two Austins, and Roebuck—did *really do much to transform the British Constitution.*' *PG*, pp. 164–5. (Italics added). Maine's conservative temperament was not likely to be receptive to such doctrines. As Crane Brinton, *The Anatomy of Revolution*, London, Cape, 1953, p. 179, noted of such new forms of nineteenth-century political radicalism: 'Neither their aims nor their methods are those that good Victorians like Bagehot and Maine could approve or sympathize with.'

25. See O. Anderson, 'The Janus Face of Mid-Nineteenth Century English Radicalism: The Administrative Reform Association of 1855', *Victorian Studies*, viii, March 1965, pp. 231–42. In recent years the whole subject of the Victorian 'revolution in administration' has been embroiled in controversy, following the publication of O.O.C.M. MacDonagh's 'The

19th Century Revolution in Government: A Reappraisal', *Historical Journal*, i, 1958, pp. 52–67. MacDonagh doubts that there was any such 'revolution', or that if there was, that abstract ideas had much bearing on events, and his argument has some relevance to Maine's own appraisal of the administrative changes taking place in his day. J. Hart, 'Nineteenth Century Social Reform: A Tory Interpretation of History', *Past and Present*, xxxi, 1965, pp. 39–61, and H. Parris, 'The 19th Century Revolution in Government: A Reappraisal Reappraised', *Historical Journal*, iii, 1960, pp. 17–37, each offer scholarly opposition to the MacDonagh thesis, while V. Cromwell, 'Interpretations of 19th Century Administration: An Analysis', *Victorian Studies*, ix, March 1966, pp. 245–55 offers a useful summary of further literature.

26. 'Head and Tail', *Sat. R.*, ii, 14 June 1856, pp. 142–3.

27. 'A Burst Bladder', *Sat. R.*, i, 1 December 1855, pp. 75–6.

28. 'Army Examinations', *Sat. R.*, i, 5 January 1856, pp. 167–8: 'We are sure that the candidates thus acquitting themselves will be as remarkable for courage, self devotion and docility as for intellectual cultivation, but we are afraid that they will be the last men whom a wise or humane Executive would send out to organize land-rental in Pegu, or to direct trench work in a Crimean winter.'

29. 'Circumlocution vs. Circumvention', *Sat. R.*, ii, 22 November 1856, pp. 649–50.

30. 'A Burst Bladder', *op. cit*, p. 76.

31. 'Eothen in the South West', *op. cit.*, p. 45. As Maine added elsewhere: 'In England, where there is no such thing as true patriotism, and where the idea of country is inextricably mixed up with the notion of paying taxes, Circumlocution may possibly be the price we pay.' 'Circumlocution vs. Circumvention', *op. cit.*, p. 650.

32. 'Io Triumphe', *Sat. R.*, ii, 9 August 1856, p. 329.

33. *Ibid.*, pp. 329–30. Elsewhere, Maine expresses a similar sentiment in writing caustically about criticisms of the British conduct of the Crimean war: 'The statement of a regimental officer who sees part of an engagement is worthier of belief than the dispatch of a general commanding, who sees it all. The story of Mr Russell, who touches up the narrative, is worthier of belief than the account of the officer who tells the tale to Mr Russell unadorned. The view of a contributor who studies the art of war in London, with the aid of a technological dictionary and a map, is worthier of belief than the version of a Correspondent who, like the pupils of Mr Squeers, not only spells "w,i,n,d,e,r,—winder", but actually goes to the Crimea to see it cleaned.' See 'The Importunity of Truth', *Sat. R.*, i, 15 December 1855, pp. 111–12.

34. 'If it really be true that Englishmen for the most part dislike theories, it must be a merciful providence which has created the distaste, for

most assuredly, when a Briton does by any accident get hold of a theory, he rides it as far as a beggar's horse.' 'Theorizing About India', *Sat. R.*, iv, 19 September 1857, pp. 254–5. Maine's distrust of abstract ideas in politics has been recently cited by W. H. Greenleaf as resembling a similar characteristic in the political thought of Professor Michael Oakeshott. In his *Oakeshott's Philosophical Politics*, London, Longmans, 1966, p. 68, he writes that 'Maine's repudiation of abstract principles of government, his historical method, and his "melancholy conservatism" (as Barker called it) very much resemble Oakeshott's point of view'. One leading difference appears in Maine's later work, however: his attempt to unite history and science, which Oakeshott would regard as involving two perpetually 'separate' modes of thought. Yet there are points of similarity in the two theorists, especially in such writings of Professor Oakeshott as his 'The Masses in Representative Democracy', in *Freedom and Serfdom: An Anthology of Western Thought*, H. Hunold, ed. Dordrecht, Holland, 1961, pp. 151–70.

35. It is not surprising that Maine was an ardent supporter of the Peelites. Their parliamentary leadership of the movement for repeal of the Corn Laws in 1846 seemed, as S. Low and L. C. Sanders point out in their *Political History of England, xii, 1837–1901*, London, Longmans, 1907, pp. 70–1, 'the natural sequence of those doctrines of freedom of contract and liberty of action which had dominated English thought since the end of the 18th century . . . it was received as an inevitable step in the process of emancipating the individual from the fetters assumed to have been artificially rivetted upon him by the misused authority of society and the state'. Moreover, Maine clearly felt an intellectual affinity with the Peelites because of their revulsion at 'the profound immorality of party' and their attachment to 'the pleasures of liberty of thought'. 'From 1840 to 1846', Maine wrote, 'and still more emphatically during the past ten years, the "Peelites" have enjoyed the luxury of thinking for themselves and of making up their minds independently on every question which came up on the carpet.' See his 'Political Dalliance', *op. cit.*, p. 673, and compare this with his rather melancholy reflections on the "passing of the Whigs" in Chapter 15, *supra*. J. B. Conacher, 'Sir Robert Peel and the Peelites, 1846–50', *English Historical Review*, lxxiii, 1958, pp. 431–52, notes that 'during these years and even from the grave after his death [Sir Robert Peel] kept the party system in a state of suspended animation'. Finally, it should be noted that Maine later became disillusioned with the intellectural heirs of the Peelites, the Manchester School of *laissez-faire* economists, over the influence they exerted upon the opinions of Liberal party Anglo-Indian administrators: see Chapters 15, 16, *supra*.

36. Along this line, a recurring theme in Maine's *Saturday Review* articles is his impatience with growing demands for greater publicity in the management of governmental affairs: 'Where is all this cynical frankness to end?', he wrote: 'Is the dirty linen of Englishmen always to be

washed in public? . . . In England, amid immense pretensions to patriotism, it really seems as if there were no impulse too trivial, no prejudice too vulgar, no interest too sordid, to overcome our sense of duty to the land which has nurtured us. Our foremost journalists have long since shown that a cry, a sensation, a class advantage, are objects which lie much nearer to their hearts than the power, or the credit, or the honour of England.' 'Mr Thackeray and the Four Georges', *op. cit.*, p. 106. On the other hand, Tocqueville, in his *Democracy in America* (P. Bradley edn.), N.Y., Vintage, 1945, ii, Part 4, pp. 342–3, concluded that complete freedom of the press was 'the only cure for the evils that equality may produce', and thus, 'the chief instrument of freedom'.

37. Compare, for example, Maine's views of party dogmatism with those expressed by Hume in his 'That Politics May be Reduced to a Science', in *Hume's Moral and Political Philosophy*, ed., H. D. Aiken, N.Y., Hafner, 1962, pp. 303–4.

38. This point is brought out in the discussion of Montesquieu contained in Kingsley Martin, *French Liberal Thought in the 18th Century*, N.Y., Harper & Row, 1963, pp. 153–67.

39. Maine left the *Saturday Review* early in 1861, apparently over an editorial dispute. Sir H. S. Cunningham, *Lord Bowen*, London, Clowes, 1896, p. 102, recalled that in 1861 an attack on Arthur Stanley caused Maine, Charles Bowen and J. F. Stephen to leave. According to Cunningham: 'Some efforts were made to start a rival journal. . . . Its editorship was offered, it would appear from one of Charles Bowen's letters, both to himself and Sir H. Maine. Both however had the wisdom to decline a dangerous and laborious post, which would have practically involved the abandonment of their profession.' Maine's departure is documented as well in H. W. Law and L.I. Law, *op. cit.*, p. 216, although reasons for his leaving are not given. W. Stebbing, *Charles Henry Pearson . . . Memorials*, London, Longmans, 1900, pp. 89–90, identifies Maine as among the 'Conservative contributors' to the *Saturday Review*, an identification which suggests a possible parallel with the circumstances of his later departure from the *Pall Mall Gazette*: see Chapter 9, n. 7, *supra*.

Chapter 5. 'Ancient Law'

1. Maine to Murray, 6 July 1860, *J. M. Arch.*

2. Maine to Murray, 11 July 1860, *J. M. Arch.*

3. Maine to Murray, 14 October 1860, *J. M. Arch.*

4. Maine to Murray, [?] February 1861, *J. M. Arch.*

5. J. A. Merivale, ed., *Autobiography and Letters of Charles Merivale*, Oxford, Hart, 1898, (privately printed), p. 321. The letter was dated 20 April 1861.

6. E. F. Fisk, ed., *Letters of John Fiske*, N.Y., Macmillan, 1940, pp. 118–19. The letter was dated 3 January 1864. For the influence of social evolutionary theory in the United States in general, see P. P. Wiener, *Evolution and the Founders of Pragmatism*, Harvard University Press, 1949, and S. Persons, ed., *Evolutionary Thought in America*, Yale University Press, 1950.

7. *Memoir*, p. 20: a review written by J. F. Stephen appeared in the October 1861 number of the *Edinburgh Review*.

8. 'Maine's *Ancient Law*', *Sat. R.*, ii, 16 February 1861, pp. 167–9.

9. *Westminster Review*, xix, April 1861, pp. 457–77. The reviewer was Frederic Harrison, who thought the book 'something special': Harrison to Morley, 18 February 1873, *Harrison Collection* LSE, File A.

10. M. Bernard, 'Maine's *Ancient Law*,' *Quarterly Review*, cx, July 1861, pp. 114–38.

11. Sir F. Pollock, ed., *Maine's Ancient Law, with Introduction and Notes*, London, Murray, 1906, p. xiv, (*Beacon Press* edn, with Introduction by Raymond Firth, Boston, 1963): all further references entered as *AL*. Further discussion of Maine's legal theory will be found in Sir F. Pollock, 'Sir Henry Maine and His Work', *Oxford Lectures and Other Discourses*, London, Macmillan, 1890, pp. 147–68, as well as his 'The History of Comparative Jurisprudence', *Journal of the Society of Comparative Legislation*, v, 1907, pp. 74–89; Sir Paul Vinogradoff, *The Teaching of Sir Henry Maine*, London, Froude, 1904; D. Thorner, 'Sir Henry Maine', in H. Ausubel, *et al.*, eds., *Some Modern Historians of Britain*, N.Y., Dryden, 1951, pp. 66–84, and in the list of critical and expository works attached to the end of the present study. For a general comparison of Roman with English materials, see W. W. Buckland and A. D. McNair, *Roman Law and Common Law*, (2nd edn, revised by F. H. Lawson), Cambridge University Press, 1965: see also B. Cohen, *Jewish and Roman Law. A Comparative Study*, N.Y., Jewish Theological Seminary, 1966 (2 vols.). For the Greeks, see R. J. Bonner, *Lawyers and Litigants in Ancient Athens*, University of Chicago Press, 1927; A. R. W. Harrison, *The Law of Athens: The Family and Property*, Oxford University Press, 1967, and J. W. Jones, *The Law and Legal Theory of the Greeks*, Oxford University Press, 1956.

12. *AL*, p. 5. But C. K. Allen, *Law in the Making*, 7th edn, Oxford, Clarendon Press, 1964, p. 120, regards the notion that judgement precedes custom as 'a . . . questionable theory', and suggests that the truth probably lies somewhere between the two.

13. *AL*, pp. 17–19.

14. *AL*, pp. 23–9.

15. *AL*, pp. 32–9. Maine defines a legal fiction as 'any assumption which conceals, or affects to conceal, the fact that a rule of law has undergone

alteration, its letter remaining unchanged, its operation being modified.'
H. F. Jolowicz, *Historical Introduction to the Study of Roman Law*, 2nd edn, Oxford, Clarendon Press, 1954, pp. 92–3, supports the view that the *respondere* 'were, in effect, very much like decisions . . . the opinions . . . helped to mould the law in a manner not entirely different from that in which judgements mould English law'. But he implies that, while the *responsa* were doubtless an important source of law during the Empire, Maine may have exaggerated their earlier importance. William Seagle, *The Quest For Law*, N.Y., Knopf, 1941, p. 66, argues that 'The common use of fictions pre-supposes a greater degree of legal sophistication than archaic people possess.' Sir F. Pollock, *op. cit.*, Note D, p. 396 suggests the qualification that: 'Perhaps Maine's exposition hardly brings out the prevailing motive for introducing fictions, the desire of obtaining a speedier or more complete remedy than the strictly appropriate form of procedure affords.'

16. *AL*, p. 25. Maine uses the term legislation in a special sense, to signify 'the enactments of a legislature which, whether it take the form of an autocratic prince or of a parliamentary assembly, is the assumed organ of the entire society, is the last of the ameliorating instrumentalities.' pp. 28–9. While critical of Bentham for his low view of the worth of legal fictions, he does share his assumption that in a mature body of law they represent 'the greatest of obstacles to symmetrical classification'. p. 26.

17. *AL*, p. 27: 'I call Equity . . . any body of rules existing by the side of the original civil law, founded on distinct principles and claiming incidentally to supercede the civil law in virtue of a superior sanctity inherent in those principles.' But J. C. Gray, in his *The Nature and Sources of the Law*, N.Y., Macmillan, 1921 (*Beacon Press* reprint, 1961), suggests that no great advantage is gained by viewing equity as a separate *source* of law in the strict sense. He points out that while it was in Roman usage primarily a frame of mind in dealing with legal questions, in England after the fourteenth century equity literally became a separate body of law, set out in courts organized for that express purpose.

18. *AL*, pp. 6–8; 28–9; 40–1: 'In the youth and infancy of a nation it is a rare thing for the legislature to be called into action for the general reform of private law.'

19. *AL*, p. 118 *et seq.* Though Maine explicitly bases his thesis on the early history of the Aryan societies, he invited later criticism by going on to comment that 'the difficulty . . . is to know where to stop, to say of what races of men it is *not* allowable to lay down that the society in which they are united was originally organized on the patriarchal model.' p. 119. At p. 133 he speaks of the Roman *patria potestas* as 'necessarily our type of the primeval paternal authority'. Further discussion will be found in Sir F. Pollock, *op. cit.*, Note K; E. M. Sait, *Political Institutions*, N.Y., Appleton-Century Crofts, 1938, pp. 115–20;

H. Sidgwick, *The Development of European Polity*, London, Macmillan, 1920, p. 47 *et seq.* and in Chapter 13, *supra*.

20. *AL*, pp. 121, 250.

21. *AL*, pp. 303–29.

22. *AL*, p. 261.

23. *AL*, pp. 264–80.

24. *AL*, p. 122.

25. *AL*, pp. 178–208.

26. *AL*, p. 124. Thus, 'Ancient jurisprudence . . . may be likened to international law, filling nothing, as it were, except the interstices between the great groups which are the atoms of society.' p. 161.

27. *AL*, p. 168.

28. *AL*, pp. 137–8.

29. *AL*, p. 150.

30. *AL*, pp. 157–61.

31. *AL*, pp. 163–5.

32. W. Friedmann, *Legal Theory*, London, Stevens, 1960, pp. 159–62; R. Pound, 'The Scope and Purpose of Sociological Jurisprudence', *Harvard Law Review*, xxv, pp. 140, 164. Maine's work, according to Pound, was 'a political type of idealistic interpretation. For a purely ethical idea of right it substitutes a political idea of individual freedom.' See also Pound's *Interpretations of Legal History*, Cambridge University Press, 1923, p. 55 *et seq.*

33. *AL*, p. 164. Maine includes as representative 'The child before years of discretion, the orphan under guardianship, the adjudged lunatic.' W. A. Robson, 'Sir Henry Maine Today', in A. L. Goodhart, *et al.*, *Modern Theories of Law*, Oxford University Press, 1933, pp. 160–79, provides an excellent summary of some facets of Maine's theories. Robson suggests that the inculcation of a sense of good faith in human societies has proceeded as much as anything through 'the instrumentality of fear and superstition, by means of oaths involving all kinds of supernatural forces and supported by a frightful carnage of human slaughter and animal sacrifice, mutilation and suffering'. Even in the modern case, as Robson argues, 'Those who speak of the "sanctity of contract" describe better than they usually know a series of phenomena which they would find it difficult to admire on closer inspection.' pp. 169–70. In this resepct, note Maine's sentimental view of the blessings of freedom of contract in Chapter 15, *supra*.

34. C. K. Allen, *Maine's Ancient Law*, Oxford University Press (World Classics), 1959, Introduction, p. xxvii.

277

35. W. Friedmann, *Law in a Changing Society*, London, Stevens, 1959, p. 124. The section on contract, pp. 90–125, provides a useful summary of recent trends in the contract law of industrialized countries.

36. But see R. H. Graveson, 'The Movement From Status to Contract', *Modern Law Review*, iv, April 1941, pp. 261–72. Graveson's discussion is based on a more orthodox legal notion of status: 'A characteristic feature of true status is its legally imposed condition', he writes, 'which cannot be got rid of at the mere will of the parties without the inter- position of some agent of the State, administrative, legislative, or judicial.' On that basis, he finds Maine's generalization neither valuable for purposes of prediction, nor even good history—holding that there is little evidence in the legal trends of medieval feudalism that would support his claims. Yet the historian Walter Ullmann, using the terms 'status to contract' in a manner roughly akin to their usage in *Ancient Law*, has concluded that Maine's thesis is substantially valid, so far as medieval feudalism is concerned: see Ullmann's *History of Political Thought: The Middle Ages*, London, Penguin, 1965, p. 147. Similarly, A. Harding, *A Social History of English Law*, London, Penguin, 1966, p. 113, adopts the view that 'We might characterize the period from 1216 to 1642 as one in which private law steadily moved its grounds from "feudal" status to "commercial" contract according to Sir Henry Maine's pattern.'

37. Sir F. Pollock, *op. cit.*, Note L, p. 423: 'Assimilation of marriage, as a personal relation, to partnership, is not within the scope of practical jurisprudence.' As R. H. Graveson, 'Movement', *op. cit.*, p. 262, puts it, in marriage 'it is not *the agreement itself* which secures the status, *but the State* alone when the agreement has been both made and performed according to its terms'.

38. Max Gluckman, *The Judicial Process Among the Barotse of Northern Nigeria*. Manchester University Press, 1955, and his *Politics, Law and Ritual in Tribal Society*, Oxford, Blackwell, 1965; R. M. MacIver and C. H. Page, *Society: An Introductory Analysis*, London, Macmillan, 1962, p. 231, found that Maine's generalization remains valid in a sociological sense, if, for 'progressive societies', we substitute 'complex societies'. Talcott Parsons suggests the rephrasing 'ascriptive' status to 'individu- ated' contract, in T. Parsons. *et al.*, *Theories of Society*, Glencoe, The Free Press, 1961, i, p. 91. Don Martindale, *Social Life and Cultural Change*, Princeton, Von Nostrand, 1962, p. 28, believes that Parson's own elaborate theory of comparative social change is itself an unwitting restatement of the theory of status to contract. S. Lipset and R. Bendix, *Social Mobility in Industrial Society*, London, Heinemann, 1959, pp. 142–3, offer the restatement that 'the status system of modern enter- prise is in part the consequence of contractual agreements among competing power groups mediated by government intervention', and conclude: 'We seem to be moving steadily towards a social order in which

278

the relations of persons will be summed up, neither in the "relations of Family", nor in the "free agreement of individuals", but in the hierarchical regulation of official duties.' Peter Drucker, *op. cit.*, pp. 358–63 suggests simply that 'the course of American history—if not of western history altogether—during the last fifty years has been from contract to status.'

39. R. Redfield, 'Maine's *Ancient Law* in the Light of Primitive Societies', *Western Political Quarterly*, iii, 1950, pp. 574–89. But E. A. Hoebel, *The Law of Primitive Man: A Study in Comparative Legal Dynamics*, Harvard University Press, 1954, pp. 328–9, has concluded that 'In surveying the truly primitive societies . . . no specific trend in the separation of the individual from his kinship group as a legal entity can really be discerned . . . The "Mainean shift" does not really become effective until after the beginning of the urban revolution in full neolithic times'. Hoebel suggests that the most important change in truly archaic societies is not, in the legal realm, the substantive shift from status to contract, but rather the great procedural transformation whereby: 'Privilege-rights and responsibility for the maintenance of the legal norms are transferred from the individual and his kinship group to the agents of the body politic as a social entity.'

40. R. H. Graveson, 'Movement', *op. cit.*, pp. 266–7, and his *Status*, *op. cit.*, Chapters v–vi. Earlier, Sir F. Pollock suggested, *op. cit.*, Note L, p. 422, that Maine's theory of status to contract is perhaps 'to be understood as limited to the law of Property, taking that term in its widest sense as inclusive of whatever has a value measurable in exchange'. On the separate question of the validity of the thesis in the context of Roman law itself, Sir William Holdsworth, *A History of English Law*, 5th edn, London, Methuen, 1942, iii, p. 455, concludes that, as applied to the Roman law of persons 'the dictum . . . is very largely true'.

41. J. Stone, *The Province and Function of Law*, London, Stevens, 1950, pp. 451–84, which includes extensive bibliographical references for further reading related to Maine's theories.

42. *AL*, p. 116: 'The rudiments of the social state, so far as they are known to us at all, are known through testimony of three sorts—accounts by contemporary observers of civilization less advanced than their own, the records which particular races have preserved concerning their primitive history, and ancient law.' See C. K. Allen, *op. cit.*, pp. ix–xvi, for discussion of intellectual conditions prevalent at the time. W. A. Robson, *op. cit.*, p. 166, emphasizes that 'It is no easy task to recreate in one's imagination the darkness which surrounded a mid-Victorian pathbreaker such as Maine, or to realize the limited amount of exact information at his disposal.' Yet as late as 1942 E. A. Hoebel could write that: 'Sir Henry Maine's *Ancient Law* still remains after eight decades the pre-eminent work on the origins and nature of primitive legal institutions.' See his 'Fundamental Legal Concepts as Applied in the Study of Primitive Law', *Yale Law Journal*, li, 1942, p. 951.

43. A. S. Diamond, *Primitive Law*, London, Longmans, 1935, (2nd edn, 1950). Diamond's main criticism of *Ancient Law* is that it does not describe truly primitive stages of legal development. Having examined the Code of Hammurabi (*c.* 2000 B.C.), the Assyrian Law and the Hittite Code discovered in this century, Diamond concludes that these contain 'no evidence to support a religious theory of the origin of law', p. 52. Among other specific criticisms, he rejects Maine's theory of the stages of legal change after codification as lacking in support in the preserved fragments of 'archaic law', pp. 206, 347–8. He feels Maine's assumption that early law was highly technical and weighed down in procedural matters is 'diametrically opposed' to the evidence, p. 346. Maine's discussion of early contractual forms is misleading, according to Diamond, for in primitive societies 'there is nothing to call for a theory of contract, or even the abstract notion of a contract', p. 401. Starting from 'simple, natural and practical beginnings,' contract 'only slowly became technical and unchanging', p. 444. His later *Evolution of Law and Order*, London, Watts, 1951, is an ambitious attempt at tracing broad stages of social development: see also his Hobhouse Memorial Lecture, *The Comparative Study of Primitive Law*, London, Athlone Press, 1965.

44. W. A. Robson, *op. cit.*, pp. 167–8. Yet Max Gluckman, *Judicial Process, op. cit.*, pp. 264–5, submits that: 'Clarity *can* be achieved by regarding "religion" as one of the sources of law in both its meanings, as a *corpus juris* and as a series of judgements on disputes. Indeed, though law and religion are different kinds of social fact, I consider that Maine was correct when he affirmed that they are closely associated in early law.'

45. E. A. Hoebel, *op. cit.*, p. 283: 'In most primitive trouble-cases the situation is surprisingly fluid, but flowing within channels that are built by the pre-existing law and moving to a reasonably predictable settlement.' There is an excellent bibliography of sources in legal anthropology at pp. 335–49.

46. Sir F. Pollock, *op cit.*, Notes E, G, H; Roscoe Pound, 'The End of Law as Developed in Juristic Thought', *Harvard Law Review*, xxx, 1917, p. 219; N. Isaacs, 'The Standardizing of Contracts', *Yale Law Journal*, xxvii, 1917–18, p. 37, and the short recent summary provided by Raymond Firth, *op. cit.*, pp. xxix–xxx.

47. J. H. Landman, 'Primitive Law, Evolution, and Sir Henry Maine', in *Michigan Law Review*, xxviii, February 1930, pp. 404–25; Irving Goldman, 'Evolution and Anthropology', *Victorian Studies*, iii, September 1959, pp. 55–75; E. A. Hoebel, *op. cit.*, p. 288. But V. G. Childe, *Social Evolution*, London, Watts, 1951; M. D. Sahlins and E. R. Service, *Evolution and Culture*, University of Michigan Press, 1960, and E. R. Service, *Primitive Social Organization*, N.Y., Random House, 1962, for example, proclaim the revival of evolutionary theory in social anthropology. In *AL* Maine shows himself aware of the problems of strictly unilinear evolutionary models: social change, he notes at p. 163,

is 'accomplished at varying rates of celerity', and elsewhere writes that 'societies do not advance concurrently, but at different rates of progress,' p. 116. See also Chapter 13, n. 26. *supra.* On the notion of 'Aryans', see F. H. Hankins, 'Aryans', in *Encyclopedia of the Social Sciences*, ed. by E. R. Seligman and A. Johnson, i, 1937, pp. 264–5; P. Giles, 'The Aryans', in *Cambridge History of India*, i, 1922, pp. 65–76; V. Gordon Childe, *The Aryans: A Story of Indo-European Origins*, N.Y., Knopf, 1926, and F. H. Hankins, *The Racial Basis of Civilization*, N.Y., Knopf, 1926.

48. F. N. House, *The Development of Sociology*, London, McGraw-Hill, 1936, p. 145. R. Redfield, *op. cit.*, p. 575 concludes that 'Maine's work is indeed a work to draw the praise of students of today. It is a work of true historical scholarship. Among books of his time on the origins and nature of institutions Maine's is outstanding in that the general ideas are referable to particular verifiable facts.'

49. A. Buchan, *The Spare Chancellor: The Life of Walter Bagehot*, London, Chatto and Windus, 1959, pp. 197, 199, 257; G. Himmelfarb, *Lord Acton*, London, Routledge and Kegan Paul, 1952, p. 239; W. C. Havard, *Henry Sidgwick: Later Utilitarian Political Philosophy*, University of Florida Press, 1959, p. 141; H. Spencer, *An Autobiography*, London, Williams and Norgate, 1904, ii, p. 289; Sir Ernest Barker, *Political Thought in England, 1848–1914*, Oxford University Press, 1959, p. 100. The resemblance between Maine's status to contract theory and Herbert Spencer's distinction, in his *Principles of Sociology*, London, Williams and Norgate, 1876, between the 'military' and the 'industrial' types of social development is striking. In D. Duncan, *Life and Letters of Herbert Spencer*, London, Methuen, 1908, Appendix B, p. 573, Spencer explained that 'The military type . . . entails compulsory co-operation, the *régime of status*, and the entire subjection of the individual; while the industrial type is characterized by voluntary co-operation, the *régime of contract*, and the independence of the the individual.' 'R. Pound, 'End of Law', *op. cit.*, pp. 222–3, suggests that 'Maine's *Ancient Law* is the principal juristic authority used in Spencer's *Justice* (1891)'. As to the influence of Maine in America, see Pound's 'Fifty Years of Jurisprudence', *Journal of the Society of Public Teachers of Law*, 1937, p. 17, and his 'End of Law' *op. cit.*, ii, *Harvard Law Review*, xxx, 1917, pp. 210–11. As Pound reflected, 'Much in American judicial decision with respect to master and servant, liberty of contract and right to pursue a lawful calling, which it has been the fashion of late to refer to the class bias of judges or to purely economic influences, is in reality merely the logical development of traditional principles of the common law by men who, if they had not been so taught, read every day in their scientific law books of the progress from status to contract and the development of law through securing and giving effect to the human will.'

50. F. W. Maitland, *Collected Papers* (ed. by H. A. L. Fisher), Cambridge University Press, 1911, ii, p. 252.

51. E. H. Barnes, ed., *An Introduction to the History of Sociology*, University of Chicago Press, 1948, pp. 233, 443. Toënnies regarded Maine as 'ein soziologisch denkender Jurist', and apparently was first lead to the idea of his classic study of *Gemeinschaft und Gesellschaft* on the basis of his reading of *Ancient Law* in 1880: see his *Soziologische Studien und Kritiken*, 1929, i, p. 54, cited in H. Alpert, *Emile Durkheim and his Sociology*, N.Y., Russell and Russell, 1961, p. 187.

52. T. Parsons *et al.*, *op. cit.*, i, p. 91; see H. Alpert, *op. cit.*, p. 185 *et seq.*

53. D. Martindale, *The Nature and Types of Sociological Theory*, London, Routledge and Kegan Paul, 1961, p. 43.

54. W. A. Robson, *Civilization and the Growth of Law*, London, Macmillan, 1935, p. xiv: 'Maine . . . may be regarded as the father of the sociology of law.' Sir F. Pollock, 'Comparative Jurisprudence', *op. cit.*, p. 88, says simply that Maine 'brought us into new and closer fellowship with our brethren in History and Arts, and helped us to understand what it is that we inherit, and what has been the part of the law and its ideas in the life of our nation.' B. N. Nelson, *The Idea or Usury*, Princeton University Press, 1949, p. 137, asserts that 'Maine must have been a central, if not the ultimate source, of many of the distinguished masters of the social sciences.'

55. Sir H. J. S. Maine, *Popular Government*, London, Murray, 1885, Introduction, pp. v–vi, p. 134: further entries as *PG*.

56. *AL*, p. 88.

57. *PG*, pp. 167–9.

58. Maine to Murray, 21 June 1861, *J. M. Arch.*

59. Sir J. E. Dalberg [after 1869, Lord Acton] to M. E. Grant Duff, April 1861, *Grant Duff Papers*, property of Mrs Sheila Sokolov-Grant.

60. Maine to Sir Charles Wood [1st Viscount Halifax], 23 July 1861, *C. W. Coll.*, Mss. Eur. F78, India Office Library.

61. Maine to Wood, 12 April 1862, *C. W. Coll.*, Mss. Eur. F78.

62. Maine to Murray, 9 May 1862, *J. M. Arch.*

63. H. J. S. Maine, 'Indian Statesmen and Indian Scribblers', *Sat. R.*, iv, 24 October 1857, p. 361.

Chapter 6. Calcutta Impressions

1. Wood to Maine, 9 October 1862, *C. W. Coll.*, Mss. Eur. F78.

2. 'Indian Statesmen and Indian Scribblers', *op. cit.*, p. 361.

3. 'Theorizing about India', *Sat. R.*, iv, 19 September 1857, p. 254. W. Stebbing, *Charles Henry Pearson . . . Memorials*, London, Longmans 1900, p. 60, notes that: 'Maine was enlisted on behalf of the East India Co. against the Liberal plan for subjecting India to the Crown.' Maine's

opposition to the transfer of Indian government to the Crown stemmed from his belief that the East India Company had a prescriptive title, whereas prominent India House advisers like J. S. Mill opposed the new scheme on the ground that a joint-stock company was a more efficient way to run a government enterprise.

4. Yet Maine, in a letter to Wood of 15 March 1863, suggested that the Legislative Council was characterized by 'its extreme independence: by which I do not mean factitiousness, but real independence. I suppose it is the only assembly in the world nominated wholly by a government in which the government has no assured majority & can only obtain one by giving genuine satisfaction to the members . . . Of course you do not *see* this, nor indeed does Lord Elgin, for it all goes on in Committee, and no questions are mooted in Council, except those on which no compromise is possible or with regard to which some member wishes to place an opinion formally on record. I am the more anxious to point this out to you, because if you did not understand it you might often misinterpret matters which occur in my own department. Legislation is with us as much a process of compromise as with you, & I foresee that measures will often have to be shaped and modified to suit the peculiarities of our Council.' *C. W. Coll.*, Mss. Eur. F78. In a letter to Sir John Lawrence of 1 August 1867, Maine expressed the view that, 'as to the susceptibility of Members of Council to opinions outside, there is no question that the open meetings of the Legislative Council have greatly increased it.' He added that 'if . . . the power of legislation without Councils were restored (as it ought to be) to the Executive Govt. of the provinces which have no legislatures (the consent of the G.G. in Council being required), the evil would be reduced to a minimum & our Council would never debate anything but Codes & Budgets.' *J. L. Coll.*, Mss. Eur. F90. India Office Library.

5. Thus, Wood reflected in a letter to Maine dated 4 May 1863: 'The value of my Council here is that it contains a much more general representation of different parts of India than the Gov. Gens. Council can contain . . . I tried to introduce broader knowledge into the Council . . . but I never could put into it such varied knowledge as the members of my Council *here* have—The only advantage the Gov. General's Council has is that it contains Natives and Europeans of *recent* experience. Many of my Councillors have left India so long that they are somewhat behind, though in such a stationary country as India that matters less than it would in most countries.' *C. W. Coll.*, Mss. Eur. F78.

6. *Memoir*, Minute of 16 March 1868, 'Government of Bengal, Simla, Calcutta', p. 377; Maine to Lord Cranborne [after April 1868, Lord Salisbury], 5 January 1867, *Salisbury Papers*, Christ Church, Oxford.

7. Maine to Wood, 16 November 1865, *C. W. Coll.*, Mss. Eur. F78: 'surely', he felt, 'not an insignificant defect if it is to be the chief seat

of a government which henceforward will probably always include a Gov. Gen. & two members of council who were never in India before in their lives.'

8. Maine to Cranborne, 14 February 1867, *Salisbury Papers.*

9. Maine to Wood, 15 March 1863, *op. cit.*: 'Bengal', he complained, 'with its permanent settlement, its feeble population, its enervating climate, its comparatively large number of European planters & its half-destroyed tenures & wholly destroyed village communities . . . is an entirely exceptional province, much more exceptional than Brittany is in reference to France.'

10. Maine to Wood, 19 March 1864, *C. W. Coll.*, Mss. Eur. F78.

11. Information in Maine to Wood, 5 July 1864, *C. W. Coll.*, Mss. Eur. F78; Maine to Cranborne, 8 February 1867, *Salisbury Papers.*

12. Maine to Wood, 5 July 1864, *op. cit.*

13. Maine to Cranborne, 23 January 1867, *Salisbury Papers.*

14. Maine to Wood, 16 September 1863, *C. W. Coll.*, Mss. Eur. F78.

15. Maine to Wood, 5 July 1864, *op. cit.*

16. *Memoir*, Minute on 'Government of Bengal, Simla, Calcutta', *op. cit.*, p. 383: Maine thought such a plan appropriate to a political system 'originating in the conquest of hot countries by persons born in cooler climates'.

17. Maine to Wood, 16 November 1865, *op. cit.*; so far as the argument that Calcutta should remain the capital because of its strategic advantages in the military view, Maine suggested in another letter to the Secretary of State, dated 20 November 1863, that: 'In fact, the capital of India for military purposes has long been, and will long be, either Simla or Lahore', and that for that reason he did not think 'that anybody who has not been in India or out of Calcutta knows how strong are the military influences brought to bear on a Gov. Genl. who goes up-country by himself.' *C. W. Coll.*, Mss. Eur. F78.

18. Maine to Wood, 5, 20, 23 November 1863, *C. W. Coll.*, Mss. Eur. F78; J. L. Morison, 'Lord Elgin in India, 1862–63', *Cambridge Historical Journal*, i, 1924, pp. 178–96. Elgin was the third Viceroy to die since 1860 (Dalhousie, d. 1860, Canning, d. 1862), prompting the remark from Maine to Wood that 'I can well imagine the state of feeling which will arise in England, not only from this single death, but from its continuing a series of deaths. I am not without fears that this apparent fatality will tell injuriously on the superstition of the Natives.'

19. A very thorough study of Wood's Indian career has recently appeared: R. J. Moore's *Sir Charles Wood's Indian Policy, 1853–66*, Manchester University Press, 1966. Maine's interests are dealt with especially at pp. 65–85, and there is an excellent list of secondary sources for further reading which is relevant to Maine's period in India, at pp. 265–73.

20. R. B. Smith, *Life of Lord Lawrence* (2 vols.), London, Smith Elder, 1883; Dharm Pal, *Administration of Sir John Lawrence in India, 1864–1869*, Simla, Minerva Book Shop, 1952.

21. Wood to Maine, 3 December 1863, *C. W. Coll.*, Mss. Eur. F78: Wood wrote further on 25 December 1863: 'Keep the peace: don't let Strachey interfere with the local govts. as to their public works & practically stop them all; don't give up taxes, or trust public companies; don't overlegislate, & you will keep India in her present state of progress.'

22. Maine to Wood, 20 November 1863, *op. cit.* Maine noted of Elgin that: 'His caution had no doubt seemed excessive to many people', but added: 'It is doubtful whether a more valuable characteristic could just now belong to anyone in Indian office . . . his experience of forms of govt. different from this had been, & was likely to be, of the greatest use to us.'

23. Maine to Wood, 5 July 1864, *op. cit.*; in a letter to his Legal Member of 26 August 1867, Lawrence submitted that 'it is my opinion that the Government of India can never be strong, but on the contrary must always be weak, which weakness will especially show itself on great occasions owing to the absence of any common bond of union between the Gov. General and the Members of his Council . . . People at home expect to have a strong Government in India with none of the elements of such a Govt.' *J. L. Coll.*, Mss. Eur. F90.

24. Wood to Maine, 25 February 1865, *C. W. Coll.*, Mss. Eur. F78: see also R. J. Moore, *op. cit.*, pp. 12–22, for an assessment of Wood's Whig outlook. Dr Moore suggests that Wood's goals, so far as law reform was concerned, were 'Abstention of the government from interference with the freedom of the individual, impartial and uniform justice, and simple legal procedures.' (p. 82). He harboured some concern that Maine's policies were too pro-European, and wrote to him on 4 May 1863: 'the chief thing I look to is the influence which you may acquire & exercise, with your knowledge of sound principles of legislation, on being able to keep it close to what is right & at any rate preventing anything very much out of the way . . . One of our great burdens in India as elsewhere has been endeavouring at once to act after English patterns—the wise thing in my belief is to adapt and improve what you find & especially in India, where the English element is so infinitesmally small in proportion to the Natives.'

25. Wood to Maine, 9 January 1863, *C. W. Coll.*, Mss. Eur. F78: 'The sympathy between different *classes* in the same country is often safeguard little enough for equal laws, but when the question is between different *races*, the safeguard is too often very, very minute.' These differences were, of course, only a matter of degree. Writing to Maine on 9 September 1864, Wood allowed that 'I am fully prepared to maintain the privileges of the white English race, but while they are to be

kept in their superior position, so as to command the obedience and respect of the natives, they must so use their power that the natives must see & feel that their power is exercised for the benefit & not for the oppression of those whom they govern.'

26. Wood to Maine, 18 February 1866, *C. W. Coll.*, Mss. Eur. F78. Wood fell from his horse while hunting and, while recuperating, announced his decision to withdraw from active politics. He was shortly afterwards created Lord Halifax, a sequence of events which prompted the droll caption to an early *Vanity Fair* print: 'He fell from his horse into the House of Lords.'

27. Maine to Wood, 2 April 1864, *C. W. Coll.*, Mss. Eur. F78. 'Your language as to the stronger and weaker races', Maine wrote, 'might apply to the Spaniards and South American Indians, but leaves out of account the calculating, astute, and wide-a-wake character of the Bengalee, who, whatever his class, knows his interests as well as the keenest Englishman, and is quite as hard a hand at a bargain. Putting aside actual physical constraint, you need never call the Bengalees the weaker race.'

28. Maine to Wood, 20 January 1864, *C. W. Coll.*, Mss. Eur. F78.

29. Maine to Elgin, 17 March 1863, *L. E. Coll.*, Mss. Eur. F83/16, India Office Library.

30. Maine to Wood, 17 November 1863, *C. W. Coll.*, Mss. Eur. F78.

31. *Memoir*, Speech of 17 December 1862, 'Breeches of Contract', p. 90.

32. B. Cohn, 'From Indian Status to British Contract', *Journal of Economic History*, xxi, 1961, pp. 613–28; J. D. M. Derrett, 'Sir Henry Maine and Law in India', *Juridical Review*, iv, 1959, pp. 40–55.

Chapter 7. European Interests

1. *Memoir*, Speech of 13 March 1868, 'Indian Municipalities'. p. 264.

2. M. Gallanter, 'Hindu Law and the Development of the Modern Indian Legal System', paper delivered before the *American Political Science Association Annual Meeting*, Chicago, 9–12 September 1964, mimeographed; J. D. M. Derrett, *Hindu Law, Past and Present*, Calcutta, A. Mukherjee, 1957; N. C. Sen-Gupta, *Evolution of Ancient Indian Law*, London, Probsthain, 1953; W. B. Hamilton, ed. *The Transfer of Institutions*, Duke University Press, 1964, Chapter 7; R. J. Moore, *op. cit.*, pp. 65–77. The most thorough account of the Company Courts before 1858 is to be found in Eric Stokes, *The English Utilitarians and India*, Oxford University Press, 1959, pp. 140–233.

3. *Memoir*, Speech of 14 December 1866, 'Overlegislation', p. 234.

4. *Memoir*, Minute of 20 February 1880, 'Memorandum . . . on the Condition of India', pp. 417–18: 'There is in fact a conflict always more

286

or less proceeding in India', Maine wrote, 'between the reign of law and a regimen of discretion . . . For my part I have the strongest sympathy with the preference of some Indian officials for discretionary administration, where the people have not outgrown it. But it is in vain to deny that this system is inconsistent with even a slight advance in the people to which it is applied, and that the area over which it is applied is constantly diminishing.' Yet while Maine saw a shift towards uniformity of administrative rule and away from the personal discretion of officials, he felt it still was the case, as he wrote to Wood on 6 November 1865, that: 'Indian law, through our codes and consolidations, is becoming quite unlike English law, nor is it only different in form. It assumes a latitude of discretion in the courts which is quite unknown in England and which a legal pedant may fearfully abuse.' *C. W. Coll.*, Mss. Eur. F78.

5. 'A visit to a Presidency like this', Maine assured Wood on 25 September 1865, while on a trip to Bombay, 'would produce in the most ambitious legislator a misgiving as to the enactment of identical laws for all India—codes and enactments declaratory of general principles always excepted.' *C. W. Coll.*, Mss. Eur. F78.

6. Maine to Wood, Note on 'Legal Education' (enclosure), 28 August, 8 December 1863, *C. W. Coll.*, Mss. Eur. F78; *Memoir*, pp. 308–10.

7. Maine to Wood, 20 January 1864, *C. W. Coll.*, Mss. Eur. F78: 'a very much larger proportion of the contracting class in this country than in any other', he complained, 'requires to be made to understand that it is *expected* by authority to perform its engagements.'

8. *Memoir*, Minute of 22 February 1864, 'Small Cause Courts', p. 311.

9. Maine to Wood, Minute on 'Contract and Rent Question' (enclosure), 3 July 1864, *C. W. Coll.*, Mss. Eur. F78.

10. Maine to Elgin, 10 April 1863, *L. E. Coll.*, Mss. Eur. F83/16. Moreover, as he wrote to the Secretary of State on 3 July 1864, *op. cit.*, 'the supreme *regulating* influence which good courts exercise and which penetrates infinitely further than the *direct* action of those courts, is almost wholly wanting in India. Of course, the new High Courts are intended to supply it, but to my mind that is beginning at the wrong end; to bring the rule of civil law home to the people, you must improve your Courts of First Instance—the only courts with which the mass of the people come in contact.'

11. *Memoir*, Speech of 16 December 1864, 'Small Case Courts', p. 213: note also Maine's amusing comment in his review of J. F. Stephen's 'Introduction to the Indian Evidence Act', *VC* (3rd edn, 1876), p. 318, that 'I have heard barristers in India assert . . . that they knew Native witnesses to be perjuring themselves whenever their toes began to twitch, and country for country, the tests which English Judges and

counsel have taught themselves to apply with practical success are hardly less singular.'

12. *Memoir*, Speech of 16 December 1864, 'Small Cause Courts', *op. cit.*, p. 216.

13. Maine to Elgin, 10 April, 23 May 1863, *L. E. Coll.*, Mss. Eur. F83/16.

14. Wood to Maine, 27 July 1863, *C. W. Coll.*, Mss. Eur. F78.

15. Maine to Wood, 30 August, 14 September 1863, *C. W. Coll.*, Mss. Eur. F78.

16. Wood to Maine, 17, 30 October 1863, *C. W. Coll.*, Mss. Eur. F78.

17. Maine to Elgin, 23 May 1863, *op. cit.*

18. Maine to Wood, 9 January 1864, Wood to Maine, 15 February 1864, *Abstract of Council Meeting* (New Civil Procedure Bill), 11 November 1864, *C. W. Coll.*, Mss. Eur. F78; Maine to Lawrence, 14 March 1864, Lawrence to Maine, 18 March 1864, *J. L. Coll.*, Mss. Eur. F90.

19. Maine to Elgin, 2 December, 12 December 1862, *L. E. Coll.*, Mss. Eur. F83/16: see also *Memoir*, Speech of 17 December 1862, 'Breaches of Contract Committed in Bad Faith', pp. 85–91.

20. Maine to Wood, 5 November 1863; *Abstract of Council Meeting* (Specific Performance), 11 November 1864, *C. W. Coll.*, Mss. Eur. F78; *Memoir*, Speech and Minute, 'Specific Performance', 11 November 1864, 9 April 1868, pp. 164–78; R. J. Moore, *op. cit.*, pp. 82–5.

21. Wood to Maine, 15 February 1864, *op. cit.*: 'I should be willing to adopt all you say', he wrote further on 2 January 1865, '*if* the contracting parties were on a decently equal footing'. During late November 1864, the Secretary of State had written that in order to prevent mischief, Maine's proposal would require '1st, that the *ryot* actually *made* and *understood* the contract; 2nd, that he had no good ground for non-performance. If you can make certain by [your] registration that the ryot enters into a *real* contract which he understands, the greater part of my difficulty is cleared off.' However, by 7 January 1865, he had renewed reservations: '1. specific performance can, in the nature of things, apply only to "exceptional cases" . . . 2. Harington proposes to confine the sp. perf. to *registered contracts*. This will be a great safe-guard *if* the registering officer satisfies himself that the *ryot* is a free agent, 3. there should be a clear time limit set upon contractual relations; 4. lastly, you insist upon *good Judges*. Where are you to get them? . . . I fear the only good laws adapted for India are such as may be fairly administered by persons of very ordinary legal or judicial powers.' *C. W. Coll.*, Mss. Eur. F78.

22. Lawrence to Maine, 4 April 1864, *J. L. Coll.*, Mss. Eur. F90.

23. Maine to Lawrence, 2 April 1864, *J. L. Coll.*, Mss. Eur. F90.

24. Maine to Wood, 5 November 1863, *op. cit.*

25. Maine to Wood, 20 January 1864, *op. cit.*

26. Maine to Elgin, 10 April 1863, *op. cit.*; Maine to Wood, 12 June 1864, *C. W. Coll.*, Mss. Eur. F78.

27. Maine to Wood, 5 November 1863, 20 January 1864, *op. cit.*

28. Wood to Maine, 7 January 1865, *op. cit.*

29. Sir Erskine Perry to Maine, 3 July 1868, *Maine Papers*, the property of Mr H. C. S. Maine.

30. *Memoir*, Speech of 17 February 1864, 'Whipping', pp. 120–6: 'The most strong deterrent of known punishment is physical pain.' Maine wrote to the Secretary of State on 19 February 1864: 'all the local governments say they must flog, chiefly because the jails are so bad. Trevelyan says "don't flog, but improve you jails up to the reforming pitch". I don't believe the alternatives to be genuine. We could not spare a tithe of the money for covering India with moderately good English jails and even if we did, it really seems to me that your English jail-system has all but broken down . . . Besides, how are you to reform a Hindoo's morality? Are you to send a Brahmin to read the Vedas to him? I truly cannot see any reformation of criminals to be practicable at present in India, except by deterring them from offences and thus breaking the habit of crime.' Wood replied on 24 March 1864: 'You certainly have me on your side in the flogging matter. I am sadly anti-modern-humanitarianism—though I by no means intended to say that flogging would set all right, I would not give up so efficient an engine of discipline for jail-birds, as it may under proper restrictions be made.' *C. W. Coll.*, Mss. Eur. F78.

31. Maine to Elgin, 31 January 1863, *L. E. Coll.*, Mss. Eur. F83/16.

32. Maine to Wood, 28 July 1864, *C. W. Coll.*, Mss. Eur. F78.

33. *Ibid.*

34. *Ibid.*

35. *Memoir*, Speech of 18 November 1864, 'Abolition of Grand Juries', pp. 179–92: Maine to Wood, 20 November 1864, *C. W. Coll.*, Mss. Eur. F78.

36. *Ibid.*, p. 190.

37. Maine to Wood, 4 December 1864, *C. W. Coll.*, Mss. Eur. F78.

38. Wood to Maine, 9, 18 January 1865, *C. W. Coll.*, Mss. Eur. F78.

39. Maine to Wood, 18 December 1864, *C. W. Coll.*, Mss. Eur. F78.

40. *Ibid.*

41. Maine to Wood, 18 October 1865, *C. W. Coll.*, Mss. Eur. F78.

Chapter 8. Indian Interests

1. Maine to Wood, 23 September 1865, *C. W. Coll.*, Mss. Eur. F78.

2. *Memoir*, Speeches of 25 November 1864, 3 March 1865, 'The Law of Succession', pp. 192–209.

3. *Ibid.*

4. *Ibid*, pp. 208–9.

5. *Memoir*, Speech of 4 November 1864, 'Re-Marriage of Native Converts', pp. 130–64. The Bishop of Calcutta found support for Maine's measure in the text of his *Pastoral Letter to the Clergy of the Diocese of Calcutta on the Remarriage of Converts Bill*, by George E. L. Cotton, (enclosure), Maine to Wood, 25 February 1865, *C. W. Coll.*, Mss. Eur. F78: 'the arguments for believing that the Apostle has sanctioned a regular divorce, including the power of remarriage, rather than a mere temporary and informal separation, are so strong, that I must accept, on scriptural grounds, the principles of Mr Maine's Bill, and maintain that the liberty which it allows to converts is consistent with a hearty obedience to the letter and spirit of the New Testament.'

6. *Memoir*, Speech of 31 March 1866, pp. 163–4.

7. Maine to Wood, 18 December 1865, *C. W. Coll.*, Mss. Eur. F78. Maine continued: 'I have been present at the late examinations and the interest & anxiety of the students are most remarkable. An examination at Oxford or Cambridge (though there is no absence of excitement about that) is nothing to it; to form an idea of anything resembling it, you must go back to the middle ages. Nor is the feeling merely one of ambition for an honour. It is an affair of bread and cheese, for a University degree, or at all events matriculation in the University, is coming to be regarded as the first condition of entrance into all the literate or semi-literate occupations which are growing up all over India.'

8. H. J. S. Maine, 'Address to the University of Calcutta', March 1866, reprinted in *VC*, (3rd edn), pp. 293–4.

9. Wood to Maine, 2 September 1864, *C. W. Coll.*, Mss. Eur. F78.

10. Maine to Wood, 5 November 1863, *C. W. Coll.*, Mss. Eur. F78.

11. See T. R. Metcalf, *The Aftermath of Revolt: India, 1857–1870*, Princeton University Press, 1964. I am indebted to Professor Metcalf's account in the following discussion.

12. Maine to Wood, 7 June 1863, *C. W. Coll.*, Mss. Eur. F78.

13. *The Englishman*,' Law Reports', 31 March 1864 (enclosure), Maine to Wood, *C. W. Coll.*, Mss. Eur. F78.

14. Maine to Wood, 4 October, 5 December 1864, *C. W. Coll.*, Mss. Eur. F78.

15. Maine to Wood, 21 March 1865, *C .W. Coll.*, Mss. Eur. F78.

16. Maine to Wood, 13 August 1865, *C. W. Coll.*, Mss. Eur. F78.

17. Wingfield to Maine, 'Memorandum on Oudh Tenure', (enclosure), Maine to Wood, 3 November, 1864, *C. W. Coll.*, Mss. Eur. F78: see also Metcalf *op. cit.*, pp. 138–58; 187–97.

18. Maine to Wood, 5 July 1864, *C. W. Coll.*, Mss. Eur. F78.

19. 'Minute on Oudh Question', 10 July 1864 (enclosure), Maine to Wood, 18 September 1864, *C. W. Coll.*, Mss. Eur. F78.

20. Wood to Maine, 24 October 1864, *C. W. Coll.*, Mss. Eur. F78.

21. T. R. Metcalf, *op. cit.*, esp. pp. 195–6.

22. *Memoir*, Minute on 'Mr Prinsep's Punjab Theories', 26 October, 1866, p. 336.

23. Maine to Lawrence, 17 October 1868, *J. L. Coll.*, Mss. Eur. F90.

24. *Memoir*, Speech of 19 October 1868, 'Punjab Tenancy', p. 271.

25. *Memoir*, Minute on 'Mr Prinsep's Punjab Theories', *op. cit.*, p. 340: Maine concluded that 'all classes connected with the soil are immeasurably better off than they were under Native Governments, and are more than compensated for any errors we may have committed in the mere adjustment of their mutual rights.' In other words, he had no paternalist doubts over whether the creation of such rights had been necessary and desirable.

26. T. R. Metcalf, *op. cit.*, p. 200.

27. J. S. Mill to Maine, 1 January 1869, in H. S. R. Elliot, ed., *The Letters of J. S. Mill*, London, Longmans, 1910, ii, pp. 169–72.

28. Thus, Maine would have shared the view of Philip Woodruff, *The Men who Ruled India: The Guardians*, London, Cape, 1954, pp. 160–1, who notes that in India during the 1860s, 'what had happened was an immense acceleration of a natural process . . . [Sir Henry Maine was pointing out that] it is natural for man to move from a society in which his status is fixed to a free society in which he finds his own level by a series of contracts. The brotherhood of the Indian village was certainly a good example of fixed status; Victorian England had gone a long way towards the free society of contract. The Punjab peasant, however, had been asked to do in a year what had taken England many centuries.'

29. See John Roach, 'James Fitzjames Stephen', *Journal of the Royal Asiatic Society*, 1956, pp. 1–16.

30. Yet commentators have usually given the lion's share of credit for post-Mutiny leadership in Indian codification to Maine's successor, J. F. Stephen. Eric Stokes, in his authoritative *The English Utilitarians and India*, Oxford University Press, 1959, p. 273, notes of Stephen that 'he counts as one of the most important figures of British Indian history in the later nineteenth century', and J. Roach, *op. cit.*, p. 1, writes that '[Stephen's] short tenure (1869–72) marks an important

stage in the completion of the Indian codes'. Maine seemed to feel, however, that Stephen got too much of the credit for the planning of codification measures. He recalled in a letter to Lord Lytton of 2 April 1878 that 'I had to insist on the examination and revision of the Commissioner's drafts to the Indian administrative officers, but this they would not submit to and finally they resigned in a huff. Then came Stephen, who was in the exceptionally advantageous position of having a stock of drafts prepared by the Commissioners, and at the same time no Commissioners to object to his amendment of their projects'. *Lytton Papers*, India Office Library, Mss. Eur. E218. See also Maine to Grant Duff, 8 April 1871, where Maine writes that 'some former Indian associates of mine have got it into their heads that Stephen scrupulously and pointedly avoids all reference to me, and never gives me credit for any share in legislation.' *Grant Duff Papers*. Stephen, however, in a letter to Lord Lytton of 6 March 1876, did acknowledge that during Maine's incumbency 'endless controversies took place between the Government of India and the Law Commissioners by which the drafts were indefinitely hung up. The quarrel lasted on till my time, & at last the Indian Law Commissioners resigned in disgust at our obstructiveness. Their resignation left me *carte blanche . . .*' *J. F. Stephen Papers*, Camb. Univ. Lib., Add. 7349, Box I. See also Maine's letter to *The Times* of 9 July 1878, p. 8, on Indian codification.

31. A contemporary discussion of the highlights of Maine's Indian career and a list of the most significant of the 211 Acts passed during his tenure of office is included in a pamphlet prepared by Sir W. W. Hunter, *Seven Years of Indian Legislation*, Calcutta, Trubner, 1870.

32. Wood to Maine, 10 March 1865, *C. W. Coll.*, Mss. Eur. F78.

33. Sir E. Perry to Maine, 17 April 1866, *Maine Papers*, the property of Mr H. C. S. Maine.

34. Maine to Wood, 19 February 1864, *C. W. Coll.*, Mss. Eur. F78.

35. *Memoir*, Speech of 14 December 1866, 'Overlegislation', pp. 227–37; Maine pursued a similar theme in a separate Minute of 1 October 1868, on 'Overlegislation', pp. 237–47.

36. Maine to Lawrence, 17 March 1867, *J. L. Coll.*, Mss. Eur. F90.

37. See discussion in E. Stokes, *op. cit.*, pp. 269–79.

38. Yet there remained important differences in the administrative philosophies of Stephen and Maine. While Stephen was a consolidator rather than a champion of abstract codification, he was still 'as strong and vehement a believer as any of his radical precedessors in the revolution to be affected by the rule of law,' according to E. Stokes, *op. cit.*, pp. 279–80. The 'revolution' he pressed for, however, was the unmitigated triumph of European values over Indian. As John Roach, *op. cit.*, p. 15, sums up the difference between Maine's approach and

Stephen's: 'Both of them felt keenly the issues raised by the interaction of Western and Eastern cultures. To Stephen, it was a one way affair, England the teacher and India the taught. To Maine, with his finer feeling for the development of institutions, there was something on both sides.' See also Chapter 15, n. 32, *supra*.

39. Maine to Lawrence, 31 July 1868, *J. L. Coll.*, Mss. Eur. F90.

40. *Ibid.* As well, Maine to Wood, 5 December 1864, *C. W. Coll.*, Mss. Eur. F78. Maine's first disagreement with the commissioners arose as early as 1863, when he urged that 'before they proceed to Contract, they should complete the whole law of Property', in a 'Demi-Official Memorandum for the Law Commissioners', 21 April 1863 (enclosure), Maine to Wood, 22 April 1863. Maine's concern was that the commissioners should make some effort to reconcile 'the two most technical systems of land law which exist in the world—English Real Property Law and the Law of Land which has grown up in Bengal since the Permanent Settlement.' At a later period Maine wrote to Lawrence, 18 February 1868: '. . . in select Committee on the Contract Law I am struggling with difficulties which cannot well bear addition. The mercantile members are opposing every single provision of the Commissioners which can decently be objected to. The ostensible reason is the inapplicability of the proposed law to the trade and circumstances of the country.' *J. L. Coll.*, Mss. Eur. F90.

41. Maine to Grant Duff, 22 December 1868, *Grant Duff Papers.*

42. Perry to Maine, 3 July 1868, *Maine Papers*, the property of Mr H. C. S. Maine. In a further letter of 1868 [n.d.], Perry reiterated the view, in noting: 'I cannot see any bond that the Govt. can exercise over such a body of men'.

43. Maine to Lytton, 2 April 1878, *Lytton Papers*, Mss. Eur. E218.

44. E. Stokes, op. cit., pp. 1–80 trace the major themes of the book. In his discussion of Maine at p. 312 et seq. Stokes sees Maine as a leading intellectual precursor of the later 'authoritarian Liberal' imperialism of Lord Cromer, which differed from the Stephen-Strachey school in its 'refusal to accept military force as by itself an adequate basis for political authority'.

45. Cited in *Memoir*, Minute on 'The Bengal Legislature', 27 February 1868, pp. 366–7. A similar Whiggish flexibility and lack of dogmatism is characteristic of much of Maine's early Indian policy: writing to Wood at the time of the Bengal rent disputes, for example, he allowed that 'I now quite forgive the authors of Act X for having framed an enactment through which Peacock was able to drive a coach and six, but at the same time I feel that, in spite of much confident assertion, the best-informed Indian officials know much less not only of the country but of each province than is commonly supposed . . . I never saw a country

in which it was so difficult to ascertain truth on any question on which men's prejudices are excited, or indeed, on which their theories are founded.' 12 June 1864, *C. W. Coll.*, Mss. Eur. F78.

46. Maine to Lawrence, 1 August 1867, *J. L. Coll.*, Mss. Eur. F90.

47. Maine to Grant Duff, 3 May 1869, *Grant Duff Papers*.

48. Perry to Maine, 20 May 1869, *Maine Papers*, the property of Mr H.C.S. Maine.

49. Lord Argyll to Stephen, 1 July, 1869, *J. F. Stephen Papers*, Camb. Univ. Lib., Add. 7349, Box 3 (misc.). As early as 24 April 1869, Stephen had written to J. S. Mill: 'A kind of rumour has grown up, I hardly know how, or why, to the effect that I am to have the offer of Maine's place when he vacates it. The whole matter is quite in the clouds as it appears to me quite uncertain whether Maine will return or not for several years to come, equally unlikely whether if he did I should have the offer of his place, & equally uncertain as to whether if I had I should accept it.' *Ibid.*

50. Cited in *Memoir*, pp. 31–2.

51. Maine to Mayo, 15 December, *Mayo Papers*, Camb. Univ. Lib., Add. 7490/90/xxiii (unmounted).

52. Merivale to Maine, 4 February 1867, *Maine Papers* (misc.), India Office Library.

53. Merivale to Maine, 21 March 1869, *Maine Papers* (misc.), India Office Library. On 9 July 1869, he wrote further that 'I met Mrs Maine last night at a W. Shaughnessy's, an old Bengal neighbour of us both—she was looking her best and enjoying the cream ices.' *Ibid.*

54. Maine to W. Harcourt, 29 November 1868, reproduced in A. G. Gardiner, *Life of Sir William Harcourt*, London, Constable, 1923, i, p. 194. Maine wrote to Harcourt that he did not consider himself 'debarred by anything which passed between us from standing for the Whewell Professorship . . . I daresay you will deem it profoundly immaterial whether I stand or not. But it would give me great pain to find myself a candidate and then to discover that you thought the step a breach of an understanding with yourself. I shall be greatly obliged to you if you will let me know your view of the situation.' Harcourt was chosen for the Professorship over J. F. Stephen. Maine apparently did not let his name go forward, and the outcome of the selection presumably influenced Stephen in his decision to accept the Legal Membership in the Viceroy's Council.

Chapter 9. 'Village Communities'

1. Sir M. E. Grant Duff, *Notes, op. cit.*, ii, p. 136.

2. A. G. Gardiner, *op. cit.*, i, p. 194; W. W. Hunter, *op. cit.*, p. 23; Maine to Salisbury, 20 November, 1885, *Salisbury Papers*; Maine to Sidgwick,

8 December 1886, *Henry Sidgwick Papers*, Trinity College Library, Cambridge.

3. Maine to Murray, 11 December 1869, *J. M. Arch.*

4. Maine to Bryce, 30 March 1871, *MSS Bryce*, Bodleian Library, Oxford: for Bryce's years at Oxford, see H. A. L. Fisher, *James Bryce*, London, Macmillan, 1927, i, pp. 130–5 *et seq.* Yet note J. F. Stephen's amusing aside in a letter to Lord Lytton of 8 July 1878 that he had been 'at Oxford, where 10 days ago I stood sweltering in a red gown under a fire of Latin compliments piled upon me by an old friend (Bryce), who sarcastically observed that I must give up for the future my bad habit of swearing at Roman Law, & declaring that Maine would probably be damned (as privately I believe he will) for reinstating it 20 years ago.' He had been awarded an Oxford D.C.L. *J. F. Stephen Papers*, Camb. Univ. Lib., Add. 7349, Box 1. For a sketch of the intellectual atmosphere of Oxford in the period, see Melvin Richter, *The Politics of Conscience: T. H. Green and His Age*, Harvard University Press, 1964, pp. 52–96.

5. Maine to W. E. Gladstone, 13 March 1872, *Gladstone Papers*, B.M. Add. Mss. 44433, ff. 293–5.

6. Maine to Bryce, 5 April, 22 June, 19 November, 7 December, 13 December 1871, *MSS Bryce*. Another nice example of Maine's professorial digressions into the realm of minor acts of 'patronage' occurs in a later letter to his publisher, dated 10 October 1884:

> Trinity Hall,
> Master's Lodge
>
> My dear Murray,
>   Staying lately with E. A. Freeman, the historian, I met his eldest daughter, who has married Arthur Evans, a rather Radical writer on Slavonic topics, but still one of the best of our younger archeologists. They have just elected him at Oxford to the Keepership of the Ashmolean Museum. Mrs Arthur Evans asked me whether I could help her in obtaining employment in Index-Making. It seems that she believes herself to have a genius for the work, having made several most elaborate indices for her father's books, and some others. I hinted to her that the occupation was not likely to be a lucrative one, but she appeared to be prepared for that.
>   I thought I might venture to ask you whether there is any chance of your having work of the kind to be done. The lady strikes me as very highly educated, clever and careful; and I should think her likely to be above the average of persons who undertake this business.
>
> J. Murray Esq.   V. truly yrs,
>   HS Maine

7. J. W. Robertson Scott. *The Story of the Pall Mall Gazette*, Oxford University Press, 1950, p. 154: 'Maine was a frequent contributor until the Radical flag was hoisted upon it in 1880 . . . Maine used

to write two or three leaders a week at special rates of pay . . . He was once described by his editor as one of two men he had known who wrote as well from the first as they ever wrote afterwards.' In the 10,000th number of the *Pall Mall*, H. D. Traill suggested: 'If two of the contributors, Sir James Fitzjames Stephen and Sir Henry Maine, were still alive and doing the same masterly work, no evening paper would have any use for it. They would have to expand it over ten pages of a high class monthly review.' Unfortunately, no marked files of the *Pall Mall*, as far as I have been able to discover, are known to exist.

8. Partial drafts of Maine's *Village Communities in East and West* are now in the *Maine Collection*. LSE, Section i. Volume 6, Item I, and Section ii, Volume 19, Item I.

9. Maine to Murray, 21 December 1870. *J. M. Arch.*

10. *VC*, (3rd edn, 1876), p. 78 *et seq.*

11. *VC*, pp. 81–2.

12. *VC*, p. 146.

13. *VC*, p. 136.

14. *VC*, pp. 141–2. See also Chapter 5, n. 36, *supra.*

15. *VC*, p. 111.

16. *VC*, p. 113.

17. *VC*, pp. 148–50.

18. *VC*, p. 164.

19. Many years later Maine wrote of Seebohm, in a letter to Alfred Lyall dated 18 October 1883: 'Is a statement made to me that a relative of yours, a lady, is going out to India to re-investigate the history of the Indian Village Communities, correct? My informant was Seebohm, a man who has published a book called the "English Village Community", a singular misnomer since his object seems to be to prove that no such thing ever existed. It is a curious mixture of learning and superficiality, learning in respect of what he has observed and read, superficiality in regard to what (not having had much of an education) he has not had time to get up. If there is really no connection between the Indian Village Community and the institution (whatever it was) out of which the English and German manor grew, it is the most singular of accidental resemblances in form.' *Maine/Lyall Letters*, India Office Library, Mss. Eur. F132/48. Maine's judgment seems to have been rather harsh, in light of the fact that Seebohm dedicated his now classic study to Maine.

20. Maine apparently entertained some early doubts about publishing his Oxford lectures. As early as 5 August 1870, he wrote in response to a request from Murray that 'I cannot say anything about my Oxford

lectures yet. The question of publishing them would depend a good deal on their quality, which, as they are not yet written, is at least doubtful.' And as late as 19 December 1870, he noted in a further letter to Murray that 'I am still hesitating about publishing,' *J. M. Arch.*

21. Maine to Murray, 12 April 1871, *J. M. Arch*; 'Maine's *Village Communities*', *Sat. R.*, xxxi, 8 April 1871, pp. 438–40.

22. Maine to Grant Duff, 12 April 1871, *Grant Duff Papers.*

23. Maine to Murray, 1 April 1871, *J. M. Arch.*

24. Maine to Murray, 12 April 1871, *J. M. Arch.*

25. J. S. Mill, 'Mr Maine on Village Communities', *Fortnightly Review*, ix, May 1871, pp. 543–56, esp. p. 544: reprinted in Mill's *Dissertations and Discussions*, London, Parker, 1875, iv, pp. 143–68. F. W. Maitland wrote shrewdly to Paul Vinogradoff of 'a queer twist of the English mind which would make me guess that the English believer in "free village communities" would very probably be a conservative—I don't mean a Tory or an aristocrat, but a conservative. On the other hand, with us the man who has the most splendid hopes for the masses is very likely to see in the past nothing but the domination of the classes', in C. A. S. Fifoot, ed., *The Letters of F. W. Maitland*, Cambridge University Press, 1965, pp. 59–60.

26. J. S. Mill, *op. cit.*, pp. 544, 549.

27. *Ibid.*, pp. 549–50.

28. E. B. Tylor, 'Maine's *Village Communities*', *Quarterly Review*, cxxxi, 1871, pp. 176–89, esp. p. 177: 'Far from overloading his arguments with heavy details, he even goes too far in suppressing them.' Similarly, the *Athenaeum*, April 15 1871, pp. 456–8, cautioned that though 'graphic and fluent', Maine's speculations 'in their present form . . . are perhaps hardly sufficiently supported by details of positive evidence.' p. 458.

29. E. B. Tylor, *op. cit.*, p. 176.

30. *Ibid.*, pp. 188–9.

31. Maine to Murray, 12 July 1871, *J. M. Arch.*

32. Harrison to Morley, 5 May 1871, *Harrison Collection*, LSE, File A (uncatalogued).

33. Sir M. E. Grant Duff, *Notes*, *op. cit.*, ii, pp. 136.

34. Sir E. Perry to Maine, 20 May 1869, *Maine Papers*, the property of Mr H. C. S. Maine. In the later stages of Maine's Indian tenure, he was also canvassed as a possible Conservative parliamentary candidate in the election of 1868. Herman Merivale wrote to Maine on 26 February 1868 that: 'This mail will take you out the news, of course anticipated by telegram, of Lord Derby's resignation. It was merely forced on him

by ill health and everybody was prepared to receive the announcement of Disraeli's succession . . . The Cambridge election was an eccentric little contest, with 2 Liberals and Cranbornites & such partisans of parties winning the day against steady Toryism. I suppose you know that some folks entertained the idea of setting you up as a candidate in your absence.' *Maine Papers*, India Office Library (uncatalogued).

35. Maine to Harrison, 18 February, 2 May 1870, *Harrison Collection*, LSE, File A (uncatalogued).

36. Maine to Grant Duff, 10 June 1870, *Grant Duff Papers*.

37. Maine to Grant Duff, 12 April 1871, *Grant Duff Papers*.

38. Maine to Grant Duff, 8 April 1871, *Grant Duff Papers*.

39. Maine to Grant Duff, 12 April, 16 May 1871, *Grant Duff Papers;* Duke of Argyll to Maine, 15 May 1871, *Maine Collection*, LSE. Maine was the first person to be appointed to the Indian Council for life, the normal appointment being for ten years, after ten years previous experience of Indian administration. *The Standard,* 6 February 1888, commenting on this unusual procedure, noted that, in securing the enabling legislation for life appointment, 'the brilliant claims of the great jurist Sir Henry Maine were not the least powerful arguments used.' A. B. Keith, *A Constitutional History of India, 1600–1935,* London, Methuen, 1936, pp. 168–9, notes that 'the terms of office of members [of the Indian Council] was reduced normally to ten years . . . this rule was modified virtually to secure the services of Sir Henry Maine, without limit of time.' It is now clear that Maine relied heavily on the political goodwill of his friend Grant Duff in seeing that his India Office interests were well represented in high places. Thus, on another occasion, when it was rumoured in Whitehall that the Permanent Under-Secretaryship of the India Office was soon to fall vacant, Maine wrote:

Private
India Office
February 6, 1874

My dear Grant Duff,

Since you left town poor Merivale has had two attacks of his ailment—the last most serious—and I hear from what seems to me a sure source that he has determined not to return to work, even if he recovers.

Circumstances have so turned out that the Government may resign before Merivale sends in his resignation, or that the Duke may not think it right to deal at all with the succession, but still, if the question of his succession is raised, I dare say I may depend on you to do what you can for my interests, as indeed, you always have done.

I say nothing of the elections till I can talk to you personally.

Very sincerely yours,
H. S. Maine

Maine was not, however, chosen for the position, as Sir Louis Mallet was appointed to succeed Merivale as permanent head of the India Office. It is, incidentally, a striking illustration of Maine's formality that, even with so close a friend as Grant Duff, he continued to the end to sign his letters 'H. S. Maine'.

40. Maine to Murray, 12 July 1871, *J. M. Arch.*

41. Maine to Murray, 30 June 1871, *J. M. Arch.*

42. Maine to Lord Lytton, 31 January 1876, *Lytton Papers*, Mss. Eur. E218.

Chapter 10. The English Patriarch

1. Wallace to Maine, 11 April 1876, *Maine Collection*, LSE, Letters (6). Sir Donald Wallace (1841–1919), head of the Foreign Department of *The Times* and later an Indian official under Lord Dufferin, published his well known *History of Russia* in 1876.

2. Maine to Murray, 4 August 1870, *J. M. Arch.* Maine's works were just beginning to be known in France by this period. He wrote to the French student of society P. Viollet on 30 June 1873 that while 'The *Ancient Law* is not, I believe, much known in France, a French economist of distinction recently informed me that he intended to translate it and to endeavour to find a publisher for it.' *Holmes Papers*, Harvard Law Library. J. C. Courcelle-Seneuil (1813–92) was the translator referred to by Maine, and his version of *L'Ancien Droit* was published by Guillaumin, Paris, during 1873. Professionally, Courcelle-Seneuil was an adherent of the French *anti-étatiste* school of economists, who argued against state interference in private enterprise.

3. Maine to Murray, 5 August 1870, *J. M. Arch.* During a leave from India, Maine had earlier written to Murray, dated 12 July 1865 that 'I do not know whether I told you that the Oxford people assured me that my book might be considered to constitute *the* ingredient of Jurisprudence in the School of Jurisprudence and Modern History, and that is rapidly becoming the favourite school after the Classical School. The Civil Service Commissioners are also going to make it necessary for Indian Civilians; Under these circumstances, I suppose a sale, though not a rapid sale, may be depended on.' *Ibid.* See also Chapter 19, *supra*, n. 22, 23.

4. Holt to Maine, 17 February 1874, *Henry Holt Archives*, Book 9 f. 431, Princeton University Library.

5. Maine to Woolsey, 29 March 1878, *Woolsey Papers*, Yale University Library.

6. Harold Laski, Explanatory Note to 'An Unpublished Maine/Adams Letter', *The Nation*, cli, 3 August 1940, pp. 94–5.

7. Mark de Wolfe Howe, *Justice Oliver Wendell Holmes: The Shaping Years, 1841–1870*, Harvard University Press, 1957, pp. 193–5.

8. Maine to Holmes, 17 June 1871, *Holmes Papers*, Harvard University Library.

9. Maine to Holmes, 23 June 1871, *Holmes Papers*, Harvard Law Library.

10. Mark de Wolfe Howe, ed., *The Holmes/Laski Letters*, London, Cumberledge, 1953, i, p. 429.

11. Maine to Holmes, 26 July 1873, *Holmes Papers*, Harvard University Library. I have assigned the year 1873 on the basis of Maine's remark that he had met Henry Adams 'this summer'.

12. W. C. Ford, ed., *Letters of Henry Adams*, London, Constable, 1930, p. 251.

13. W. H. Jordy, *Henry Adams: Scientific Historian*, Yale University Press, 1952, p. 34 *et seq.*

14. W. C. Ford, *op. cit.*, p. 236.

15. See E. Samuel's definitive *The Young Henry Adams*, London, Cumberledge, 1948, p. 232.

16. See Karl Resek's recent *L. H. Morgan: American Scholar*, University of Chicago Press, 1960, for further detail of Morgan's career. An earlier biography is B. J. Stern's *Lewis Henry Morgan: Social Evolutionist*, University of Chicago Press, 1931.

17. A. L. White, ed., *Extracts From the European Travel Journal of L. H. Morgan*, in *Rochester Historical Society Publications*, xvi, ii, 1937, pp. 374–5. John Fiske, the positivist historian who was at the time a history lecturer at Harvard, met Maine in 1873, and described him as 'plump and good natured', rather than 'good sized', but their impressions parallel one another. E. F. Fisk, *op. cit.*, p. 284.

18. Maine to Morgan, 31 July 1871, *Morgan Papers*, University of Rochester. The paper Morgan had sent was apparently his 'Stone and Bone Instruments of the Aricknarees', *New York State Museum Reports*, xxi, 1871, pp. 25–46. The larger work referred to was his important *Systems of Consanguinity and Affinity of the Human Family*, Washington, D.C., Smithsonian Institute, 1870–71.

19. Trends were indicated in 'Mr Murray's List of New Works' for April 1872, when Tylor's *Primitive Culture*, Maine's *Village Communities*, and Darwin's *Origin of Species* were advertised together. In March of the same year, Sir John Lubbock's American publisher wrote that his *Prehistoric Times* had sold nearly 1,000 copies in two days, which would be a respectable sales figure today for a book as serious in subject matter: Appleton Publishing Company to Lubbock, 8 March 1872, *Avebury Papers*, B.M., Add. Mss. 49642.

Chapter 11. Critics

1. *The Athenaeum*, 15 April 1871, pp. 456–8.

2. Stephen to Lytton, 27 July 1876, *J. F. Stephen Papers*, Camb. Univ. Lib., Add.Mss. 7349. Box 1.

3. Mill to Cairnes, 2 August, 1872, in H. S. R. Elliot, *op. cit.*, 343.

4. Morley to Mill, 2 March 1873, *Mill-Taylor Collection*, LSE, ii, Item 241.

5. Harrison to Morley, *Harrison Collection*, LSE, File A.

6. *VC*, p. 16.

7. Maine to Murray, 23 October 1872, *J. M. Arch.* Maine's reference to the 'curious dislike' of conservative Roman Catholics for *AL* presumably stems from his discussion of natural law as a mere *legal* concept having no intrinsic moral value.

8. J. O'Connell, 'Maine on Ancient Law', *Law Magazine and Review, for both branches of the legal profession at home and abroad*, October 1872, p. 756.

9. *Ibid.*, November 1872, p. 887.

10. Maine to Murray, 27 October 1872, *J. M. Arch.*

11. T. E. Cliffe Leslie, 'Maine's *Ancient Law*', *Law Magazine, op. cit.*, December 1872, p. 1054.

12. *Schweizer Lexicon*, i, 1954, p. 778; J. J. Bachofen, *Das Mutterecht: eine Untersuchung uber die Gynaikokratie der alten Welt nach ihrer religiosen und recht lichen Natur*, Stuttgart, Krais & Hoffmann, 1861.

13. Bachofen included a lengthy preface to his even more lengthy treatise, which summarized the general points of his argument while omitting the detailed sources of the text itself. This was published separately in Paris by the *Groupe Francais d'Etudes Feministes* in 1903 as *Le Droit de la Mere dans l'antiquite*. See also the discussion of Bachofen in J. F. McLennan's *Studies in Ancient History*, London, Quaritch, 1876, p. 320 *et seq.*

14. J. F. McLennan, *op. cit.*, Chapter 1, *ibid.*, p. 320.

15. *Ibid.*, Chapter 7.

16. J. F. McLennan, *op. cit.*, p. 92. Thomas Hobbes, in his *Leviathan* (1651), Part ii, ch. 20, wrote: 'if there be no contract, the dominion is in the mother. For in the condition of mere nature, where there are no matrimonial laws, it cannot be known who is the father, unless it be declared by the mother; and therefore the right of dominion over the child dependeth on her will, and is consequently hers.'

17. *Ibid.*, p. 104.

18. *Ibid.*, p. 125.

19. *Ibid.*, p. 154.

20. *Ibid.*, pp. 154–5.

21. Sir H. J. S. Maine, *Early History of Institutions*, London, Murray, 1875, p. 310: further entries as *EHI*.

22. *EHI*. pp. 306–41, esp. 340. Maine had completed the lecture by early 1873, as in a letter to Murray of 9 May 1873, he noted that: 'The lecture referred to in the accompanying letter is in fact a chapter of a book very much resembling *Ancient Law* which may one day appear. Would my allowing these ladies to reprint it—which I would like to do—in any way effect its copyright, or could this be avoided by proper stipulations?' *J. M. Arch.* The essay was first published by the feminist group, unnamed in Maine's letter, as 'The Early History of the Property of Married Women, as Collected from Roman and Hindoo Law', Manchester, Ireland, 1873.

23. T. E. Cliffe Leslie, 'The History of the Property of Women', *The Athenaeum*, 9 May 1873, pp. 693–5.

24. J. F. McLennan, *op. cit.*, p. 126. McLennan came later to the view that patriarchalism had been adopted *only* at Rome and was therefore, in the comparative view, an outright aberration.

25. *EHI*, Introduction. p. viii.

26. Maine to Murray, 13 October 1873, *J.M. Arch. The Times*, 13 October 1873, p. 9.

27. Maine to Murray, 10 September 1874, *J. M. Arch.*

28. *EHI*, pp. 20–1.

29. *EHI*, esp. pp. 64–97, 214–17.

30. T. E. Cliffe Leslie, 'Maine on the *Early History of Institutions*', *Fortnightly Review*, xvii, March 1875, pp. 305–20.

31. J. E. Cairnes, 'Mr Spencer on Social Evolution', *Fortnightly Review*, xvii, pp. 63–82.

32. Stephen to Lady Grant Duff, 20 February 1875, *J. F. Stephen Papers*, Camb. Univ. Lib., Add. 7349, Box 1. Stephen was not above being caught up in the spirit of anthropological speculation himself, for all his protest. Following a dinner party at Lubbock's, for example, he wrote to Lady Grant Duff on 27 June 1874 that: 'The only difference that arose between us (& it was not a very bad one) was owing to my expressing some doubts whether the practice of honeymoon tours (being peculiar to England & a modern institution) could properly be regarded as a vestige of the barbaric theory of marriage, which was that the man carried off his wife, much as the Romans did from the Sabines. I think he thought I displayed an improper levity on this subject, but we soon made up!' *Ibid.*

33. W. R. W. Stephens, *Life and Letters of Edward A. Freeman*, London, Macmillan, 1895, p. 100.

34. Maine to Grant Duff, 30 March 1874, *Grant Duff Papers*.

35. Henry Holt to Maine, [n.d.], *Henry Holt Archives*, Book 12, f. 248.

36. Henry Adams to Maine, 22 February 1875, first published with Explanatory Note by Harold Laski in *The Nation*, cli, 3 August 1940, pp. 94–5.

Chapter 12. Scientific Conservatism

1. P. M. Laurence, *Collectanea: Essays, Addresses and Reviews*, London, Macmillan, 1899, pp. 208–9.

2. *The Times*, 25 May 1875, p. 9.

3. B. N. Nelson, *op. cit.*, pp. 137–8.

4. Sir H. J. S. Maine, 'The Effects of Observation of India on Modern European Thought", reprinted in *VC*, (3rd revised edn, 1876), pp. 2–5–39 (215).

5. *VC*, p. 222.

6. *VC*, p. 224.

7. *VC*, pp. 210–1.

8. *VC*, pp. 229–30.

9. *VC*, p. 231.

10. *VC*, p. 232.

11. *VC*, p. 233.

12. *VC*, p. 237.

13. *The Nation*, xx, 1 April 1875, pp. 225–6.

14. Henry Holt to Maine, 10 October 1875, *Henry Holt Archives*, Book 12, f. 426.

15. Holt to Maine, 30 November 1875, *Henry Holt Archives*, Book 12, f. 491.

16. Maine to Murray, 13 December 1875, *J. M. Arch.*

17. 'Sovereignty' and 'Sovereignty and Empire', in *EHI*, pp. 342–70; pp. 371–400. Maine's lectures on sovereignty have no immediate bearing on the preceding chapters on early Irish law, which seems to add credence to the view that he preferred to make his most important answers to critics indirectly and discreetly: it is notable that immediately preceding these two lectures is Sir Henry's paper on 'The Early History of the Settled Property of Married Women', pp. 306–41, which while having little to do with the Irish material, is an indirect answer to J. F. McLennan's criticisms of his patriarchal thesis.

18. *EHI*, p. 360: for further criticisms by Maine of Bentham, see his 'Ancient Ideas Respecting the Arrangement of Codes', *Fortnightly Review*, xxv, May, 1879, p. 763 *et seq.*

19. *EHI*, pp. 388–9.

20. *EHI*, p. 398.

21. *EHI*, p. 364, (italics added).

22. *EHI*, pp. 364–5, (italics added).

23. *EHI*, p. 359.

Chapter 13. Patriarchs—or Matriarchs?

1. J. F. McLennan, *op. cit.*, Preface, pp. xii-xiii.

2. *Ibid.*, pp. 354–8.

3. *Maine Collection*, LSE, Section i, Volume 10, Item N.

4. Maine to Morgan, 30 July 1876, *Morgan Papers*. The letter is partially reproduced in B. J. Stern, *op. cit.*, p. 137.

5. K. Resek, *op. cit.*, p. 137 *et seq.*

6. H. R. Hays, *From Ape to Angel: An Informal History of Social Anthropology*, London, Methuen, 1959, p. 74, suggests that Morgan came close to being 'the Darwin of social anthropology'.

7. L. H. Morgan, *Ancient Society: or, Researches in the Lines of Human Progress from Savagery Through Barbarism to Civilization*, N.Y., Holt, 1877, p. 62 (Belknap Press of Harvard University Press editions, 1964, with Introduction by L. A. White).

8. *Ibid.*, Preface, p. viii.

9. *Ibid.*, p. 150.

10. *Ibid.*, p. 63.

11. *Ibid.*, p. 383.

12. *Ibid.*, p. 500.

13. *Ibid.*, p. 552.

14. At any rate Maine wrote to Oliver Wendell Holmes on 8 October 1876, to apologize for not replying to an earlier letter, 'owing', he said, 'to a sharp attack of a fever originally caught in India', and adding that he was 'even now scarcely in a condition to do more than acknowledge the paper which you have been good enough to send me'. *Holmes Papers*, Harvard Law Library.

15. Maine to Morgan, 30 July 1877, in B. J. Stern, *op. cit.*, p. 142.

16. Sir J. Lubbock, 'Ancient Society', *Sat. R.*, 5 January 1878, cited in Karl Resek, *op. cit.*, pp. 143 fn.

17. Maine to Morgan, 30 April 1878, *Morgan Papers*.

18. Morgan to Maine, 14 May 1878, *Maine Collection*, LSE, Letters (9).

19. Maine to Tylor, 27 May 1878, reproduced in *Man*, li, July 1951, p. 104. Tylor's paper on Morgan appeared in the *Academy*, xiv, 1878, pp. 67–8.

20. Maine to Morgan, 8 November 1880, *Morgan Papers*. The letter is partially reproduced in B. J. Stern, *op. cit.*, p. 144.

21. McLennan to Maine, 21 October 1880, *Maine Collection*, LSE, Letters (10).

22. Sir H. J. S. Maine, *Dissertations on Early Law and Custom*, London, Murray, 1883, p. 196. Further entries given as *ELC*.

23. *ELC*, p. 192.

24. *ELC*, p. 127.

25. *ELC*, p. 216.

26. *ELC*, p. 219.

27. *ELC*, p. 231.

28. *The Athenaeum*, 31 March 1883, pp. 399–400.

29. Lang to Maine, March/April 1883 [undated], *Maine Collection*, LSE, Letters (14). The 'clock-bell' reference is to Maine's criticisms of McLennan's unilateral evolutionary views. The 'jealousy' allusion is in answer to Maine's assertion that, in order for the matriarchal theory to be fully plausible, the instinct of sexual jealously in the human species must be assumed to have been curtailed for lengthy periods.

30. F. Engels, 'The Origin of the Family, Private Property and The State', London, 1884, reproduced in *Karl Marx and Frederick Engels: Selected Works*, Moscow, Foreign Languages Press, 1958, pp. 117–327. McLennan fared no better than Maine, being summarily dismissed as 'the dry-as-dust lawyer.'

31. E. R. Bulwer [First Earl Lytton] to Maine, 8 May 1883, *Maine Collection*, LSE, Letters (13). E. B. Tylor wrote on 15 March 1883 'with many thanks for the book', noting that: 'When I set to work on the anthropological museum at Oxford, there are several things I shall want to trouble the India Office about. It is too bad that the Aramic wood-drill for making the sacred fire should not be to be seen in England, and there are other Hindu things we have no specimens of. It is a pity that one can only put dry dead specimens in cases: would it were possible to have a suttee to show.' *Ibid., Letters* (12).

32. E. B. Tylor, 'The Matriarchal Theory', *Nineteenth Century*, xl, July, 1896, pp. 84–5.

33. K. R. V. Wikman, 'Letters from E. B. Tylor and Alfred Russell to Edward Westermarck', in *Abo Akademi, Acta Academiae Aboensis, Humaniora*, xiii, (7).

34. Robin Fox, *Kinship and Marriage*, London, Penguin, 1967, p. 18, has recently suggested that the historical and evolutionary perspective of the nineteenth century pioneers in kinship studies frequently led them to conclusions 'quite staggeringly without foundation'.

35. *Memoir*, pp. 48–9.

36. Spencer to Youmans, 17 May, 1883, in D. Duncan, *op. cit.*, pp. 232–3.

37. For Spencer's analysis and critique of Maine's patriarchal thesis, see his comments in *The Principles of Sociology*, London, Williams and Norgate, 1906, i, pp. 681–92.

Chapter 14. Return to Cambridge

1. Much of this lecture material is in the *Maine Collection*, LSE, Section ii, Vol. 20, Item 4, synopsis and text of two courses of nine lectures each on 'Gaius and Early Institutions'. The first series is headed 'Law of Persons', the second 'Law of Things'.

2. Maine to Holmes, 24 August 1878, *Holmes Papers*, Harvard Law Library: 'I trust F. Pollock Jr., whom I think you know, will be elected . . . He is of all men in this country most likely to rewrite the history of English law, which urgently needs re-writing.'

3. L. Stephen, ed., *Letters of John Richard Green*, London, Macmillan, 1901, pp. 423–4. Mrs Humphrey Ward recalled that Green's house at 14 Kensington Square, London, was after 1800 'the centre of a small society such as England produces much more rarely than France. Mr. Lecky came—Sir Henry Maine, Mr. Freeman, Mr. Bryce, Bishop Stubbs, sometimes, and Mr. Stopford Brooke, and many more.' p. 397.

4. Maine to Lord Lytton, 26 August 1876, *Lytton Papers*, Mss. Eur. E218.

5. Lord Derby to Maine, 24 April 1876, *Maine Collection*, LSE, Letters, (7).

6. Maine to Lord Salisbury, 28 December 1877, *Salisbury Papers*; *The Times*, 4 January 1878, p. 9.

7. Stephen to Lady Grant Duff, 15 December 1881, *J. F. Stephen Papers*, Camb. Univ. Lib., Add. 7349, Box 1. In a letter to Lord Lytton of 10 January 1879, Stephen wrote even more strongly: 'I think he is in most ways the cleverest man I ever knew, but in nothing has he shown more ability than in his wonderful economy of labour for many years. I doubt whether he has done a real hard days work since he went to India in 1862, but he somehow manages to do just as much and just as well as if he did work, & he is at the top of the tree of respectability and splendour'. *J. F. Stephen Papers*, Camb. Univ. Lib., Add 7349, Box 1. On the other hand, one must take into account that Maine and Stephen, while very close friends, were not above backbiting. Maine, for example, wrote rather uncharitably to Lytton on 2 August 1878, noting that: 'Stephen . . . has succeeded in getting the Chancellor with his back

to the wall & extracting from him as clear a promise of a Judgeship as a Chancellor can make. This is in consequence of Stephen's English work: I fear no Indian work would command a similar reward.' *Lytton Papers*, Mss. Eur. E218. Stephen was appointed a Judge of the High Court on 3 January 1879.

8. Stephen to Lady Grant Duff, 29 December 1881, *J. F. Stephen Papers*, Camb. Univ. Lib., Add. 7349, Box 1.

9. Stephen to Lady Grant Duff, 15 December 1881, 12 January 1882, *J. F. Stephen Papers*, Camb. Univ. Lib., Add. 7349, Box 1.

10. *The Times*, 8 November 1882, p. 9.

11. Thompson to Maine, 8 November 1882, *Maine Collection*, LSE, Letters, (11); Walpole's letter of resignation was printed in *The Times*, 8 November 1882, p. 8.

12. The *Spectator*, iv, 2 December 1882, p. 1531.

13. *ELC*, pp. 174–5; originally published under Maine's signature in the *Fortnightly Review*, xxx, November 1881, p. 603 *et seq.*

14. *ELC*, p. 191.

15. *ELC*, p. 133; originally published in the *Fortnightly Review*, xxxi, February 1882, p. 180 *et seq.*

16. *ELC*, p. 159.

17. Lord Acton to Mary Gladstone, 7 January, 19 January 1882, in H. Paul, ed., *Letters of Lord Acton to Mary Gladstone*, London, Allen, 1904, pp. 118–19.

18. *Ibid*, p. 26. In the original, Acton added: 'there is a handsome, un-interesting Lady Maine.' In a letter to Mary Gladstone of 30 March 1884, Acton noted of Maine's wife that 'otherwise, I do not stand in his wife's books quite where I should wish.' *Mary Gladstone Papers*, B.M. Add. Mss. 46239. Poor Lady Maine seems a perpetual outsider with Maine's friends. J. F. Stephen confided in a letter to Emily Cunningham of 1 April 1875 that he was so thankful to have married well, for had he chosen 'even a stupid commonplace woman like 50 people—Lady Maine, say—my life would really be clouded.' *J. F. Stephen Papers*, Camb. Univ. Lib., Add. 7349, Box 2.

19. Acton to Mary Gladstone, 8 August 1880, in H . Paul, *op. cit.*, p. 29.

20. Maine left a personal estate valued at £46,715 6s 7d., according to his Will. Aside from Maine's legal fees, India Office income, and profes-sorial stipend, he mentions in a letter of 7 February 1871 certain 'Indian Railway Shares', and in a further letter to his publisher of 9 February 1871, of a 'call made on the shareholders of the Oudh and Rohiland Railway'. *J. M. Arch.* Other income derived from his publications.

21. *Quarterly Review*, clii, July, 1881, p. 75, attributed to Maine on internal evidence: in the *Quarterly Review*, clvi, July 1883, a quotation is cited from the same dispatch and Maine is named as its author.

Chapter 15. 'Imperium et Libertas'

1. Stephen to Lord Lytton, 6 March 1876, *J. F. Stephen Papers*, Camb. Univ. Lib., Add. 7349, Box 1.

2. Cited in L. Stephen, *Life of J. F. Stephen*, London, Smith Elder, 1895, p. 300.

3. Stephen to Emily Cunningham [Lady Egerton], 25 April 1872, *J. F. Stephen Papers*, Camb. Univ. Lib., Add. 7349, Box 2. The reference to the 'P.M.G.' is the *Pall Mall Gazette*.

4. Stephen to Emily Cunningham, 1 May 1872, *J. F. Stephen Papers*, Camb. Univ. Lib., Add. 7349, Box 2.

5. Stephen to Lytton, 2 May 1876, *J. F. Stephen Papers*, Camb. Univ. Lib., Add. 7349, Box 1; see discussion in L. Stephen, *op. cit.*, pp. 306–40.

6. J. F. Stephen, *Liberty, Equality, Fraternity*, London, Smith Elder, 1873, (2nd edn, 1874): p. 54 *et seq*. Subsequent references are to this edition, and entered as *LEF*.

7. *LEF*, p. 132.

8. *LEF*, p. 133.

9. *LEF*, p. 339.

10. Stephen to Lytton, 2 May 1876, *J. F. Stephen Papers*, *op. cit.*: 'I wish you would remember to tell me whether you ever saw a small book of mine called "Liberty, Equality, Fraternity". My daughter christened it "*Frequality*", which is a much better name.'

11. Stephen to Lytton, 4 September 1879, cited in J. P. C. Roach, *Sir James Fitzjames Stephen: A Study of His Thought and Life*, unpublished Ph.D. dissertation, Cambridge University, 1953, no. 2399, p. 225.

12. *LEF*, pp. 353–4. The quotation 'Be strong and of good courage' is taken from *Deuteronomy* 31:6–7.

13. See for example J. C. Rees, *Mill and His Early Critics*, Leicester University Press, 1956, which argues effectively the case that Mill's authority 'had been challenged and his central thesis called in question before Stephen had decided to fire his broadside'. p. 4. For varying reception of Stephen's own book, see the *Saturday Review*, xxxv, April 19 1873, pp. 517–18; the *Athenaeum*, no. 2377, May 17 1873, pp. 627–8; the *Westminster Review*, c, July 1873, pp. 212–14; the *Quarterly Review*, cxxxv, June 1873, pp. 178–89.

14. A. Carlyle, ed., *New Letters of Thomas Carlyle*, London, Lane, 1904, ii, p. 291: In a letter of 23 December 1872, Carlyle wrote of Stephen that

'He volunteers weekly to visit me on Sunday with a long walk and long intelligent discourse, which however relates mainly to objects rather foreign to me: Indian matters, effete English Officiality in the Home Departments, projects of codification, etc.' Stephen's interests, he says in a letter of 2 November 1872, 'though really important to the world, are not so to me'.

15. Stephen to Emily Cunningham, 29 December 1873, *J. F. Stephen Papers*, Camb. Univ. Lib., Add. 7349, Box 2.

16. F. Harrison, 'The Religion of Inhumanity', *Fortnightly Review*, xiv, June 1873, pp. 677–99. Morley had set the tone in his introductory 'The Death of Mr Mill', *ibid.*, pp. 669–76: 'The most eminent of those who are now fast becoming the front line, as death mows down the veterans, all bear trace of his influence, whether they are avowed disciples or avowed opponents.' p. 670. Harrison had written to Morley on 19 April 1873, of his intention to 'skin [Stephen]', and to entitle his article the 'Religion of Inhumanity', which, he thought, 'would slay Stephen with one blow'. *Harrison Collection*, LSE, File B.

17. F. Harrison, *op. cit.*, p. 677: Harrison wrote to Morley on 3 May 1873 that 'There is a picture of Heaven and Hell a la Stephen which makes me laugh in the night. I have found him out. Stephen is a Calvinist who has lost his belief in Christianity. I see him in the pulpit and gown of John Knox thundering about the wrath to come. I notice he has not a Gospel in his hand, but a new edition of Bentham.' *Harrison Collection*, LSE, File B.

18. F. Harrison, *op. cit.*, p. 693.

19. J. Morley, 'Mr Mill's Doctrine of Liberty', *Fortnightly Review*, xiv, August 1873, pp. 234–56.

20. Harrison to Morley, 8 April 1873, *Harrison Collection*, LSE, File B. Harrison's reference to Stephen's 'argument as to the equality of the sexes' refers to the rebuttal, in *LEF*, p. 219 *et seq.*, of Mill's *Essay on the Subjection of Women* (1869).

21. F. Harrison, 'The Revival of Authority', *Fortnightly Review*, xiii, January 1873, pp. 1–26.

22. Morley to Harrison, 20 April 1873, *Harrison Collection*, LSE, File B.

23. Morley to Harrison, 22 April 1873, *Harrison Collection*, LSE, File B. The animosity was largely intellectual: Stephen wrote to Lord Lytton, 2 May 1876, that 'I also saw Morley the other day in the street & walked with him a bit . . . He is the best of good fellows & I like him exceedingly. He is fair, truthful, & thoroughly manly & honourable, but he is a bit of a fanatic . . . he & several other young fellows, as Meredith would say, give me the *queerest* feeling whenever I talk to them.' *J. F. Stephen Papers*, Camb. Univ. Lib., Add. 7349, Box 1.

24. *LEF*, Preface (2nd edn), p. xvii.

25. *LEF*, p. xxx. For a brief summary of the leading tenets of Comte's 'Religion of Humanity', see J. Bowle, *Politics and Opinion in the Nineteenth Century*, London, Cape, 1954, pp. 117–33.

26. Harrison to Morley, 9 April 1873, *Harrison Collection*, LSE, File B. Harrison wrote to Morley on 24 April 1873: ' I met Stephen the other night at a wrangle about codes and digests between him & Reilly. He was most friendly to me. I told him I was going to pitch in to him, which he rather wished & certainly expected. I told him he knew nothing of Comte, to which he assented. He said it was curious how many enemies he made; "well", I said, "you take pains to do so," "Oh" said he, "but on every side one treads on people's corns." F.H.: "Well!, that is your religion, isn't it?" J.F.S.: "No, not exactly—perhaps it's my mode of worship." He hopes Mill is not pained and wishes to be thought a good fellow in private life.' *Ibid*, File A.

27. *PG*, p. 58. See *LEF*, pp. 198–9; 256–7, for important similarities.

28. *LEF*, p. 1. Stephen's position had been anticipated by Alexis de Tocqueville, *Democracy in America*, ii, Chs. 2, 5, (Phillips Bradley edn), Vintage, 1960.

29. Sir H. J. S. Maine, 'Mr Fitzjames Stephen's Introduction to the Indian Evidence Act', *Fortnightly Review*, xiii, January 1873, pp. 51–67; reprinted in *VC* (3rd ed, 1876), pp. 295–329.

30. *VC*, pp. 299–300.

31. *VC*, pp. 323–4.

32. Sir W. W. Hunter, *Life of Lord Mayo*, London, Smith Elder, 1876, ii, pp. 165–6; part of this passage is cited in E. Stokes, *op. cit.*, p. 280. Yet Stephen's aggressive 'Anglicism' was offset by his Benthamist desire to be objective and impartial: thus, he was not always consistent with himself in his appraisals—compare his rather impatient assessment of the pedigree of the Indian village community with his defence of Maine's *Village Communities* against Mill in *LEF*, p. 242: 'Sir Henry Maine's account of the matter—is as interesting as it is ingenious—in this, as in other cases, he confines himself to an investigation of or to speculations about matters of fact; and neither says, nor, as it seems to me, assumes, as Mr Mill always does, that to show that the course of events has in fact led from A to B, and appears to be in the direction of C, proves that B is better than A, and that C is better than B.' Perhaps he affords the best explanation in his unpublished autobiography when he says of Maine and himself that 'at last I came to recognize, not only his wonderful gifts, but the fact that at bottom & substantially he & I agreed fundamentally though it cost us both a good deal of trouble to find it out.' *J. F. Stephen Papers*, Camb. Univ. Lib., Add 7349, Box 2, f. 39. Note also Leslie Stephen's comment, *op. cit.*, pp. 413–14 that as time passed Stephen 'may be said to have been recruited, almost in spite of himself, by the historical school'.

33. Or at least 'change', for Stephen can not really be said to have been a supporter of the notion of historical progress. *LEF*, pp. 236–45.

34. L. Stephen, *op. cit.*, p. 398; E. Stokes, *op. cit.*, p. 306.

35. E. Stokes, *op. cit.*, p. 307. Professor Stokes has an enlightening discussion on the philosophical roots of nineteenth-century British imperialism and its connection with utilitarianism, at p. 288 *et seq.*

36. *Ibid.*, pp. 306–11; 312– 20. R. Iyer, 'Utilitarianism and All That: The Political Theory of British Imperialism', *Saint Antony's College Papers on South Asian Affairs*, no. 8, London, 1960, p. 23, discerns at least four separate strains of British imperialist philosophy: (*a*) the Burkean doctrine of imperial trusteeship; (*b*) the utilitarian theory of state activity propounded mainly by Bentham and the two Mills; (*c*) the Platonic conception of a ruling elite acting like wise guardians; (*d*) the Evangelical hope of spreading the gospel of western Christianity and western institutions.

Chapter 16. India and Party Politics

1. Stephen to Emily Cunningham, 17 March 1875, *J. F. Stephen Papers*, Camb. Univ. Lib., Add. 7349, Box 2. Donald Southgate, *The Passing of the Whigs, 1832–1886*, London, Macmillan, 1965, p. 336, suggests that 'The participation of the old governing class in Liberal politics declined steadily from 1868 onwards. Whiggery was told very clearly that is was a nuisance.'

2. Maine to Lytton, 7 April 1876, *Lytton Papers*, Mss. Eur. E218.

3. Maine to Lytton, 7 April 1876, *Lytton Papers*, Mss. Eur. E218. Maine had written to complain of the lack of consultation between the Whig Viceroy and the Indian Council in London. The creation of the Council as a second branch of Anglo-Indian government, he wrote, 'was the fruit, first of all, of a feeling that, if the Home Branch [of the Indian Government] was worth anything, it was good for knowing everything that was going on in India'.

4. As Secretary for India, 1868–74, Argyll caused friction with his councillors by going over their heads to deal directly with the Viceroy. When Maine wrote to Sir Erskine Perry for information on a legal matter on 20 May 1869, for example, Perry wrote back rather crisply that 'our Duke does not seek counsel from us in these matters'. *Maine Papers* (misc.) India Office Library. Argyll was instrumental in having the provisions of the 1858 Act that created the Council revised so as to limit tenure of membership to ten years. Previous to this charge in 1869, membership was held 'during good behaviour but without limit of time', and thus the Argyll amendment had the effect of enhancing the Secretary's power. The older arrangement, at least for certain members of Council, was eventually reinstated in 1876: see n. 47, *supra*. Argyll's successor, Lord Salisbury, was perhaps even more firm

in his interpretation of the Secretary's position in relation to the Council, but Maine seems to have felt that his own voice was listened to more readily by the Tory statesman. For a brief and reliable discussion of the background party issues involved, see R. J. Moore, *Liberalism and Indian Politics, 1872–1922*, London, Arnold, 1966, p. 16 *et seq.* The book contains an excellent short bibliography. I draw substantially on Dr Moore's account of the transitions in Indian politics during this period in the discussion of this chapter. Argyll, like Northbrook, was an aristocratic Whig who carried intact his British party concern for 'liberty and property' to the arena of Indian affairs. He thus felt towards Maine, as had Sir Charles Wood, that he was not always a reliable ally. While working on the papers for amending the Punjab Tenancy Act of 1868, for example, he wrote to Northbrook that he intended 'to fire a shot across the bows of the school, now so strong and active, which deprecates all property in land, and advocates a land revenue system, destructive of proprietorship, as distinguished from mere occupancy. . . . I do not think Maine will like it, because he is rather of the Mill school on these questions.' Duchess of Argyll, *George Douglas, Eighth Duke of Argyll; Autobiography and Memoirs*, London, Murray, 1906, ii, pp. 282–3. He seems to have misunderstood Maine's position, which was that the special conditions of India required a flexibility on the part of the administrative class that might not always be consistent with British party views. When *The Times*, 14 February 1870, p. 9, noted that the Punjab Tenancy Act of 1868 had been passed against the wishes of the 'landlord school' because Maine 'clung to the principle of prescription at all hazards, and enabled the school of confiscation . . . to gain a numerical victory', Sir Henry retorted in a letter to the editor that when the full facts became known, he would be 'greatly surprised if [readers] are of the opinion that the gentlemen with whom I acted are exactly the persons against whom the charge of confiscation should be brought.' See also H. S. R. Elliot, op. cit., ii, pp. 169–72. In domestic British politics, Maine and Argyll stood closer together, especially on such issues as Irish land reform: see D. Southgate, *op. cit.*, pp. 373–6. For Maine's correspondence with Salisbury on the consolidation of Indian statute law, I have consulted Maine to Salisbury, 5 March, 18 May, 27 May, 31 December 1874, *Salisbury Papers*. See also L. Stephen, *op. cit.*, pp. 354–5.

5. Maine to Salisbury, 31 December 1874, *Salisbury Papers*. The plan to include himself on the new Commission, he wrote, 'really only arose from my recollection of the awkwardnesses which were caused by the relation of the old Commissioners corresponding with the India Office through their Secretary, and with the Government of India through the India Office. All sorts of needless difficulties seemed to me to arise from the want of a short-cut to authentic information.'

6. Cited in J. L. Hammond and L. T. Hobhouse, *Lord Hobhouse: A Memoir*, London, Arnold, 1906, pp. 93–4.

7. Maine to Salisbury, 15 June 1874, *Salisbury Papers*.

8. *ELC*, p. 389.

9. Maine to Lytton, 2 April 1878, *Lytton Papers*, Mss. Eur. E218. The letter was devoted to a series of reminiscences on the problems of continuing the codification schemes under Lytton's predecessor, Lord Northbrook.

10. R. J. Moore, *op. cit.*, p. 17, who feels that the friction between Northbrook and Salisbury 'opened a decade in which Indian affairs were to be the subject of bitter conflicts between the parties at home'. B. Mallet, *Thomas George, Earl of Northbrook*, London, Longmans, 1908, Chapter 2. Mallet's sympathetic treatment of Northbrook's Indian career notes that after the period of 'severe' reforming energy following the Mutiny, 'the progress made . . . had at this time somewhat outstripped the actual requirements of the people . . . a period of comparative rest was required, and . . . the political instincts and the personal character of the new Viceroy enabled him to recognize and act upon this truth.' p. 65.

11. Stephen to Lytton, 6 March 1876, *J. F. Stephen Papers*, Camb. Univ. Lib., Add. 7349, Box 1. Like Maine, Stephen urged upon the new Viceroy that codification 'might succeed if Hobhouse's successor was favourable, & could be worked with'.

12. Maine to Lytton, 26 August, 26 September 1876, *Lytton Papers*, Mss. Eur. E218. Maine had earlier tried unsuccessfully to persuade Stephen to return to Calcutta. Stephen wrote to Lytton, 24 June 1876: 'Since I began this letter, or rather this article, I got a letter from Maine asking me point blank to tell him in writing for Lord S's information whether "I would go to India next spring or not".' *J. F. Stephen Papers*, Camb. Univ. Lib., Add. 7349, Box 1. Maine thus was apparently very eager to take advantage of the new political situation that united a strong Tory Secretary of State with a willing Tory Viceroy. As he had written earlier to Salisbury of the Northbrook regime: 'this whole tone of complaint on the part of the Government of India is quite new to me. I feel sure that if Lord Lawrence's government felt inclined to complain of anything it was the indecisive tone of the home authorities on important matters, and I myself had a special grievance in the Secretary of State's practice of sending us out the drafts of the Indian Law Commissioners, without a single word to tell us whether he agreed or not with their sometimes most formidable suggestions. Many a difficulty would have been got over in my time, if the Secretary of State would only have given a distinct opinion.' *Salisbury Papers*, 3 November 1874.

13. Whitley Stokes, *The Anglo-Indian Codes* (2 vols.), Oxford, Clarendon Press, 1887–8, General Introduction, pp. i–xxviii.

14. Maine to Salisbury, 4 February 1878, *Salisbury Papers*.

15. Maine to Lytton, 28 June 1878, *Lytton Papers*, Mss. Eur. E218. Maine's view, as he wrote further to Lytton in a letter of 20 February 1880, was that codification by select committee was preferable to nothing at all, and that to forego all further efforts in the face of opposition to a Commission was 'to be niggard of almost the only unquestionable boon which the British Government is enforcing in India.' *Ibid.*

16. Maine to Lytton, 2 August, 30 August 1878, *Lytton Papers*, Mss. Eur. E218.

17. Cited in *Memoir*, pp. 49–61; *The Times*, 9 July 1878, p. 8

18. W. Stokes, op. cit., pp. xx–xxi. At the outset of Lord Ripon's viceroyalty in 1880, Stokes wrote to Ripon that 'yesterday I received a letter from Sir H. Maine exulting that the prospects of codification are looking up here, & saying that things have also improved at the India Office, from the codifiers point of view.' 5 November 1881, *Ripon Papers*, B.M. Add. Mss. 43610. f. 41 (cxx). Yet once Stokes's first batch of measures, mostly prepared under Lytton, had been enacted, the further projects were set aside. Courtenay Ilbert wrote to Ripon on 25 May 1882 that: 'Before leaving England I had some talk with Sir H. Maine about Indian codification. Two things seem pretty clear. First, that the work is too important to be dropped & secondly, that it is inexpedient to press any further codifying measures on the Legislative Council just at present.' *Ripon Papers*, B.M. Add. Mss. 43610. f. 9 (cxi).

19. Stephen to Lytton, 27 July 1876, *J. F. Stephen Papers*, Camb. Univ. Lib., Add. 7349, Box 1.

20. *Memoir*, Minute of 12 November 1875, 'Selection and Training of Candidates for the Indian Civil Service', pp. 402–11; Maine to Salisbury, 31 May 1877. Maine noted that 'from what I hear, the Parliamentary attack on the reduction of age seems likely to be formidable.' *Salisbury Papers*. See also R. J. Moore, *op. cit.*, pp. 19–21.

21. Maine to Lytton, 7 June 1878, *Lytton Papers*, Mss. Eur. E218.

22. Lady Betty Balfour, *The History of Lord Lytton's Indian Administration*, London, Longmans, 1899, pp. 518–19: when the measure was considered before the Indian Council in London, only three members recorded Minutes of dissent, Sir William Muir, Sir Erskine Perry and Colonel Yule.

23. Maine to Lytton, 7 June 1878, *Lytton Papers*, Mss. Eur. E218.

24. H. Paul, *op. cit.*, p. 26: Lord Acton in this letter to Mary Gladstone noted that Maine was 'not at heart a Liberal', adding that 'He considers . . . that the party, especially Lowe, has treated him less well than Salisbury'.

25. The standard work on Ripon's Indian career is S. Gopal, *The Viceroyalty of Lord Ripon, 1880–1884*, Oxford University Press, 1953, which I have relied on in the discussion which follows.

26. S. Gopal, *op. cit.*, p. 70. The act was repealed 19 January 1882.

27. *Ibid.*, pp. 84–5.

28. *Ibid.*, p. 169.

29. Stephen to Lytton, November [?] 1882, *J. F. Stephen Papers*, Camb. Univ. Lib., Add. 7349, Box 1.

30. S. Gopal, *op. cit.*, p. 190 *et seq.*

31. R. J. Moore, *op. cit.*, pp. 33–5.

32. Sir Richard Cross to Ripon, 16 March 1883, *Ripon Papers*, B.M. Add. Mss. 43633, ff. 55–6 (cxliii). As early as 15 December 1869, Maine had written to Lord Mayo: 'the Supreme Legislative Council was only intended to be the local legislature of the Non-Regulation provinces *ad interim*, and it was expected that local councils would be rapidly established all over India. But all authorities are agreed that this turns out to be impossible for the present, and that being so, I believe the conjoint action of the Supreme and local Executive Governments to be altogether a better transitional machinery for legislation than recourse to the Viceroy's Legislative Council.' *Mayo Papers*, Camb. Univ. Lib., Add. 7490/55/xxiii.

33. Maine to Ilbert, 11 April 1883, *Maine/Ilbert Letters*, India Office Library, Mss. Eur. D594. Maine refers to a passage in Ripon's 'Resolution on Local Self-Government' of May 1882, in which the Viceroy commented that: 'It is not primarily with a view to improvement in administration that this measure is put forward and supported. It is chiefly desirable as an instrument of political and popular education.' Cited in R. J. Moore, *op. cit.*, p. 33.

34. S. Gopal, op. cit., pp. 113–66.

35. Maine to Alfred Lyall, 28 March 1883, *Maine/Lyall Letters*, India Office Library, Mss. Eur. F132/48.

36. Maine to Ilbert, 7 June 1883: Maine wrote that 'strangely enough, Lord Hartington must have *imagined* that he had sent the caution we supposed to Lord Ripon. For, after he left the India Office, he told me that he had written to India in the sense of my note. But, after hearing from you what he *did* write, I have no doubt that his memory played him false and that he confounded what he actually wrote with what he perhaps intended to write when he left town.' It is a curious fact that the Ilbert controversy, which had such an important bearing on the emergence of Indian nationalism, was in a sense related to Maine's ill health. It was the reason for his absence in Paris when the Ilbert papers came home: he was still in precarious health later that same year when he wrote to Ilbert on 8 August that 'I am just leaving England for Hambourg, where I am going to drink the waters. I have not been very well lately, possibly through having brought out a book in addition to

315

my ordinary work.' The book was *ELC*. In a further letter of 4 September 1883, he speaks of the 'bodily and mental depression produced by the Hambourg waters'. *Maine/Ilbert Letters*, Mss. Eur. D594. S. Gopal (*Ripon, op. cit.*), pp. 132–3 thinks it unlikely, however, that even if Maine's views had been available to Ripon, that the Viceroy would have heeded them. As Gopal says, 'Ripon always had much contempt for the "old fogies in the Indian Council".'

37. Maine to Lyall, 28 March 1883, *Maine/Lyall Letters*, Mss. Eur. F132/48.

38. Cited in L. Stephen, *op. cit.*, p. 461. The letters to *The Times* were dated 1, 2 March, 9 June 1883.

39. Grant Duff to Ripon, 2 April 1883, *Ripon Papers*, B.M. Add. Mss. 43588. ff. 241–2 (xcviii). '*Personally*', he added, 'I am devoted to Stephen, but I have just sent him a message through Arthur Russell to the effect that he is *politically* "a child of the devil and getting more silly every day".'

40. Maine to Ilbert, 8 August 1883. 'It seems to me' he wrote in a further letter to Ilbert dated 4 September 1883, 'that many of the opinions current in India and even in the Indian Government about the Sect. of State in Council are mere delusions, owing in part to pedantry or want of courage in asking for explanations in the proper quarter.' *Maine/Ilbert Letters*, Mss. Eur. D594.

41. Maine to Ilbert, 7 June 1883: 'the old law Commission which existed in my time would infallibly have asked for an opportunity of seeing and considering such a measure as yours, modifying a Code, as an important measure.' Writing on 8 August, he added that 'You say that English opinion ought to be brought to bear on the question, and in a certain sense I agree with you, but then I doubt the possibility of bringing it to bear by any other agency than a Commission. What has lately taken place here is striking evidence of the impossiblity of settling the question in either sense by popular agitation.' *Maine/Ilbert Letters*, Mss. Eur. D594.

42. Ilbert to Ripon, 23 November 1883, *Ripon Papers*, B.M. Add. Mss. 43601 (cxi): 'Maine says "I was very glad to read in a later letter from your Govt. that you proposed to pass the Bill when you reached Calcutta, for disjunctory rumours to a contrary effect had been current".'

43. Maine to Lyall, 28 March 1883, *Maine/Lyall Letters*, Mss. Eur. F132/48. See also Chapter 4, n. 33, *supra*.

44. Maine to Ilbert, 11 April 1883. In a further letter of 25 August, Maine wrote rather stiffly that 'I think I gave you before my opinion that the Indian Government is from end to end an Act of Parliament Government, and cannot go an inch beyond its statutory powers.' *Maine/Ilbert Letters*. Mss. Eur. D594.

45. Maine to Lyall, 28 March 1883, *Maine/Lyall Letters*, Mss. Eur. F132/48.

46. Maine to Ilbert, 26 April 1883, *Maine/Ilbert Letters*, Mss. Eur. D594.

47. Maine to Salisbury, 1 February, 28 September, I October 1875, *Salisbury Papers*. Maine's proposal, enacted early in 1876, extended during good behaviour the tenure on Council of those members whose initial appointment had been made before they had accumulated ten years Indian service. While Maine was a champion of the role of the India Council as an advisory body, he was also a strong supporter of the supremacy of the Secretary of State in cases of conflict between the home government and the Indian authorities. Thus, on the subject of financial control, Maine wrote to Lord Randolph Churchill that: 'The idea that the Council is the sole judge in such matters has a tendency to weaken the Secretary of States' sense of responsibility in the exercise of this control, which Parliament deliberately intended to be serious and heavy, and which could not doubtless be exercised unless the Secretary of State considered and gave all due weight to the views of his financial advisers here.' 8 October 1885, *Lord Randolph Churchill Papers*, Chartwell, viii, no. 955. See also R. J. Moore, *op. cit.*, p. 16.

48. Maine to Lytton, 7 June 1878, *op. cit.* See also Chapter 6, n. 5, *supra*.

49. Maine to Lyall, 20 March 1885, *Maine/Lyall Letters*, Mss. Eur. F132/48.

50. Maine to Lyall, 16 September 1885, *Maine/Lyall Letters*, Mss. Eur. F132/48.

51. Maine to Lord Randolph Churchill, 5 August 1885, 9 January 1886, *Lord Randolph Churchill Papers*, vi, no. 769; xi, no. 1267. See also R. J. Moore, *op. cit.*, p. 51.

52. Maine to Lord Randolph Churchill, 29 November, 7, 24, 28 December 1885, *Lord Randolph Churchill Papers*, x, nos. 1114, 1204, and 1217.

53. Maine to Lord Randolph Churchill, 27 December 1885; 13 January 1886, *Lord Randolph Churchill Papers*, x, no. 1216; xi, no. 1287.

54. Lyall to Maine, 21 August 1885, *Maine/Lyall Letters*, Mss. Eur. F132/48.

55. Maine to Lyall, 18 October 1883, *Maine/Lyall Letters*, Mss. Eur. F132/48.

56. Maine to Lyall, 16 September 1885. Maine had been entertaining serious thoughts of leaving the Indian Council altogether during this period. He wrote to Lyall on 20 January 1883: 'I should myself seize any fair opportunity of going. I am strong of opinion that nobody should stay in Council too long, even though the law permit it, as it does in my case.' *Maine/Lyall Letters*, Mss. Eur. F132/48.

Chapter 17. The 'St James's Gazette'

1. Cited in F. W. Hurst, *Early Life and Letters of John Morley*, London, Macmillan, 1927, ii, p. 90.

2. Cited in S. Maccoby, *English Radicalism, 1853–1886*, London, George Allen & Unwin, 1938, p. 254

3. Harrison to Dilke, 5 April 1880, *Charles Dilke Collection*, B.M. Add. Mss. 43898.

4. Sir H. J. S. Maine, 'The Future of Political Ignorance', *St James's Gazette*, i, 31 May 1880, p. 3: subsequent entries as *St J.G.*

5. Stephen to Lady Grant Duff, 25 November 1881, *J. F. Stephen Papers*, Camb. Univ. Lib., Add. 7349, Box 1.

6. Morley to Gladstone, 7 April 1880, *Gladstone Papers*, B.M. Add. Mss. 44255. f. 13.

7. J. W. Robertson Scott, *op. cit.*, p. 154: see Chapter 9, n. 7, *supra*.

8. *Ibid.*, p. 236.

9. Acton to Mary Gladstone, 23 May 1880, *Mary Gladstone Papers*, B.M. Add. Mss. 46239. See also J. W. Robertson Scott, *op. cit.*, p. 256 *et seq.*

10. *Maine Collection*, LSE, Section ii, Vol. 22, Item 8.

11. Discussion based on S. Low and L. C. Sanders, *op. cit.*, xii, pp. 239–43; See also D. Southgate, *op. cit.*, pp. 343–7; 370–8.

12. 'Landlordism', *St J.G.*, i, 17 June 1880, p. 244.

13. 'Rewarding and Punishing By Legislation', *St J.G.*, i, 21 June 1880, p. 291. In a further article on 'Dubitations About Private Property', *St J.G.*, i, 16 July 1880, p. 643, Maine observes that 'the spokesmen of the International Association always said that practical Communism would have its first chance in the British Empire, and that the point in the social edifice at which it would make its way inwards was the ownership of land in these islands'.

14. 'Property, Contract, and the Prosperity of England', *St J.G.*, i, 2 August 1880, p. 867.

15. 'The Irish Land Court as a School of Liberty', *St J.G.*, ii, 13 May 1881, p. 1795.

16. 'Alternatives in Legislation', *St J.G.*, iii, 4 October 1881, p. 1299.

17. 'The Agitation Against Private Property', *St J. G.*, i, 24 November 1880, pp. 2443–4. For T. H. Green's essay on 'Liberal Legislation and Freedom of Contract', see J. R. Rodman, ed., *The Political Theory of T. H. Green*, N.Y., Appleton-Century-Crofts, 1964, pp. 43–73. Note in this connection the interesting aside of Crane Brinton, *English Political Thought in the Nineteenth Century*, London, Benn, 1933, p. 279, that

Maine's later political writings mark an important turning point in British conservative thought, for: 'Just as Green is a liberal who, in spite of certain qualifications, trusts the State, . . . so Maine is a conservative who distrusts the State.' See also M. Richter, *op. cit.*, pp. 267–91.

18. 'Radicalism Old and New', *St J.G.*, ii, 25 January 1881, pp. 331–2.

19. *Ibid.*, p. 332.

20. 'Radical Patriarchalism', *St J.G.*, i, 18 June 1880, p. 260. Elsewhere, in 'The Goal of Democratic Progress', *St J.G.*, i, 8 June 1880, Maine had noted that: 'It is quite possible to hold with Bentham as a moralist, that the greatest happiness of the greatest number is the proper standard of morality and law, and yet to refuse to allow to Bentham as a political philosopher that the opinion of the greatest number is conclusive as to what is best for their happiness.' p. 116. He added: 'If legislation were to go on for any length of time with the average opinion of the great mixed multitude of Englishmen as its standard, the final result would be to arrest everything which Liberals associate with their creed.'

21. *Ibid.* In the original draft, Maine gives a slightly different rendition: 'A privileged class arises: lives on fat of land and leaves lean to others. Civilizes itself then & rejoices in strength. At last what it has learned is diffused to others & a larger class is reared on crumbs which fall from rich man's table. Sometimes peacefully, sometimes by revolution, old privileged order expelled from monopoly, but new class is aristocracy, only another kind. *This is just as true of normally democratic societies as any others. The democracy of U.S. does not extend to property & by inequalities of property, they have prospered.*' (Italics added). *Maine Collection*, LSE, Section i, Vol. 7, Item J.

22. 'Hereditary Legislators', *St J.G.*, i, 13 September 1880, p. 1443. Maine's belief in the 'circulation of elites', by means of the admission of talent from outside, carried over to his discussion of property. Thus, in his article on 'Landlordism' (*op. cit.*), p. 244, he noted: 'There has always been plenty of land for sale in England since the Reformation. The number of great English families which were founded by lawyers, by Turkey merchants, by City scriveners, and by the successful men of similar classes, has always been remarked, and in fact they make up the bulk of the English aristocracy . . . As the oarsman or railway traveller passes along the valley of the Thames, dotted with mansions not very long ago thought to be the choicest in the country, he will discover that hardly one of them belongs to the family to which it is attributed in Horace Walpole's or other similar memoirs.'

23. 'Signs of the Times'. *St J.G.*, ii, 21 March 1881, p. 1075; 'The Past and Future of Democratic Government', *St J.G.*, iii, 5 September 1881, p. 899.

24. 'The Survival of the Unfittest', *St J.G.*, i, 22 December 1880, p. 2819.

25. 'Malthusianism and Modern Politics', *St J.G.*, i, 7 July 1880, p. 524. By 'force' Maine means, as he suggested in 'The Future of Constitutionalism', *St J.G.*, ii, 24 February 1881, pp. 747–8, sheer numbers. Thus, in his estimation, the chief claim of democracy to power is 'the palpable fact that, as a rule, majorities are stronger than minorities, the multitide than a class, the many than the few.' What worried him was that while authority in a democracy 'is in its essence the authority of the strongest . . . there are several communities in which the Army is really stronger than the great majority of the nation, and might govern by the same right by which the feudal aristocracies governed—that is, by the fact of being so armed that no other class, however multitudinous, had any chance against them.' p. 748.

26. 'Electoral Corruption', *St J.G.*, i, 18 October 1880, p. 1923.

27. 'The Goal of Democratic Progress', *op. cit.*, p. 115.

28. 'Electoral Corruption', *op. cit.*, p. 1923.

29. *Ibid.*

30. 'Remedies for Electoral Corruption', *St J.G.*, ii, 21 January 1881, p. 275.

31. 'The Whigs', *St J.G.*, i, 20 August 1880, p. 1123; see also G. L. Goodman, 'Liberal Unionism: The Revolt of the Whigs', *Victorian Studies*, iii, December, 1959, pp. 173–89. For a concise interpretation of the parliamentary philosophy of the Whigs, see Chapter 1, 'Old Tory and Old Whig Politics', in S. Beer, *British Politics in the Collectivist Age*, N.Y., Knopf, 1965.

32. Maine certainly opposed Irish Home Rule. In his 'Franchises and Opinions in Ireland', *St J.G.*, i, 14 June 1880, pp. 195–6, Sir Henry reflected that 'offensive as the assertion may be to Irish ears, it is simply the English Government which stands between Ireland and moral and material stagnation.' In his Irish Land Court as a School of Liberty'', *op. cit.*, p. 1795, he had further noted that 'nobody who has attempted to picture to himself what the state of Ireland would be if she were really enfranchised from the authority of Great Britain has ever supposed that she would be a country with free institutions.' For a general discussion of the Whig flight from the Liberals over Home Rule, see D. Southgate, *op. cit.*, pp. 381–416.

33. 'How the Jacobins Conquer a Nation', *St J.G.*, ii, 17 May 1881, pp. 1851–2.

34. 'Hereditary Legislators', *op. cit.*, p. 1443; 'The House of Lords', *St J.G.*, ii, 13 June 1881, p. 2211.

35. 'Hereditary Legislators', *op. cit.*, p. 1443.

36. 'Principles of Parliamentary Procedure', *St J.G.*, iii, 29 December 1881, p. 2483.

37. *Maine Collection*, LSE, Section i, Vol. 14, Item U.

38. Acton to Mary Gladstone, 10 July 1880, cited in H. Paul, *op. cit.*, p. 26.

320

39. L. Stephen, *op. cit.*, p. 460.

40. Maine's total scholarly *oeuvre*, nonetheless, represents an important contribution to the growth of more rigorous approaches to the study of political institutions. For this aspect of his influence, see E. A. Freeman's pioneering *Comparative Politics*, London, Macmillan, 1873; Sir J. R. Seeley's *Introduction to Political Science*, London, Macmillan, 1896 (reprint, edited by Henry Sidgwick, 1923); Henry Sidgwick's *Development of European Polity*, London, Macmillan, 1896, (2nd edn, 1920), all of which were influenced by Maine's new 'historical and comparative' methods. Further discussion of relevance here will be found in W. Graham, *English Political Philosophy from Hobbes to Maine*, London, Arnold, 1926, p. 376 *et seq.*; E. M. Sait, *op. cit.*, pp. 115–20, and Peter Viereck, *Conservatism From John Adams to Churchill*, N.Y., Anvil Books, 1956, who notes that 'Burke left the systematizing of his ideas to disciples of more talent, less genius, notably Sir Henry Maine. Maine's *Popular Government* (1885) systematized the Burkean approach into a consistent philosophy, *gave it a scholarly basis*, and applied it to the post-Burkean problem of modern industrialism.' (Italics added).

Chapter 18. A Manual of Unacknowledged Conservatism

1. Stephen to Lady Grant Duff, 16 March 1882, *J. F. Stephen Papers*, Camb. Univ. Lib., Add. 7349, Box 1.

2. Sir H. J. S. Maine, 'The Prospects of Popular Government', *Quarterly Review*, clv, April 1883, pp. 551–76. The essay was reprinted in *PG*, pp. 1–55.

3. *PG*, p. 51. Note J. F. Stephen's comment in *LEF*, p. 249, that: 'The truth is that the change . . . from status to contract is very far indeed from being universally favourable to equality'. Concerning the stability of democracy in the U.S., Maine noted in his 'The Past and Future of Democratic Government', *St J.G.*, iii, 5 September 1881, p. 899 that even though 'assisted . . . by an enormous material prosperity, the American Constitution has required the bloodiest civil war of modern times to keep it from dissolution; [and] . . . half the American States were for six years under an absolute military Government, which has even now only partially ended'.

4. *PG*, p. 22. The same principle, Maine thought, applied to the new 'share of power' given to the mob by the destructive inventions of modern scientific warfare: 'the mob has obtained new arms', he wrote, 'and among the newly discovered modes of putting an end to human life on a large scale, the most effective and terrible is a manipulation of explosive compounds quite unknown till the other day. The bomb of nitro-glycerine and the parcel of dynamite are . . . characteristic of the new enemies of government.' p. 25.

5. *PG*, p. 29: there are strong similarities with the argument of J. F. Stephen's *LEF*, pp. 256–72.

6. *PG*, pp. 32–3. What concerned Maine, that is, was that while the ideas were 'commonplace', they would be held by partisans with militaristic fervour. Maine coins the term 'Irreconcileable parties' to describe this new type of ideological politics. 'Irreconcileables', he says at p. 25, 'are associations of men who hold political opinions as men once held religious opinions.'

7. *PG*, pp. 34–7. Maine enlists the support of Darwin for his criticisms of mass democracy. As he wrote in 'Signs of the Times', *St J.G.*, ii, 21 March 1881, p. 1075: 'Aristocracy, translated into scientific language, is the same thing as the survival of the fittest. If there be any fragment of truth in the most famous of modern scientific theories, it must mean that the government of the future belongs not to all mankind, but to a portion of it; not to the whole of a community, but to a part selected naturally from among the rest; not to the Many, but to the Few.' Yet Maine did not strictly speaking *owe* his ideas as a political thinker to Darwin, as we know he was writing similar things in the *Saturday Review* before the appearance of the *Origin of the Species* in 1859 or *The Descent of Man* in 1872.

8. *PG*, p. 50.

9. *PG*, p. 55. In his 'The Goal of Democratic Progress', *St J.G.*, i, 8 June 1880, p. 115, Maine puts the same thought somewhat more bluntly: 'no prediction is safer than that when any society has been firmly cemented down to [this] new basis, there will follow paralysis, silence and death'.

10. Sir H. J. S. Maine, 'The Constitution of the United States', *Quarterly Review*, clvii, January 1884, pp. 1–31: reprinted as the final essay of *PG*, pp. 196–254.

11. *PG*, p. 239.

12. *PG*, pp. 239–40.

13. *PG*, p. 254. Yet note in this respect that Maine, in his 'Hereditary Legislators', *St J.G.*, i, 13 September 1880, p. 1443, expressly says that 'the materials for a copy of the Constitution of the United States are not to be found in Great Britain. A British Constitution reformed in the spirit of democracy would have little resemblance to American institutions.'

14. Sir H. J. S. Maine, 'The Nature of Democracy', *Quarterly Review*, clviii, October 1884, pp. 297–333, reprinted as the second essay of *PG*, pp. 56–126.

15. *PG*, p. 75. Maine says that in order to appreciate Rousseau's influence, one must 'read, not so much the writings of the sage, as the countless essays printed in France by his disciples just before 1879'. Yet a recent study by Joan MacDonald, *Rousseau and the French Revolution*, London, Athlone Press, 1965, argues that the influence of Rousseau on the French Revolution has been very much exaggerated. While Maine held Rous-

seau to be the spiritual source of modern democracy, he thought
Bentham's political theory potentially even more dangerous. Rousseau
never believed men always knew their own interest, while Bentham
explicitly began with that assumption. 'On this point', Maine felt, 'it
must be owned that Rousseau shows himself wiser that Bentham.' *PG*,
p. 166.

16. *PG*, p. 78: the words 'an audience quite ready under very slightly
altered conditions to "'eave" many an "'arf-brick" at the platform' were
omitted in the reprinted version.

17. *PG*, p. 99. Maine must surely be one of the earliest modern analysts
of party: 'No force acting on mankind has been less carefully examined
than Party', he reflected (p. 98), 'and yet none better deserves examination.' Applying his anthropological perspective elsewhere in the book,
Sir Henry suggested that: 'Party feeling is probably far more a survival
of the primitive combativeness of mankind than a consequence of
conscious intellectual differences between man and man.' p. 31.

18. Sir H. J. S. Maine, 'The Age of Progress', *Quarterly Review*, clix, April
1885, pp. 267–98, reprinted as the third essay of *PG*, pp. 127–95. The
final mss of the essay, dated 'Feb. 28, /85', is in the Yale University
Library, a gift of the late Professor Harold Laski in 1946.

19. *PG*, pp. 188–9. Maine's view that democracy 'gives birth to despotism
with the greatest facility' is not unlike the argument of Bertrand de
Jouvenel's *Sovereignty: An Inquiry Into the Political Good* (trans. J. F.
Huntington), Cambridge University Press, 1957. De Jouvenel suggests
that while in the days of so-called absolute monarchy the king was
always supposed to be *bound* by customary and religious law, this
moral safeguard has been eradicated by the unrestricted power of
modern legislatures. With the advent of political democracies, theoretical absolutism has actually been extended, not lessened, for 'whoever
is able to vary at will the rules of action need never infringe them.'

20. Cited in A. Sidgwick and G. M. S. Sidgwick, *Henry Sidgwick*: *A
Memoir*, London, Macmillan, 1906, pp. 392–3. W. C. Havard, *Henry
Sidgwick and Later Utilitarian Political Philosophy*, University of
Florida Press, 1959, p. 141 notes the similarity between Sidgwick's
own political thought and that of Maine, especially in their common
acceptance of 'the thesis of gradualism and empiricism'.

21. Sidgwick to Bryce, 26 August 1884, 22 January 1885, *MSS Bryce*,
ff. 20–1; 22–3.

22. Stephen to Lytton, 7 September 1884, *J. F. Stephen Papers*, Camb.
Univ. Lib., Add. 7349, Box 1.

23. H. F. Lowry, K. Young and W. H. Dunn, eds., *The Notebooks of
Matthew Arnold*, Oxford University Press, 1952, p. 409; K. Allott,
Five Uncollected Essays of Matthew Arnold, Liverpool University
Press, 1953, pp. 25–31.

24. *The Times*, 15 April 1885, p. 9.

25. Acton wrote to Mary Gladstone on 9 February 1884, noting that he had been reading 'the first article in the *Quarterly Review*'. He added that 'I wrote eight pages of criticism and should have liked to send them to you, instead of Maine, but perhaps you have not read him.' H. Paul, *op. cit.*, p. 175; see also the Preface, p. xii, *PG*.

26. Acton to Mary Gladstone, 27 April 1885, H. Paul, *op. cit.*, p. 209.

27. Maine to Murray, 1 August 1886, *J.M. Arch*. Earlier, in a letter to Murray of 19 September 1885, he observed that: 'It cannot of course be denied that the book is short, but I have no 5th Essay, and the four printed complete the treatment of the subject as sufficiently analysed by me. Also, I am inclined to believe that the volume contains as much as people will care to read on abstract politics. If I *do* get hold of a new class of redress, I do not think they will complain.' Yet Sir Alfred Lyall wrote in his diary: 'I have been reading Maine's book on popular government; it makes one or two good points . . . but . . . Maine won't take enough trouble . . . I could add a good chapter by applying his ideas to the subject of Oriental government, and to the English attempt to govern India on modern principles'. Cited in Sir M. Durand, *Life of Sir A. C. Lyall*, London, Blackwood, 1913, p. 309.

28. Maine to Murray, 19 July 1885, *J.M. Arch*.

29. *The Times*, 22 October 1885, p. 13: 'It is absolutely certain, is it not', Maine wrote to his publisher on 21 October 1885, 'that your early copies of my book included the Editor of *The Times*?', and added, in a telegram sent from Mosler Road, Queen's Gate at 9:00 a.m. the next morning: '*Times* today proves my doubts unfounded. Maine.' *J.M. Arch*. For further general discussion of Maine's *Popular Government*, see B. Lippincott, *Victorian Critics of Democracy*, University of Minnesota Press, 1938, pp. 179–206; Crane Brinton, *op. cit.*, pp. 266–81,; K. B. Smellie, 'Sir Henry Maine', *Economica*, March, 1928, pp. 64–94; J. E. G. de Montmorency, 'Sir Henry Maine and the Historical Jurists', in F. J. C. Hearnshaw, ed., *The Social and Political Ideas of Some Representative Thinkers of the Victorian Age*, London, Harrap, 1933, pp. 84–99; Sir E. Barker, *Political Thought in England, 1848–1914*, Oxford University Press, 1959 (first pub. 1915), pp. 140–60; J. Bowle, *Politics and Opinion in the Nineteenth Century*, London, Cape, 1954, pp. 248–73.

30. Acton to Mary Gladstone, 28 November 1885, *Mary Gladstone Papers*, B. M. Add. Mss. 46239.

31. Acton to Mary Gladstone, 11 November 1885, cited in H. Paul, *op. cit.*, pp. 212–13.

32. Maine to Murray, 3 November 1885, *J.M. Arch*. Maine's reference to Dilke's review was apparently prompted by the contrast between the coolness of the first paragraph—'his articles are weakened by a lack of

the scholarly thoroughness and that philosophical caution which he has taught us to expect from him'—and the straightforward elucidation of the leading themes of *PG* which followed: see *The Athenaeum*, 30 October 1885, pp. 563–4.

33. Maine to Murray, 8 November 1885, *J.M. Arch.*

34. Maine to J. K. Stephen, 14 November 1885, Camb. Univ. Lib., Add. 4403 (BB). J. F. Stephen, in a letter to Lady Grant Duff of 9 December 1881, wrote of his son that: 'He is a dangerously clever fellow, a cleverer fellow than ever his father was—and his father is not by any means disposed to underrate himself.' *J. F. Stephen Papers*, Camb. Univ. Lib., Add. 7349, Box 1. J. K. Stephen, (1859–92) was a promising writer and poet, author of *Lapsus Calami* 1891. L. Stephen, *op. cit.*, writes that 'He wrote a good deal for Mr Greenwood in the 'St James's Gazette' . . . James once wrote a leading article in the train between Paddington and Maidenhead.' p. 474. He suffered severe head injuries in a freak accident in 1886, from which he never fully recovered, and he died in 1892 at the early age of thirty-three.

35. H. Spencer, *The Man versus The State*, London, Williams & Norgate, 1884, Preface, p. i.

36. *Ibid.*, pp. 1–17. see also Chapter 5, n. 49, *supra*.

37. Yet note that D. Southgate, *op. cit.*, in citing *Popular Government* in his Preface, p. xvi, suggests that in practical political terms, by the date of its publication 'it was time for the Whigs to be gone'.

38. J. Bowle, *op. cit.*, p. 255.

39. W. A. Robson, in A. L. Goodhart, ed., *op. cit.*, p. 173.

40. Two excellent surveys of the points touched on here can be found in Giovanni Sartori's *Democratic Theory*, Wayne State University Press, 1962, and H. B. Mayo's *An Introduction to Democratic Theory*, Oxford University Press, 1960, esp. Chapter 6.

41. Maine to Cross, 9 July 1885, *Cross Papers*, B. M. Add. Mss. 51274, xii, (unmounted).

42. Maine to Cross, 14 July 1885, *Cross Papers*, B. M. Add. Mss., 51274, xii; *The Times*, 14 July 1885, p. 10.

43. *Ibid.*, (*Cross Papers*, xii).

44. Maine to Salisbury, 17 July 1885, *Salisbury Papers*.

45. Maine to Grant Duff, 15 August 1885, *Grant Duff Papers*.

46. *Ibid.* Churchill, the leading exponent of 'Tory Democracy' after Disraeli's death in 1881, apparently pressed Maine to try and extend his *Popular Government* essays to 'tap a lower and larger stratum'. Sir Henry, however, wrote to his publisher that 'I think it premature to

325

enter upon any such plan for the present. The book is primarily intended for educated readers, and it has yet to be seen what is the extent of their interest in it.' *J.M. Arch.*

47. Maine to Salisbury, 20 November 1885, *Salisbury Papers*. In a letter to Murray dated 11 September 1885 Maine observed: 'I have a good many suggestions that the new book should appear before the general election.' *J.M. Arch.* In a letter to Bryce of 26 April 1886, Acton noted: 'They tell me that May has quite come around to H.R. If so, he comes from afar. I have not seen what is to be done for him, and hope that his health is not breaking. Maine, I presume, is a contemptuous opponent of all our policy.' *MSS Bryce*, i. f. 26. 'H.R.' refers to Irish Home Rule. May was created Lord Farnborough in early 1886, but died shortly afterwards.

48. Stephen to Lady Grant Duff, 15 December 1881, *J. F. Stephen Papers*, Camb. Univ. Lib., Add. 7349, Box 1.

49. Stephen to Lytton, 10 January 1879, *J. F. Stephen Papers*, Camb. Univ. Lib., Add. 7349, Box 1: in his letter to Lytton of 6 March 1876, Stephen reflected that 'Maine . . . certainly is one of the ablest men I know, but he never of late years had much liking for laborious work, or much strength for it.' See also Chapter 14, n. 7, *supra*.

50. Stephen to Lady Grant Duff, 20 February 1875, *J. F. Stephen Papers*, Camb. Univ. Lib., Add 7349, Box 1 (italics added). In an obituary notice which appeared in the *Saturday Review* on 11 February 1888, Stephen acknowledged that 'Till [Maine] was forty years old he hovered on the verge of being an invalid, and had several most trying and tedious illnesses.' To compensate for his constitutional handicap, Stephen felt, Maine had 'an almost preternatural quickness of understanding and facility of expression. Sir Henry Maine could read a thick volume . . . whilst an ordinary man read a hundred pages' (cited in *Memoir*, pp. 79–80).

51. Thus, Maine to Edward Atkinson, Vice-Chancellor of Cambridge and Master of Clare College, 13 December [?]: 'I am afraid I cannot be at the Meeting which, if I remember rightly, is to be held at 3 PM today. I have a headache which would be turned into a very bad one by the Meeting, as I know by long experience. But I should suppose the proceedings would be almost formal.' *Atkinson Letters*, Camb. Univ. Lib., Add. 6584. f. 615. Again, on 21 May [?]: 'I am only sorry to say that I cannot be at the meeting of Heads today. I have to go to town on urgent official business.' *Ibid.*, Add. 6584. f. 684. In India, Maine wrote to Lord Lawrence to excuse himself from a Meeting on 7 July 1864: 'I am suffering from a terrible headache caused partly by Council, but partly by lying in the sun at the Cricket-ground.' *J.L. Coll.*, Mss. Eur. F90. Both of the Atkinson letters, while undated, are from the period *c.* 1880.

52. Maine to Lawrence, 2 January 1865, *J.L. Coll.*, Mss. Eur. F90.

53. Maine to Lawrence, 30 May 1868, *J.L. Coll.*, Mss. Eur. F90.

54. Stephen to Lady Grant Duff, 15 December 1881, *J. F. Stephen Papers*, Camb. Univ. Lib., Add. 7349, Box 1.

55. Maine to Ilbert, 25 August 1883, *Maine/Ilbert Letters*, Mss.Eur. D594.

56. Stokes to Ripon, 5 November 1881, *Ripon Papers*, B.M. Add. Mss. 43610. f. 41 (cxx).

57. Acton to Mary Gladstone, 8 August 1880, cited in H. Paul, *op. cit.*, pp. 29–31.

58. Maine to Dr Rost, 26 January 1877 (misc. letters), Wellcome Foundation Medical Library, Euston Road, London, W.C.1.

59. Maine to Lytton, 28 June 1878, *Lytton Papers*, Mss. Eur. E218. Maine's second son, Henry Hallam, was admitted as a Pensioner of Pembroke College, Cambridge, in 1880, but never graduated. He later removed to Ireland, where he lived at Owenstown, Dundrum County.

60. Lord Granville to C. S. Maine, 9 October 1880, *Maine Papers*, the property of Mr H. C. S. Maine.

61. C. S. Maine, 'The International Tribunals of Egypt', *Fortnightly Review*, xxxviii, August 1885, pp. 166–77.

62. *The Times*, 16 September 1884, p. 1.

63. Lady Maine to Lady Campbell-Bannerman, 2 November 1884, B.M. Add. Mss. 41246. f. 207.

64. William Hartwick to C. S. Maine, 8 July 1885, *Maine Papers*, the property of H. C. S. Maine.

65. Miss C. E. Searle to C. S. Maine, 15 July 1885, *Maine Papers*, the property of H. C. S. Maine.

66. S. M. Searle to C. S. Maine, 2 July 1885, *Maine Papers*, the property of H. C. S. Maine.

Chapter 19. Final Years

1. Reeve to Maine, 13 November 1885, *Maine Collection*, LSE, Letters, (15).

2. Eliza Maine to Holt, 26 March 1886, *Henry Holt Archives*. She added: 'We all remember you very well—it isn't so *very* long since you were here, is it? Lady Maine has had very bad health indeed lately, but this year she is stronger and more able to see people and go a little more into society—They still go to Cambridge for about three months every year. Charlie Maine is married and lives in Surrey. This is the first winter he has been in England for a long time, & as it has been a very long & trying one, & he has kept quite well, I think he must be much stronger. His wife was a widow & had one little boy. She is very nice looking & also very nice & bright—and she has some money which did no harm! Charlie himself got a little permanent

appointment wh. is easy work & makes it pleasant for him. They have a baby boy of which my sister is very fond. She has gone to stay with them, otherwise I am sure she would send a message . . . I seem to have given up writing which is perhaps stupid of me. But to tell the truth I do *hate* reviews, even if favourable, and it would be uphill work starting under another name, & yet I never will write another line under my own. I sometimes think I would like to write a novel & say what I *really* thought! But I don't suppose anybody would take it.'

3. *Contemporary Review*, xlix, January 1886, p. 151.

4. *Westminster Review*, lxii, January 1886, pp. 237–9; the Whiggish *Edinburgh Review*, clxiii, January, 1886, pp. 266–91, in a lengthy article, thought *Popular Government* 'a book which deserves to rank with the best and wisest productions of English political literature'.

5. *The Nation*, xlii, 25 March, 1 April 1886, pp. 263–4; pp. 281–2.

6. E. L. Godkin, 'An American View of *Popular Government*', *Nineteenth Century*, xix, February 1886, pp. 177–90 (181).

7. *Ibid.*, p. 186.

8. *Ibid.*, p. 187 *et seq.*

9. J. Morley, 'Sir H. Maine on Popular Government', *Fortnightly Review*, xxxix, 1 February 1886, pp. 153–73 (155).

10. *Ibid.*, p. 169.

11. Sir H. J. S. Maine, 'Mr Godkin on Popular Government', *Nineteenth Century*, xix, March 1886, pp. 366–79 (368).

12. *Ibid.*, p. 370. Mill's desire to protect minority rights, Maine observes, 'closely corresponds to my own'.

13. Acton to Bryce, 26 April 1886, *MSS Bryce*, i. f. 26; Acton to Mary Gladstone, 23 June 1886, *Mary Gladstone Papers*, B. M. Add. Mss., 46239.

14. Bryce to Sidgwick, 12 September 1887, *MSS Bryce*, xv. f. 117–8.

15. Johnson [Cory] to Cornish, 11 July 1886, cited in F. W. Cornish, *op. cit.*, pp. 520–1.

16. Sir H. J. S. Maine, 'India', in T. H. Ward, ed., *The Reign of Queen Victoria: A survey of Fifty Years of Progress*, London, Smith Elder, 1887, i, pp. 460–528. Maine may very well be referring to the 'Irish problem' here: for further discussion of Ireland in relation to Indian politics in this period, see R. J. Moore, *op. cit.*, pp. 52–3.

17. Maine to Sidgwick, 8 December 1886, *Henry Sidgwick Papers*; see also Chapter 8, n. 54, *supra*. Maine's decision to gradually sever his London commitments is hinted at in his resignation from the Senate of London University during 1885. Lord Granville wrote to Sir Richard Cross on 31 October 1885 that: 'You will have been informed by the Registrar

of Sir Henry Maine having resigned his seat on the Senate of the University of London. This is a cause of great regret to us.' *Cross Papers,* B.M. Add. Mss. 51274. xii.

18. Maine to Sidgwick, 26 February 1887, *Henry Sidgwick Papers.* Yet Sir Henry noted that 'I too have been reading the statutes of the International Professorship and there seems to me to be no doubt that the founder of the Professorship contemplated the Professor being engaged in non-academical pursuits.'

19. Maine to Sidgwick, 1 December 1887, *Henry Sidgwick Papers.* Maine commented that by the date of this letter he had 'prepared and delivered a course of lectures on International Law'. Sir Charles Aitchison (1832–96) was at the time Lieutenant-Governor of the Punjab. The Commission he chaired, which chiefly concerned Maine here, recommended in its report that the minimum and maximum age limits for candidates for the I.C.S. be altered to 19 and 23 respectively, but opposed the holding of competitive examinations in India itself; further discussion can be found in R. J. Moore, *op. cit.,* pp. 60–1.

20. A. Tighe, 'Sir H. Maine and the Patriarchal Theory', *The Nation,* xlii, 15 April 1886, p. 317.

21. Sir H. J. S. Maine, 'The Patriarchal Theory', *Quarterly Review,* clxii, January 1886, pp. 181–209: see also J. D. Mayne, 'The Patriarchal Theory', *Law Quarterly Review,* 1 October 1885, pp. 485–95. In a letter to Alfred Lyall of 20 March 1885, Sir Henry commented that 'I wonder whether you are likely to see McLennan's "Patriarchal Theory".? It is a highly controversial though not crucial attack on the 5th Chapter of my "Ancient Law", displaying (as usual) a good deal of cleverness but betraying some curious ignorance and particularly, as it seems to me, a total misapprehension of the Comparative Method. He appears to have thought that, in order to prove that Aryan society once had a patriarchal shell, it was necessary to shew that an exact counterpart of the Roman family was to be found in all Aryan society.' *Maine/Lyall Letters,* Mss. Eur. F132/48.

22. Maine to Murray, 21 November 1886, *J.M. Arch.*

23. Maine to Murray, 20 January 1884, *J.M. Arch.* The relative decline of analytical jurisprudence was due in part to a growing interest in British legal history among younger jurists. Thus, in a letter of 6 November 1887, Sir Henry wrote to a 'Mr Maitland' that 'I am sincerely obliged to you for sending me your book on Bracton. I once lectured at Oxford on Glanvill, and took in enough knowledge of a period and time on which your volumes have a bearing to be immensely interested by them. At the same time, I have only read the first fully at present.' The letter was written, of course, to F. W. Maitland (1850–1906), who was at the time Reader in English Law at Cambridge: he had just brought out his *Bracton's Note Book* (3 vols., 1887). I am indebted to

Professor C. H. S. Fifoot for bringing this letter, which is in Cambridge University Library, to my attention.

24. Acton to W. E. Gladstone, 19 January 1888, *Gladstone Papers*, B.M. Add. Mss. 44094. f. 1.

25. Acton to Mary Gladstone, 18 February 1888, *Mary Gladstone Papers*, B.M. Add. Mss. 46239.

26. Acton to C. S. Maine, 13 February 1888, *Maine Papers*, the property of H. C. S. Maine. On 22 February 1888, Grant Duff wrote in his diary: 'Not long ago I wrote to Acton that I thought Maine, in spite of his exceedingly troublesome health, would live to be 80, but he has gone from us at 66.' Sir M. E. Grant Duff, *Notes, op. cit.*, viii, pp. 33–5.

27. Acton to C. S. Maine, 23 February 1888, *Maine Papers*, the property of H. C. S. Maine. Acton asked Charlie Maine 'to bear in mind, some day, in looking over his shelves, that he had one or two volumes of mine in hand. They are not of the least importance; but they have one peculiarity which will be my excuse with you, that they are pencil-marked by me, so that if they are ever found and returned, these copies would save me a good deal of time. I only remember a thin unbound volume or tract on Rousseau, entitled, perhaps, *Hommes et Choses*; a volume or two of Post, in German, on Comparative Jurisprudence; and J. S. Mill's Inaugural Lecture, in cloth. This little book was at Montfleury, and I fancy Miss Searle had no means of knowing what the pencil marks implied.'

28. *The Times*, 6 February, pp. 6, 8; 7 February, p. 9; 9 February, p. 6; 9 June, p. 16; 21 June, p. 12; 25 December, p. 5, 1888. For fuller notices of Maine, see Sir A. Lyall, 'Life and Speeches of Sir Henry Maine', *Quarterly Review*, clxxvi, April 1893, pp. 287–316; Sir F. Pollock, *Oxford Lectures and Other Discourses*, London, Macmillan, 1890, pp. 147–68; Sir C. L. Tupper, 'India and Sir Henry Maine', *Journal of the Society of Arts*, xlvi, 18 March 1898, pp. 390–405.

29. Sir M. E. Grant Duff, *Notes, op. cit.*, viii, p. 119; ix, p. 195.

Bibliography

1. Manuscript Collections

Acton Papers, Cambridge University Library.
Atkinson Papers, Cambridge University Library.
Avebury Papers, British Museum.
Bryce Manuscripts, Bodleian Library, Oxford.
Cross Papers, British Museum.
Randolph Churchill Papers, Chartwell.
Elgin Collection, India Office Library.
Gladstone Papers, British Museum.
Grant Duff Papers, property of Mrs Sheila Sokolov-Grant.
Harrison Collection, London School of Economics and Political Science.
Holmes Papers, Harvard University Library and Harvard Law Library.
Holt Archives, Princeton University Library.
Lawrence Collection, India Office Library.
Maine Collection, London School of Economics and Political Science.
Maine/Ilbert Letters, India Office Library.
Maine/Lyall Letters, India Office Library.
Maine/Lytton Letters, India Office Library.
Maine/Merivale Letters, India Office Library.
Maine Papers (misc.), India Office Library.
Maine Papers (misc.), property of H. C. S. Maine, C.M.G., M.V.O.
Mary Gladstone Papers, British Museum.
Mayo Papers, Cambridge University Library.
Mill Papers, London School of Economics and Political Science.
Morgan Papers, University of Rochester Library.
Murray Archives, John Murray Publishing Company.
Ripon Papers, British Museum.
Salisbury Papers, Christ Church, Oxford.
Sidgwick Papers, Trinity College, Cambridge.
Stephen Papers, Cambridge University Library.
Wood Collection, India Office Library.
Woolsey Papers, Yale University Library.

2. Chronological List of the Publications of Sir Henry Maine

1842. 'The Birth of the Prince of Wales, a poem which obtained the

Chancellor's Medal in the University of Cambridge', in *Prolusiones Academicae*, Cambridge (1842).

'Caesar and Rubiconem Constitit', Latin Poem, *ibid.*

'Navis ornata atque armata in aquam deducitur (Carmen Latinum numismate annus dignatum)', *ibid.*

1848. 'Midsummer Night's Dream', *Edinburgh Review*, lxxxvii, April, 1848, 418–29 [unsigned].

1851. 'H. F. Hallam: A Memoir', London, Spottiswoode and Shaw (1851), for private circulation; reprinted in H. Hallam, ed., *A. H. Hallam: Remains in Verse and Prose* (1863).

1855. 'The Conception of Sovereignty and Its Importance in International Law', a paper read on 16 April 1855, in *Papers Read Before the Juridical Society, 1855–1858*, London (1858), i, 26–45.

1856. 'Roman Law and Legal Education', in *Cambridge Essays* (1856), reprinted in *VC*, (3rd edn, 1876), 330–83.

1855–58. A partial list of Maine's contributions to the *Saturday Review*, given in M. M. Bevington, *The Saturday Review, 1855–1868* (1941). All the articles were unsigned.

'Our Relations With the United States', i, 3 Nov., 1855, 2.

'Our Newspaper Institutions', i, 3 Nov., 1855, 2.

'Memoirs of James Gordon Bennett and His Times', i, 3 Nov., 1855, 15.

'Southwark and Public Opinion', i, 10 Nov., 1855, 27.

'Laid up in Lavender', i, 17 Nov., 1855, 41.

'The War Policy of the American Government', i, 24 Nov., 1855, 58.

'A Burst Bladder', i, 1 Dec., 1855, 75.

'The Inns of Court', i, 1 Dec., 1855, 76.

'Bible Burning', i, 8 Dec., 1855, 90.

'Mr. Thackeray and the Four Georges', i, 15 Dec., 1855, 106.

'The Importunity of Truth', i, 15 Dec., 1855, 111.

'American Parties', i, 22 Dec., 1855, 133.

'The Sound Dues', i, 29 Dec., 1855, 147.

'Jeanne de Vaudreuil', i, 29 Dec., 1855, 157.

'Army Examinations', i, 5 Jan., 1856, 167.

'A Political Deadlock', i, 12 Jan., 1856, 183.

'President Pierce and His Message', i, 19 Jan., 1856, 202.

'Lectures For Senators', i, 26 Jan., 1856, 222.

'A Parallel', i, 26 Jan., 1856, 227.

'Mistakes of Daily Occurrence in Speaking and Writing', i, 2 Feb., 1856, 261.

'Publicity and the Peace', i, 9 Feb., 1856, 265.

'The Moral of McNeill', i, 16 Feb., 1856, 285.

'The Crimea Commission', i, 23 Feb., 1856, 310.

'The Division List on Sabbath Observance', i, 1 Mar., 1856, 334.

'Your Petitioners Will Ever Pray, etc.,' i, 8 Mar., 1856, 358.

'Our Cousin Veronica', i, 8 Mar., 1856, 372.

'Lord Stratford and General Williams', i, 15 Mar., 1856, 382.

'Leaves of Grass', i, 15 Mar., 1856, 393.

'French Sketches of English Character', i, 5 April, 1856, 459.

On internal evidence, the following further articles may be attributed to

Maine. Essays entered with a question mark indicate doubt as to his authorship:

'Mr Disraeli on India,' iv, 1 Aug., 1857, 97.
'Wild Justice', iv, 8 Aug., 1857, 121.
'The Solvency of the East India Company', iv, 15 Aug., 1857, 147.
'Reactions of Public Opinion about Public Men', iv, 22 Aug., 1857, 170.
'Lost Illusions', iv, 5 Sept., 1857, 214.
'Religious Influences in Hindostan', iv, 12 Sept., 1857, 233. [?]
'Indian Government', iv, 3 Oct., 1857, 294.
'The Opposition on the Indian Crisis', iv, 10 Oct., 1857, 317. [?]
'New Schemes of Indian Government', iv, 17 Oct., 1857, 340.
'The Indian Press', iv, 14 Nov., 1857, 435.
'European Opinion on Bengal', iv, 21 Nov., 1857, 457. [?]
'More Assertions and Less Facts', iv, 21 Nov., 1857, 463.
'The Abolition of the Double Government', iv, 5 Dec., 1857, 501.
'Control and Responsibility', iv, 19 Dec., 1857, 553.
'Religion and India', iv, 26 Dec., 1857, 575. [?]
'The New Indian Department', v, 2 Jan., 1858, 1.
'Why is there to be an India Bill Next Session?', v, 16 Jan., 1858, 55.
'The Petition of the East India Company', v, 23 Jan., 1858, 78.
'The Incorporation of India and England', v, 30 Jan., 1858, 101.
'The New Circumlocution Office', v, 20 Feb., 1858, 177,
'Progress of Opinion on the Indian Question', v, 27 Feb., 1858, 207.
'Squeezable Materials', v, 6 Mar., 1858, 232.
'What is to be done with the new India Bill?', v, 3 April, 1858, 336.
'The Friend in Need', v, 17 April, 1858, 385. [?]
'The India Resolutions', v, 24 April, 1858, 409.
'Indian Legislation', v, 1 May, 1858, 434.
'Mumbo-Jumbo in Parliament', v, 8 May, 1858, 462.
'A Responsible Indian Minister', v, 15 May, 1858, 489. [?]
'The Moral of the Ellenborough Debate', v, 29 May, 1858, 548.

1861. *Ancient Law, Its Connection With the Early History of Society and its Relation to Modern Ideas,* London, Murray, (1861); 2nd edn (1863); 3rd edn (1866); 4th edn (1870); 5th edn (1873), with mss Notes; 6th edn (1876); 7th edn (1878); 9th edn (1883); 10th edn (1885); 11th edn (1887); 14th edn (1891); 'Cheap Edition', Murray (1905); Pollock's edn with Notes (1906), reprinted, with further notes, 1907, 1909, 1912, 1927; new edn (1930). New Universal Library edn (1905); Everyman's Library edn (1906), with Introduction by J. H. Morgan, reprints 1907, 1931, 1954, 1960; Oxford University Press edn, World's Classics, (1931), with Introduction by C. K. Allen. K. C. Banerji, edn (1912), Allahabad; translated by J. C. Courcelle-Seneuil as *L'Ancien Droit Considere dans ses Rapporte avec l'histoire de la societie primitive et avec les idees modernes,* Paris, Guillaumin (1873); Russian edn (1873); Hungarian edn, translated by A. Pulszky as *A Jog Oskora* (1875); first American edn from 2nd London edn, Scribner, N.Y. (1864), with Introduction by T. W. Dwight, reprint 1870; 3rd American edn from 5th London edn,

N.Y., Holt, (1877), reprint 1878, 1880 [?], 1888; Beacon Press paperback edn, Boston (1963), from Pollock edn with Notes (1906), with new Preface by Raymond Firth.

1862–69. [Speeches] *Abstracts of the Proceedings of the Council of the Governor-General of India, Assembled for the Purpose of Making Laws and Regulations*, Calcutta, (1863–70).

1866. 'Short Essays and Reviews on the Educational Policy of the Government of India, as expounded by Henry Sumner Maine, in his address to the undergraduates of Calcutta University, 19 March 1866, etc.' Calcutta, (1866), reprinted in 3rd edn of *VC* (1876).

1871. *Village Communities in the East and West*, London, Murray, (1871), 'six lectures delivered at Oxford'; 2nd edn (1872); 3rd edn, 'to which are added other lectures, addresses and essays', including the Rede Lecture of 1875, (1876); 7th edn (1895). First American edn from 3rd London edn, Holt (1876), reprinted 1880, 1889.

'A Mahometan Revival', *Cornhill Magazine*, xxiv, October 1871, 421–37 [unsigned].

1873. 'Mr Fitzjames Stephen's Introduction to the Indian Evidence Act', *Fortnightly Review*, xiii, January, 1873, 51–67, reprinted in *VC*, 3rd edn (1876), 295–329.

'The Early History of the Property of Married Women', A lecture delivered at Oxford, Manchester, Ireland (1873); reprinted as Chapter 11 of *EHI* (1875), 306–41.

1875. *Lectures on the Early History of Institutions*, London, Murray, (1875); American edn Holt (1875); in French as *Etudes sur l'histoire des institutions primitives*, translated, with a Preface by Joseph Durieu de Leyritz, and with an Introduction by d'Arbois de Jubainville, Paris, Thorin, (1880).

'The Effects of Observation of India on Modern European Thought', the Rede Lecture, London, Murray, (1875), reprinted in *VC*, 3rd edn (1876), 203–39.

1877. 'The Decay of Feudal Property in France and England', a lecture delivered at the Royal Institution, published in the *Fortnightly Review*, xxi, April 1877, 460–77; in French as '*Des Causes de la decadence de la propriete féodale en France et en Angleterre*', Paris, Thorin (1877), reprinted from *Revue Generale Du Droit*; reprinted in English in *ELC* (1883), 291–328.

'South Slavonians and Rajpoots', in *Nineteenth Century*, ii, December, 1877, 796–819; in French as '*De l'organization juridique de la famille chez les Slaves du sud et chez les Rajpoutes*', Paris, Thorin, (1879), reprinted from *Revue Generale Du Droit*; reprinted in English as Chapter 8 of *ELC* (1883).

1879. 'Ancient Ideas Respecting the Arrangement of Codes', *Fortnightly Review*, xxv, May, 1879, 763–77, reprinted as Chapter 11, 'Classifications of Legal Rules', of *ELC* (1883), 362–92.

1880–81. In the *Maine Collection*, Vol. xxii, Item viii, is included a hand-written list, entitled 'Statement of Contributions from Sir Henry Maine to *St James's Gazette* from 31st May 1880 to 31st Dec. 1881.' Throughout Maine's association with the newspaper, none of his articles were signed.

'The Future of Political Ignorance', i, 31 May, 1880, 3.
'Hares and Rabbits', i, 4 June, 1880, 76.
'Goal of Democratic Progress', i, 8 June, 1880, 115–16.
'Franchises and Opinions in Ireland', i, 14 June, 1880, 195–6.
'Landlordism', i, 17 June, 1880, 243–4.
'Radical Patriarchalism', i, 18 June, 1880, 259–60.
'Rewarding and Punishing by Legislation', i, 21 June, 1880, 291.
'Small Pox and Small Beer', i, 22 June, 1880, 316.
'Law, Conscience, and Mr Bradlaugh', i, 28 June, 1880, 395–6.
'Irish Land and English Justice', i, 29 June, 1880, 403.
'Sabbatarianism and Spirit Drinking', i, 5 July, 1880, 491–2.
'Malthusianism and Modern Politics', i, 7 July, 1880, 524–5.
'Clergymen and Laymen at the Universities', i, 12 July 1880, 579.
'The Lesson to Liberals', i, 14 July, 1880, 611-12.
'Dubitations about Private Property', i, 16 July, 1880, 643.
'Possible Surprises From the Far East', i, 22 July 1880, 723–4.
'Lost Political Lessons', i, 23 July, 1880, 739.
'Imaginary Indian Grievances', i, 27 July, 1880, 796.
'Property, Contract, and the Prosperity of England', i, 2 Aug., 1880, 867.
'Probable Effects of Past Blunders', i, 9 Aug., 1880, 963.
'The House of Lords', i, 11 Aug., 1880, 995.
'The House of Commons and Its Business', i, 16 Aug., 1880, 1059.
'The Whigs', i, 20 Aug., 1880, 1123.
'The Misfortune of Ireland', i, 30 Aug., 1880, 1259–60.
'The Age of Plebiscites', i, 6 Sept., 1880, 1356.
'The Farmer's Friends', i, 9 Sept., 1880, 1395.
'Hereditary Legislators', i, 13 Sept., 1880, 1443.
'Irish Distress', i, 14 Sept., 1880, 1459.
'National Debts', i, 18 Sept., 1880, 1523.
'Irish Agitators and the Church of Rome', i, 27 Sept., 1880, 1635.
'Law and Law Amendment in Ireland', i, 5 Oct., 1880, 1755–6.
'Now and Then', i, 11 Oct., 1880, 1827.
'Some Results of Nonconformist Success', i, 14 Oct., 1880, 1883–4.
'Electoral Corruption', i, 18 Oct., 1880, 1923.
'Irish Disease and Quack Remedies for It', i, 21 Oct., 1880, 1979–80.
'Bertrand and Raton', i, 25 Oct., 1880, 2019.
'England Under a New Dispensation', i, 4 Nov., 1880, 2165.
'Ecclesiastical Politics and Ecclesiastical Teaching', i, 5 Nov., 1880, 2187–8.
'Some Advantages of the Recognition of Barbarism', i, 10 Nov., 1880, 2251–2.
'The Judgement of the United States on Free Trade', i, 12 Nov., 1880, 2275.
'The Eccentricities of the University Commissions', i, 13 Nov., 1880, 2299–300.

'Catilinarian Victories and Their Fruits', i, 16 Nov., 1880, 2332.
'Mr Bright's Political and Historical Philosophy', i, 19 Nov., 1880, 2379–80.
'The Agitation Against Private Property', i, 24 Nov., 1880, 2443–4.
'Irish Facts and English Emotions', i, 1 Dec., 1880, 2531.
'Medicine for the Irish Malady', i, 7 Dec., 1880, 2611.
'Why the Revolution Makes Way', i, 10 Dec., 1880, 2659.
'Extraordinary Law', i, 18 Dec., 1880, 2771.
'Unnoticed Dangers of the Irish Example', i, 20 Dec., 1880, 2795–6.
'The Survival of the Unfittest', i, 22 Dec., 1880, 2819.
'The Superstition of Ordinary Law', i, 31 Dec., 1880, 2931.
'French Opinion on Irish Affairs', ii, 4 Jan., 1881, 35–6.
'The Dependence of Ireland on Great Britain', ii, 10 Jan., 1881, 115.
'The Two Voices', ii, 11 Jan., 1881, 139–40.
'Mr Froude and his Critics', ii, 17 Jan., 1881, 211.
'Remedies for Electoral Corruption', ii, 21 Jan., 1881, 275.
'Radicalism, Old and New', ii, 25 Jan., 1881, 331–2.
'The Populousness of the United States', ii, 28 Jan., 1881, 379–80.
'The Work of the University Commissioners', ii, 4 Feb., 1881, 475–6.
'The Ordinary Law of Ireland and What Should be Done With It', ii, 10
    Feb., 1881, 517.
'Disillusion', ii, 17 Feb., 1881, 643.
'The Land League and the Catholic Bishops', ii, 21 Feb., 1880, 692.
'Mr Parnell and Foreign Opinion', ii, 22 Feb., 1881, 716.
'The Future of Constitutionalism', ii, 24 Feb., 1881, 747–8.
'Budgets and Land Bills', ii, 2 March, 1881, 819.
'Wiping Out Conservatism', ii, 8 March, 1881, 899.
'The Measure of English Responsibility for Ireland', ii, 9 March, 1881,
    915.
'The Irish Nightmare', ii, 15 March, 1881, 1004.
'Signs of the Times', ii, 21 March, 1881, 1075.
'The Latest National Humiliation', ii, 24 March, 1881, 1123.
'Pax Britannica', ii, 4 April, 1881, 1267.
'The Russian Conquests in Central Asia', ii, 5 April, 1881, 1291.
'Death Duties', ii, 7 April, 1881, 1323–4.
'The Projected Economic Revolution in Ireland', ii, 12 April, 1881, 1379–
    80.
'Some Certain Results of the Land Bill', ii, 14 April, 1881, 1411.
'Patriarchal Radicalism', ii, 19 April, 1881, 1467–8.
'The Medicines and the Quackeries of the Land Bill', ii, 23 April, 1881,
    1531–2.
'The Disraeli of Foreign Opinion', ii, 29 April, 1881, 1611–12.
'Opium', ii, 2 May, 1881, 1635–6.
'Missions and Their Results', ii, 7 May, 1881, 1724.
'The Theory of Liberationism', ii, 9 May, 1881, 1739–40.
'The Irish Land Court as a School of Liberty', ii, 13 May, 1881, 1795.
'How the Jacobins Conquer a Nation', ii, 17 May, 1881, 1851–2.
'The New Opinion of the Constituencies', ii, 23 May, 1881, 1923–4.

337

'The Revision of the New Testament', ii, 27 May, 1881, 1987–8.
'The Price of a Commercial Treaty', ii, 30 May, 1881, 2019.
'The Moral of Monte Carlo', ii, 2 June, 1881, 2075–6.
'The Precedent of Fifty Years Since', ii, 8 June, 1881, 2147.
'The House of Lords', ii, 13 June, 1881, 2211.
'Constitutional Government in Eastern Europe', ii, 14 June, 1881, 2227–8.
'Providence and Political Economy', ii, 18 June, 1881, 2291.
'Modern Mysteries', ii, 23 June, 1881, 2355.
'The War Against Disease', ii, 27 June, 1881, 2411–12.
'The Hanoverian Stage of Italian Politics', iii, 1 July, 1881, 3–4.
'Veracity in Politics', iii, 4 July, 1881, 35–6.
'The Crime of Guiteau', iii, 7 July, 1881, 83.
'The Belief of the Original Free Traders', iii, 11 July, 1881, 131.
'The Irish Land Bill as a Source of Revolution', iii, 18 July, 1881, 227–8.
'Free Trade and Foreign Tariffs', iii, 21 July, 1881, 275.
'The True History of Free Trade', iii, 26 July, 1881, 339–40.
'A Message to a Wrong Address', iii, 4 Aug., 1881, 467–8.
'British Trade and British Markets', iii, 5 Aug., 1881, 483.
'Free Contract and Free Trade', iii, 10 Aug., 1881, 547.
'The House of Commons and the French Treaty', iii, 16 Aug., 1881, 627.
'New Theories of the Constitution', iii, 20 Aug., 1881, 691.
'Orating and Legislating', iii, 22 Aug., 1881, 707.
'Our Commercial Difficulties With France', iii, 24 Aug., 1881, 739.
'British Prosperity and Fiscal Legislation', iii, 31 Aug., 1881, 835.
'Social Safeguards in France and England', iii, 2 Sept., 1881, 867.
'The Past and Future of Democratic Government', iii, 5 Sept., 1881, 899.
'The Position of the Radicals', iii, 7 Sept., 1881, 931.
'New Economical Facts For Consideration', iii, 13 Sept., 1881, 1011.
'The Farmer and His Friends', iii, 14 Sept., 1881, 1027.
'The Radicals and The Farmers', iii, 21 Sept., 1881, 1123.
'Landed Properties, Large and Small', iii, 26 Sept., 1881, 1187–8.
'Orthodoxy and Heresy in Economics', iii, 30 Sept., 1881, 1251.
'Alternatives in Legislation', iii, 4 Oct., 1881, 1299. .
'The Demoralization of a People', iii, 7 Oct., 1881, 1317.
'Logic at Leeds', iii, 11 Oct., 1881, 1403–4.
'What the Boers Really Want', iii, 14 Oct., 1881, 1443–4.
'Remedies for Agricultural Distress', iii, 22 Oct., 1881, 1555.
'The Opium Trade Between India and China', iii, 24 Oct., 1881, 1571–2.
'The Russian Return to Orientalism', iii, 1 Nov., 1881, 1691–2.
'Perils of Old and New Wealth', iii, 4 Nov., 1881, 1731–2.
'Free Trade and How it is Threatened', iii, 11 Nov., 1881, 1827.
'Mr Bright and His Triumphs', iii, 17 Nov., 1881, 1907–8.
'Confusion of Thought About the Land', iii, 22 Nov., 1881, 1979–80.
'Surreptitious Revolution', iii, 1 Dec., 1881, 2099.
'The Irish Paradox', iii, 5 Dec., 1881, 2155–6.

'The North Borneo Company', iii, 6 Dec., 1881, 2163.
'Paying the Educational Piper', iii, 8 Dec., 1881, 2195.
'The New Nation', iii, 21 Dec., 1881, 2371.
'Realities of Indian Taxation', iii, 22 Dec., 1881, 2387–8.
'The Principles of Parliamentary Procedure', iii, 29 Dec., 1881, 2483.
'The Periodical Trick', iii, 31 Dec., 1881, 2523.
'The King and His Relation to Early Civil Justice', Royal Institution, *Notices of Proceedings*, ix; reprinted in *Fortnightly Review*, xxx, November, 1881, 603–7, and as Chapter 6 of *ELC* (1883), 160–91.

1882. 'The King and His Successor', *Fortnightly Review*, xxxi, February, 1882, 180–94, reprinted as Chapter 5, entitled 'Royal Succession and the Salic Law', of *ELC* (1883), 125–59.

1883. *Dissertations on Early Law and Custom*, London, Murray, (1883), including an important Chapter on 'Theories of Primitive Society'; new edn (1891); (1901); French translation by M. Rene de Kerallain, as *Etudes sur l'ancien droit et la coutume primitive*, Paris, Toulouse, (1884); in Spanish as *El Antiguo Derecho y la Costumbre Primitive*, Madrid, La Espana Moderna, (188–?); 1st American edn, Holt, (1886).
'The Prospects of Popular Government', *Quarterly Review*, clv, April 1883, 551–76 [unsigned]; reprinted as Essay 1 of *PG* (1885), 1–55.

1884. 'The Constitution of the United States', *Quarterly Review*, clvii, January, 1884, 1–31 [unsigned]; reprinted as Essay 4 of *PG* (1885), 196–254.
'The Nature of Democracy', *Quarterly Review*, clviii, October, 1884, 297–333 [unsigned]; reprinted as Essay 2 of *PG* (1885), 56–126.

1885. 'The Age of Progress', *Quarterly Review*, clix, April 1885, 267–98 [unsigned]; reprinted as Essay 3 of *PG* (1885), 127–95.
Popular Government, London, Murray, (1885); 2nd edn (1885); 3rd edn (1886); 4th edn (1890); 5th edn (1897); 'Popular edn' (1909); 6th edn (1918); 1st American edn Holt (1886); in French, translator Rene de Kerallain, as *Essais sur le gouvernement populaire*, Paris, Thorin, (1887); in Spanish, translator Siro Garcia del Mazo, as *El Gobierno Popular*, Seville, (1888).

1886. 'The Patriarchal Theory', *Quarterly Review*, clxii, January, 1886, 181–209 [unsigned].
'Mr Godkin on Popular Government', *Nineteenth Century*, March 1886, 266–79.

1887. 'India', in T. H. Ward, ed., *The Reign of Queen Victoria: A Survey of Fifty Years of Progress*, London, Smith Elder, (1887), i, 460–528.

1888. *International Law: The Whewell Lectures*, London, Murray, (1888), edited for publication by Frederick Pollock and Frederic Harrison, Sir Henry Maine's literary executors; 2nd edn (1894); 1st American edn Holt (1888); 1st French edn Thorin (1889).

1889. Government of India, Legislative Department, *Minutes By the Right Honourable Sir Henry Maine, 1862–1869, with a Note on Indian Codification Dated 17 July 1879*, Calcutta, Superintendent of Government Printing (1889).

3. Select List of Secondary Studies

a. Maine and his work:

BURROW, J. W., *Evolution and Society: A Study in Victorian Social Theory*, Cambridge University Press, 1966.

COHN, B., 'From Indian Status to British Contract', *Journal of Economic History*, xxi, 1961, pp. 613–28.

CRANSTON, M., 'A Dialogue on Democracy: Arnold, Maine, Morley', in his *Political Dialogues*, London, B.B.C. Publications, 1968.

DERRETT, J. D. M., 'Sir Henry Maine and Law in India', *Juridical Review*, iv, 1959, pp. 4—55.

EVANS, M. O., *Theories and Criticisms of Sir Henry Maine*, London, Stevens and Haynes, 1896.

FEAVER, G. A., 'The Political Attitudes of Sir Henry Maine', *Journal of Politics*, xxvii, May 1965, pp. 290–317.

GODKIN, E. L., 'An American View of *Popular Government*', *Nineteenth Century*, xix, February 1886, pp. 177–90, reprinted in M. Keller, ed., *Problems of Modern Democracy: Political and Economic Essays by E. L. Godkin*, Harvard University Press, 1966, pp. 68–97.

GRANT DUFF, SIR M. E., *Sir Henry Maine: A Brief Memoir of His Life, With Selections From His Indian Speeches and Minutes*, edited by *Whitley Stokes*, London, Murray, 1892.

GRAVESON, R. H., 'The Movement From Status to Contract', *Modern Law Review*, iv, April 1941, pp. 261–72.

HARRISON, F., 'The English School of Jurisprudence', *Fortnightly Review*, xxv, January 1879, pp. 114–30.

HOEBEL, E. A., 'Fundamental Legal Concepts as Applied in the Study of Primitive Law', *Yale Law Journal*, li, 1942, pp. 951–66.

HOLDSWORTH, SIR W. S., *Some Makers of English Law*, Cambridge University Press, 1938.

HUNTER, W. W., 'Seven Years of Indian Legislation', Calcutta, Trubner, 1870.

LANDMAN, J. H., 'Primitive Law, Evolution, and Sir Henry Maine', *Michigan Law Review*, xxviii, 1930, pp. 404–25.

LESLIE, T. E. C., 'Maine's *Early History of Institutions*', *Fortnightly Review*, xvii, March 1875, pp. 303–20.

LYALL, SIR A., 'Life and Speeches of Sir Henry Maine', *Quarterly Review*, clxxvi, April 1893, pp. 287–316 [unsigned]

— 'Sir Henry Maine', *Law Quarterly Review*, xiv, April 1888, pp. 129–38.

MAYNE, J. D., 'The Patriarchal Theory', *Law Quarterly Review*, i, October 1885, pp. 485–95.

MILL, J. S., 'Mr Maine on Village Communities', *Fortnightly Review*, ix, May 1871, pp. 543–56, reprinted in his *Dissertations and Discussions*, London, Parker, 1875, iv, pp. 143–68.

MORLEY, J., 'Sir Henry Maine on Popular Government', *Fortnightly Review*, xxxix, February 1886, pp. 153–73.

OLDHAM, J. B., *Analysis of Maine's Ancient Law, With Notes*, Oxford, Blackwell, 1913.

PILLAI, PURNALINGAM, *An Epitome of Maine's Ancient Law and Austin's Jurisprudence*, Madras, 1915.

POLLOCK, SIR F., *Introduction and Notes to Sir Henry Maine's Ancient Law*, London, Murray, 1906.

— 'Sir Henry Maine and His Work', in his *Oxford Lectures and Other Discourses*, London, Macmillan, 1890, pp. 147–68.

— 'Sir Henry Maine as a Jurist', *Edinburgh Review*, clxxvii, July 1893, pp. 100–21 [unsigned].

SMELLIE, K. B., 'Sir Henry Maine', *Economica*, viii, March 1928, pp. 64–94.

SMITH, B. C., 'Maine's Concept of Progress', *Journal of the History of Ideas*, July/September, 1963, pp. 407–12.

SOYEDA, J., 'A Comparison Between Japanese Village Communities and Those Described by Sir Henry Maine', Cambridge University Press, 1886.

STEPHEN, SIR J. F., 'English Jurisprudence', *Edinburgh Review*, ccxxxii, October, 1861. pp. 480–1.

REDFIELD, R., 'Maine's *Ancient Law* in the Light of Primitive Societies', *Western Political Quarterly*, iii, 1950, pp. 574–89.

ROBSON, W. A., 'Sir Henry Maine Today', in A. L. Goodhart, *et al.*, eds., *Modern Theories of Law*, Oxford University Press, 1933.

THORNER, D., 'Sir Henry Maine', in H. Ausubel, *et al.*, eds., *Some Modern Historians of Britain*, N.Y., Dryden Press, 1951, pp. 66–84.

TUPPER, SIR C. L., 'India and Sir Henry Maine', *Journal of the Society of Arts*, xlvi, March 1898, pp. 390–405.

TYLOR, E. B., 'Review of Maine's *Village Communities*', *Quarterly Review*, cxxxi, July 1871, pp. 176–89.

VINOGRADOFF, SIR P. G., 'The Teaching of Sir Henry Maine', An Inaugural Lecture delivered at Corpus Christi College Hall, London, Froude, 1904.

WILSON, W., 'A Lawyer With a Style', *Atlantic Monthly*, lxxxii, September 1898, pp. 363–74.

b. Background sources:

AARSLEFF, H., *The Study of Language in England, 1780–1860*, Oxford University Press, 1967.

ACTON, SIR JOHN EDWARD DALBERG, [First Baron Acton], *The History of Freedom in Antiquity*, Bridgnorth, Edkins, 1877.

— *The History of Freedom in Christianity*, Bridgnorth, Edkins, 1877.

— *A Lecture on the Study of History*, London, Macmillan, 1895.

— *Lectures on the French Revolution*, (ed. by J. N. Figgis and R. V. Laurence), London, Macmillan, 1901.

— *Lord Acton on Nationality and Socialism, . . . with an appendix on Burke*, (ed. by G. E. Fasnacht), Oxford University Press, 1949.

AGNELLI, A., *John Austin alle origini del positivismo giuridico*, Turin, Publications of the Institute of Political Science of the University of Turin, 1959.

ANNAN, N. G., *The Curious Strength of Positivism in English Political Thought* (L. T. Hobhouse Memorial Lecture, no. 28), Oxford University Press, 1959.

AUSTIN, J., *A Plea for the Constitution*, London, Murray, 1859.

— *The Province of Jurisprudence Determined*, London, Murray, 1832 (2nd edn, with additions edited by Sarah Austin, 3 vols., London, Murray, 1861–3: see also *The Province of Jurisprudence Determined and The Uses of the Study of Jurisprudence*, with an Introduction by H. L. A. Hart, London, Weidenfeld and Nicolson, 1954).

BACHOFEN, J. J., *Das Mutterecht, eine Untersuchung uber die Gynaikokratie der alten Welt nach ihrer religiosen und rechtlichen Natur*, Stuttgart, Krais & Hoffmann, 1861. Translated by R. Manheim, with a Preface by George Boas and an Introduction by Joseph Campbell, as *Myth, Religion and Mother Right*, London, Routledge and Kegan Paul, 1968.

BAGEHOT, W., *The English Constitution*, London, Chapman and Hall, 1867.

— *Physics and Politics*, London, King, 1872.

BARKER, SIR E., *Political Thought in England, 1848–1914*, Oxford University Press, 1959, 'The Lawyers', pp. 140–60.

BAUDET, H., *Paradise on Earth: Some Thoughts on European Images of Non-European Man*, Yale University Press, 1964.

BAUMGARDT, D., *Bentham and the Ethics of Today*, Princeton University Press, 1952.

BEARCE, G., *British Attitudes Towards India, 1784–1858*, Oxford University Press, 1961.

BENN, A. W., 'The Historical Method', in his *The History of English Rationalism in the Nineteenth Century*, ii, London, Russell & Russell, 1906.

BENTHAM, J., *The Works* (11 vols., ed. by J. Bowring), Edinburgh, Tait, 1843.

BEVINGTON, M. M., *The Saturday Review, 1855–1858*, N.Y., Columbia University Press, 1941.

BOWLE, J., *Politics and Opinion in the Nineteenth Century*, London, Cape, 1954, pp. 249–57.

BRINTON, C., *English Political Thought in the Nineteenth Century*, London, Benn, 1933, pp. 266–81.

BRYCE, J., *The American Commonwealth* (3 vols.), London, Macmillan, 1888.

— *Modern Democracies* (2 vols.), London, Macmillan, 1921.

— *Studies in History and Jurisprudence* (2 vols.), Oxford, Clarendon Press, 1901.

BURKE, E., *The Works* (6 vols., with Introductions by W. Willis, F. W. Rafferty and F. H. Willis), Oxford University Press, 1906, 1907.

BURNS, J. H., 'J. S. Mill and Democracy, 1829–61', *Political Studies*, v, 1957, nos. 2, 3; pp. 158–75, 281–95.

Cambridge History of the British Empire [*Cambridge History of India*, ed. H. H. Dodwell], v, *British India, 1497–1858*, Cambridge University Press, 1929.

— vi, *The Indian Empire, 1858–1918*, Cambridge University Press, 1932.

342

CATTANEO, M. A., *Il positivismo guiridico inglese: Hobbes, Bentham, Austin*, Milan, Publications of the Faculty of Jurisprudence of the University of Milan, 1962.

CLÉREL DE TOCQUEVILLE, COUNT ALEXIS CHARLES, *Oeuvres Complètes*, Paris, Gallimard (sous la direction de M. J. P. Mayer), 1961, etc.

COBBAN, A. B. C. *Rousseau and the Modern State*, London, George Allen and Unwin, 1964 (2nd edn).

COLLINS, J. C., *Voltaire, Montesquieu and Rousseau in England*, London, Nash, 1908.

COURTNEY, C. P., *Montesquieu and Burke*, Oxford, Blackwell, 1963.

COWLING, M., 1867: *Disraeli, Gladstone and Revolution*, Cambridge University Press, 1967.

— *Mill and Liberalism*, Cambridge University Press, 1963.

DARWIN, C., *The Origin of Species*, London, Murray, 1859.

— *The Descent of Man* (2 vols.), London, Murray, 1871.

DICEY, A. V., *Lectures on . . . Law and Public Opinion During the Nineteenth Century*, London, Macmillan, 1905.

DURKHEIM, E., *Montesquieu and Rousseau: Forerunners of Sociology*, (trans. by George Davy), University of Michigan Press, 1960.

EASTWOOD, R. A., and G. W. KEETON, *The Austinian Theories of Law and Sovereignty*, London, Methuen, 1929.

FERGUSON, A., *An Essay on the History of Civil Society*, Edinburgh, Bell, 1767 (ed., with an Introduction, by Duncan Forbes, Edinburgh University Press, 1966).

FRIEDMANN, W., *Legal Theory*, London, Stevens, 1960.

FUSTEL DE COULANGES, *La cité antique*, Paris, 1861.

GOPAL, S., *British Policy in India, 1858–1905*, Cambridge University Press, 1965.

— *The Viceroyalty of Lord Ripon, 1880–1884*, Oxford University Press, 1953.

GRAHAM, W., *English Political Philosophy from Hobbes to Maine*, London, Arnold, 1926, pp. 348–415.

GRANT DUFF, SIR M. E., *Notes From a Diary* (12 vols.), London, Murray, 1897.

GUÉHENNO, J., *Jean-Jacques Rousseau*, Paris, Grasset, 1962 (2nd edn). Translated by J. and D. Weightman (2 vols), London, Routledge and Kegan Paul, 1966.

HART, H. L. A., *The Concept of Law*, Oxford, Clarendon Press, 1961.

HAVARD, W., *Henry Sidgwick and Later Utilitarian Political Philosophy*, University of Florida Press, 1959.

HAYS, H. R., *From Ape to Angel: An Informal History of Social Anthropology*, London, Methuen, 1959.

HERRICK, J., *The Historical Thought of Fustel de Coulanges*, Catholic University of America Press, 1954.

HOBBES, T., *De corpore politico: or, The Elements of Law, Natural and Politick*, London, 1650 (ed., with Preface and Critical Notes by F. Toënnies), Cambridge University Press, 1928. First published 1889.

— *Leviathan*, London, 1651 (ed., with Introduction, by M. J. Oakeshott, Oxford, Blackwell, 1946).

HOBSBAWM, E. J., *Primitive Rebels: Studies in Archaic Forms of Social Movement in the 19th and 20th Centuries*, Manchester University Press, 1959.

KANTOROWICZ, H., 'Savigny and the Historical School of Jurisprudence', *Law Quarterly Review*, liii, pp. 326–43.

KNICKERBOCKER, F. W., *Free Minds: John Morley and His Friends*, Harvard University Press, 1943.

KRADER, L., ed., *Anthropology and Early Law*, N.Y., Basic Books, 1966.

LASLETT, P., *The World We Have Lost*, London, Methuen, 1965.

LAWSON, F. H., *The Oxford Law School, 1850–1965*, Oxford University Press, 1968.

LECKY, W. E. H., *Democracy and Liberty*, London, Longmans, 1896.

— *History of European Morals from Augustus to Charlemagne*, (2 vols.), London, Longmans, 1911. First published 1896.

— *History of the Rise and Influence of the Spirit of Rationalism in Europe*, (2 vols.), London, Watts, 1910. First published 1865.

— *The Empire: Its Value and Its Growth*, London, Longmans, 1893.

— *The Political Value of History*, Birmingham and Midland Institute Presidential Address, 1892.

LETWIN, S., *The Pursuit of Certainty*, Cambridge University Press, 1965.

LEVIN, L. M., *The Political Doctrine of Montesquieu's Esprit des Lois: Its Classical Background*, Columbia University Press, 1936.

LIPPINCOTT, B., *Victorian Critics of Democracy*, University of Minnesota Press, 1938.

LLOYD, T., *The General Election of 1880*, Oxford University Press, 1968.

LUBBOCK, SIR J., *Prehistoric Times*, London, Williams and Norgate, 1865.

— *The Origin of Civilization*, London, Williams and Norgate, 1870.

MACK, M., *Jeremy Bentham: An Odyssey of Ideas, 1748–1792*, London, Heinemann, 1962.

MACPHERSON, C. B., *The Political Theory of Possessive Individualism*, Oxford University Press, 1962.

MALLOCK, W. H., *Aristocracy and Evolution: A Study of the Rights, the Origin and the Social Functions of the Wealthier Classes*, London, Black, 1898.

— *The Limits of Pure Democracy*, London, Chapman and Hall, 1918.

— *Property and Progress*, London, Murray, 1884.

— *The New Republic*, London, Chatto and Windus, 1889 (first published 1877).

MANSFIELD, H. C., *Statesmanship and Party Government: A Study of Burke and Bolingbroke*, University of Chicago Press, 1965.

MARCUSE, H., *Reason and Revolution: Hegel and the Rise of Social Theory*, Oxford University Press, 1941.

MAYER, J. P., *Alexis de Tocqueville: A Biographical Study in Political Science*, N.Y., Harper and Row, 1960.

MAYO, H. B., *An Introduction to Democratic Theory*, Oxford University Press, 1960.

MCLENNAN, J. F., *Primitive Marriage*, Edinburgh, Longmans, 1865.

— *Studies in Ancient History*, London, Quaritch, 1876.

— *Studies in Ancient History* (2nd series, ed., by his widow, E. A. McLennan), London, Macmillan, 1896.

— *The Patriarchal Theory*, (ed. by Donald McLennan). London, Macmillan, 1885.

METCALF, T. R., *The Aftermath of Revolt*, Princeton University Press, 1964.

MILL, JAMES, *The History of British India* (3 vols.), London, Baldwin, 1818.

MILL, J. S., *Auguste Comte and Positivism*, reprinted from the *Westminster Review*, London, 1865.

— 'Austin on Jurisprudence', *Edinburgh Review*, cxviii, October 1863, pp. 439–52.

— *Considerations on Representative Government*, London, Parker, 1861.

— *Memorandum on the Improvements in the Administration of India during the last 30 Years, and the Petition of the East India Company to Parliament*, London, 1858.

— *Mill on Bentham and Coleridge*, (ed. by F. R. Leavis) London, Chatto and Windus, 1950.

— 'Recent Writers on Reform', *Fraser's Magazine*, lix, April 1859, pp. 489–508.

— *Utilitarianism, On Liberty, Essays on Bentham, Together With Selected Writings of Jeremy Bentham and John Austin* (ed., with Introduction, by Mary Warnock) London, Collins, 1962.

MOORE, R. J., *Sir Charles Wood's Indian Policy, 1853–1866*, Manchester University Press, 1966.

— *Liberalism and Indian Politics, 1872–1922*, London, Arnold, 1966.

MORGAN, L. H., *Ancient Society*, N.Y., Holt, 1877 (ed., with Introduction, by L. A. White), Belknap Press of Harvard University Press, 1964.

— *Systems of Consanguinity and Affinity of the Human Family*, Washington, D.C., Smithsonian Institute, 1870, 1871.

MURRAY, R. H., *English Social and Political Thinkers of the Nineteenth Century*, Cambridge, Heffer, 1929.

PACKE, M. ST J., *Life of John Stuart Mill*, London, Secker and Warburg, 1954.

PAL, DHARM, *Administration of Sir John Lawrence in India, 1864–1869*, Simla, Minerva Bookshop, 1952.

PINTO-DUSCHINSKY, *The Political Thought of Lord Salisbury, 1854–1868*, London, Constable, 1967.

PLAMENATZ, J., *The English Utilitarians*, Oxford, Blackwell, 1949.

— *Man and Society*, (2 vols.), London, Longmans, 1963.

POLLOCK, SIR F., *An Introduction to the History of the Science of Politics*, London, Macmillan, 1895.

RICHTER, M., *The Politics of Conscience: T. H. Green and His Age*, Harvard University Press, 1964.

345

ROACH, J. P. C., 'Liberalism and the Victorian Intelligentsia', *Cambridge Historical Journal*, xiii, 1957, pp. 58–81.

— 'James Fitzjames Stephen', *Journal of the Royal Asiatic Society*, 1956, pp. 1–16.

ROBERTSON SCOTT, J. W., *The Story of the Pall Mall Gazette*, Oxford University Press, 1950.

ROTHBLATT, S., *The Revolution of the Dons*, London, Faber and Faber, 1968.

ROUSSEAU, J. J., *The Political Writings* (ed. by C. E. Vaughan), Oxford, Blackwell, 1962.

RUMNEY, J., *Herbert Spencer's Sociology: A Study in the History of Social Theory*, London, Williams and Norgate, 1934.

SECONDAT, CHARLES LOUIS DE, BARON DE MONTESQUIEU, *Oeuvres Complètes* (sous la direction de M. André Masson), 3 vols., Paris, Nagel, 1950–55.

SMITH, F. B., *The Making of the Second Reform Bill*, Cambridge University Press, 1966.

SMITH, R. E., *Life of Lord Lawrence* (2 vols.), London, Smith Elder, 1883.

SMITH, P., *Disraelian Conservatism and Social Reform*, London, Routledge and Kegan Paul, 1967.

SPAHR, M.,'Mill on Paternalism in Its Place', C. J. Friedrich, ed., *Nomos IV: Liberty*, N.Y., Atherton Press, 1962, pp. 162–175.

SPENCER, H., *Social Statics*, London, Williams and Norgate, 1851.

— *The Man Versus The State*, London, Williams and Norgate, 1884.

— *The Principles of Sociology* (3 vols.), London, Williams and Norgate, 1876.

STANLIS, P. J., *Edmund Burke and the Natural Law*, University of Michigan Press, 1958.

STEPHEN, J. F., *Horae Sabbaticae*, London, Macmillan, 1891, 1892.

— *Liberty, Equality, Fraternity*, London, Smith Elder, 1873, (new edn R. J. White, ed., Cambridge University Press, 1968).

— *The Story of Nuncomar, and the Impeachment of Sir Elijah Impey* (2 vols.), London, Macmillan, 1885.

STEPHEN, L., *The English Utilitarians* (3 vols.), London, Duckworth, 1900.

— *Life of Sir James Fitzjames Stephen*, London, Smith Elder, 1895.

SOUTHGATE, D., *The Passing of the Whigs, 1832–1886*, London, Macmillan, 1962.

STOKES, E., *The English Utilitarians and India*, Oxford, Clarendon Press, 1959.

TYLOR, E. B., *Anahuac*, London, Longmans, 1861.

— *Primitive Culture* (2 vols.), London, Murray, 1871.

— *Researches into the Early History of Mankind and the Development of Civilization*, London, Murray, 1865.

WOODRUFF, P., *The Men Who Ruled India: The Guardians*, London, Cape, 1954.

YOUNG, G. M., *Victorian England: Portrait of an Age*, Oxford University Press, 1949.

Index

Subheads are given in book-page sequence, except for Maine's life, where a chronological listing has been adopted. Approximate dates are provided for members of Maine's family. Bracketed numbers stand for entries in the foot-note section. Thus, '276(6)' refers the reader to page 276, note 6.

Athenaeum Club, The, 12, 62, 64, 107, 112, 131, 134, 137, 164, 165, 246

Athenaeum, The, on *Village Communities,* 136; on Maine's defense of patriarchal thesis, 143, 167–8; on *Early History of Institutions,* 144, 145; on *Popular Government,* 237

Austin, John, 114; as a lecturer, 19; Maine on his *Province of Jurisprudence Determined,* 27–28, 156–8, 193, 258; and Bentham, 45; reputation compared to Maine's, 128; his theory of sovereignty used by J. F. Stephen in attacking Mill's *On Liberty,* 184, 191

Avebury, 1st Baron, *see* Lubbock, Sir John

Avignon, 187

Bachofen, J. J., his *Das Mutterecht,* 139 *pass.,* 301(13)

Baden-Powell, B. H., 119

Bagehot, W., 58, 231

Balfour, Lady, 314(22)

Bancroft, Charles, Maine on, 230

Barker, Sir E., 324(29)

Barnes, E. H., 282(51)

Beaconsfield, 1st Earl of, *see* Disraeli, Benjamin

Beadon, Cecil, 79

Benares, 70

Bendix, R., 278(38)

Bengal, government of, 66, 79; Maine thinks it unrepresentative of India, 67, 284(9); its close-knit European community a source of pressure on the authorities, 68; attitude of its native inhabitants to British rulers, 82, 286(27); their adaptability, 89; land tenure controversy in, 91–93, 95, 96, 104, 217; indigenous social institutions of, 146

Bennett, J. G., 36

Bentham, Jeremy, and John Austin,

19, 27; and reform legislation in England, 20, 35, 46, 49, 59, 271(24); influence of in British legal studies, 25, 44–45, 101, 120, 128; and Benthamism, 32, 36, 60–61, 217; and legal fictions, 48; influence of in Indian administration, 77, 100, 102, 104–6; Maine on, 152, 156–8, 304(18), 319(20); Chauncey Wright defends, 154; his felicific principle, 233

Beresford-Hope, A. J. B., 30

Bernard, M., on *Ancient Law,* 45, 114, 268(27)

Best, R. I., 268(27)

Bevington, M. M., 31

Biarritz, 249

'Black Act' sentiment, Maine accused of in India, 84–5

Blackstone, Sir William, 19, 128

Board of Legal Studies, The, 112

Bodleian Library, Oxford, 5, 112

Boehm, Sir Edgar, his marble medallion of Maine, 261–2

Bombay, government of, 66; Maine compares it favourably with Bengal, 67, 70–71, 87; J. F. Stephen's rendezvous with Maine at, 106–7; Maine departs for England from, 108, 182; and uniform legislation, 287(5)

Bonner, R. J., 275(11)

Bowle, J., 310(25), 324(29)

Bradlaugh case, The, 218

Bradley, George, Dean, 261

Brehon Code, 144, 145, 159

Bright, Dr, 247, 260

Bright, John, Maine on his type in parliament, 31; J. F. Stephen's concern over policies of, 185; and Lord Ripon, 207; Maine's disapproval of his inclusion in Gladstone's 1880 Cabinet, 212

Brinton, Crane, 271(24), 318(17), 324(29)

169–70; in J. F. Stephen's thought, 188

Feroze, The, 110

Fifoot, C. H. S., 297(25), 330(23)

Firth, G. B., 211

Fisher, H. A. L., 281(50), 295

Fiske, J., 43–44, 300(17); his enthusiasm for Maine's *Ancient Law,* 43–44; meets Maine, 300(1)

Ford, W. C., 300(12)

Foreign Office, Law Under-Secretaryship of offered to Maine, 110, 172

Fortnightly Review, The, J. S. Mill's review of *Village Communities* in, 119, 120, 122; John Morley as editor of, 137; notice of Maine's *Early History of Institutions* in, 145; Morley on *Liberty, Equality, Fraternity* in, 187, 189; Maine on J. F. Stephen in, 191; Morley on Liberal's 1880 victory in, 211; his review of *Popular Government* in, 238, 253; Charles Maine in, 248

Fox Bourne, H. R., 269(3)

Fox, Robin, on theory of kinship in early anthropology, 306(34)

Frazer, Sir James, 57

Freeman, E. A., 171, 295(6), 321 (40); on Aryans, 146

Free Trade, 39, 152; *see also* Peelites, Political Economy, Manchester School of

French Revolution, The, 178, 224; Maine on possibility of similar events in England, 222

Friedmann, W., 55, 277(32), 278 (35)

From status to contract, 53; and Maine's political views, 39, 59, 60, 154, 214–16; reception of thesis by Maine's contemporaries, 53–54; later appraisal of, 55–56; and Maine's Indian policy, 73, 76–77, 82, 88–89, 92–93, 201, 286 (32), 291(28); and *Village Com-*

munities, 115–16; and F. Engels, 168; J. F. Stephen on, 193, 321(3); Herbert Spencer on, 281(49), 239; *see also under* Roman law, Development of

Froude, J. A., 182

Gaius, 52

Gallanter, M., 286(2)

Galton, Sir Francis, 12, 165

Gardiner, A. G., 294(54)

Gaskell, C. M., 132

Geldart, Dr James, 20–21

Geldart, Dr Thomas, 173

Gibbs, F., 13

Gladstone, Mary (Mrs Drew), 179, 180, 213, 225, 236, 237, 254, 259

Gladstone, W. E., 31, 188; and the Peelites, 29; his Government of 1868, 101, 197; Maine to, on Roman law, 112; Maine's opposition to his domestic reform policies, 196; and to his Indian policy, 196, 203, 208; and to his Irish policy, 204; his Government of 1880, 211, 212; Maine's attack on, 214 *pass.,* 224–6; and the *Pall Mall Gazette,* 213; his Government of 1886, 245, 255

Glover, Serjeant, 30

Gluckman, Max, 278(38), 280(44)

Godkin, E. L., his critique of *Popular Government,* 252–3

Goethe, von, Johann, compared to J. S. Mill, 186

Goldman, I., 280(47)

Gopal, S., on Viceroyalty of Lord Ripon, 314(25) *pass.*

Governor-General (or Viceroy) of India: *see under* individual incumbents: Canning, Charles Earl; Dufferin, 1st Marquis of; Elgin, 8th Earl of; Lawrence, John Laird, 1st Baron; Lytton, 1st Earl of; Mayo, 6th Earl of; Northbrook, 1st Earl of; Ripon, 1st Marquis

353

Maine's Oxford lectures, 111, 118; and *Village Communities*, 117; criticisms of, 136–7, 159, 169, 241–2, 329(21); and *Early History of Institutions*, 144–5; and Rede lecture of 1875, 151–2; conservative results of in Maine's work, 152–3, 158, 190–1, 192–3, 222–3, 226; and racial tolerance, 152, 208–9; and Indian policy, 153, 192, 210; and Benthamism, 154–8; and political studies in England, 321(40)

Hittite Law, 56

Hobbes, Thomas, his theory of sovereignty, 27; and J. F. Stephen, 107, 184, 193; and Maine, 228; on matriarchalism, 301(16)

Hobhouse, Arthur, J. F. Stephen on, 182; as Law Member of Viceroy's Council, 197–9

Hockcliffe, Bedfordshire, 3

Hoebel, A. E., 57, 279(39, 42), 280(45)

Holdsworth, Sir W., 19, 279(40)

Holmes, Oliver Wendell, Jr, meets Maine, 130–1, 304(14); influence of Maine on his *The Common Law*, 132, 148

Holt, Henry, 252; admires Maine's work, 130; on reception of *Early History of Institutions* in America, 146–7; Henry Adams on, 148; on Maine's criticisms of Bentham, 154–6

Home Office, Permanent Under-Secretaryship at offered to Maine, 242, 243–4

House, F. N., 281(48)

House of Commons, view of in Maine's *St James's Gazette* articles, 223; *Popular Government* treatment of, 231–2, 235, 240; Maine seeks Chief Clerkship of, 244–5, 251; and political representation, 270(18)

Howe, Mark de Wolfe, 300(7, 10)

Hugo, Gustav, 46, 150

Hume, David, 39, 49

Hunter, Sir W., 193, 292(31)

Hurst, F. W., 318(1)

Ihering, von, Rudolph, 46

Ilbert, Sir Courtenay, 246–7; as Law Member of Viceroy's Council under Ripon, 205; his controversial Criminal Jurisdiction Bill, 205–6, 207, 209–10, 315(36); on Indian codification, 314(18)

Imperialism, 107, 153, 181, 311 (35–36); in thought of J. F. Stephen, 183, 185–6, 193–5; of Maine, 195, 202 *pass.*, 208–10, 293(44); and party politics in England, 206–7, 226; and Khedive's Suez Canal shares, 213

India: under East India Company, 36; remnants of indigenous legal system of, 47, 64, 114, 116–17, 150 *pass.*; hardships of climate, 62, 63, 68; Maine's articles on, 64, 65–66, 74, 282(3); British ignorance of, 65; relations between Anglo-India officials and Europeans, 67, 68, 85; unsuitability of Calcutta as capital of, 67 *pass.*, 87, 284(7); relations between Indians and Europeans, 72–73, 77, 81–82, 83, 84, 86, 91–93, 209, 285(25); landlord and tenant in, 91–98, 115, 117, 214; and British party politics, 196 *pass.*, 207, 210; relations between Viceroy's and home government, 197–9, 204–5, 207–8, 311(3), 313(12), 316(40)

Anglo-Indian government: Governor General's (or Viceroy's) Council, 64, 66, 67–73, 75, 77, 88, 89, 92, 94, 95, 96, 97, 98, 100, 101, 104, 107, 108, 124, 182, 199, 200, 207, 283(4), 315(32), 316(44); Law Member of, 18, 62, 65 *pass.*; Legislative Department

Juridical Society of Moscow, The, 170

Keith, A. B., 298(39)
Kell, Rev. Mr, 22
Kelso, Roxburghshire, ancestral home of Sir Henry Maine, 1–7 *pass.*, 22, 258
Kingship, *see* Monarchy
Knowles, James, 260

la Californie, Lord Acton's villa at, 259
Lahore, 70
Lamb, Mrs, 5
Landman, J. H., 280(47)
Lang, Andrew, 111, 132, 168
Laski, Harold, 130, 132, 227; and Maine's papers, *xix*
Latham, R. H., Maine's colleague at Trinity Hall, 173, 176; and memorial service for Maine at Trinity Hall Chapel, 261, 265(7)
Law, H. W., 269(3)
Law Magazine, The, 137 *pass.*
Lawrence, John Laird, 1st Baron, 108; as Viceroy of India, 68, 69, 81, 106, 110, 246; Maine's impressions of, 71–72; and racial exploitation, 81, 91; in tenure controversies, 94–97; his paternalism, 104, 285(23)
Legal education, state of in England during 1840s, 19–20; Maine on, 20–21, 24, 27–28, 45; of Indian civil servants, 76; use of *Ancient Law* in, 128–9
Legislatures, and legislation, 276(16); relative lateness of as source of legal reform, 47, 49, 155, 157, 178, 191, 198–9, 276(18); and democracy, 60; significance in Roman legal history, 145; Maine recommends use of comparative method in,

152–3; opposition of Indian Judges to power of, 200; and single chambers, 222–3
Leslie, T. E. C., 138–9, 143, 145
Leverrier, Urbain, 18
Liberals, 34, 177, 184, 220, 239, 242; and the *Morning Chronicle*, 30; and J. S. Mill, 120; and Sir M. E. Grant Duff, 122; and Manchester School of political economy, 154, 191, 195; and Lord Acton, 178; Maine's disagreements with, 179, 237, 314 (24); and John Morley, 189; Indian policy of under Gladstone, 196, 202 *pass.*, 208, 211–12, 226; and the *Pall Mall Gazette*, 213; domestic policy of, 214 *pass.*; Liberal Hundreds, 221; and *Popular Government*, 236, 245, 253, 254; Charles Maine on, 248–9; *see also* Radicals, Whigs
Liberty, Equality, Fraternity, *see* Stephen, Sir J. F.
Life Peerages Bill, The, 110
Lindley, Nathaniel, his *Introduction to the Study of Jurisprudence* (1855), 20
Lippincott, B., 324(29)
Lipset, S., 278(38)
Locke, John, 39
Lodge, Henry Cabot, 133
London Institute, The, 178, 236
London University, 13, 176; use of Austin's *Jurisprudence* at, 258–9; Maine on Senate of, 328(17)
Low, S., 273(35)
Lubbock, Sir John, 134, 135; his uncharitable review of Morgan's *Ancient Society*, 163; M.P. for London University, 176; American sales of his *Prehistoric Times*, 300(19)
Lucknow, 70
Lushington, Franklin, 12, 13, 171
Lyall, Sir A., 175, 205, 206, 207, 208, 261; on rising expectations

at India Office, 298(39); appointed life member of Council of India, 125; publishes *Early History of Institutions*, 144; chosen Rede lecturer at Cambridge University for 1875, 149; controversy over his theory of primitive patriarchalism, 137–43, 159 *pass.*; honours, 170; rejects offer of Under-Secretaryship at Foreign Office, 172–3; elected to Mastership of Trinity Hall, Cambridge, 173; resigns Corpus Professorship of Jurisprudence, 171; leader writer on the *St James's Gazette*, 1880–1, 213–26; publishes *Early Law and Custom*, 166; publishes attack on democracy, *Popular Government*, in 1885, 237; accepts, then resigns, Under-Secretaryship at Home Office, 242; rejects offer of Chief Clerkship of House of Commons, 245; his recurring ill health, 245–8; named to Whewell Professorship of International Law, Cambridge, 1887, 256; death at Cannes, 1888, 259; his estate, 307(20)

Works: Ancient Law, 14, 26, 31, **41-61**, 62, 64, 65, 72, 73, 80, 88, 92, 98, 104, 105, 109, 111, 114, 115, 120, 128, 129, 130, 131, 132, 134, 135, 137, 138, 139, 143, 144, 145, 147, 151, 154, 166, 192, 194, 199, 214, 216, 226, 234, 252, 256, 258, 299(2–3)

Village Communities in the East and West, 27, 50, **114–18**, 120, 128, 132, 136, 137, 147, 151, 154, 155, 156, 171, 258, 296(20)

Early History of Institutions, 26, **144–8**, 154, 156–8, 159, 171, 302(22)

Early Law and Custom, **166–9**, 171

Popular Government, 59, 60, 158, 181, 190, 219, 223–5, 226,

227–42, 244, 245, 251–5, 324(27) *pass.*

International Law, 257 comprehensive list of Maine's publications, 331–9

Maine, Lady (*neé* Jane Morton Main, 1827–1920), 3, 30, 108, 131, 148; and Maine's papers, xviii–xix; family and birth, 1–2; marriage to first cousin, 7, 22; as Cambridge hostess, 22–23; her health, 43, 64, 110, 327(2); as a grandmother, 249–50; and death of Sir Henry, 259 *pass.*; her death, 261; Herman Merivale on, 294(53); Lord Acton and J. F. Stephen on, 307(18)

Maine, Rev. Lewin George, 3, 249, 264(7)

Maine, Nevill, 249

Maitland, F., on Maine's influence in Europe, 58; on political implications of British legal anthropology, 297(25); Maine to on *Bracton's Note Book*, 329(23)

Malinowski, B., 57

Mallet, B., 313(10)

Mallet, Sir Louis, 299(39)

Malthus, Thomas, 220

Mane, John, 1

Manu, Code of, 47, 145

Marienbad, 172

Married Women's Property Acts, The, and *Ancient Law*, 54

Marseilles, 108

Martindale, Don, 278(38), 282(53)

Martin, Sir J. R., Maine's physician, 62, 247

Martin, K., 274(38)

Matriarchal family, 135, 167–8, 169; L. H. Morgan on, 134, 162, 164; J. Bachofen on, 139–40; J. F. McLennan on, 140–2; Maine's critique of, 142–3, 166–7; *see also* J. F. Bachofen, J. McLennan, L. H. Morgan

Maurer, von, G. L., 115, 116

May, Sir Erskine, 244, 326(47)

Mayne, J. D., defends patriarchal thesis, 329(21)

Mayo, H. B., 325(40)

Mayo, 6th Earl of, as Viceroy of India, 106; praises Maine's Indian achievements, 107; the assassination of, 108, 197; Maine supports his plan for financial decentralization in India, 204

McLennan, Donald, 258

McLennan, J. F., 134, 168; his *Primitive Marriage*, 139, 140–2; 147; his *Studies in Ancient History*, 159–60; Maine on, 164, 165, 258, 303(17), 329(21); his death, 166

McNair, A. D., 275

Merivale, Charles, 43

Merivale, Herman, 108

Michels, R., 219

Middle Temple, Maine's association with, 24 *pass.*, 30, 41, 42, 43, 111, 256; and *Ancient Law*, 268(31)

Midsummer Night's Dream, *A*, Maine's Apostles' Club essay on, 14

Mill, James, 153, 271(23)

Mill, J. S., 39, 119, 308(13); his interest in historical and comparative studies, 20, 58; compared with Maine as Indian counsellor, 97–98, 153; his critique of *Village Communities*, 120–1, 130; on danger of historical approach, 136–7; J. F. Stephen's attack on, 183–9; Maine's interpretation of, 217, 239, 254

Mofussil, Anglo-India court system in, 75, 78, 83, 205, 206; British planters in, 92

Moltke, von, Count, 139

Monarchy, Maine on, differences between Britain and America traceable to, 35; and Maine's political thought, 40; and early law, 46, 116, 177–8; and moral safeguards, 323(19)

Montesquieu, Charles Louis de Secondat, Baron de, gradual acceptance of his approach to study of society in England, 20; and Maine, 39, 44, 150, 261; on British political institutions, 231

Montfleury Hotel, Cannes, 259

Montriou, Mr, 92

Moore, R. J., 284(19), 285(24), 312(4), 313(10)

Morgan, L. H., first meets Maine, 133–5; his *Systems of Consanguinity of the Human Family*, 133 *pass.*, 160; his *Ancient Society*, 161 *pass.*; Maine on, 163–4, 165, 167; death, 166; defended by Engels, 168

Morison, J. L., 284(18)

Morley, John Viscount, 122, 190, 213, 222; his criticism of historical method, 137; defends J. S. Mill against J. F. Stephen, 187, 189; on Liberal victory of 1880, 211; on academic critics of democracy, 212–13; on Maine's *Popular Government*, 238, 253, 254; J. F. Stephen on, 309(23)

Morning Chronicle, The, Maine as contributor to, 29; change in ownership of, 30; unsigned articles characteristic of, 31

Mosca, G., 219

Muktirs, 78

Müller, Max, 26, 111, 166

Munro, Sir Thomas, 104

Munsifs, 77, 79, 80

Murray, John, 64, 111, 114, 119, 144, 155, 237, 258, 295(6); publisher of *Ancient Law*, 41–43, 61, 137–8; Maine to on *Popular Government*, 236

Murray, Mrs, 43

Murray, R. H., 266(1)

Mysore, 66

Napier, Robert, 1st Baron, 85

359

161; J. F. McLennan on, 142; in Ireland, 145

Sokolov-Grant, Mrs Sheila, 25

Southgate, D., 311(1), 325(37)

Sovereignty, Maine's critique of command theory of, 27, 46, 156–8, 193; and democracy, 32, 60, 227–8, 323(19); in India, 67, 191; J. F. Stephen on, 184

Spectator, The, on results of Cambridge parliamentary election of 1882, 177; on *Popular Government*, 237

Spencer, Herbert, John Fiske on, 44; compared with Maine, 58, 145–6, 170, 239, 281(49); on Maine, 306(37)

Stanley's *Eastern Church*, 43

Star and Garter Inn, Richmond, annual banquet of Apostles' Club at, 15, 182

Stebbing, W., 274(39), 282(3)

Stephen, Sir J. F., 26, 203, 225, 238, 249; on Maine's background, 4; first meets Maine, 13–14; on Maine's appointment to Regius Professorship at Cambridge, 19; on Maine as a jurist, 24, 136, 146; on the *Morning Chronicle*, 29; as contributor to the *Saturday Review*, 31; on *Ancient Law*, 44; and Indian codification, 98, 197, 199; his philosophy of Anglo-Indian administration compared with Maine's, 101, 191–5, 202, 209, 292(38); as Legal Member of Viceroy's Council, 103, 106, 110, 294(49); friction with Maine, 125, 174, 291(30), 306(7); as Trinity Hall guest of Maine, 175; influence of India on political thought of Stephen, 183, 185 *pass.*, 190, 210; his *Liberty, Equality, Fraternity* (1873), 183–191, 193, 195, 308(10) *pass.*; its influence on Maine's political thought, 190–1, 217, 228, 321(5);

Maine's review of his *Introduction to the Indian Evidence Act*, 191–2, 287(11); Stephen's dislike of political parties, 196; on Ripon's Indian policy, 206; his disgust at British political trends, 212, 227; on *Popular Government*, 235; on Maine's health, 245, 246, 326 (49–50); Maine's influence on, 266(10), 310(32); Stephen as an amateur anthropologist, 302(32); possible renewal of Indian tenure of, 313(12)

Stephen, J. K., 238, 325(34)

Stephen, Leslie, on his brother's attitude towards the historical school of jurisprudence, 183, 310 (32); his *Life* of James Fitzjames, 194; his essay on Maine for the *Dictionary of National Biography*, 225

Stern, B. J., 300(16)

Stevens, R., 267(6)

Stokes, Eric, 104, 195, 286(2), 291(30), 292(37), 293(44), 311 (35–36)

Stokes, Whitley, as student under Maine, 25–26; Maine recommends him as Legal Member of Viceroy's Council, 199; his period of office, 200, 314(18); dedication of his *Anglo-Indian Codes* to Maine, 201; on Maine, 247

Stone Building, Lincoln's Inn, Maine's chambers at, 26, 41

Stone, J., 56, 279(41)

Strachey, Sir John, 146, 175

Strachey, Sir Richard, 175, 203

Stuart, Prof., 177

Stubbs, William, 111, 132

Sumner, John Bird, Maine's godfather, 4; and St. Margaret's, Mapledurham, 5, 22

Taluqdars, and tenure of land in Oudh, 93–94, 96

Taylor, Harriet, 119

GLASSBORO STATE COLLEGE